harvest

'...whatsoever a man soweth, that he shall also reap.' GALATIANS 6:7

Published in 2009 by Murdoch Books Pty Limited

Murdoch Books Australia
Pier 8/9
23 Hickson Road
Millers Point NSW 2000
Phone: +61 (0) 2 8220 2000
Fax: +61 (0) 2 8220 2558
www.murdochbooks.com.au

Murdoch Books UK Limited
Erico House, 6th Floor
93–99 Upper Richmond Road
Putney, London SW15 2TG
Phone: +44 (0) 20 8785 5995
Fax: +44 (0) 20 8785 5985
www.murdochbooks.co.uk

Publisher: Kay Scarlett

Project Editor: Sarah Baker
Designer: Alex Frampton

ISBN: 9781741967128

A catalogue record for this book is available from the British Library.

Printed by 1010 Printing International in 2009. PRINTED IN CHINA.

Readers of this book must ensure that any work or project undertaken complies with local legislative
and approval requirements relevant to their particular circumstances. Furthermore, this work is necessarily
of a general nature and cannot be a substitute for appropriate professional advice.

harvest

A complete guide
to the edible garden

Meredith Kirton

MURDOCH BOOKS

Contents

Ground rules.   *Eco-principles.*

the kitchen garden

Practicalities and possibilities.   Plant, promise, harvest.

Contents

growing edibles

A growing number of people want to dedicate areas of their garden to vegetable patches, herb gardens or orchards so they can enjoy the superior taste and convenience of homegrown, seasonal produce. They might want to grow their produce organically, so they can avoid the use of chemicals and reduce their reliance on fossil fuels, or they might want their children to see where food comes from — and it's much easier to grow carrots than to keep a goat!

So if you want to grow your own produce, where do you start? The best advice is to start small.

Growing your own food is a real commitment that involves hard work, and the quality and quantity of your produce tends to depend on the effort you put into it.

In other words, planting is just one of a series of tasks involved in the whole process.

You might start off simply, perhaps by growing a few culinary herbs near the kitchen door, or you could reorganise your life so that all you grow and how you do it become part of a daily philosophy. But whatever you decide, enjoy the process as well as the pleasure of growing your own produce.

The basics

To grow most fruit, vegetables and herbs you need an area of open, level ground with friable, well drained soil that is enriched with compost or manure. You also need up to eight hours' sun per day, ready access to water and the time to tend your edible garden properly.

tip

Look for storage containers on castors, then drill holes in the bottom before planting up your mobile gardens.

Below: Protect vulnerable plants from heat or cold with a cloche.

Opposite: Plant seedlings in newspaper pots and the paper will rot down into the soil.

Climate and aspect

Basically, most edible plants need full sun. Shade from trees and buildings and even root competition from other plants will affect the success of your edible garden, so choose an open, sunny spot, preferably facing the equator, although east–west is also acceptable.

Few edible plants will grow in deep shade, but many of the root and leaf crops will cope well in part shade, especially in hot weather. You can improve a shady area by trimming tree branches to admit more sun, or by using a light-coloured wall or mulch to reflect more light onto the plants.

Leafy greens such as salad vegetables, spinach and silver beet cope with more shade because they don't need the sun to flower and fruit like other crops, such as tomatoes and eggplant. Peas, beans, leek and summer squash will tolerate some shade. Herbs that grow in partial shade include lemon balm, lemon verbena, mint, chives, thyme, sage, dill, parsley and basil.

Fooling nature

Temperature is another important factor in determining what you can grow. If it's too hot or too cold in your area, many plants will either die or not be able to fruit or flower. But there are ways of modifying temperature.

If you live in a cool climate, you can plant against sunny walls in order to benefit from the reflected heat. Raised garden beds will also help the soil warm up, as will dark-coloured mulch applied after the warming process has begun. You may also want to consider using cold frames, plastic tunnels, glasshouses, cloches and even hothouses.

A time-honoured way of growing plants out of their climate is to grow them in pots, then move them either inside when the weather is too cold or under shade when it gets too hot. In cold areas you could grow citrus trees and shrubs in mobile planter boxes, then simply move them into a sunroom over winter. Even tropicals can be grown in a cooler climate if they're given shelter in the cold months.

Some particularly cold-sensitive crops — such as tomatoes, basil, eggplants and many cucurbits — can be raised from seeds earlier in the season if they are kept in a protected place. Jiffy pots, which expand after watering to grow into a peaty pod that's perfect for germinating seedlings, are ideal for this (see page 14). You can then plant your edibles straight into the soil once the weather is right and germination is complete.

Alternatively, you could use rolls of newspaper (see opposite) or pots made

Planting seeds in peat pods

Plant tomato seeds in peat pods, then place them in a mini glasshouse until the seeds germinate.

1 Moisten the peat pods with a little water. They will start to plump up.

2 Plant seeds in each peat pod.

3 Place the peat pods in a mini glasshouse. Before planting out, acclimatise the plants by keeping the lid off for a week.

out of recycled cardboard. Then protect the seedlings with a mini glasshouse, clear plastic tray, glass bell jar, sheet of glass or even a clear plastic shopping bag.

Plant selection

Clever and appropriate plant selection is usually the simplest way of working with climate and site restraints. Snow peas, rhubarb and spinach are the ultimate cold-season vegetable crops. Other good contenders are the brassicas, such as broccoli and cabbages. Carrots and beets like cool weather, while apples, pears, nuts and many berries also grow in the cold.

At the other end of the scale, chillis, capsicums, okra, legumes, corn, peanuts, pumpkins, squash, sweet potatoes, watermelon and tomatoes are all heat-loving crops. Sunflowers, Jerusalem artichokes, gourds, yacon and many tropical fruits, such as pineapple, are also easy to grow in hot areas. But don't forget compost, which helps the soil hold water, and a thick layer of mulch (see pages 16–17) to cool both the soil and the roots of plants.

Protecting plants with shade cloth, or planting tall crops to cast some shade on shorter ones during the afternoon, can also help. (See 'Companion planting', page 46.)

Lots of soil moisture is seldom a problem unless the drainage is poor,

which could be due to a couple of factors: the site is lying at the lowest point in the surrounding landscape, or the soil is just very heavy and takes some time to aerate. To compensate for this, you could plant those few plants that tolerate 'wet feet' (see 'Aquatics' on page 358) or elderberry, mint or garden cress.

You could also build a raised garden bed filled with good soil. This raised system can be as simple as an area surrounded by a low log or a brick retaining wall.

Frost protection

To avoid problems with frost, try not to plant your edibles in a depression or at the foot of a slope, as this is where frost is most likely to settle and cause cold burn. In very cold areas, consider growing frost-tender plants such as tomatoes and cucumber in a glasshouse or conservatory, or protect them with cloches and hotbeds in a similar fashion until the last chance of frost is over. You can also apply certain foliar sprays prior to frost to give plants some protection from cold burn.

Lack of water can also be a problem in the edible garden. Many herbs are drought-resistant once they reach full size, while drought-tolerant vegetables include tepary beans (*Phaseolus acutifolius*), which have deep root systems. Strawberries, beets, Swiss chard, New Zealand spinach, potatoes, carrots, rutabaga and radishes do well in sandy soil if compost has been added and the beds mulched.

Soil and cultivation

The key to a successful harvest is great soil, so consider its texture and structure, its pH and fertility, and how well it drains.

Texture and structure

Soil texture refers to the amount of sand, clay and silt in your soil. You can do a simple texture test (see box, at right) to work out the various components of each, but, in general, the more sand, the better the drainage; the more clay, the richer the soil; and the more silt, the more you need to improve the soil for better drainage.

Improving the soil

In most cases, adding plenty of organic matter — including animal manure, leaf litter, grass clippings and even the roots of plants themselves — play an important part in the life of your soil. Together with bacteria, fungi, soil microbes, worms and beneficial nematodes, they eventually transform the organic matter into humus, which holds moisture, contains air pockets and absorbs liquid nutrients, releasing them back to plants.

Other soil improvement strategies include installing raised garden beds and gradually adding household and garden scraps as compost and worm castings. You could also plant some clover as a cover crop, digging it under to add organic

Soil texture tests

There are two methods for testing the texture of your soil.

First, try the 'worm test' (below right). Squeeze a small amount of moist soil. A pure clay sample will feel smooth and sticky and you'll be able to roll it into a long, thin worm. Silt is also smooth, but a silt 'worm' will start to break up after it reaches about 3 cm (1 in) in length. Sand will crumble, but loams, or mixtures, will form a worm before breaking.

For the other test you need a small, clear jar filled with water. Place your sample in the jar and shake vigorously, then allow it to settle. The components will eventually fall to the bottom of the jar — the clay, the heaviest, will sit on the bottom; then the silt; and finally, sand, the lightest, will float on top of the water. This test will also show you the proportions of sand, clay, organic matter and silt in your soil.

matter. Finally, apply a thick layer of mulch that will keep the surface of the soil from forming a hard crust. It will eventually rot down into the soil.

But if improving your soil seems like a huge obstacle, or you just can't wait to start planting, you can simply plant edibles that are already suitable for your particular soil.

For example, many of the common herbs used in cooking originated in the Mediterranean region and do quite well in sandy soil with a high pH. Beans, peanuts,

tip

Use a test kit to test your soil's pH. If it is alkaline, the pH will range from 7 to 14, but an acid soil will be less than 7.

Planting seedlings

Made from recycled paper, eco mat suppresses weeds but lets water and air reach the soil before decomposing.

1 Rake the soil into a fine tilth, moisten it, then lay the eco mat.

2 For each plant, cut a cross-shaped hole in the eco mat.

3 Add some potting mix to each hole.

4 Plant into the hole and smooth down the corners of the mat.

chives, nasturtiums and sweet potatoes will also grow in sandy soil. If you have clay soil, try broccoli, cabbages, cauliflower or mustard greens, but first raise them in seed-raising mix, as poor drainage in these soils can rot the seedlings.

Mulch

Mulch suppresses weeds and helps keep water in the soil by cutting down on the amount of evaporation. It comes in a wide variety of forms. In the kitchen garden, which will be dug over frequently, it makes sense to use a mulch that will break down quickly into the soil as well as add to its richness and water-holding capacity. Use high-nitrogen mulches such as manure, lucerne hay, pea straw and the leafy tops of sugar cane.

·Longer-lasting mulches, which have less nitrogen and more carbon, include pine flake, pine bark, wood chip and leaf litter. These work well where you're not likely to be digging over garden beds — for example, around fruit trees. They don't fertilise the soil, but the solution is simple — just add slow-release manure pellets.

Sometimes, however, you'll need to keep weeds down in a large area such as an orchard, where there's a lot of foot traffic. In this case you need something more heavy-duty. However, if you need to access the soil you'll have to roll up the carpet, but as the soil around fruit trees doesn't need digging over, it can be ideal.

Inorganic mulches, such as pebbles and gravel, can be a maintenance problem wherever plants, especially annuals (like most vegetables), are growing, as these beds will need to be turned.

Drainage

The type of soil you have will greatly affect its ability to drain. Sandy soil tends to drain freely, while heavier soils such as clay hold water, which is why they expand so much. Clay soils with good texture, which have formed peds or flocculated into balls with the addition of organic matter and cultivation, will also drain well.

Low-lying areas, where water naturally collects, are best avoided. If there is no other option, in these areas it may be necessary to install raised beds or agricultural drainage pipes, which will remove water from the site.

The importance of worms

Worms are an essential part of your garden's soil. Along with their relatives, such as nematodes, they work their way through soil and organic matter, bacteria and fungus, producing deliciously rich castings, or worm poo, which is an essential building block for life-giving soil.

Millipedes and slaters also process a fair amount of dead and decaying organic matter and, along with centipedes (which can bite and sting), eat slugs and snails. They are the ultimate recyclers. All these creatures live in leaf litter, so remember to keep a few leaves lying around on your garden floor.

Worm farms

You can buy worm farms, or simply make your own out of polystyrene boxes that stack easily on top of each other. Worms need shade and shelter, moisture and drainage, and any system you use will need three layers:

1 a working layer at the top, where you deposit the scraps;
2 a bedding layer, with moist shredded newspaper and compost; and, finally,
3 a bottom layer, where the worm castings will collect.

In the worm farm kit, slots allow for the run-off of worm wee, which is useful as a liquid fertiliser base. If you're making your own worm farm, just punch holes into each layer. Once the worms have eaten their way through the organic matter, use the castings as a fertiliser on your plants.

Composting

Compost is a rich resource for your garden, a natural tonic for plants and a great way to turn kitchen scraps and garden waste into enriched soil; it also overcomes two problems — landfill and soil degradation — at the same time. Many nutrients can be recycled through composting and, thanks to a complex web of micro-organisms, can be made accessible to plants once again.

Compost bins and tumblers

These are ideal for limited spaces, but they have no direct contact with the soil, so earthworms and microbes have no way of entering the bin unless you add them. Add compost worms and some rotted animal manure to kick-start the system.

Some bins are stationary while others can be flipped or turned. The bins that rotate on the long axis of the barrel are by far the most stable as, once moist, the weight of compost can be substantial.

tip

To check your drainage, dig a few holes 60 cm (2 ft) deep and fill them with water. They should empty in a few hours.

Below left: A worm farm.

Below: Worm 'wee'.

Below: You can buy stationary compost bins that are bottomless so that worms and other organisms can come up through the soil.

Below right: If the carbon to nitrogen ratio in an open compost pile is correct, then it should rot down fairly quickly.

Compost heaps or piles

The basic rule for building a compost heap is to create layers of various wet and dry ingredients, each with its own carbon to nitrogen ratio, which aid in the speed of their decomposition: the nitrogen feeds the bacteria that break down organic matter. To maintain a healthy, efficient compost heap, you need to keep the carbon to nitrogen ratio at about 25–30:1.

Layer a 'wet' ingredient, such as grass clippings or vegetable scraps (nitrogen), between 'dry' ingredients, such as leaf litter or shredded newspaper and wood chips (carbon). Add comfrey leaves, a natural accelerant, and lime, which helps sweeten an acidic compost pile, as well as a few handfuls of ready-made compost or rotted animal manure, as these all give you a supply of the micro-organisms required for the compost to work efficiently.

Finally, keep your compost damp and aerate it regularly, so that the organic matter can break down quickly and reach the temperature that's required to kill off any pathogens.

Compost bags

Once you have the ingredients in place, you can start your next pile. But if you're running out of space or time, you could bag your organic matter to use later. Although these bags of compost decompose without oxygen, they can still provide your soil with essential nutrients and organic content.

1 Assemble organic matter, such as fallen leaves, grass clippings, shredded newspaper and kitchen scraps.
2 Place a roughly even layer of each into a heavy-duty black plastic garbage bag, interspersing each layer with either compost or blood and bone.
3 Wet the pile until it's completely moist.
4 Mix the whole lot together with gloved hands, then tie off. Place the bag or bags in the sun so the black plastic will absorb the heat and hasten the composting process. About three months later, you should have compost.

Soil fertility

Various soil elements are essential for plant growth. The best known of these

— N (nitrogen), P (phosphorus) and K (potassium) — are listed on all fertiliser packets as the N:P:K ratio. These, along with sulfur, calcium and magnesium, are known as macronutrients, because your plants need so much of them to survive.

Micronutrients are needed in smaller amounts, but are still essential for plant growth. These include molybdenum, sodium, boron, copper, cobalt, manganese, zinc and iron.

Most organic-aligned methodologies recommend building up the soil itself with organic matter rather than fertilising the plants. In that way, the plants are then able to draw on all the nutrients as they need them, and this strategy has its advantages (see page 36).

Like humans, overfed plants can develop various problems, as they produce sappy growth that tends to be vulnerable to pest and disease attack. Overfeeding can also lead to other elements being unavailable, as it can change the soil pH or, worse still, the availability of heavy metals.

Nitrogen

Plants obtain nitrogen naturally from the breakdown of organic matter, or chemically from fertilisers such as urea and sulfate of ammonia. Nitrogen is responsible for green growth, so a deficiency can result in yellowing leaves as well as older leaves yellowing and dropping. Too much nitrogen can cause sappy, leggy growth that is susceptible to diseases and insect attack.

Phosphorus

Phosphorus is mainly needed for good root growth, which is important for young plants when they are establishing a root system. It is found organically mainly in blood and bone, and hoof and horn and bone dust, but small amounts of it are also

Above: To speed up the decomposition of your compost pile, dig up some comfrey and add it to the pile.

contained in animal manures, especially poultry, but in much larger quantities in guano (sea bird and bat manure).

Chemically, phosphorus is usually supplied as superphosphate, which is not certified by organic organisations.

Potassium

Potassium is responsible for flowers and fruit, as well as the general health and wellbeing of plants. It makes plants more resistant to pests and diseases, as well as to stresses from drought. Animal manure contains sufficient levels of potassium; however, excess quantities of potassium can cause magnesium deficiencies.

Calcium

Calcium occurs naturally in most soils, but it's not always available. This may be due to the soil pH, or to extremely wet or dry conditions, which can lock calcium away from plants. It works by creating strong cellular growth in plants, so a deficiency first shows up as stunted new growth.

It's usually applied in lime, which also improves the structure of both clay and sandy soils. The safest way to apply lime is in slow-acting ground limestone. Apply it a few months before you plant the beds to give the lime time to start breaking down.

Magnesium

Excessive use of magnesium, essential for developing chlorophyll, which is in turn required for photosynthesis, can result in magnesium deficiency. In very acid soils, this is problematic. It shows up on older leaves as yellowing from the tip down in a characteristic V-marking.

The quick-fix chemical application of liquid magnesium sulfate, or Epsom salts, will immediately rectify leaf drop, but checking soil pH and perhaps using limes that contain magnesium, such as gypsum, are better longer-term strategies.

Too much salt

Chemical fertilisers are, in fact, basically salts of various forms. If you live near the ocean, however, you may be aware that too much soil salt can actually burn plants. Asparagus, potatoes and many herbs are salt-tolerant, while shallow-rooted crops, such as lettuce and other greens, may do well since their roots stay above the salty groundwater. Raised beds are sometimes helpful in this case.

If you use seaweed as a mulch in the garden, make sure you rinse it thoroughly in fresh water before using it. Alternatively, rinse it, then steep it in water until it decomposes and becomes an excellent homemade liquid fertiliser.

Fertilisers

If you still want to feed your plants, first understand what's in a product and how that works. Commercial fertilisers are available in both organic and chemical forms, and the macro- and micronutrients of all fertilisers should be shown in an analysis table on the packet.

Commonly available mixes include chemical fertilisers, water-soluble plant foods and fertilisers that are designed for specific groups of plants — for example, citrus and fruit tree fertiliser contains an N:P:K ration of 8:3:7 as well as calcium and sulfur, but excessive use can result in excess cadmium and mercury.

Organic fertilisers

Organic fruit care foliar concentrates are new fertilisers that also contain amino acids; naturally occurring plant extracts, which are growth and flowering stimulants; and beneficial micro-organisms. They are said to provide pest and disease resistance as well as strong, vigorous growth.

Pelletised manure products also come in slightly modified or boosted products, such as those specially made for tomatoes (and other fruiting plants such as chilli, capsicums, melons, eggplants and corn).

Watering your garden

Failing to water your garden effectively can result in edible plants losing their fruit, their leaves tasting bitter or, ultimately, the death of the whole plant. Here are some basic guidelines to follow.

- Water the roots instead of spraying the foliage or soaking the subsoil, which can result in shallow-rooted plants and also wash away plant nutrients, leaching them from the soil into the water table.
- To minimise the amount of water loss from evaporation or run-off, water in the evening when the air is still, or first thing in the morning, and use a sprinkler that soaks in slowly, or a dripper system. (If you live in an area with water restrictions, you could run a sprinkler system off a water tank.)
- Young plants are more vulnerable to dry conditions, but they only need small amounts of water to keep them going, so increase the volume but decrease the regularity as they mature.

Deficiencies

Without trace elements in the soil, all sorts of strange diseases and problems can result. A deficiency usually shows up as abnormal growth, but it can also lead to diseases such as club root and cracking, which is caused by, among other things, a boron deficiency.

You can often just read your plant's leaves and make an educated guess as to the problem. For example, acid soils can be a problem for all brassicas, when whiptail occurs as a result of molybdenum becoming unavailable at these low levels. On cauliflowers, for instance, the leaves become smaller, puckered and ribbon-like.

One solution is to lime the soil to raise the pH, but a faster solution is to treat the soil with a liquid form of molybdenum (3 g/^{1}/$_{10}$ oz ammonium molybdate per 5 litres/9 pt of water) and a wetting agent. Liming acid soils can also help treat infestations of club root in brassicas; it can be quite a severe problem in swedes.

Calcium deficiency

Lacking calcium can cause problems too. For example, tomatoes and capsicums can both develop blossom end rot if the available calcium is simply not present in the soil, or if too much sodium, potassium and nitrate fertilisers are in the soil: your plants will take them up in preference, much to the fruit's detriment.

Uneven watering can also be a contributing factor. An apple disease, known as bitter pit, causes small sunken spots on the fruit when the calcium supply is sporadic or watering uneven.

Chlorosis

Other common deficiencies include chlorosis, the yellowing of acid-loving plants grown in soil to which too much lime has been added. The green veins and yellow leaves are symptomatic of this problem, which can sometimes occur on citrus, especially on new growth. Rectify the acidity around these plants to a pH of below 6 by applying iron chelates every few weeks until the problem disappears.

Zinc and magnesium deficiencies

Sometimes citrus is not able to take up enough zinc, especially in very sandy soils where the zinc is often leached out. The symptoms of zinc deficiency include dieback, narrow foliage on both new and older growth, and a distinctive pale yellow marking between the veins that gives it an almost zebra-like look. It may be necessary to apply zinc as trace elements, along with urea, which helps the soil's uptake of zinc. Added organic matter usually doesn't help in this case; in fact, it can make it more extreme.

Magnesium deficiency, also common in citrus, occurs in low-acidity soils. It looks similar to zinc deficiency, but the leaves remain their normal size. Epsom salts (1 g/^{1}/$_{30}$ oz manganese sulfate per 1 litre/1^3/$_4$ pt water) applied to the foliage can help.

Above: Fruit tree fertiliser contains trace elements.

Left: A magnesium deficiency is evident on the leaves of a lemonade tree.

- Weed regularly, as the weeds themselves compete against other plants for water.
- Keep an eye on the mulch. Mulching creates a physical barrier between the soil and the air, cutting down the amount of evaporation of water from the soil and keeping the soil cool. But it will also absorb any light showers or watering, while the soil below the mulch may remain dry.
- Adjust your watering techniques to suit your soil type. Clay soil will hold water longer, whereas sandy soil will dry out quickly as it is so porous.
- Check your soil with the ideal water gauge — poke your finger into the soil, a few knuckle joints down, to see if it is dry. During dry spells, use a rainwater tank, recycled shower water or another environmentally friendly approach to saving water.

Water tanks and grey water

With changing weather patterns resulting in drought and water restrictions, many people have installed water tanks and/ or use grey water. Tanks come in various shapes, colours and sizes and can be rigid or flexible, expanding as the water arrives after each shower.

The rules for harvesting rainwater and using it on the garden are simple. First, check if you need building approval from your local authority, and then consult an expert for advice on where to position it. Other factors to consider include screening entry points to exclude mosquitoes and other insects.

Local government rules also apply to grey water — that is, water from the bath, shower and laundry — but these will vary from area to area. The general rule is not to use this water on vegetables but otherwise to use it straightaway, before

Hydroponics

Hydroponics was invented in 1929 by Professor William Gericke, who grew 8-m (26-ft) tomatoes in mineral nutrient solutions instead of soil. The concept of hydroponics came about as an extension of the nineteenth century discovery that plants absorb their nutrients as ions dissolved in water; the ions usually come from the soil but can also be supplied artificially. The soil itself also acts as an anchor for the roots, but in hydroponics this is replaced by an inert medium such as perlite, gravel, mineral wool or vermiculite.

Today almost any plant can be grown this way, and the advantages are twofold. Not only can plants consistently access as many nutrients and as much water as they need, but they can also be kept hygienically free of many soil-spread diseases. Thus the home gardener can grow plants anywhere, even indoors, provided there is adequate lighting.

bacteria can grow in it. And always use the rinsing water from the washing machine as well as environmentally friendly phosphate-free detergents, otherwise you may inadvertently change the soil's structure and chemical balance with added detergents.

Below left: Try to position a water tank near a downpipe, on the cool side of the house.

Below: Use a rain gauge to measure the amount of rainfall in your garden.

Opposite: Avoid using grey water on vegetables, especially leafy greens.

Planting and harvesting times

Most vegetables and some herbs and fruiting plants are annuals with a maximum six-month life cycle, but all are grouped into warm-season and cold-season crops.

Annuals

Plant warm-season crops in spring, when all chance of frost has finished, and they will bear fruit (such as beans, tomatoes, corn, squash, eggplants, chillis, rockmelon and watermelon) throughout summer and into early autumn.

Replace cool-season crops — such as broad beans, peas, broccoli, cabbages, onions, potatoes, carrots, spinach and lettuces — at the end of autumn, then harvest them throughout winter into early spring.

Harvesting annuals

Some vegetables, such as leafy greens, are very fast growers and can be harvested after a month, while others take three months to mature or start bearing fruit; one example is corn, which takes about 12 to 16 weeks to mature.

Others, like carrots, can be successively harvested throughout the year, from baby through to 'grown up' carrots, especially if you sow them every two weeks, from spring onwards. Ten to twelve weeks is a good rule of thumb, however, from seed to feed, although in cooler weather it could take sixteen weeks.

Perennials

Depending on the climate, many plants are known as perennial, which means they survive from one season to the next. Including perennials in your edible garden makes planting far less onerous each season, but it also probably means that for a time some areas of your garden will be taken up with plants that are not actually cropping.

Here are some perennials to consider including in your vegetable garden:

- root vegetables, such as fennel, scorzonera, Jerusalem artichoke, yam, yacon, oca, Chinese artichoke, tree onion, spring onion and chives;
- herbs, such as sage, thyme, winter savory, perennial basil, oregano, various mints, marjoram, tarragon and curry plant; and
- leafy greens and stems such as sorrel, rhubarb, water spinach, watercress, Lebanese cress and asparagus.

Unusual additions to the edible garden, such as lima beans, mushroom plant, globe artichoke, pepper and even vanilla bean orchid can also be perennial, depending on the climate.

Above: The globe artichoke is actually a perennial thistle.

Opposite: A vegetable patch planted with warm-season crops such as beans and corn.

Planting and harvesting guide

FRUIT AND NUTS

Plant	Planting time	Time to harvesting
Almond	Winter	6–7 years
Avocado	Spring to autumn	3 years, in autumn or spring, depending on the variety
Banana	Any time	10–13 months in frost-free climate; usually late summer
Berries (cuttings)	Winter	2 years for most, less for strawberries. Harvest in late spring to late summer, depending on the variety
Cape gooseberry	Spring	3–4 months, summer and autumn
Chestnut	Late winter, early spring	5–7 years, autumn
Citrus trees	Spring Autumn	2 years 2–3 years, winter
Cranberry seedlings	Spring	3 years, autumn
Custard apple	Spring	7 years, late autumn to early spring, depending on fruit set
Feijoa	Spring	3–4 years, autumn
Fig	Winter	4 years, summer and autumn
Grape (cuttings)	Winter	2–3 years, summer and autumn
Guava	Spring to autumn	18 months, autumn
Hazelnut	Early winter	5–7 years, autumn
Kiwi fruit (cuttings)	Winter	3–4 years, autumn or winter
Lilly pillies	Any time	2 years, summer and autumn
Longan	Late summer, early winter	3–4 years, late summer
Lychee	Spring	4–6 months, summer
Macadamia	Autumn and winter	5 years
Mango	Spring	2–3 years, summer and autumn
Mulberry (cuttings)	Spring	2–3 years, spring
Olive	Autumn to spring	5 years
Passionfruit	Spring	6–8 months, summer and autumn
Pawpaw	Late summer	18 months, all year, depending on fruit set
Pecan and hickory	Winter	5–7 years, autumn
Persimmon	Winter	3 years, autumn
Pineapple	Any time	2 years
Pistachio	Winter	5 years, autumn
Plantain	Autumn, winter	As banana
Pome fruit	Winter	3–5 years
Pomegranate (cuttings)	Winter	4–5 years, autumn
Pomegranate (seeds)	Spring	5–6 years, autumn
Rambutan	Spring	2–3 years, midsummer
Rockmelon	Spring, summer	14–16 weeks
Sapodilla	Spring and summer	5–8 years
Star fruit	Spring to summer	If grafted, 18 months. Late summer to late winter
Stone fruit	Winter	3–4 years
Walnut	Winter	10–15 years, autumn
Watermelon	Spring, summer	14–16 weeks

VEGETABLES

Plant	Planting time	Time to harvesting
Amaranthus	Spring, summer	10–14 weeks
Asparagus	Spring, summer	2 years
Beans (broad)	Autumn	10–12 weeks
Beans (climbing)	Spring	10–12 weeks
	Summer	12–14 weeks
Beans (dwarf)	Spring	8–10 weeks
	Summer	10–12 weeks
Beetroot	Spring, autumn, winter	10–12 weeks
Broccoli	Summer, autumn	12–16 weeks
Brussels sprouts	Summer, autumn, winter	12–16 weeks
Cabbage	Summer, autumn, winter	8–16 weeks
Capsicum and chilli	Spring, summer	10–16 weeks
Carrot	All year	12–16 weeks
Cauliflower	Summer, autumn, winter	14–26 weeks
Celeriac	Spring, autumn, winter	16–22 weeks
Celery	All year	20–22 weeks
Chia	Spring	10–14 weeks
Chickpea	Autumn, winter	12–14 weeks
Chicory	Summer, autumn, winter	16–20 weeks
Chives	Spring, summer	12 weeks +
Choko	Spring	18–20 weeks
Corn	Spring, summer	12–16 weeks
Cress	Spring	4–6 weeks
Cucumber	Spring, summer	8–12 weeks
Eggplant	Spring, summer	14–16 weeks
Endive	Spring, autumn, winter	8–12 weeks
Florence fennel	Summer, autumn, winter	18–24 weeks
Garlic	Spring	24 weeks
Globe artichoke (seed)	Spring	30 weeks
Gourd	Spring, summer	14–16 weeks
Hamburg parsley	Spring, summer	12–18 weeks
Jerusalem artichoke	Spring	24–30 weeks
Kale	Spring, autumn, winter	8–16 weeks
Kohlrabi	Spring, autumn, winter	8–10 weeks
Leek	Spring, autumn, winter	12–20 weeks
Lentil	Spring, summer	8 weeks +
Lettuce	All year	8–12 weeks
Linseed	Autumn, winter	20 weeks
Mizuna	Autumn, winter	8 weeks
Mustard	Autumn, winter	2–4 weeks
Okra	Summer	16–20 weeks

VEGETABLES

Plant	Planting time	Time to harvesting
Onion	Summer, autumn, winter	24–32 weeks
Parsnip	Spring	16–22 weeks
	Summer, autumn	16–20 weeks
	Winter	20 weeks
Pea	Autumn, winter	12–16 weeks
Potato	Spring	16–20 weeks
Pumpkin	Spring	14–16 weeks
Quinoa	Spring, summer	16–20 weeks
Radicchio	Spring, autumn, winter	8–12 weeks
Radish	Spring	8–12 weeks
	Autumn, winter	6–8 weeks
Rhubarb	Spring	8–12 weeks
	Autumn, winter	8–20 weeks
Rice	Spring	14–16 weeks
Rocket	Spring	4–6 weeks
	Autumn	6–8 weeks
	Winter	8–10 weeks
Rye	Autumn	16 weeks
Salsify	Spring	8–10 weeks
	Autumn	20–22 weeks
	Winter	20–22 weeks
Sesame	Summer	16 weeks
Shallots	Spring, autumn, winter	12–14 weeks
Silver beet	Summer, autumn	8–12 weeks
Soya beans	Spring	12–16 weeks
Spelt	Autumn, winter	20 weeks
Spinach	Spring	12–16 weeks
	Autumn, winter	8–10 weeks
Spring onions	Summer	8–12 weeks
Squash	Spring, summer	12–16 weeks
Sunflower	Spring, summer	20–24 weeks
Swede	Spring	12–20 weeks
	Autumn, winter	12–16 weeks
Tomato	Spring, summer	14–16 weeks
Turnip	Autumn, winter	10–12 weeks
Watercress	Spring	8–14 weeks
	Autumn	8 weeks +
	Winter	8 weeks +
Wheat	Autumn, winter	24 weeks
Yacon	Spring	20–24 weeks
Zucchini	Spring, summer	8–14 weeks

HERBS

Plant	Planting time	Time to harvesting
Angelica	Autumn	14 weeks +
Anise	Autumn, winter	30 weeks +
Arrowroot	Spring	6 months +
Basil	Spring, summer	12–20 weeks
Calendula	Autumn, winter	10–12 weeks
Caraway	Spring, summer	12 weeks +
Celery herb	Spring	12–14 weeks
Chervil	Autumn, winter	12–20 weeks
Chinese keys	Spring	6 months
Coriander	Spring, summer, autumn	8–22 weeks
Curry plant	Spring to autumn	8 weeks +
Dandelion	Spring, autumn, winter	6–22 weeks
Dill	Spring, autumn, winter	12–20 weeks
Fennel	Summer, autumn, winter	18–24 weeks
Fenugreek	Autumn, winter	2 weeks as sprouts
Galangal	Spring	6 months +
Ginger	Spring	6 months +
Horseradish and wasabi	Spring	6 months +
Hyssop	Spring, autumn, winter	8 weeks +
Lemon balm	Spring, summer, autumn	8 weeks +
Lemon grass	Spring	6 months +
Lovage	Autumn	8 months +
Mace	Spring	20 weeks +
Marjoram	Spring, autumn, winter	12–20 weeks
Mint	Spring, summer, autumn	8 weeks +
Nasturtium	Spring, autumn, winter	8–20 weeks
Orache	Spring, summer	12–24 weeks
Oregano	Spring, summer, autumn	8 weeks +
Parsley	Spring, autumn, winter	6 weeks +
Perilla	Spring	20 weeks +
Purslane	Spring, summer	6–8 weeks
Rosella	Spring	20–22 weeks
Rosemary	Any time	8–12 weeks +
Sage	Spring, autumn, winter	6 weeks +
Salad burnet	Spring, autumn, winter	12–14 weeks
Savory	Spring	16 weeks
Sweet cicely	Autumn	10 weeks +
Tarragon	Spring	10 weeks +
Thyme	Spring, autumn, winter	6 weeks +
Turmeric	Spring	6 months

Growing methods

Ask ten people the best way to grow a plant and they're likely to give ten different answers. It may be that you are trying to build a philosophy into your food production, or simply want to grow a couple of carrots, so don't be bullied in your own backyard. Take the time to do some research, then make informed decisions that suit your lifestyle.

Starting from scratch

If you're establishing a vegetable patch for the first time, start off by removing all the rocks and rubbish, then add manure or compost to your soil (see the information on soil health on pages 15 to 21). Then consider how you're going to grow your edibles. (Fruit and nut trees have their own requirements, so consult those sections on pages 76 to 227.)

All the methods discussed in this section rely upon a commitment to an edible garden, or at least to a section of your garden. But you could just include edible plants as incidentals among standard ornamentals. This can be the best option for those who want a little taste test, so to speak, before they commit themselves to a full-on kitchen garden.

This option can be as simple as growing a passionfruit vine over your fence or a few tubs of citrus, or may involve more considered design options, such as growing strawberries as groundcovers, or fruiting plants such as guavas as hedges. Even feature plants can be edible — for example, the striking form of pineapples makes them very attractive tub specimens.

A kitchen garden can be fitted in almost anywhere. Growing smaller plants from ranges of miniature vegetables

available in seeds and seedlings is one option, but bear in mind that they'll produce either full-sized produce on dwarf-sized plants, or miniature-sized produce on small plants, so choosing the right selection may mean you can cram a larger variety into a small space.

Another clever tactic is to grow plants that mature quickly so you can harvest more than one crop per season. You can also utilise space by planting climbing plants such as climbing beans, cucumbers and tomatoes and training them up a trellis or wall.

Potted produce

And there's no reason why you can't have a mini garden in pots or even small, halved rainwater tanks, filled with planter mix instead of water. A container-grown edible garden is great if you rent and want to take your garden with you when you move. It's also convenient, as you can place pots on the doorstep or windowsill.

Make sure your containers — whether they're polystyrene boxes, olive oil tins or the latest in fashion — have drainage holes. If they don't, drill some. Next, fill them with the best potting mix you can afford, first checking that it meets any relevant standards.

Above: Always keep your gardening tools sharp and neatly stored, and they'll serve you well.

Opposite: Asian greens, rocket and strawberries grow among a selection of herbs, such as varieties of basil and parsley.

Pots work really well with most leaf crops — such as lettuce, rocket and herbs — and even with larger growers such as tomatoes, eggplants and peas trained up totems, but root vegetables need really deep containers in order to succeed. Many fruits and vegetables are also suitable for hanging baskets. If you have only a sun-filled balcony, try 'Tumbling Red' tomatoes; the exotic dragon fruit, a succulent that bears night-scented blooms; strawberries; and some peas, such as 'Sugar Pod'.

'Divide and conquer' method

While you might think it's impossible to have too much garden, it's not, and your high hopes may soon be dashed as the reality of limited resources (mostly time) start playing havoc with your patch.

The simplest way to deal with this is the 'divide and conquer' method. Cut the space in half: use one half for your edibles and the other for a green manure crop, such as clover, which can be tilled under to enrich the soil. Then swap the two halves over the following year.

If this seems a waste of space, try growing cucurbits. A single plant of a large-sized variety of pumpkin can cover 10 m (33 ft) or more, and its huge leaves will shade out the weeds. But remember to always bulk up the soil afterwards with plenty of manure or compost, as they are big eaters, and leave the area fallow until the following spring. Other large sprawlers, such as sweet potatoes, can also be used this way in warm climates.

No-dig garden method

Another popular method of raising beds is what's known as a 'lasagne' or 'no-dig' garden. Just build up layers of newspaper, soil, compost, blood and bone, straw and manure, layer upon layer, as if you were layering pasta sheets with bolognaise and béchamel sauces to make lasagne, but instead of finishing with grated cheese, cover the lot with mulch or more straw.

Plant vegetable seedlings into a handful of either soil or premium potting mix, and their roots will tunnel through the layers as they become larger and stronger. Worms will come up through the ground after the manure and compost, and do the 'digging' for you (see also pages 16–17).

Obviously, you'll need to support the beds in some way — as for the raised garden bed (see page 14), use railway sleepers, logs, bricks or even bales of straw pegged into place. Raising the beds like this is good not only for the soil, but also for your back, so it's worth considering.

Traditional approaches

After humans settled down to growing crops, they eventually applied a system of grids to growing plants. It made access easier, irrigating via canals simpler and

Right: You can keep seedlings warm in winter by placing the punnets and trays on top of an electric blanket, which should be set at about 21°C (70°F), depending on the crop.

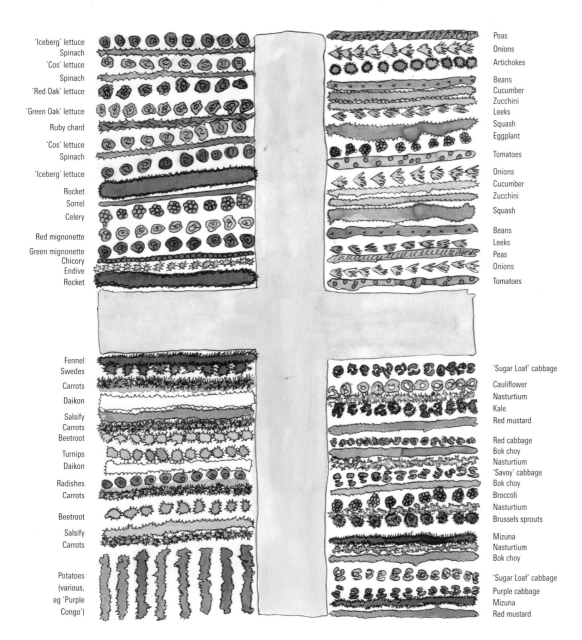

'Iceberg' lettuce
Spinach
'Cos' lettuce
Spinach
'Red Oak' lettuce

'Green Oak' lettuce

Ruby chard

'Cos' lettuce
Spinach

'Iceberg' lettuce

Rocket
Sorrel
Celery

Red mignonette

Green mignonette
Chicory
Endive
Rocket

Peas
Onions
Artichokes

Beans
Cucumber
Zucchini
Leeks
Squash
Eggplant

Tomatoes

Onions
Cucumber
Zucchini

Squash

Beans
Leeks
Peas
Onions

Tomatoes

Fennel
Swedes
Carrots
Daikon

Salsify
Carrots
Beetroot

Turnips
Daikon

Radishes
Carrots

Beetroot

Salsify
Carrots

Potatoes
(various,
eg 'Purple
Congo')

'Sugar Loaf' cabbage

Cauliflower
Nasturtium
Kale
Red mustard

Red cabbage
Bok choy
Nasturtium
'Savoy' cabbage
Bok choy
Broccoli
Nasturtium
Brussels sprouts

Mizuna
Nasturtium
Bok choy

'Sugar Loaf' cabbage
Purple cabbage
Mizuna
Red mustard

Above: A typical method of crop rotation is to divide your vegetable patch into four rectangles.

generally suited our geometric mindset. But even in ancient times we were aware that growing the same thing over and over again in the one place would wear out the soil, or deplete the same nutrients, so a system of leaving the land fallow once every seven years developed.

Crop rotation — moving plants from one section of land to another — is a logical extension of this. It not only keeps the soil more balanced but also prevents the accumulation of many diseases, such as club root rot (see page 255), and some pests, such as russet mite (see 'Mites', page 56) and root knot nematode (page 59).

Rows and rotation

The most common method of crop rotation is to divide your patch into four parts, and rotate your crops from one section to the

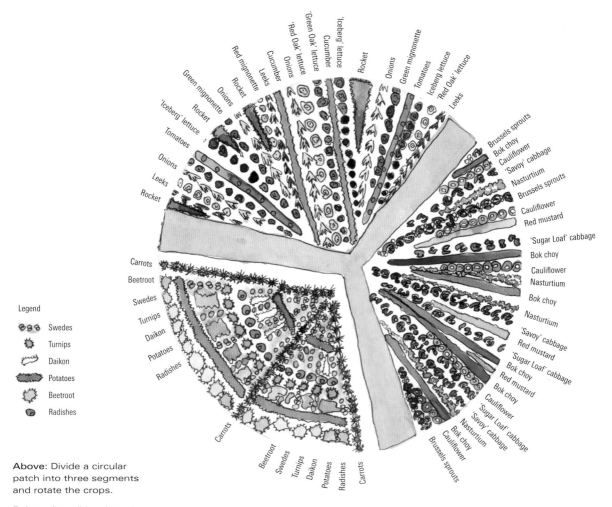

Green mignonette
Onions
Rocket
'Iceberg' lettuce
Tomatoes
Onions
Leeks
Rocket
Red mignonette
Rocket
Leeks
Cucumber
Onions
Cucumber
'Red Oak' lettuce
'Green Oak' lettuce
'Iceberg' lettuce
Cucumber
Rocket
Onions
Green mignonette
Tomatoes
Iceberg lettuce
'Red Oak' lettuce
Leeks

Brussels sprouts
Bok choy
Cauliflower
'Savoy' cabbage
Nasturtium
Brussels sprouts
Cauliflower
Red mustard
'Sugar Loaf' cabbage
Bok choy
Cauliflower
Nasturtium
Bok choy
Nasturtium
'Savoy' cabbage
Red mustard
'Sugar Loaf' cabbage
Bok choy
Red mustard
Bok choy
Cauliflower
Nasturtium
'Sugar Loaf' cabbage
'Savoy' cabbage
Bok choy
Cauliflower
Brussels sprouts

Carrots
Beetroot
Swedes
Turnips
Daikon
Potatoes
Radishes

Carrots
Beetroot
Swedes
Turnips
Daikon
Potatoes
Radishes
Carrots

Legend

🦪🦪🦪 Swedes

🌼 Turnips

〰️ Daikon

🟫 Potatoes

🌸 Beetroot

🔴 Radishes

Above: Divide a circular patch into three segments and rotate the crops.

Below: A traditional patch planted in rows.

next so that plants with the same nutrient requirements don't eat up all the available food. For example, in the first section, after you've added manure, plant beans and peas. In the next section, dig in some lime and add, in season, cabbages, cauliflower or brussels sprouts. In the next plot, plant salad greens, tomatoes, eggplants, onions and leeks and, in the last section, plant carrots, beetroot, radishes and potatoes (the range of gourmet potatoes is huge; see pages 282–3).

The following season move everything along — that is, plant the cabbages where the peas were, the salad greens where the cabbages were, and so on.

Alternatively, you could divide your patch into threes, as shown in the illustration opposite. Try to organise it so that legumes (peas and beans) are followed by brassicas (cabbages, broccoli and brussels sprouts). Then follow them with root crops, or add plenty of manure again before planting leafy greens or fruiting plants such as eggplants and tomatoes — all vegetables that will enjoy more food. This also means that plants that like lime — for example, legumes and brassicas — grow in the limed section before lime-sensitive plants are planted.

The square foot method

This method utilises a grid method rather than rows. Each square within the grid is 1 x 1 m (3 x 3 ft) and edged by a hard path. These squares are then further divided into 30-cm (1-ft) squares. Once you've harvested a square, replant it immediately with new seeds or seedlings; depending on what you plant, each square contains up to sixteen plants.

The benefit of this method is that your vegetable patch produces a maximum crop for the space, and you won't compact the soil as you stand and work from the paths. The condition of the soil is crucial, however, as a 'hard-working' plot like this requires well conditioned soil with lots of added organic matter.

The grid still needs to follow basic plant size rules. For example, only one cabbage or tomato plant can go in each 30-cm (1-ft) box. These can be dotted about your squares, however, so that the likelihood of cabbage moth attack is diminished, in much the same way as a traditional organic or permaculture system works (see page 36). But you could fit up to nine smaller vegetables such as beetroot in each square.

Planning an orchard

Obviously orchardists set out their orchards in a similar grid-like pattern to maximise the number of trees they can grow and to make it easier for the harvester to move down the rows. However, the drawback with this type of system is that it generally creates a monoculture, which means that plants are growing by themselves with their own kind rather than in a mixed system.

You can partly remedy this by planting some other plants among your orchard rows. They might be insect-attracting plants, green manure crops or just flowers for the house. You could also mix some flowering groundcovers with grass to help attract bees, which will pollinate any self-sterile trees.

A rambling rose will attract bees and butterflies to this old orchard.

Left: Before you start planting vegetables, lay down some string lines to use as guides. This bed, which is part of a four-bed system, has lain fallow but is now ready to plant with seedlings.

Organic gardening

To garden organically is to believe that you are interconnected with natural processes, and that your inputs and outputs need to be natural rather than artificial to have integrity. It's a matter of looking at gardening holistically, even of considering the world as one large living organism…Gaia.

Above: Pumpkins, alliums and dill grow together in an organic garden.

Opposite: Organically grown white and orange carrots, parsnips and heirloom sugar beet.

A way of life

Advocates of organic gardening will tell you that we have to go organic in order for the world to survive, while skeptics will insist that the world can't be fed in an organic model, and that global starvation will be the inevitable result.

No doubt the truth is probably somewhere in between, but if you want to make lifestyle changes by using fewer chemicals and fossil fuels, and by increasing biodiversity in your own garden, then perhaps this is your opportunity to make a difference. After all, the environmentalists' mantra is 'Think globally, act locally', so why not start in your own backyard?

Many believe there are health and culinary benefits — that organically grown food not only tastes better but is healthier, containing higher levels of antioxidants. What is undisputable is that the fresher your produce, the more vitamins and minerals it contains, so eating homegrown produce that hasn't been sprayed with pesticides is definitely an advantage.

Organic farms have to comply with rigorous standards applied to both their food production and processing techniques in order to gain accreditation, but the home gardener is constrained by no such red tape.

While using naturally derived compost, fertilisers, animal manures and worm products is fairly straightforward, the weak point of maintaining the organic model is usually pest control. Try removing pests by hand and using organic products such as diatomaceous earth and oil sprays until your garden builds its own ecosystem, where predator wildlife and natural checks and balances are in place. But be patient, as most experts say this can take about three years; in the meantime you'll need to be vigilant.

Permaculture

Permaculture is an abbreviation of the term 'permanent agriculture', which relates to the sustainable use of the land in the production of food and use of resources. It conjures up images of country-scaled properties, begging the question: 'What does this have to do with the average suburban backyard?' Like organic gardeners, permaculturalists believe in using only natural fertilisers and pesticides.

The term 'permaculture' itself was coined in the 1970s by two Australians, David Holmgren and Bill Mollison. Their concept was defined further when they published *Permaculture One* in 1978. According to this work, permaculture

Poultry

You don't have to own a farm to experience the unique taste and colour of fresh eggs from your own free-ranging chickens or ducks, as the average backyard is large enough for at least a couple of birds, which will supply your daily needs.

Chickens

Chickens need water and chicken pellets daily, and will happily scratch and forage around your garden, eating grubs and insects as they go. They also love kitchen scraps, making them the ultimate recyclers, but they will need some work too: their coops must be cleaned out weekly and they need worming every three months. Healthy birds will live for about ten years, but lay better when they are young. Make sure you don't buy a rooster: not only do they not lay, but they are also banned in residential areas due to their antisocial dawn crowing.

Coops and tractors

You can buy A-frame kit coops, known as 'tractors', which are easy to erect and have the added advantage of being mobile: just move them around the garden on their rear wheels so the chickens won't wear out a patch of lawn. You can change their position, depending on the season, making sure your chickens always have some shade and shelter where they can escape hot or wet weather. You can also run a mobile coop up and down your vegetable patch so the chickens eat out sections where vegetables have gone to seed.

Another great alternative is round chicken houses, where the chickens can't corner and peck each other as easily. This bullying occurs whenever you introduce another bird to the coop; until a 'pecking' order is established, the new bird may be attacked quite badly.

Ducks

For slug and snail policing, it's hard to go past ducks. One of the best backyard types is Khaki Campbell, which will lay more than 300 eggs a year. Muscovy ducks are quieter and don't need a pond although, obviously, they will need water. They can be used for egg laying too.

This spread: You must provide chickens with a well ventilated shelter that gives them protection from the heat and cold winds. They also benefit from ground-covers under foot, even if it's only grass.

is not only a sustainable system of agriculture but also a holistic system of design for all human needs. It's most often applied to basic human needs such as water, food and shelter, but it is also used to design more abstract systems, such as community and economic structures.

In relation to the urban garden, the basic principles of permaculture cover the input and output of resources. These include using rainwater tanks to catch roof water (instead of sending it into the stormwater system), which is then used to water vegetables; grey-water tanks that divert household water to trees; poultry that can convert scraps into fowl manure; compost heaps that turn vegetable matter into a valuable soil conditioner; and worm farms that process paper and vegetable matter into soil conditioners and liquid feed. In other words, this system basically reuses resources, sometimes reinventing them to have other useful purposes.

In the average suburban backyard, the permaculture set-up usually involves a seven-tiered forest. Each tier produces food, as follows.

1 The top layer is the canopy, made up of fruit and nut trees.
2 The next layer consists of smaller fruit trees and dwarf cultivars.
3 The third layer is smaller shrubs, such as currants and berries.
4 These fruit-bearing shrubs are planted among herbs, the fourth layer.
5 The next layer is the root zone, where root crops are grown.
6 The sixth layer comprises ground-covering plants, such as clover, sweet potatoes and strawberries.
7 The last layer is the vertical one, where climbing plants, such as fruiting vines and peas and beans, grow.

Producing edibles in your own environment means your food goes straight from the garden to the table, so neither transport nor fuel is involved in the process. Producing crops organically in a diverse ecosystem also means that no environmental poisons and toxins are released into the environment, and there is also room for birds, insects and other beneficial organisms such as lizards and frogs in the system.

Biodynamics

Developed more than 65 years ago, bio-dynamics — a farming technique that is all about soil fertility, soil organisms and building plant health from the ground up — closely follows moon alignments and planetary positions. Early supporters of biodynamics, such as Rudolf Steiner, were key players in the development of these theories, including using 'preparations' (see box, below right), which are soil activators made from farm-sourced materials. They also firmly believed in living systems being affected by celestial cycles.

The moon has long been used as a planting guide, with the waxing and waning cycles indicating the timing of various gardening jobs, such as planting out, sowing seeds, feeding and watering. This may sound a bit strange, but lunar gardeners will tell you that if the moon can affect gravity enough to cause tidal action, why wouldn't it also affect the flow of water in the water table and thus soil moisture itself, and therefore be fundamental to plant growth?

These age-old practices may have more validity than we realise, even though we don't understand them yet. They are ancient techniques that take into account such things as the position of the planets: trees, for instance, have a ruling planet, so there are better times for planting each type, depending on whether or not its planet is in an ascendant position.

The basic guidelines, however, are that you should sow plants that crop above the ground during the waxing moon, sow plants that crop under the ground (bulbs and roots) during the waning moon, and annuals during the waxing moon, as this is its fertile phase and encourages quick growth. Biennials, perennials and shrubs, on the other hand, should be planted during the waning moon, which is the moon's quiet period; this allows the maximum time for root growth.

Other principles include not sowing or transplanting on days when there is a new moon, full moon or quarter moon. Transplanting is best done between the new and full moon (waxing), as is grafting and mowing. Weeding is better done between the last quarter and the new moon, when the moon is in its barren phase. Any digging and tilling should be done in this phase too. Seed collection should be done at full moon.

Above: A compost pile, one of the biodynamic Compost Preparations.

Opposite: According to the philosophy of permaculture, sharing surplus with neighbours is not only an act of generosity, but also helps spread the cause.

Biodynamic preparations

These preparations are not supposed to take the place of other organic gardening practices, such as composting and manuring, crop rotation and using poultry and other livestock as recyclers, but rather to assist soils with their fertility cycles.

The three basic preparation groups are Horn Manure Preparation (500), Horn Silica Preparation (501) and Compost Preparations (502 to 507). The Horn Manure Preparation — where a cow horn is filled with cow manure then buried in the ground from autumn to spring — is designed to enliven the soil, boosting the microflora and availability of nutrients, including trace elements. The Horn Silica Preparation is supposed to lead to better fruit and seed development as well as an improvement in its nutrition and flavour, while the Compost Preparations help with soil and material breakdown.

Garden wildlife

One of the main reasons for keeping your garden as free as possible of pesticides is to protect beneficial insects and other wildlife, whether they're breaking down organic matter into fertiliser for plants, ridding your garden of pests or fertilising your flowers so they will produce fruit.

Above: A green lacewing.

Opposite: A healthy garden is a balanced ecosystem, where pests are kept under control by their natural predators. Encourage birds into the garden with a birdbath.

Beneficial insects and other wildlife

The typical garden is home to many different types of insect, and in a way they're all beneficial, as they are all part of the food chain. But beneficial insects, as gardeners call them, are those that help out with pest control, eating insects that would otherwise be eating their way through your plants.

Some are well known, and include ladybirds, praying mantis, lacewings and predatory mites. Encouraging them into your garden is worth a bit of effort. It may be a simple matter of letting some parsley go to seed or not mowing your grass quite so short, but probably the best thing you can do is not spray your garden in case you accidentally kill off the beneficial insects.

Earwigs, hoverflies, wasps, dragonflies and even predatory insects are all doing you a great service by keeping other insects in check. But don't forget that many others, such as bees, butterflies and even the humble fly are working hard, pollinating your crops so, wherever possible, they should be protected.

Our understanding of the environment and the average garden's ecosystem is still developing, but we do know that about 90 per cent of garden wildlife are invertebrates, most of which you probably rarely see. As we still have so much to learn, it's important to 'tread lightly on the earth', starting in your own garden.

Lacewings

With their fragile wings, pale green adult lacewings (*Chrysopa* sp.) are quite pretty. The female will feed only on nectar, so always include some flowers in your patch for her. She lays up to 200 eggs on individual strands of fine hair-like silk so that when they hatch, the little dears don't eat each other. Her laying technique also protects the eggs from ants. The larvae will happily munch on moth eggs, aphids, scale, mealybugs and even hard to control pests such as mites, thrips and white flies.

Above, from left to right: A fungus-eating ladybird; praying mantis; fruit bats, also known as flying foxes, asleep in the daytime; and a blue tongue lizard.

Ladybirds

Ladybirds (*Coccinella* sp.) come in many shapes, colours and spot counts, with over 3000 different species worldwide and at least 400 native to Australia alone, but one thing almost all of them have in common is that they are the gardener's fabulous friend. Both adult and larval forms of this insect love nothing more than to feast on aphids and other soft-bodied invertebrates.

Praying mantis

Svelte praying mantis (*Mantis religiosa*) are the panthers of the insect world, quickly pouncing on and devouring many other insects in the garden, even those bigger than themselves. And they are renowned for their sexual conquests: after mating, the female mantis is quite likely to dine on her now superfluous partner. Luckily for gardeners, these stick-like insects also munch on grasshoppers, bugs, crickets and anything else they can find.

Birds and fruit bats

Birds and fruit bats are often reviled for the damage they cause to precious fruit trees. What normally goes unnoticed, however, is all the hard work they also invest in keeping insect populations down. They eat vast quantities of insects and are integral to the pest patrol in your garden.

In Australia, fruit bats or flying foxes are protected native animals, so it's illegal to harm them. To deter them, use effective barriers such as netting or even sensory-triggered flood lights.

Nets can be either permanent or temporary throws, depending on the grade of material. Make sure they are proper bird nets, however, with about 15-mm ($1/2$-in) diamond mesh, which is the correct size for excluding, rather than trapping, birds and bats. For more ideas, see page 50.

While you might need to net fruit trees and fruiting vines to keep birds away from your produce, encouraging them into your garden certainly has more benefits than disadvantages. Grow a mix of native

Leaf-eating ladybirds

If the leaves of your cucurbits, potatoes, beans or tomatoes start to exhibit skeletonised damage, then chances are the 28-spotted ladybird (*Henosepilachna* sp.) is responsible. In the home garden, both the adults, which have 28 spots on a light orange background, and the larvae, a creamy yellow colour covered in black spines, can be picked off by hand.

The 28-spotted ladybird.

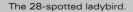

plants to encourage birds into the garden, bearing in mind that you may have to utilise different approaches to attract lots of different species. Some birds like trees, others low-growing shrubs and grasses.

All birds need water, so a birdbath in a safe place will also encourage them to linger, bathe and feed. If your water feature is deep, put something in the centre for them to stand on. (See also the box on 'Attracting wildlife', page 46.)

Lizards

Lizards love eating slugs and snails, arguably garden enemy number one, so actively including lizards in your garden management plan makes great sense. You stand a good chance of having a healthy lizard population if you refrain from using toxic snail bait (don't forget lizards will unwittingly eat poisoned pests) and keep pets (especially cats) under control, by either keeping them inside or making sure they wear mirrored collars with at least a bell to alert lizards of their approach.

Making sure there is plenty of ground cover and a sunny place or well protected rock where they can bask as well as following a pesticide-free policy in your own backyard — hopefully your neighbours will too — should allow the lizards to go about their beneficial work of eating insects, snails and slugs.

Sex in the garden

Many fruit trees can only produce fruit if their flowers are fertilised. This is where cross-pollination comes in. Sometimes you need to plant different cultivars, or trees with flowers of different sexes so that the flowers of one tree pollinate the other. Even partly self-fertile plants often produce much more fruit if they're grown near another plant.

These pollen transfers can be carried by wind, but more often they are carried by insects — primarily bees and butterflies — while they gather pollen for honey or feast on nectar-filled blooms. Encouraging these insects into your garden makes good sense. Avoiding chemicals is the first step, but if you have to spray, make sure you don't do it when the bees are actively foraging, so first thing in the morning is usually safest. The other thing to remember is to attract bees and butterflies to your garden by planting other flowers with your fruiting crops so they'll fertilise your flowering fruit and vegetables.

Some people with larger plots also like to put beehives in their garden or orchard. Bear in mind though that bees need regular attention, and they also have stingers. Some apiarists will set up a hive on your property and then look after it for you, even supplying you with the odd bottle of honey.

Attract butterflies to your garden so they'll pollinate your edibles.

Spiders

If you suffer from arachnophobia, then perhaps it's time to take a fresh look at spiders and start appreciating all the work they do in the garden. Even the beauty of a dew-dripping web is reason enough to encourage spiders into the garden.

Spiders eat moths and butterflies, the adult stages of caterpillars, as well as flies and beetles. They also provide nutritious snacks for lizards, birds and the garden superstar, praying mantis. While it's true that some spiders are poisonous to humans, most simply don't have fangs that are strong enough to pierce skin, let alone gardening gloves.

Taking the simple precaution of wearing gloves as well as closed-in shoes will protect you from most things you'll find in the garden, while being cautious when walking about at night or first thing in the morning will help prevent those sticky web entanglements.

Companion planting

Plants themselves can be used to help control and manage pests. Some plants, especially herbs, are known for their pungent aroma, which has traditionally been very useful for repelling insects. Rue (*Ruta* sp.), wormwood (*Artemisia* sp.), basil (*Ocimum basilicum*), pennyroyal (*Mentha pulegium*) and the other mints are just some of the better known herbs.

Planting natural pesticides such as pyrethrum among your crops can be used in isolation, or in a complementary manner, to either deter pests or mask desirable plants with other scents. This system of planting is one aspect of 'companion planting', which offers an environmentally friendly solution to keeping your garden healthy while, at the same time, encouraging biodiversity.

In the garden, companion plants work in different ways. There are masking plants, such as sage, oregano and thyme,

Attracting wildlife

Adding water to your garden is a great way to start creating a sanctuary for garden wildlife. Obviously animals such as frogs will benefit, but so will birds, dragonflies, lizards and damsel flies. When they're not sunning themselves by the pool, they will happily eat any pests in your garden.

Frogs love flies, mosquitoes and other insects we love to hate, so it makes good gardening sense to try and include a place for frogs in your garden. This might mean installing a frog pond, which should have shallow edges and a flat base at least 50 cm (20 in) deep to allow frogs both easy access in and out of the pond and enough depth in which to breed happily. A position in half sun, half shade is ideal. Placing logs and rocks in the pool will also give the frogs safe places in which to bathe and breed.

A well designed frog pond can be a beautiful garden feature.

which produce strong, pungent oils that 'mask' other plants likely to be attacked by insects. You can also plant lavender (*Lavandula* sp.), which has an incredibly strong scent, to protect nearby vulnerable plants like beans from pests such as white flies. It also helps to repel aphids.

And there are pest-repellent plants, which you can use in various ways. You can plant tansy (*Tanacetum vulgare*), for example, near doorways to repel flies, or scatter the leaves around to repel ants. Basil is another companion plant that is often used to repel aphids, but if you grow a pot near your barbecue area it will also help keep flies and mosquitoes away.

Wormwood has an incredibly strong scent that can be used to repel insects, as has sage (*Salvia* sp.). Plant either of these herbs around cabbages to repel the cabbage moth (*Plutella xylostella*) (see page 257).

Insect-attracting plants such as elder (*Sambucus* sp.), dill (*Anethum graveolens*) and fennel (*Foeniculum vulgare*) all have pretty flowers; grow these to attract hoverflies, which eat other pests in the garden.

'Nurse' plants

Often these relationships are mutually beneficial. For example, Native Americans follow a traditional companion planting practice called the Three Sisters. They plant corn, beans and squash close together: corn provides a support for the beans to climb; beans return nitrogen to the soil; and with its large leaves covering the soil, squash controls weeds and deters pests. Traditionally, rotten fish were buried when the corn seeds were planted, although you could use a fish emulsion fertiliser instead. After the last frost in your area, try using the Three Sisters method in your garden.

Phenology

This is the study of the times of recurring natural phenomena, such as the dates when leaves or flowers emerge, even when insects emerge from their cocoons or migratory birds make their first flight. The founder of this science was Robert Marsham (1708–1797). A keen naturalist from Norfolk in the United Kingdom, he was the first to record the coming of spring according to 27 key indicators, rather than the conventional date itself (1 September in the southern hemisphere, 1 March in the northern). These days scientists are keen to study whole systems like this, using them as indicators for other things, such as global warming.

'Trap' plants

Another practice is to grow sunflowers as 'trap' plants with beans, thus using one plant as a lure for certain insects. The sunflowers attract the sapsuckers first, leaving the beans, which are prone to aphid attack, relatively pest-free. Nasturtiums can also be used as a trap crop with aphids, as can chives.

Complementary plants

Another way to use plants as companions is to plant those with different needs next to each other. For example, shallow-rooted plants will compete for moisture with other shallow-rooted plants, but may be suitable for growing next to a deep-rooted crop. This works for plants such as carrots and tomatoes, where the carrots help break up the soil and allow the tomatoes greater access to deep soil moisture. Obviously, growing plants that are prone to the same pest or disease together is poor practice, and crop rotation can break these cycles.

While many of these relationships are still hearsay, planting even some of these herbs will not only diversify your garden design but also add attractive, interesting and aromatic elements to it.

Above: A bean plant climbing up corn, a traditional 'nurse' plant.

Common pests

A wide range of insects and other pests may be a problem in your edible garden, but understanding how they eat and breed will help you to either deter them or co-exist with them.

Ants

Ants like nesting in dry areas, such as in the sand between pavers and even in pot plants, but it's when they team up with aphids, scales and mealybugs that the trouble really starts.

These sap-sucking insects, which produce honeydew (see page 59), are often protected from attacks by other insects by the ants, which are keen to harvest their sweet excretion. On the other hand, ants also help to recycle organic matter, aerate the soil while building their tunnels and are themselves a food source for many other creatures.

If your garden is plagued by these pests, taking care of the ants may well be a necessary evil. However, many ant sprays are quite toxic and will kill other beneficial insects too, so try pouring boiling water on their trails, putting out tubs of borax mixed with sugar or even kicking their nests over so they are forced to use their resources to make repairs.

Beetles

Beetles have six legs, like all insects, and hardened forewings, and all have chewing mouth parts.

Asparagus beetles

You can easily control this black and orange bug (*Crioceris asparagi*) by picking it off by hand. Also, because the adults overwinter in leaf litter, you can keep them at bay with thorough winter clear-outs. There is also a natural predator, a metallic green wasp, so don't spray asparagus beetles as these will also be affected.

Dried fruit beetles

Carpophilus hemipterus attack a wide range of fruit, including stone fruit and tomatoes. Their presence is mostly due to unwanted, perhaps damaged, fruit not being picked or cleared away from the ground. The beetles themselves are dark brown and only a few millimetres long, looking a bit like passionfruit seeds.

While they are in their larval stage, feeding inside the fruit, any contact sprays will be ineffective, but they can work in winter when the beetles usually shelter in the bark and crevices of the tree trunk.

Fig beetles

Fig tree leaf beetle (*Poneridia semipullata*) is an Australian native beetle that likes exotic figs. Attacking in groups, it quickly skeletonises the leaves, which then fall prematurely. Both the larval and adult stages can cause damage, and they usually start work in early summer. In late winter, look for groups of pale yellow eggs, then squash them by hand.

Fig bark beetle (*Aricerus eichhoffi*), another Australian pest, tunnels into the tips of shoots. Cut off any damaged shoots.

Opposite: An outline of a cat with marble eyes, which catch the light, will help frighten birds away from your crops.

Longicorn beetles

Adult longicorn beetles, which have a square shape and long antennae, eat very little. They vary in size from 5 mm (1/5 in) to 6 cm (2¼ in), depending on the species, and different species attack different trees; many only eat deadwood and fallen trees rather than living tissue.

The cream larvae usually feed on the phloem and cambial region just under the bark. In a healthy tree, the larvae are usually trapped in sap, but on a stressed tree they might be able to get a foothold and even ring-bark your tree.

Trees can be weakened by a number of causes — drought or poor drainage; mechanical injury from a lawn mower, for example; grass growing too close to the trunk and taking the feed and water from the tree; or simply old age.

Birds and bats

Birds can also turn from friend to foe, quickly devouring your crops. There are many ways to scare them away.

Scarecrows are perhaps the most common method. Stuff some old clothes with straw, and use a broom handle or two for the spine and/or arms, finishing off with an old hat and boots. Give them 'accessories' such as glistening beads, dangling bells and even shiny paper or foil vests that reflect the light as well as the movement of other things.

Another option is to use replicas of their natural predators — for example, metal cut-outs of hawks, eagles and even cats with marbles for eyes, placed near your orchard or kitchen garden. Careful netting and screening of either the whole patch, the whole tree in fruit or just the fruits themselves are other tactics for protecting your harvest (see page 44).

Borers

The larvae of some moths can also damage fruit trees, especially stone fruit. Of particular concern is the fruit tree borer, which lays its eggs in the branch junctions between stems and branches. The larvae eat the soft bark surrounding their hole and come out at night to feed on some of the leaves. The signs of their activity are oozing sap, webbing and frass (their droppings) in the branch junctions and, in severe cases, ring-barking of tree limbs.

To control borers, remove any webbing or frass. Poke wires down the holes and try to stab the grubs. Be vigilant and keep your tree healthy and vigorous.

Pod borers are caterpillars that attack beans. The easiest way to remove them is by hand, but breaking their life cycle by rotating your crops, so that you grow a non-legume in between seasons, will also help. If you have to spray, try using neem oil, which is extracted from the fruit and seeds of the neem tree (*Azadirachta indica*). It is approved by organic organisations.

The large auger beetle (*Bostrychopsis jesuita*) hastens the death of already dying trees by tunnelling into the sapwood.

Below: Toy rubber snakes, placed strategically in fruit trees, may deter birds.

Below right: Inflate empty wine bladders and hang them near your crops.

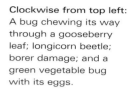
Clockwise from top left: A bug chewing its way through a gooseberry leaf; longicorn beetle; borer damage; and a green vegetable bug with its eggs.

Bugs

Unlike beetles, bugs suck up sap through a straw-like appendage called a proboscis. Not all bugs eat plants, however. Look out for the pirate bug, which eats moth eggs and thrips; the big-eyed bug, which dines on mites; and the pointy shoulder 'stink' or shield bug. A simple examination with a magnifying glass should reveal whether they're eating other bugs or your plants.

Fruit-spotting bugs

Native to Australia, *Ambypelta* sp. munch on guavas, pecans, passionfruit, stone fruit, custard apples, avocados, persimmons, papaws, lychees and macadamias, even citrus. They cause fruit drop and spotting. Be vigilant at flowering and fruiting times when they are most likely to be present. They are about 1.5 cm (1/2 in) long, green when adult and orange-red when young.

Green vegetable bugs

In the edible garden, the biggest pest is the green vegetable bug (*Nezara viridula*), which has a triangular thorax with three tiny yellow spots across its back. About 1.5 cm (1/2 in) long, it can suck bean pods dry or leave splotch marks on your tomatoes.

These bugs also like pumpkins, spinach, capsicums, peas, passionfruit, oranges and potatoes. Removing spent fruit and old plants as well as keeping beds weeded will help control this bug, as the young bugs prefer foliage to fruit.

Harlequin bugs

Dindymus versicolor also likes fruit and vegetables, with apples, figs, grapes, oranges, rhubarb, pumpkins, tomatoes and melons their favourites. Their bodies have triangular yellow and green markings, often with red and black highlights.

Just over 1 cm (1/2 in) long, they travel in packs and feed on new growth, causing wilted leaves and fruit, leaving it blemished. They overwinter in junk heaps, piles of wood and near fences, so patrolling these areas and squashing them will help minimise the possibility of a spring attack. Weeds also attract them so, again, controlling these will help.

tip

If you improve the vigour of your tree, you'll improve its chances of overcoming the longicorn beetle and other borers.

Olive lace bugs

Froggattia olivinia is an Australian native pest that sucks sap, leaving the leaves mottled yellow. Thoroughly spray the underside of the leaves with pyrethrum.

Rutherglen bugs

A dirty grey colour, *Nysius vinitor* travel along roadsides and degraded areas, feeding off weeds and grass until it dries off. The problems occur when they stumble into your place, and the comparative feast helps their numbers to quickly increase.

Once they're in your garden, their favourites are grapes, strawberries, beans, lettuce, tomatoes, onions, carrots and potatoes. They also don't mind stone fruit, even if it's unripe; look for long threads of sap dripping from your crop.

Earwigs

You'll find earwigs under loose bark, rock piles and timber. They mainly feed on lettuces, but also like some other vegetables such as cauliflower and celery. Luckily, they're easy to trap. Simply scrunch up some newspaper and put it into a terracotta pot, then pop it among your crops or near their hiding holes. Once they're in the pot, set the newspaper alight,

then replace it with fresh newspaper for the next round. (Don't use this method if you live in a bushfire-prone area and/or there is a fire danger warning in place.)

Flies

The common fly is part of the *Diptera* family, which includes mosquitoes, robber flies and hoverflies. Sawflies, on the other hand, are part of the *Hymenoptera* family, which includes bees, wasps and ants.

Bean flies

Ophiomyia phaseoli is a small but very troublesome pest that attacks French (dwarf) and climbing beans. This 3-mm (1/10-in) black fly lays its eggs on bean foliage during warm, humid weather.

Above right: The colour yellow is attractive to many insects, including grasshoppers. You can buy sticky traps for this purpose or make your own. You can even make traps by covering yellow plastic containers with a layer of molasses or petroleum jelly.

Below: You can also fill a yellow container with water, and they will drown.

Below centre: Turning over a piece of bark may reveal an earwig.

Below right: A fruit fly on an orange.

Once hatched, the larvae tunnel their way inside the stems, making the plants wilt and yellow. When you harvest the beans, bits will break off easily or the whole plant may fall over. Regularly check your plants and give them a quick spray of white oil every few weeks in the growing season.

Carrot flies

Chamaepsila rosae is a problem in the northern hemisphere, particularly in the United Kingdom, where it attacks not just carrots, but also parsnips and celery. This fly lays its eggs around developing crops and, as the creamy yellow maggots hatch, they feed on the outer layers of the roots, creating rusty brown tunnels and rendering the crop useless as they cause more damage throughout autumn.

The best control is to prevent the female from coming in contact with the roots in the first place: simply erect a small tunnel of horticultural fleece that will stop the fly entering. Newer resistant varieties of carrot such as 'Flyaway' are also being bred to combat this pest.

Fruit flies

For the fruit grower, fruit fly is undoubtedly one of the worst pests. It affects tomatoes and many citrus, stone and pome fruit as well as other fruit-like vegetables. This tricky pest overwinters on trees, such as loquats, where they hide over the cooler months when most food sources are short.

Monitoring for evidence of this pest is the first step towards its control. You can hang baits of various types in trees, from the home-made yeast baits to scientifically designed pheromone baits (see the step by step sequence above), which attract the males by luring them with a female-like scent. But it's important to realise that it's the females that lay the eggs in your crops

and, once these hatch, the maggots start eating and damaging your fruit.

There is a product that contains a bacteria-derived insecticide, called spinosad, which is registered for use with fruit fly (both Mediterranean fruit fly, or *Ceratitis capitata*, and Queensland fruit fly, or *Bactrocera tryoni*). It also has the green tick of approval from eco-organisations. You can apply it in baits or as a band or spot spray to the trunk or lower foliage of trees or plants within the orchard.

Pear and cherry slugs

Pear and cherry slug is actually the larval stage of black sawfly (*Caliroa cerasi*). You can easily hose them off affected trees, such as pears, apples, plums, cherries, quinces and crabapples. (See page 165.)

Setting up pheromone baits

Attract male fruit fly into a trap by using pheromone baits that mimic the smell of the female fruit fly.

1 Place the felt containing the chemical in the slot on the lid.

2 Punch a hole in the side of the container. The insects will fly in through this hole.

3 Punch another hole in the bottom so that water can escape.

4 Hang the bait in your fruit tree.

White flies

Of more concern to the kitchen gardener is white fly, a pest that attacks, depending on the variety, citrus, sugar cane and, in the case of greenhouse white fly, beans and tomatoes. These are about 3 mm (1/10 in) long and feed by sucking sap from the underside of leaves.

White flies are parasitised by the parasitic wasp (*Encarsia formosa*) and are usually kept in check naturally; however, if this is not the case in your garden, hang sticky yellow traps in susceptible crops, such as beans and tomatoes, as white flies are attracted by the colour yellow.

Fungus gnats

Often mistakenly called black fly, fungus gnats look like mosquitoes. They are about 3 mm (1/10 in) long, and feed on decaying organic matter as well as soft-fleshed fruit such as nectarines. The larvae can feed on the fine root hairs of seedlings, causing wilt. You can afford to ignore them, unless they appear in plague numbers.

Grasshoppers, crickets and katydids

Inland katydids (*Caedicia simplex*) look very much like green grasshoppers and usually eat leaves of various plants but, as adults, can also attack the fruit of peaches, apples, pears and grapes. They are not usually a concern, however, as sprays that are used in most commercial orchards keep their numbers down, which in turn keep them under control elsewhere. If things get bad, try a chilli or garlic spray as a deterrent.

Crickets, such as the black field cricket (*Teleogryllus commodus*), can also diverge from their normal diet of pasture grasses and attack fruit, such as strawberries. They can be a problem, especially if the plants are young and vulnerable. Keeping the soil well watered and mulched will stop it cracking and providing hiding holes for them. You can limit the damage caused by bad infestations by covering susceptible crops with nets until they pass by.

Not all grasshoppers are plant eaters. Those with sharp, spiny front legs are actually predators and will eat some of your garden bugs, so check before you squash them.

For the others, it's best to look for them in the morning, before the day warms up and the short-horned type becomes active. The long-horned grasshoppers eat at night time, but can fall prey to birds, sugar gliders, lizards, snakes, frogs and assassin bugs. Robber flies, paper wasps and parasitic wasps also work hard in this regard, but can be encouraged further if you plant nectar-producing plants (see page 45) and even sweet Alice and clover.

Other biological ways of keeping their numbers down include keeping chickens. The eggs of grasshoppers can, however, lie in the soil for years until it rains, then hatch and cause devastation, especially in inland areas, before vacating the area for another. When this happens, cover anything precious and wait until they pass before replanting.

Garden soldier flies

Sometimes called a garden maggot, *Neoexaireta spinigera* is not a pest in the garden. The adults, about 12 mm (1/2 in) long, are very common and can often be found trapped inside by flyscreens. Like fungus gnats, they usually feed only on decaying fruit, so you don't need to control them.

Clockwise from top left:
A leaf-eating caterpillar;
codling moth on an apple;
another type of leaf-eating
caterpillar; and a cricket.

Grubs, moths and caterpillars

Except for fruit-sucking moths, which affect citrus, tomatoes, melons and custard apples, the damaging part of a moth's life cycle is the larval stage. Freshly hatched caterpillars usually skeletonise leaves, leaving the main venation intact, but as their mouths grow, so does their strength, increasing the damage they can cause to foliage and even stems.

Citrus butterflies

Other caterpillars that can cause grief in the orchard are the small (*Papilio anactus*) and large citrus butterfly (*Papilio aegeus*), the grapevine moth, the grapevine hawk moth (*Hippotion celerio*) and the currant borer moth (*Synanthedon tipuliformis*).

The large citrus butterfly is black with a pale yellow band at the tip of its forewing while the young larvae look like bird poo. It can eat quite a lot of foliage, but can be easily removed by hand. The small citrus

butterfly looks similar and has white, grey and black markings with orange spots on its hind wings. It lays eggs singly and can also be easily picked off by hand.

Codling moths

Cydia pomonella is probably the worst pest in this family. In Australia, its control is statutory in many areas, and affected fruit must be destroyed immediately. The small (2 cm/³⁄₄ in across) greyish brown moth lays its eggs into pome fruit, some stone fruit and even immature walnuts, so the larvae have plenty to eat as they grow.

Oriental fruit moths

Grapholita molesta lays its eggs on the underside of new leaves and shoots, and as the larvae grow, they tunnel into the new shoots, eventually making them wither and die, but in the process they may ooze gum. This moth is most likely to attack your peaches and nectarines as well as apples, quinces and pears.

tip

Suitable for using against caterpillars and other chewing insects on crops such as tomatoes, spinosad is also available as a dust or liquid concentrate, but it has a small withholding period.

Painted apple moths

Also a pest in apple orchards is the Australian native pest called painted apple moth (*Teia anartoides*), which can give you a very nasty sting if it lands on your bare skin. Also called spitfires, they tend to stagnate in the one area, as the female is wingless, and can therefore build up to quite large numbers. Banding around affected tree trunks is an easy way to control them.

Other caterpillars and grubs

Watch out for tomato grub or corn earworm (*Helicoverpa arigera*), cluster caterpillar (*Spodoptera litura*) and green looper (*Chrysodeixis eriosoma*). Control these by manual removal, bio-insecticides or *Bacillus thuringiensis*, an organic spray that won't affect birds or bees. The latter, a naturally occurring bacteria that can be sprayed onto leaf surfaces, is registered for use on many caterpillars.

A ring-barking grub drills a hole into the trunk of guava and then feeds off the cambium, disguising the damage with frass. To control it, scrape off the frass and put a few drops of pyrethrum into the entrance hole to poison it.

Lucerne fleas

Smithurus viridis can be a problem in some legume crops. They are tiny, greenish yellow bugs that jump when approached. They usually hatch in the warm, wet weather of autumn, and they prefer heavy soils; in fact, they cannot cope with sandy soils. A predatory mite is being developed for their control, which can be difficult, especially in agriculture.

Mites

The mite most gardeners recognise is two-spotted mite (*Tetranychus urticae*). This mite is a real problem for glasshouse growers and can kill plants if its numbers grow to large enough populations.

Clockwise from top left: An infestation of two-spotted mite, also known as red spider mite; mite damage on bean leaves; and rust mite on mandarins.

These pests quickly build up resistance to sprays, rendering them useless. The other big problem is that the predatory mites also get wiped out in the attack, and therefore insects such as *Phytosiulus permilis*, which can eat 20 to 30 mites a day, are no longer able to keep their numbers down naturally. A better solution is to keep the foliage of susceptible crops, especially the undersides, thoroughly washed with water, as the average mite hates bath time.

You can keep the pest mites under control using an oil-based spray. These oils have no withholding periods and are registered for use by organic farmers. They act as a mild insect repellent on the leaf's surface as well as block the breathing parts (spiracles) and clog the skin (exoskeleton) of the mites, making it hard for them to expel carbon dioxide, so the mites effectively poison themselves.

These oils won't damage any beneficial insects in your garden's ecosystem, as they work to protect your crops. If you see problems arising from tomato russet mites (*Aculops lycopersici*), two-spotted mites or earth mites, try an oil-based spray on fruit trees, tomatoes, cucumbers, capsicums and strawberries.

Grape blister mite (*Colomerus vitis*), which is most active in wet spring weather, causes felt-like patches on grapes. Lime sulfur sprays in winter combined with good hygiene will keep this pest in check.

Sapsuckers

The term 'sapsuckers' refers to the way these insects feed through their straw-like proboscises. Quite prevalent in the garden, they include aphids, mealybugs and scale insects, many of which target only a few different plants.

There are a couple of different organic methods for trying to keep them at bay.

Making your own white oil

Try making up your own safe oil spray. Mix 500 ml (17 fl oz/2 cups) of sunflower oil with 125 ml (4 fl oz/½ cup) of environmentally friendly dishwashing liquid, then shake thoroughly. Add 1 tablespoon of this concentrate to 1 litre (34 fl oz/4 cups) of water and apply it in the cool of the evening or first thing in the morning, but never in hot or windy conditions, as you can easily burn your plants. This will help control sapsuckers such as aphids and mealybugs.

Leaf miner damage on an artichoke leaf.

1. Apply a soap spray at weekly intervals. Just dissolve 3 tablespoons of soap flakes or 2 teaspoons of mild detergent in 4 litres (140 fl oz/16 cups) of water, then spray any infested plants either first thing in the morning or late in the afternoon.

2. Apply some protective oil coverings, another organically approved and reasonably successful strategy. But you must reapply the oil regularly. Also, the oil sprays will only work on the young, nymphal stages of the scale's life cycle.

tip

Before you use a chemical in the garden, remember that when one pest disappears, another usually takes its place, and it may be an even worse problem than the original one.

Scale insects

The worst offenders in the kitchen garden include San Jose scale, black scale (citrus, olives and passionfruit), louse scale (citrus), mango scale, pink wax scale (citrus, avocados, custard apples and mangoes), woolly aphids and black and green peach aphids. Other types of scale include grapevine scale and frosted scale (which can attack stone fruit).

Scale insects are divided into those with soft shells and those with hard scales. In the latter group fall Californian red scale, San Jose scale (in some areas of Australia, its control is required by law), white louse scale and apple mussel scale, and these scales don't produce any honeydew. They still suck sap, however, and are a particular problem on citrus.

Black scale attacks are most troublesome on olives, citrus and passionfruit. They reproduce quickly, producing copious amounts of honeydew, so in summer their populations can quickly explode and leave your trees covered in sooty mould. Control them when they are still juvenile, before their numbers get out of hand.

To control scale, you can spray oils on deciduous trees when the scales are dormant in winter. However, you may need to add poison to white oil before you spray it on evergreens, as the straight oil only works on the crawler or nymphal stage of hard scales.

You can deal with soft scales quite effectively with ant control (see page 49) and a timely oil spray, although make sure you use one that doesn't harm their arch enemies — parasitic wasps, lacewings and ladybird larvae.

Sooty mould

This black substance looks just like soot and grows on the honeydew excreted by scales, mealybugs and aphids. It causes its own problems, as it can become so thick that it stops leaves from photosynthesising properly. The treatment is twofold: treat the scales or aphids themselves to stop the production of honeydew, and physically remove the sooty mould with soapy water.

Aphids

Aphids can reproduce without males and give birth to live young; in fact, depending on the temperature, they can produce up to six young per day. But if winter is approaching, they will usually mate in order to produce eggs that will overwinter. It is this adaptability that enables a few aphids to become an infestation. You may

did you know? French marigolds (*Tagetes* sp.) can be used to help clear the ground of nematodes. The nematodes are attracted to the roots of the marigold, where they are unable to breed. The next generation of nematodes is then greatly reduced or eliminated.

notice that new growth is often twisted
and puckered, and that buds will fail to
open properly, or open prematurely, which
obviously affects fruit trees.

Both the cherry aphid and the woolly
aphid will eat the roots of your tree too.
And then there is the problem of black
sooty mould, which grows on the resultant
honeydew. Try dealing with any ants (see
page 49 for some ideas), encouraging
beneficial insects, spot spraying with oil
and cleaning up weeds so these pests
have nowhere to hide.

Mealybugs

Mealybugs look a bit like tiny hairy white
slaters, have six legs and are covered in a
waxy, protective white coating that renders
many chemical sprays useless. If they are
not kept under control by predators such
as lacewings and ladybird larvae, they can
get out of control.

In summer, mealybugs are usually
seen in the crux of leaves and stems.
They produce honeydew, which ants help
them to produce (see page 49). A targeted
method of control is to dab them with
matchsticks wrapped in cotton wool that
has been soaked in methylated spirits.
Otherwise, wipe down badly affected
leaves with warm, soapy water and then
use an oil-based spray to smother them.

Slugs and snails

Snails and slugs are gastropods that chew
their way through leaves, especially the
new growth of freshly planted seedlings or
the young growth on trees such as citrus.
While some species are very specific to
certain plants and not a pest to edibles,
and others are carnivorous and eat pests,
the majority of snails and slugs love eating
your homegrown produce.

First, protect your seedlings, where
possible — put up a barrier around them,
destroy the gastropods' hiding holes and
encourage creatures such as lizards, which

Root knot nematodes

Root knot nematodes attack edibles such as potatoes,
gooseberries and passionfruit, damaging the roots and
causing the growth of lumps and bumps. In good weather,
where adequate water is supplied, the damaged roots may be
able to keep up with a plant's supply. It is in periods of water
stress that the follow-on effects of stunted growth, wilting in
hot weather and even pale, nutrient-starved foliage can result.

If you do have an infestation of these micro worms, remove
and destroy the affected plants. Leave your soil fallow and
bare for a period, then plant resistant crops such as corn,
onions, cabbages and cauliflowers. To help keep nematodes
at bay, be diligent in your crop rotation practices and avoid
reinfecting the area with dirty boots or tools and mud.

Right: Ducks love to feast on snails and slugs.

love to eat them. Snails and slugs live and breed in moist areas, coming out at night to feed. Inspect under damp leaves and rocks daily, and patrol at night or after rain, squashing gastropods as you go.

However, if your snail and slug problem is getting out of control, try a low-toxic approach first, such as spraying coffee around susceptible plants (see the steps below) and putting out beer traps.

If you want to start poisoning them with commercial snail baits, it's best to research the many different types first, as some are quite toxic to pets.

Thrips

Thrips feed by rasping and scratching, then sucking the plant's juices as they 'bleed'. Their damage therefore is usually fairly disfiguring, leaving marks on petals, fruit and foliage, depending on the type of thrip.

Greenhouse thrips

Outside, in warmer areas, greenhouse thrips (*Heliothrips haemorrhoidalis*), which are black and about 1.5 mm (1/20 in) long, can be a problem for persimmons, the fruit of 'Valencia' oranges, grapes and passionfruit vines. These thrips feed

Spraying snails and slugs

Don't waste your leftover plunger or espresso coffee. Dilute coffee with water, then pour the solution into a spray bottle. Cover the soil and leaves of any plants likely to be attacked, then repeat weekly, or after any rain, when they will come out of their hiding holes.

1 Pour 1 part of espresso into 3 parts of water.

2 Pour the coffee solution into a spray bottle.

3 Spray onto the foliage.

under the leaves, and create a silvering effect similar to the damage caused by olive lace bug and two-spotted mite. They too prefer dry, dusty conditions, so watering under the leaves of affected plants, especially those growing under overhanging eaves, can help considerably.

Onion thrips

One of the biggest pests in the kitchen garden is the onion thrip (*Thrips tabaci*), which is yellowish to brown-grey. It attacks onions, lettuce, beans, peas, potatoes and the whole Brassica family.

The best way to control it is with regular watering, especially under the leaves, as well as managing weeds, as they will harbour onion thrips too. Cold winters usually kill off these and other thrips, or at least reduce their numbers but, conversely, warm weather increases their numbers significantly.

Pyrethrum is usually used to keep them under control, and also to stop the spread of viral diseases they can carry, such as spotted wilt virus (see page 71). Avoid using this poison when bees are foraging, and be careful with cold-blooded animals

Above: Plague thrips on a young liquidambar leaf.

such as lizards, which are also affected by this chemical, even though it's naturally derived from *Pyrethrum* sp.

Plague thrips

Thrips imaginis, which are yellow and about 1 mm (^{3}/100 in) long, attack the flowers of many members of the Rosaceae family, including stone fruit, pome fruit and raspberries. The effects of their attacks depend on the plant, but range from flower drop to fruit damage and reduced level of fruit set. Thrips are not usually a problem with grapes, citrus, plums or pears, but can be a significant one on berrying plants.

tip

Parasitic wasps (Ceranisus sp.) will also assist with the management of greenhouse thrips.

Trap slugs (far left) and snails (left) in beer baits — lay a bottle, about half full of beer, on its side in the garden.

Weevils

These snout-nosed beetles are a brownish grey colour. Different types of weevil attack various plants. Elephant weevil (*Orthorhinus cylindrirostris*) can attack grapes, citrus, apples, apricots and peaches, especially if these plants are already stressed.

The fruit tree root weevil's larvae (*Leptopius robustus*) cause damage to a wide range of plants, including apples, pears, figs and citrus, chewing on their roots and weakening the tree. Luckily, they are easy to outwit: after they have pupated in the soil, the adult climbs the tree to feed on the leaves and lay its eggs, so it's a simple matter of banding troubled trees — that is, wrapping their trunks with big swathes of foil or greasy cloth such as hessian that they can't climb, thereby interrupting their life cycle. Once you find adults stuck in the fabric, you can simply squash them.

Other weevils attack smaller plants — for example, the Fullers rose weevil (*Asynonychus cervinus*) attacks the roots of tomatoes as well as the leaves of plants such as citrus, passionfruit, blackberries, peaches and cherries. Practising general winter hygiene — removing old leaves and clearing weeds — should remove most of the eggs before they hatch.

Although they're not true weevils, pea weevils (*Bruchus pisorum*) have a very similar appearance and feed on flowers, young leaves and pods. They lay their eggs inside a pea pod so that the larvae lives inside the developing pea.

Pea weevils are a particular nuisance if you're trying to grow legumes for dry storage, as these pests can survive for many months. Regular inspection from the flowering stage onwards, manually removing them and protecting plants with a fine net are the easiest and safest methods of control.

If your olive tree looks like it's been put through the paper shredder, then chances are it's been attacked by adult black vine weevils (*Otiorhynchus sulcatus*). The larvae have just as big an appetite but are much harder to spot, as they tunnel into the soil and feed off the roots. As yet, there are no effective controls for this pest on olives, although insecticides used on the trunks of grapevines, before the adults have had a chance to lay eggs, have had some success.

Pesticides and other chemical controls

In the 1940s, when DDT and its allies were introduced, growers thought their problems were solved with a simple spray. But 70 years or so later, we know that these sprays have wrought vast environmental damage due to the toxic and persistent effects of these organochlorides.

These days, most people understand that a couple of spots and the odd bite mark are part of sharing their garden within a broader environment. But some gardeners still want a quick fix. Even though the chemical controls we use now are less deadly and more rigorously tested, there is a growing band of supporters for alternative approaches. These range from the 'organic or bust' group to those who strive for an 'integrated' approach.

The first step towards successful gardening is to understand the life cycles of insects as well as the systems in which plants can best cope with insects and other problems. So even if you have no qualms about reaching for the bug gun, be armed with the right chemicals and understand the consequences of your actions.

These consequences may include killing off natural predators, so the pest itself grows in numbers, or becomes chemically resistant to sprays.

tip

Withholding periods are always on the poison's registration panel, and you must adhere to them.

Understanding poisons

If, however, you feel that you have 'shared' enough, then intervening may be your only option. Even so, what you use and how you use it are still pertinent issues.

For example, blanket spraying all your crop is likely to kill off all the beneficial insects, while target spraying the worst affected plants will not only save the good guys but overall have a better result. Spraying in the early morning too is less likely to cause damage to plants and more likely to actually hit the pest or disease. It also means you're less likely to inadvertently spray foraging bees.

How chemical sprays work

It's important to understand how various sprays are classified, and the different ways they work on your plants.

1 Contact sprays work on contact with the pest itself. In order for them to be effective, you must spray either the pest or the disease itself. This may mean spraying at a time when the pest is active, or getting under the leaves if that's where they hide or feed, so you can actually hit them with the chemical.

2 Penetrant poisons act through ingestion of a leaf (or fruit) that has been sprayed, so that anything that eats the leaf or fruit will ingest the poison too.

3 Systemic poisons work by absorbing the chemical into the whole plant, so that if you spray the foliage, the roots, fruit and flowers will also carry the effects of the chemical. That's great if the problem you're dealing with is hard to reach — for example, mealybugs on the roots of your plants — but the poison may also affect your crop. Depending on the withholding period of the chemical, this could mean you can't eat the fruit.

Above: If you do choose to use chemical sprays against pests, you'll also endanger beneficial insects, such as bees.

Toxicity

The toxicity of a chemical can be measured in two ways — how it affects you if you inhale or ingest it, and how it affects you through your skin.

Usually the most poisonous to humans is given the ranking of 'Highly toxic', and should have 'Danger' on the label. 'Moderately toxic' has to carry the word 'Warning', and those less toxic still must show the word 'Caution'.

Try to limit yourself to those pesticides marked 'Caution'. Read the label carefully and only apply it during a safe window. This means never spraying when it is windy; wearing protective gear, such as long sleeves and long pants, boots, gloves, goggles and a mask if required; and sticking to any warnings about withholding periods for fish and bees.

did you know? In 1962, Rachel Carson, an American marine biologist and nature writer, published a book called *Silent Spring*, in which she exposed the devastating long-term effects of DDT on the environment. The book has been widely credited with launching the environmental movement.

Remember too that just because a product is naturally derived or indeed a plant product, such as pyrethrum, it can still affect a pest's nervous system and can also potentially be dangerous to you, so always handle pesticides with great care. Dedicate one sprayer to weedicides, if you use them, and another to any other

Below: Birds will become accustomed to scarecrows unless you regularly move them around the garden.

pest and disease problems. Accidentally spraying your favourite grandmother's rose bush with black spot spray, which contains glyphosate residues, can thus be avoided. After use, flush away any residue by thoroughly washing out your equipment, including the nozzle, at least three times.

Integrated pest management (IPM)

Embraced by most people in agriculture and horticulture, IPM is an ecological method of controlling pests. It helps nature maintain a healthy balance by regarding the whole garden as an ecosystem in its own right.

IPM is all about analysing the problem — for example, looking at whether or not the particular problem is damaging the edible part of your plant, or only affecting its aesthetic value.

And there are other questions you need to ask yourself. Will healthy populations of predators, such as praying mantis (see page 44), be affected, even by the 'organic' sprays allowed in, say, an organic set-up? What's the flow-on effect of this pest's demise? Are other bugs waiting for the opportunity to present itself?

Answering these questions intelligently, outwitting the pests and finding a balance is the essence of the IPM philosophy.

The first step towards having a pest- and disease-free garden is growing healthy plants — giving them the right amount of water and nutrients; not subjecting them to positional stress from severe winds, drought or cold; and employing sensible hygiene habits and watering rituals (see page 20). Other tactics include not growing some plants that you know have problems, or not mass planting the susceptible, as this only flags their presence to pests.

Animal barriers and deterrents

Possums, rabbits, deer, rats, mice, bandicoots and raccoons are just some of the animals that have cleverly adapted to the suburban landscape so they can make short work of your edibles. Aside from the fact that these animals are sometimes protected species, it stands to reason that perhaps we humans can simply outwit them.

The first step is to correctly identify the problem. Some burrowing animals, like rabbits, will need to be kept out of your garden with a fence that goes down into the ground. Jumpers, like wallabies, may need high fences to keep them out.

Skilful climbers, like mice, may be impossible to deter, but easier to control. They damage young trees by nibbling on the bark, especially when food is scarce over winter, and inadvertently ring-bark your saplings. If this is the case, a sheath of agricultural pipe with a slit down one side (so it can expand as the tree grows) may be all that is needed to eliminate the problem until the tree matures.

Repellents, which are sprayed onto your plants as a protective barrier, taste awful. There are all sorts of safe home remedies, from using chilli powder or cayenne pepper to spice up your plants so much that animals stay clear, to making horribly bitter teas from the likes of wormwood, quassia and other foul-tasting plants.

If deer are a problem in your garden, you can even buy predator scents to hang in your trees so the deer think it's an unsafe area and move on. All these repellents and deterrents will need to be replaced after any rainfall or snow.

Light and sound can also help scare off animals. You could try wind chimes, movement-activated lights and even water sprayers, which detect an animal's approach and give them a blast of water from a specially designed sprinkler, or ultrasounds, which are inaudible

Above: Barberry (*Berberis* sp.), an attractive shrub that bears thorns, makes a good barrier plant.

to humans but deter many animals. Hanging CDs from trees, using humming lines and also balloons with eyes drawn on them can also scare them away.

None of these options will work for longer than a short period, however, so you need to mix them up and move them around so the problem animal never works out what you're up to.

Another environmentally friendly solution for keeping animals out of your garden is to plant animal-resistant shrubs and plants, or prickly plants that will make it uncomfortable for them to stay and graze. Deer don't like leaves with a fuzzy texture — lamb's ear and lungwort, for example — while sharp-edged shrubs such as barberry, roses, rough lemons (see page 178) and mahonia can be good barrier plantings.

Common problems

Like animals, plants can suffer from many different problems that have nothing to do with pests. Deficiencies, bacterial infections and viral and fungal diseases can all cause damage in the garden, but you must execute any solutions very carefully so that the crop you are trying to grow does not itself become inedible or poisonous.

Above: This pea plant is suffering from a bad case of powdery mildew.

Opposite: Saving seeds and replanting them is one way of ensuring that you grow disease-free plants. Shown here are the dried seed heads of Chinese mustard greens.

Fungal diseases

Fungal problems tend to have similar symptoms but different root causes. This means that while many plants may suffer from, say, black spot, each black spot tends to be a specific species of fungus. So, what may be useful on beans may not work on roses, and so on.

The most common fungal problems of vegetables are leaf spots, blights, anthracnose, black spots, rusts, mildews and root rots.

Anthracnose

This is a fungus that results in black sunken spots on the leaves, twigs and fruit of many plants. Particularly affected is the avocado, where the problem starts off as small brown spots on the fruit and then goes into a holding pattern until the fruit ripens or the weather conditions are moist. Then the spots darken and go beneath the skin, causing rounded spots on the flesh.

Monthly copper sprays from flowering until harvest can keep this disease in check, as can planting less susceptible varieties in the first place. Mangoes and macadamias also suffer from anthracnose and, as with avocados, the spores can be harboured on the deadwood of trees, so regularly pruning out deadwood helps prevent the build-up of spores.

Many beans also suffer from anthracnose. They too develop sunken black spots, and the leaf venation turns dark. Cucurbits, tomatoes and lettuces can all suffer, but you can help avoid the problem by buying disease-free seeds in the first place. Again, planting disease-resistant varieties and rotating crops are both good preventative measures. In wet, humid weather look for the telltale spots and, if necessary, harvest fruit early, then remove and destroy any remaining crops.

Downy mildew

Downy mildew can occur on cucurbits, brassicas, grapes, lettuces, onions, peas and many other vegetables. The spots usually show up first on the upper surface of the leaf, but on the underside you will see a furry or downy growth, which can be purplish in colour.

This fungal disease needs high humidity to germinate and grow, but you can control it by cutting off the affected parts and destroying them as well as by increasing air circulation and avoiding overhead watering. Practise crop rotation regularly, thin crops to increase air circulation and avoid overplanting.

tip

Grey mould (botrytis) can be a problem on fruit such as tomatoes and berries, infecting the leaves, flowers and fruit with a fuzzy fungus, especially in warm, humid weather. Increase the air circulation around plants by judicious pruning and adequate spacing and remove and destroy any damaged parts.

Fruit rot

This is a problem for hermaphrodite pawpaws, although a variety called 'Richter' is resistant. Otherwise, spray with copper hydroxide in hot, humid weather and pick fruit early before letting it ripen inside.

Fusarium wilt

Fusarium wilt (*Fusarium oxysporum*) tends to be a secondary pathogen that invades plant tissue that is damaged in some way, possibly by another rot or by mechanical means. It is a real problem when crop rotation isn't practised or when susceptible varieties are grown instead of resistant ones, as the fungus can remain in the soil for years. Characterised by slow growth, rapid wilting on hot days and, eventually, by death, it attacks a wide range of edible plants, but especially tomatoes, rockmelon and watermelon. If you split open the stems, closer inspection will reveal a brownish red discolouration inside.

Leaf blights

Celery, potatoes, carrots, strawberries and sweet corn are all prone to various types of this fungal disease. The splotch-like damage usually starts on the outer edges of the leaf and then spreads, gradually making the leaf rot as it does so. Leaf blights are spread by water but, in most cases, can be kept in check with a copper spray. Crop rotation, plant hygiene and certification of seed are other good preventative measures.

Leaf spots

You can usually identify leaf spots by small, circular yellow spots with a red margin turning black inside. These include angular leaf spot, a problem for French beans, which is usually the result of using disease-infected seed, so always buy from a reliable source. Leaf spots also affect peas, bananas, blackcurrants, mulberries, rhubarb and strawberries, as well as, of course, roses.

An emulsifiable botanical oil is registered for rose leaf spot and works by forming a protective coating on the leaves that the fungal spores find difficult to impregnate. Repeat every ten days or so if conditions are bad.

Phytophora

Phytophora is a soil-borne fungus that has a devastating effect on a wide range of plants, but particularly susceptible in the edible garden are young seedlings as well as trees such as citrus, avocado and mango. The disease develops very quickly

Below, from left to right: Leaf blight on blackcurrant; leaf spot; and collar rot caused by phytophora.

in moist soils, and as these occur in the tropics and during germination, they can quickly get out of control and cause death, collar rot or tree cankers. If only part of the root system is attacked, it is quite typical for only the corresponding branches above ground to wilt and die.

This fungus attacks the fine hair roots first before rapidly making its way to larger roots and the tree or seedling's 'collar' — that is, the space where the stem or trunk becomes root at ground level.

Phytophora usually spreads through water or soil, so good drainage and good hygiene will be your best options for keeping this problem at bay. Cutting away diseased or affected wood and removing affected seedlings are other first-line measures in stopping the spread of the disease. You can also use soil drenches to kill off the fungus temporarily, but if the conditions are still right, reinfection can occur.

Powdery mildew

Powdery mildew of various types will affect many edibles, including apples, peas, cucurbits, grapes, pawpaws, mangoes and strawberries. The characteristic damage caused by this fungus is an icing sugar-like white film that spreads across foliage in humid weather, distorting the leaves of young plants. On apples, the disease can spread across the fruit as well. On strawberries and grapes the fruit set is likely to be poor, while on cucurbits the size of the fruit may be affected.

To control the spread of this fungus on grapes, you can use a food-grade potassium bicarbonate, which is best combined with a plant oil, such as a canola oil-based product that has been enhanced with tea tree and eucalyptus. This is also registered for strawberries (and roses), and

trials show success with cucurbits. Repeat every ten days or so if conditions are bad.

If you'd like to experiment with another home remedy, mix 250 ml (9 fl oz/1 cup) of cow's milk to 1.25 litres (44 fl oz/5 cups) of water, then spray the solution all over your cucurbits, on top and below the leaves. Repeat every week (or after any rain) to help control powdery and downy mildew. You could also try Bordeaux spray (see the step by step sequence on page 147).

Rust

As its name suggests, rust looks much more reddish or yellowish than anthracnose and black spot. The small spots first appear on the upper surface of older leaves, then below this spot a pustule develops before spreading to the new growth. Buy only disease-free seed and pick off any leaves as symptoms appear. Silver beet and beetroot are both prone to rust, as are beans, peaches, raspberries and many others.

Violet root rot

Violet root rot (*Helicobasidium brebissonii*) is a soil-borne fungus that occurs when rotations of potatoes, carrots and other root crops are too frequent, especially in sandy or peat-based soils. The surface of roots develop a dark purple rot, which spreads upwards across the top layer. Secondary rots, such as fusarium, can then attack, causing more damage.

Bacterial diseases

These diseases are usually highly infectious, which is why commercial growers often have to adhere to strict hygiene codes. Simple house rules, such as destroying damaged plants immediately and only using certified seed (or at least treating your own seed; see page 71) will

Above, from top to bottom: Powdery mildew on a plane tree; rust on leek foliage; and shot hole on a plum tree.

go a long way towards staving them off. As many bacterias are spread in water droplets as they're splashed from one plant to another, it's worth choosing mulch types carefully and looking at the way you irrigate.

Bacterial canker

This is another infection whose incidence can be dramatically reduced by crop rotation and planting disease-free certified seeds. It affects tomatoes and stone fruit, although different bacteria cause the damage. On tomatoes the effects don't show up until your plants are nearly at fruiting age, when they can suddenly start to wilt and the leaves shrivel. In worst case scenarios, the stems will split and the fruit develop small, raised white spots that then go brown.

Destroy the entire plant, and then wash your hands thoroughly and change your clothes before returning to the garden.

Bacterial leaf spot

Cucurbits, especially Lebanese cucumbers, also suffer from a bacterial infection that results in the same sort of damage as leaf spot. If you notice it, remove any affected plants immediately. Lettuces can also become infected with this bacteria, which eventually causes the veins to blacken and finally the whole leaf to collapse. Splashing water will spread it from one infected plant to another. Buying certified disease-free seeds is the best preventative measure.

Bacterial soft rots

Bacterial soft rots — which affect potatoes and other vegetables such as celery, lettuce and brassicas — are more likely to cause damage when conditions are damp. For this reason it's not recommended that you dig up potatoes in wet weather, as you can easily damage the tubers and spread this smelly bacterial disease, which is usually associated with slimy areas.

Late blight

You can avoid late blight, which affects potatoes, by planting disease-free tubers. This disease shows up on the leaves as brown spots and on the tubers as purplish black spots that become sunken. Humid weather and rain favour this disease.

Potato scab

Also called common scab, potato scab develops if the soil is too alkaline and is not kept moist while the tubers are developing. It starts off as small brown spots but quickly develops into a corky, raised brown 'scab'. Try to avoid this problem by purchasing seed potatoes that are certified disease-free.

Shot hole

Shot hole, which attacks stone fruit, causing fine holes in the foliage, has a similar reddish appearance to rust, but the hole's centre drops out. It can also cover the fruit. Remove and destroy any damaged leaves.

Viral diseases

Viral attacks on plants are dire. As there is no spray you can use, your only action is to remove and destroy the affected plants. The best way to cope with viruses is to prevent them in the first place. They're usually spread via insects, water splashes and infected propagation materials. The safest options are usually as follows.

- Keep insects under control.
- Use seed treatments (see opposite).
- Plant healthy tubers and cuttings.
- Follow good hygiene practices, such as keeping splashing under control.

tip

To limit the spread of shot hole, a viral disease that affects stone fruit, don't irrigate trees from overhead in case splashing spreads the disease.

Seed saving

One way of ensuring your crops are not susceptible to disease is to save your own disease-free seeds and plant them in the next season. Sunflowers, for example, are really easy to grow from seed. To collect the edible seeds, cut off the browning flower heads and shake them in a sieve, or tie a brown paper bag around their heads and then shake these. Save some seeds to sow back into your patch when you're ready for your next crop, and eat the rest — they're very nutritious.

Another option is to keep your plants well fed on compost (see 'Composting', page 17). As compost is made up of many beneficial micro-organisms, organic gardeners believe that it encourages the growth of microflora, whereby 'bad' viruses (and bacteria) are met by their natural enemies. However, as yet there is no definitive research supporting this theory, especially on plants.

Mosaic virus

Often spread by sap-sucking insects, especially aphids, mosaic virus results in mottled yellow damage on the foliage of many plants, such as cucurbits, potatoes and brassicas. This virus is a problem with leaf crops but the main outcome on fruiting crops is loss of vigour. Plant certified seeds and control sapsuckers.

Spotted wilt

A common virus affecting edibles is spotted wilt, which affects potatoes, tomatoes and capsicums as well as lettuces and many ornamentals and weeds. As the name suggests, plants can suddenly wilt and die. The first symptoms depend on the plant it's attacking, but the signs vary from spotting, in the case of tomatoes, to yellow lines or concentric rings (capsicums). Onion thrips (see page 61) usually spread the disease, and as these insects are most prevalent in dry weather, you need to watch out for them during hot summers.

Seed treatments

You can kill many diseases by treating seeds with hot water; however, the time span (20 to 30 minutes) and the temperature (45 to 50°C/113 to 122°F) are specific to each type of plant, so do your research first. If you overdo the treatment, you'll destroy germination.

Place the seeds and a pebble (to weigh them down) in a nylon stocking, then place the stocking in a saucepan of water with a thermometer for the desired time. After the seed has been treated in this way, plunge it into cold water, spread it out on paper towel to dry off completely in the shade, then store it in an airtight container.

Below: Mosaic virus.

Seasonal jobs in the kitchen garden

| | JOBS | | |
Season	Fruit and nuts	Vegetables	Herbs
Spring	Prune loquat.	Clean up winter debris and top-dress with blood and bone.	Take root cuttings of bergamot, mint, tarragon, hyssop and sweet cicely.
	Prune dead and diseased wood from avocados, chestnuts, macadamias, pecans and Cape gooseberries.	Take suckers of artichoke.	Layer sage and thyme.
	Hard prune avocados (staghorning).	Plant crowns of asparagus and rhubarb.	Cut back rosemary and lavender after flowering.
	Cut back elder after flowering.	Plant tubers of Chinese artichoke.	Transplant marjoram, oregano, mint and lemon balm if necessary.
	Feed mangoes, passionfruit, almonds and pomegranates.	Manure prior to planting where necessary.	Prune bay, winter savory, hyssop, lavender, wormwood and thyme.
	Apply dolomite and compost to bananas.	Weed around chives.	Weed around mint and tarragon as they take off.
	Feed pawpaws with chicken manure.	Keep weeds clear of emerging shoots of asparagus.	Take cuttings of mint, sage, winter savory, lavender, rosemary, cotton lavender and curry plant.
	Mulch berries with rotted manure.	Remove any covers from forced vegetables such as cardoon and chicory.	Transplant out frost-sensitive basil once last chance of cold has gone.
	Feed blueberries with azalea and camellia food, cow manure or worm castings.	Dig back into the ground any spent pea crops.	Raise annual herbs such as coriander, dill and basil.
	Fertilise avocados.	Graft eggplants and tomatoes.	
	Feed chestnuts, pecans and macadamia nuts.	Hill up beans as they grow.	
	Feed and prune tamarillos.	Thin seedlings of squash, cucumber and melons to the strongest plants.	
	Prune cherries.		
	At bud swell, spray peaches and nectarines with copper oxychloride.		

Seasonal jobs in the kitchen garden (continued)

	JOBS		
Season	Fruit and nuts	Vegetables	Herbs
Summer	Feed pawpaws with chicken manure.	Hill up over beans as they grow.	Layer rosemary.
	Prune blueberries.	Shorten the tendrils of melons, cucumbers and pumpkins to keep them more compact.	Keep cutting (or using) your herbs to stop them from flowering and going to seed.
	Prune and feed lychees.	Thin out crops to increase air circulation and decrease likelihood of fungus.	Trim cotton lavender after flowering, or before if you don't mind losing the flowers.
	Prune blackberries.	Remove laterals from tomatoes and stake them as they grow.	Weed around herbs.
	Fertilise cherries, avocados, bananas, custard apples, mangoes, pawpaws, passionfruit, pineapples and blueberries.	Bag fruit fly-susceptible vegetables, eg tomatoes and capsicum.	Pick most herbs for fresh foliage.
	Protect fruit from birds by netting trees.	Cover heat-susceptible leafy greens with shade cloth.	Crystallise two-year-old growth on angelica.
	Bag fruit to protect it from fruit fly.	Sow catch crops after harvesting first spring-sown vegetables.	Harvest and dry sage, tarragon, lavender, marjoram and thyme.
	Keep water up to avocado trees.		
	Cover fruit for protection from birds.		
	Feed passionfruit.		
	Use a white oil spray on citrus to deter stink bugs and leaf miners.		
Autumn	Feed pawpaws with chicken manure.	Manure prior to planting where necessary.	Take semi-hardwood cuttings of perennial herbs such as rosemary.
	Plant cranberry seedlings.	Take suckers of artichoke.	Harvest and freeze dandelion roots, parsley and mint.
	Prune and feed mangoes.	Feed vegetables with liquid fertiliser to keep them growing quickly.	Collect seeds of anise, caraway, coriander and dill.
	Prune Cape gooseberries.	Cut back asparagus and mulch heavily with poultry manure.	Preserve tarragon and dill in vinegars.
	Prune lychees and mangoes.	Prepare beds for potatoes.	Lift and divide horseradish.
	Fertilise mangoes and custard apples.	Wrap celery as it grows to blanch the stems.	Pinch out flowers on basil.
	Feed pineapples.	Prepare onion beds to a fine tilth.	
	Cover fruit to protect it from birds.		

Seasonal jobs in the kitchen garden (continued)

	JOBS		
Season	Fruit and nuts	Vegetables	Herbs
Winter	Spray lime sulfur on pruned grapes and deciduous fruit trees.	Divide rhubarb and force by blocking out the light.	Lift and store any cold-susceptible herbs, eg mint.
	Prune deadwood out of citrus, blueberries, grapes, berries, almonds, pome fruit and stone fruit (except cherries).	Divide suckers of artichoke.	Reduce watering on herbs.
	Prune pineapples.	Divide crowns of asparagus.	Tidy up dead annuals.
	Feed pomegranate with citrus food.	Train broad beans within their confines.	Trim out old wood.
	Feed and prune fig trees.	Cover frost-susceptible vegetables with cloches.	Cut back perennials.
	Prune mulberry if required.	Mulch over perennial herbaceous vegetables.	
	Feed bananas with banana compost.	Tie outer cauliflower leaves over each head to keep it snowy white.	
	Cut back old foliage on strawberries.	Mulch over fallow areas to prevent weeds taking over.	
	Feed and prune kiwi fruit.	Make frames for climbers out of fruit-tree prunings.	
	Fertilise citrus and prune any dead or diseased wood.		
	Prune stone fruit.		
	Prune pome fruit.		
	Prune grapes.		
	Prune berries.		
	Feed and prune olive trees if necessary.		

Mouth-watering.   Crunchy, creamy.

fruit and nuts

Sweet and succulent.   Seasonal delights.   Plenty.

Contents

the age of exploration

Fruit and nuts have come a long way over the ages, from the earliest days when gathering berries and wild fruit from the bush and forest was part of our subsistence culture, to a more settled life, when animals were kept and crops cultivated.

As trading between countries and, indeed, continents developed, the Silk Road opened up, and the East and the West started trading. Spice routes were developed, and fruit too made journeys, so successfully sometimes that its place of origin has become somewhat obscured.

During the Age of Discovery, in the sixteenth, seventeenth and eighteenth centuries, as European imperialist powers such as Spain, Portugal and Britain continued to 'discover' new lands, fruit such as pineapples, bananas, mangoes and even melons from Africa became the toast of dinner tables as well as prized possessions in European conservatories.

Citrus, pome and stone fruit have became staples throughout the world, and today there is hardly a lunchbox in the Western world that doesn't have a piece of fruit from Asia inside it.

Fruit from the New World has also featured in our diets, and many are among the most popular fresh fruit eaten in the world today — citrus, watermelon, bananas, grapes, apples, coconuts, mangoes, pears, peaches and nectarines.

Nuts are also invaluable food sources, and they can be stored for long periods, over winter or during drought.

Berries

Berries are a special summer treat to be enjoyed when they are in season. And as they are often expensive, with poor shelf lives, it makes sense to try growing them at home. Fortunately for the home gardener, they produce quite efficiently per square metre and are very adaptable in their habit.

Choosing soft fruit

Growing berries, or soft fruit as they are sometimes called, is not difficult, provided you select varieties that are suitable for your climate. And with new crossbreeds being released all the time, you can choose from a wonderful range — from boysenberries and silvanberries to loganberries and currants.

Berries have always been popular in cool climates that receive regular frosts, and members of the *Ribes* genus — which includes the English gooseberry and currants (red, white and black) — do extremely well in these, despite the cold weather. Other cool-climate lovers include the *Rubus* genus — boysenberries, loganberries, youngberries, blackberries and raspberries. These do best in tableland and mountainous areas as well as in cooler coastal regions, but can be grown in other climates if they're protected from strong winds and planted in semi-shade to shield them from excessive heat.

Above: As blueberries ripen, they develop from a pale green to dark blue or indigo.

Left: The large, elongated developing fruit of a pink-flowering strawberry.

That certainly doesn't mean you'll miss out if you live in a warm climate. Strawberries produce well in a wide range of climates, as does the elderberry, a famous ingredient in wines and cordial, while the evergreen (rabbit-eye type) blueberries are also adaptable to warmer areas. Add to these the Cape gooseberries, white and red mulberries, Barbados cherry (*Malpighia glabra*), Brazilian cherry (*Eugenia uniflora*, also known as jaboticaba; see page 127) and tazzleberry (*Myrtus* sp.) and you'll have the ingredients for a delicious summer fruit platter.

If you don't have room in your garden, try growing some berries in containers. Cranberries like a cold climate, but have an unusual prostrate habit that is perfect for rockeries and hanging baskets. Gooseberries, blueberries and currants are all suitable for tubs that are about 40 cm (16 in) across. Mulberries can also be grown in larger pots; the weeping, grafted sort is a particularly beautiful ornamental tree, suitable as a feature in the garden.

Trailing or cane fruit

Members of the genus *Rubus* are known collectively as trailing or cane fruit. Although there are 250 different species, all bear berries. Most have prickly stems and are shrubs (either rambling or upright) belonging to the same family as roses (Rosaceae), which are cultivated all over the world. The fruit are delicious, which is why gardeners put up with the thorns and go to so much trouble to grow them. They are fabulous eaten fresh, or in jams and preserves, stewed or brewed into liquors, or you can simply freeze them for later.

The best known members of this genus are blackberry (*R. fruticosus*) and raspberry (*R. idaeus*), although some hybrid crosses of the two, which have been around for nearly 100 years, are also commonly grown. These include the loganberry (*R. loganobaccus*), a cross between 'Red Antwerp' raspberry and 'Aughinburgh' blackberry. This hybrid has bigger fruit than either parent and is less rampant than blackberry, which can err on the weedy side in many climates.

tip

Berries are usually available as bare-rooted plants in winter via mail order or direct from your nursery. If they are not wrapped in moist material such as hay, moss or sawdust, keep them heeled into the ground or in a pot until you are ready to plant them, otherwise their roots will dry out.

1

2

3

4

5

6

7

8

berries

1 Elder flower 2 Green elder 3 Loganberry 4 'Aurea' elder 5 Unripe elderberry
6 'Guincho Purple' elder 7 Ripe elderberry 8 Blueberry and raspberry 9 Blackberry
10 Strawberry 11 Australian native raspberry 12 Pink-flowered strawberry

Other hybrids with these two parents include tayberry (*R. fruticosus* x *R. idaeus* 'Tayberry'), which has bigger, redder fruit than loganberry; tummelberry, which is an even redder 'Tayberry' hybrid cross; and marionberry (*R. loganobaccus* x *R. fruticosus* x *R. idaeus*), which over a two-month season produces fruit that looks rather like a giant blackberry.

Other unusual berry species include boysenberry (*R. ursinus* x *R. idaeus*), dewberry (*R. caesius*), blackcap (*R. occidentalis*), wineberry (*R. phoenicolasius*) and cloudberry (*R. chamaemorus*). There is even an Australian native raspberry, also called brambleberry (*R. rosifolius*).

For the home gardener, *Rubus* berries represent good value for the space they occupy, with many types producing quite heavy yields. For example, two canes usually bear enough fruit for an average-sized family. The easiest types to grow at home are the thornless members of this group. Thornless blackberries are sold under the names 'Thornfree', 'Merton' and 'Oregon', and there are also thornless loganberry cultivars. But try not to limit yourself to these, as some of the most delicious fruit grow on thorny canes designed to protect them from predators.

Cultivating trailing or cane fruit

Culturally, *Rubus* species vary in their climatic requirements, with raspberry needing the cold and a proper winter dormancy to bear fruit, while those species

Top: To pick raspberries, gently grasp each one between your thumb and forefinger and pull it away from its core.

Far left: The Australian native raspberry.

Left: The white flower of the loganberry.

Planting brambles

The first thing to do before planting trailing berries is to make sure the area is grass- and weed-free, with perennial and bulbous weeds killed off completely. Dealing with weeds around prickly plants is no fun, so the more thoroughly you do this, the easier future maintenance will be. Also, before planting, take the opportunity to enrich the soil with added manure, compost or worm castings and a few handfuls each of blood and bone, urea and superphosphate.

1 Keep plants 'heeled in' until you're ready to plant them.

2 A healthy young plant showing the green stem and roots.

3 You'll need to plant your brambles next to a strong support. A fence post is ideal, as you can use the fence wire to support its trailing habit.

4 Backfill, keeping the plant and stake upright, then water in.

with more blackberry in them can adapt to warm coastal areas. They all like a well drained soil with plenty of summer moisture while the fruit is forming. Shelter from wind is desirable and protection from birds essential, as they are the number one pest when it comes to growing soft fruit.

Feeding

Dress cane fruit annually with more manure, and maintain a thick layer of mulch to discourage weeds. Use a complete plant food each winter, keeping it away from the base of the plant. Raspberries like plenty of lime, which can be applied in winter.

Pruning

To increase your yield, just remove old fruiting canes — any older than, say, three years — but don't cut back to the ground each year, as the new growth won't produce fruit until it's a year old or 'ripe'.

Harvesting

Pick ripe raspberries in the morning every few days and eat them fresh, or make them into jam, bottle or freeze them. If you are going to freeze them, don't wash them or they'll become soggy. Just place them on a tray, then put the tray in the freezer. Once they are frozen, transfer them to a plastic bag and they will easily stay separate.

tip

Don't plant blackberry bushes and then neglect them, as they can become a serious weed.

Pruning loganberry

In the first year of planting a trailing berry, choose one strong leader and remove any others. We pruned a loganberry, but the method is standard for all trailing berries. In the following winter, cut this leader back to about 15 cm (6 in) above ground level, which will then encourage water shoots and another crop of canes. When your plant is two years old, be fairly brutal with your winter prune, cutting back to ground level all but a few of the most vigorous canes. For all subsequent prunes, remove the canes during the growing season, after they fruit, and let the new growth just trail along the ground, and tie it in winter. The next winter pruning will encourage lots of fruit and maximise air circulation around the plant, thus minimising the likelihood of disease and ensuring ease of picking.

1 This loganberry is in need of a good winter prune.

2 Remove any weak canes or those that might be damaged or rubbing by cutting them at the base.

3 In winter, tie the strongest of these back up to the trellis or wire in an open fan shape, and completely remove the weaker canes.

4 Once pruned and trained, trailing berries will produce well.

Problems

Birds will want to feast on your fruit, so protect the berries with nets. To lift the nets above the bushes, you'll need to use canes with bottles on the ends to protect your eyes, and peg the edges to the ground.

Hailstorms can cause havoc when berries are in flower or fruit, so in bad weather protect them with a sheet.

These tender fruits can suffer from various fungal problems, including those listed below.

- Anthracnose: page 66.
- Grey mould: page 68.
- Yellow rust: page 69.

Strawberries

Versatile and easy to grow and harvest, strawberries take up little space in the home garden.

There are basically two types of strawberry — the annual or alpine strawberry (*Fragaria vesca*) and the perennial type (*F.* x *ananassa*). There are also perennial varieties that crop once a year in early summer with large fruit, or successive cropping types that keep producing slightly smaller fruit throughout summer and autumn. In the home garden, it's probably best to grow smaller, more regular crops.

Strawberries are a groundcover plant, growing only about 20 cm (8 in) tall but able to spread rapidly via their runners. The fruit is unusual in that the seeds are borne on the outside of the flesh, which can be red, white or golden.

You can grow strawberries in dedicated beds, strawberry pots and hanging baskets, as a groundcover and, in the case of the alpine strawberry, as a border. There are pink-flowered strawberries, such as 'Pink Panda', and variegated leaf types. Both types make very pretty features.

Cultivating strawberries

Strawberries are either planted as crowns in late autumn and winter, or as seedlings in spring. Prepare the bed a few months in advance by digging in well rotted manure or compost, and adding some slow-release complete plant food, raking it in until the bed is even again. Strawberries are acid-lovers, so never add lime to the soil where you are growing, or planning to grow, them.

Strawberries are best grown away from the soil, which is why they have the name 'straw' berry, as straw was traditionally used as a mulch to stop the fruit from spoiling. Strawberries suffer from many problems, but the main concerns are fungal diseases that rot the fruit, and weeds, which are difficult to eradicate due to the ground-covering nature of the plant.

Placing 1-m (3-ft) strips of woven weed control mat deals effectively with both these problems. It won't stop water and air getting to the soil but it will control weeds and stop fruit rot. Alternatively, you can grow strawberries in hanging baskets or raised beds filled with sterile medium, or plant them in raised ridges, then mulch them heavily between the rows with hay, straw or pine needles in an effort to protect the fruit from the ground.

Below left: Strawberries don't ripen after they've been picked, so either eat them straightaway, or freeze them for later use.

Below: The white flower of the perennial type.

Bottom: The pink-flowering strawberry is a pretty choice for borders.

Right: Little bamboo canes have been pushed into this strawberry patch to deter birds.

Strawberry sorbet

345 g (12 oz/1¹/₂ cups) caster (superfine) sugar
750 ml (26 fl oz/3 cups) fresh strawberry purée
strawberries and whipped cream, to serve (optional)

Put the sugar and 250 ml (9 fl oz/1 cup) of water in a saucepan. Stir over low heat until the sugar has dissolved. Remove from the heat and allow to cool.

Stir the strawberry purée into the cooled sugar syrup and pour into a metal tin. Put in the freezer until cold.

Transfer to an ice cream machine and follow the manufacturer's instructions, Freeze overnight. Store in the freezer until ready to serve.

Makes 1 litre (35 fl oz/4 cups).

Whatever method you choose, bear in mind that strawberries usually grow in the same bed for about three years, so don't skimp on the initial preparation. They yield best in their second and third years, with reducing harvests in subsequent years, so they are usually replanted.

This can be done with plants taken from your established crowns. Simply choose the first few developing plants of each runner, pin them to the ground or pot them up, then remove the 'mother' plant once the new ones have settled into their new position.

Feeding

Whenever you plant new strawberry runners, add some more slow-release fertiliser to the soil. Provided you prepared the soil thoroughly, no other feeding

Planting strawberries

Lay out strips of weed control mat (which normally comes in about 1.2-m/4-ft widths) onto level, well prepared soil.

1 Separate the crowns.

2 With a sharp knife, cut a cross in the plastic and peel back the corners to make a hole.

3 Plant crowns in each hole, and mulch well.

is required. Too much nitrogen-based fertiliser, such as blood and bone, can result in lots of leaves at the expense of fruit. For this reason, if you are going to feed your plants, do it in winter.

Pruning

Cut back all the old foliage at the end of each berry season, leaving only the fresh new leaves. Remove any surplus runners.

Harvesting

The fruit bruises easily, so always pick strawberries by their stems. Wait until the fruit is ripe before picking so you taste their full sweetness and flavour. Strawberries can be eaten fresh, made into jams or bottled, and even frozen, then used in recipes when they're still frozen. Although they don't defrost well at room temperature, they are fine to use in cooked dishes, such as cakes, muffins, pies and crumbles.

Problems

You'll need to keep birds away from the fruit with nets or, if your patch is small, place each truss in a glass jar lying on its side to keep the water out, thus avoiding fruit rot while letting in the sun.

Currants and gooseberries

Currants and gooseberries, both members of the *Ribes* genus, are just two of some 150 species of berrying plants that enjoy cool climates. Deciduous shrubs that burst into growth in early spring, they have delicate racemes of flowers, followed by berries. The best known is probably the blackcurrant; its syrup is a constituent in a popular cordial that contains high levels of vitamin C.

Currants are popular not only for their fresh fruit but also for their dried

Wild strawberry

Although wild or alpine strawberries (*Fragaria vesca*) produce much smaller berries, these are fragrant, with an intense flavour. They come in either red, creamy white ('Fructo Albo') or yellow fruiting types. 'Semperflorens', the cultivar usually grown, rarely has runners, so the only way to grow it is by raising seed; however, their petite size and sweet fruit make it worth the effort.

Sow them in autumn in seedling trays under a sheet of glass. Prick the seedlings out and plant into individual pots or under a frame to overwinter in a protected position, then plant them out in spring. They fruit throughout late spring, summer and autumn.

The red type of wild strawberry, which grows wild in European woodlands, bears white flowers and small, rounded scarlet fruit.

Left: Protect ripening strawberries from birds by inserting them into a clear glass jar.

Above: The developing fruit of the blackcurrant (*Ribes nigrum*).

Above right and below: Gooseberries have a high citric acid content, and are at their best when unripe.

Centre: A red currant cultivar, *Ribes rubrum* 'Jonker van Tets', which grows to about 1 m (3 ft).

form, which is used in baked goods such as fruitcakes and mince tarts. There are red (*R. rubrum*), gold (*R. aureum*), white (*R. rubrum* 'White Versailles' and 'White Dutch') and black (*R. nigrum*) currants, all of which grow to about 1.5 m (5 ft). Currants have a sharp taste that makes them ideal for jams. They are also very pretty, bearing lovely chain-like bunches of small round fruit with a jelly-like translucency, rather like miniature grapes.

Gooseberries (*Ribes uva-crispa*) are smaller, growing to about 1 m (3 ft), and have quite a tart flavour. The berries are greenish, although some of the cultivars have red or yellow tinges or stripes — for instance, 'Roaring Lion' goes dark red when it's ripe.

Cultivating currants and gooseberries

Neither currants nor gooseberries are self-fertile, so you need to plant them in mixed groups of different varieties to ensure that

fruit develops. But that is not their only requirement: they are both cool-climate plants that need a high chilling winter and a cool summer. They also need protection from winds and a rich, well dug, acid soil, plus shade from the hottest sun. Otherwise, they're easy to grow.

Both currants and gooseberries should be planted when dormant, in winter, but after the worst frosts are likely to have finished. You'll buy them as bare-rooted plants, so take care not to let them dry out before you plant them. A couple of months before planting, dig in compost and well rotted manure, then discourage weeds with a 20-cm (8-in) layer of mulch. Water them well, especially at fruiting time.

Feeding

Feed *Ribes* berries in winter with complete plant food, but don't overdo it, as too much food promotes leaf growth at the expense of fruit. Topping up with rich organic mulches is a better strategy.

Pruning

When planting gooseberry shrubs, encourage an open habit by cutting them back to about 30 cm (1 ft) tall, to an outer facing bud. This will make them easier to pick and ensure maximum cropping.

With blackcurrants, prune back all the older canes to encourage new growth. Red currants, however, fruit on spurs that are over a year old, so make sure you don't prune them all back.

Harvesting

When they're ripe, the fruit of currants and gooseberries have a glassy translucency that makes them very beautiful, and this luminescence is the key factor in determining when your berry is ripe and ready to pick. The season starts with red currants in late spring, then a few weeks later blackcurrants and gooseberries are in season. Gooseberries have quite vicious thorns, so wear gloves and be careful when you pick them.

Problems

- Cover the plants with nets to protect them from birds: page 44.
- Cut off any canes that are affected by currant borer moth at ground level and destroy them.
- Encourage air circulation as much as possible to reduce the likelihood of anthracnose and grey mould, powdery mildew and leaf spot: pages 66–9.

Above left: Red currant (*Ribes rubrum*) in flower.

Above: Blackcurrants (*Ribes nigrum*) will keep in the fridge for up to four days.

Unusual species and hybrids

There are two widely known crosses between currants and gooseberries. One, the jostaberry (*Ribes nigrum* x *R. uva-crispa*), looks more like a blackcurrant; the other, worcester berry (*Ribes divaricatum*), a hybrid with blackcurrant, looks like a gooseberry blushed with purple. It grows taller than both parents, fruits well and is not affected by mildew. North American species include the buffalo currant (*R. odoratum*), which has perfumed flowers followed by black fruit, and the mountain gooseberry (*R. oxyacanthoides*), which has delightful mauve flowers and purple-red, edible berries.

Above: For Thanksgiving dinners in the United States, cranberry sauce is traditionally served with turkey.

Vaccinium berries

Vaccinium is a genus containing berries from the northern hemisphere (in particular North America) — cranberries, whortleberries, huckleberries and blueberries. All members of the Heath family, Ericaceae, they are true acid-loving plants, preferring a soil pH of about 4.8 to 5.3 (see page 15).

Blueberries

The blueberry genus contains a few different species, but the most commonly grown are the highbush type (*Vaccinium corymbosum*) and rabbit-eye (*V. ashei*), both of which are bushy shrubs. Highly ornamental plants, with dainty pink or white flowers, glossy green foliage and blue berries, they can withstand both cold and warm climates, depending on the cultivar: 'Earliblue' is great for cool conditions, while 'Sharpblue', one of the hybrids, is suitable for warm zones and coastal areas.

Perfect for the home garden, blueberries are self-fertile, although growing a selection of cultivars will improve cropping. They can also be grown in pots, and need no special pruning other than shaping. Like most berries, they require regular watering during fruit set as well as annual dressings of organic mulch. They are acid-loving plants, so you can feed them with azalea and camellia fertiliser once each spring or, if you prefer an organic approach, with cow manure and worm castings.

Cranberries

The cranberry plant (*V. macrocarpon*) is a groundcover that takes root and binds the soil as it grows. It has mauve flowers that develop into tart red fruit that are used a lot in juices. Commercial growers harvest cranberries by flooding the field: the berries float to the surface where they are scooped up, like leaves skimmed from the surface of a swimming pool. Bears adore this fruit, however, so should you ever find yourself harvesting cranberries in the wilds of North America, watch your back!

Below: The pink flower of 'Delight', which is a blueberry cultivar.

Below right: The silvery bloom on blueberries, a sign of freshness, protects them from the sun.

Harvesting from the wild

Foraging for berries is becoming a lost art, but as it's often a case of trial and error, sometimes resulting in tragedy, perhaps it's no wonder. In the hedgerows of the UK countryside, berry hunting is enjoying a revival of sorts, with many a family spending summer days searching for fruit from these wild storehouses. Many of the plants we grow as ornamentals in our gardens actually produce edible fruit.

The barberry (*Berberis vulgaris*) is one such plant. Although the berries are edible, they can cause mild stomach cramps if you eat too many. This plant is usually grown for its fabulous foliage — some cultivars have wonderful pink, purple and spotted leaves.

Native to central and southern Europe, Africa and Asia, the barberry is a very spiky shrub to about 4 m (13 ft) tall. In late summer it bears edible red fruit that is very sour, but rich in vitamin C. Known as *zareshk* in Iran, these berries are used in Afghan rice dishes, preserves, jams and syrups.

In the same family is *Mahonia* sp., sometimes called grapeberry or holly grape. Growing to about 2 m (6½ ft), its spiky ornamental foliage is very useful for shady spots in the garden. It bears yellow flowers, which are followed by bluish black berries that hang in a long raceme, covered in a white powdery bloom like the one on black grapes.

Also in the Berberidaceae family is the May apple (*Podophyllum* sp.). Used by Native Americans to treat intestinal worms and constipation, it has egg-shaped or plum-like fruit.

Mountain ash or rowan (*Sorbus* sp.) is another berry tree used for food. Traditionally the berries are made into jelly (either with apples or on their own) and served with game.

Star gooseberry (*Phyllanthus acidus*) is an unusual berry from India that is used in pickles; strangely, it comes from the *Euphorbia* family, which is mostly highly toxic. The pale greenish yellow fruit that appear after the spring flush of red flowers are edible, although they won't appeal to everyone. They are juicy and very acidic, so they're rarely eaten fresh. Instead, they're usually made into a sauce or syrup. The plant itself grows into a 9-m (29½-ft) tree and likes a frost-free position.

Top: The hollow stems of the elder have traditionally been used for making flute-like instruments.

Centre and bottom: *Mahonia* (centre) and *Berberis* (bottom) are both members of the Berberidaceae family.

Hedgerow culture

In the last twenty years, British hedgerows have been recognised as an important habitat worthy of protection. These hedgerows typically include wildflowers such as Queen Anne's lace (*Daucus carota*) and berrying plants such as the sloeberry (*Prunus spinosa*), which produces prune-like black fruit protected by sharp spines; the elderberry; hazelnut or filbert; and other bramble fruit such as rosehip, blackberry and raspberry.

These summer crops are harvested from the wild and then made into jams, wines and other condiments to be enjoyed when fresh fruit is not in season. Sloe gin, for example, is a traditional Christmas treat made with sloeberries and served during Yuletide.

Also grown in hedgerows are hawthorns (*Crataegus* sp.). While most of these are inedible, there is an apple-flavoured edible hawthorn (*C. azarolus*) and also an intergeneric hybrid called *Crataegomespilus* sp., which is a medlar and hawthorn cross. An intergeneric hybrid is a cross between two genera. This is most unusual, as usually crosses occur between two species within the same genus. This type of hybrid is a bit like the plant equivalent of crossing a donkey and a horse, which results in the infertile but useful animal known as the mule.

Elder

Elder is a very pretty shrub, with two species mainly grown for fruit — *Sambucus nigra*, or black elder, from Europe, and *S. canadensis*, or sweet elder, from North America. Both are deciduous in cold climates, but the elder can be evergreen in warm areas, and even a pest in certain wet conditions where there is no period of dormancy, when it can sucker too readily. Elders make a good hedging plant as long as they are pruned regularly and you have the space.

However, it is the beautiful flowers, edible berries and sometimes striking foliage that have made this plant so popular as an ornamental and edible plant. Some wonderful foliage varieties include 'Aurea', with golden yellow leaves; 'Aureomarginata', with variegated leaves; and 'Guincho Purple', which has very dark leaves, providing interest and contrast to a height of about 3 m (10 ft). Don't eat elderberries or drink their juice without cooking them slightly first.

Pruning elder

With their suckering habit, elders can grow a bit too easily in some frost-free areas, spreading a fair way across the ground. To help contain this plant, try to hack it back to the ground every 2 to 3 years.

Using either a pruning saw, or even a chainsaw if you have very large clumps, cut stems down to about 30 cm (1 ft) off the ground. These stems are quite light wood, so the job is not as arduous as it sounds.

Leave the base stalks, as these will reshoot as the suckers come up, so in no time your plant will be thick and bushy, and producing many berries.

Opposite, clockwise from top left: Rose hip (*Rosa* sp.); *Rosa rugosa*; elder flower; and elderberry. Both the fruit and the flower of the elder can be made into wine.

Cranberries take about three years to start bearing. In the first couple of years they produce runners rather than the upright growth that's responsible for flowers and then fruit. They can be planted out as young seedlings in either spring or autumn into soil enriched with plenty of peat moss and a handful or two of blood and bone. Feed cranberries monthly with fish emulsion.

Harvest berries in autumn once they are red and before any hard frosts arrive, although they will cope with light frosts. Protect plants from hard frosts over winter with either a cloche or a layer of dry leaves, and every couple of years add a layer of sand to your bed to encourage it to produce new runners and uprights.

Huckleberries and whortleberries

Collectively known as bilberries, both huckleberry (*V. ovatum*) and whortleberry (*V. myrtillus*) have blue-black fruit. The latter is extremely cold-tolerant, as it's native to subarctic regions, and its fruit tastes similar to the blueberry, while red huckleberry (*V. parvifolium*), which is endemic to Alaska, has pink berries.

Bilberries have very similar growing requirements to blueberries, liking the same acid soil, but both are very difficult to grow. In alkaline areas, grow them in pots.

Below right: Cape gooseberries look like cherry tomatoes with golden orange skins.

Deadly nightshade family

While many berries belong to the rose family, Rosaceae, others are members of the deadly nightshade family, Solanaceae, which includes potatoes and tomatoes.

Cape gooseberries

One such plant is the Cape gooseberry, native to South America. Also known as golden berry (*Physalis peruviana*), it is a small herbaceous shrub, 1 x 1 m (3 x 3 ft), which dies down each winter to a permanent rootstock. The flowers are similar to tomato flowers — yellow and bell-shaped, with a purple-green calyx. As the fruit opens, the calyx turns papery and yellow, hiding the yellow fruit.

Tamarillos

Tamarillos (*Solanum betaceum*), or tree tomatoes as they are also known, are quick and easy plants to grow in any frost-free area, or in a protected position in a marginal climate. They only grow to about 3 m (10 ft), so they're not really trees at all. Their very large leaves look like heart-shaped tobacco foliage, while the pale pink bell-shaped flowers appear in spring and summer, followed by egg-shaped fruit that develop a reddish orange tinge as they ripen. Inside, the fruit looks like a cross between a tomato and a passionfruit, with a sweet taste that has a bit of an afterbite.

Poisonous berries

Some berries are highly toxic: the pokeberry (*Phytolacca americana*), a pretty but deadly perennial; green poison berry (*Cestrum parqui*); and *Acokanthera* sp., whose fruit, which look like black olives, are used to make poison darts. The berries of the highly ornamental and popular cotoneaster and pyracantha have both upset many a child's belly.

As with other members of this family, regular water throughout the growing season will benefit their cropping ability and vigour.

Other relations

Sunberry (*Solanum guineense* x *S. villosum*) is also a member of the nightshade family, but was bred in the early 1900s by Luther Burbank, who especially selected species that would produce a very sweet blue berry that is slightly larger than a pea. After he sold the rights to this plant, they became known as wonderberries (*S. burbankii*).

Wonderberries are ripe when they turn black and lose their glossy sheen. Also known as solanberry and black-berried nightshade, this member of the Solanaceae family produces tiny white flowers that are very similar to those on eggplants and chillis. Many consider the fruit bland and tasteless, but a judicious amount of sugar and lemon juice makes all the difference if you use the berries in jam and pie fillings.

The plant itself grows to 1 m (3 ft) and should bear fruit in less than three months. Grow it as you would tomatoes (see page 331).

Other relations include the Chinese lantern (*Physalis alkekengi*), tomatillo or jamberry (*P. philadelphica* syn. *P. ixocarpa*) and North American ground cherry (*P. pruinosa*).

See other Solanum fruit such as eggplants, on pages 326–7, and tomatoes and bush tomatoes, on pages 331–5.

Above left: The unripe fruit of the cape gooseberry is protected by its calyx, or husk.

Above: Once the husk becomes papery, the fruit is ready to eat.

Top left and left: Tamarillos are delicious eaten while still warm from the tree.

Goji berries

Lycium sp., Solanaceae family

Goji berries (*Lycium barbarum* and *L. chinense*) are of huge commercial interest since being marketed as a 'superfood' due to, among other things, their high vitamin C content. Known also as wolfberries, they are actually an Asian member of the potato family. Goji berries have been used in Chinese medicine for hundreds of years and, worldwide, China is the major supplier.

Climate: Goji berries can survive both cool winters and hot summers.

Culture: With their pretty flowers and berries, goji berries can make a nice shrub and are also suitable for growing in a conservatory. Prune back heavily to keep the plants looking bushy and to promote flowering and fruiting.

Height: 1 to 2 m (3 to 6 1/2 ft) with long, sappy growth.

Colours: The flowers are very similar to the trumpet blooms of eggplants, and appear throughout summer. These plants flower white and purple simultaneously before developing into red fruits that are about 2 cm (3/4 in) long.

Planting time: Spring through to late autumn as potted specimens.

Soil: These berries are not fussy about soil, but will flower and fruit better in a well drained soil that's moderately fertile.

Position: Full sun to semi-shade is best.

Planting spacing: 1 to 2 m (3 to 6 1/2 ft) apart.

Fertiliser: Slow-release fertiliser in spring.

Pests and diseases: Prone to attack by grazing animals such as deer and rabbits, so may need fencing.

Propagation: Germinate fresh berries or plant soft-tip cuttings, and plant out in spring.

Harvesting and storing: The berries appear throughout late summer and autumn, right up until the first frost. The fresh berries are best, but they can also be dried (pictured at right), juiced or frozen. You can start harvesting when the plant is two years old, but it produces most heavily from 4 to 5 years.

tip

Avoid digging the soil around fig trees as they have shallow roots that can be easily damaged.

Fruit from the ancient world

Many types of berry fruit have been cultivated since ancient times. While the blackthorn or sloe has been used in hedgerows for thousands of years in its native Europe, Eurasia and North Africa, there are also many other examples, such as figs, mulberries and pomegranates, which have an equally interesting history.

Mulberries

Many people have fond childhood memories of mulberry trees (*Morus nigra*) — of climbing their branches, picking fruit in late spring or simply smuggling leaves into a cardboard box to feed silkworms. If you already have a mulberry tree in your garden, you may already be familiar with the problem of clean washing stained with

been cultivated in China for centuries. The weeping form ('Pendula') is a very attractive specimen in the garden and bears fruit that is first white, before gradually changing to pink, then red. 'Shahtoot' is a delicious non-staining, white-fruited cultivar. Its fruit looks a bit like a caterpillar, but once you taste it, you'll find it very sweet and juicy.

Above and opposite: Mulberries can be stewed or made into jams, wine or a delicious sorbet.

Cultivating mulberries

Seedling trees should start cropping the year after planting, and be setting decent-sized crops by their third year. You can also plant what are known as truncheons, or large pieces of branch, about 1.5 m (5 ft) long, in either spring or autumn. Just bury them about 50 cm (20 in) into the earth so they are self-supporting. They will sprout roots spontaneously.

For best results, water the trees well in summer. Once they are established, they seem to develop a vigorous root system and are adept at finding their own ground water.

Grafted weeping trees are on *M. alba* rootstocks, generally 1 to 2 m (3 to 6½ ft) in height, with smaller fruit. They make a lovely specimen tree in any garden, but are especially useful in small spaces, even large tubs, as they never outgrow the allotted space.

Feeding

Any reasonably fertile soil will sustain growth naturally on mulberry trees. If your tree is growing in poor soil, apply a complete plant food each spring to encourage more vigour.

mulberry juice, courtesy of either fallen fruit or bird droppings.

So before planting a mulberry, consider the position, making sure it won't become a nuisance. Children love to pick the ripening fruit from low branches, but if your tree overhangs a path, fruit fall will become a messy hazard.

Most species of *Morus*, all members of the Moraceae family, are native to Asia, although some are from central Africa and North America. The species that is commonly cultivated is actually native to Iran, but for some strange reason it's known there as the black English mulberry (*M. nigra*).

The lesser known red mulberry or 'Hicks Fancy' (*M. rubra*) is native to the eastern United States and Canada, while the white mulberry (*M. alba*) has

did you know? You can remove a mulberry stain by rubbing it with half a lemon, then washing it in soapy water.

did you know? 'Here We Go Round the Mulberry Bush' is thought to be derived from a nursery rhyme sung by female prisoners at HMP Wakefield in Yorkshire, England, who entertained their children by walking around a mulberry bush within the prison area.

Pruning

Mulberries grow to about 10 m (33 ft), with an open crown. Prune your tree once it reaches about 1.3 m (4 ft) to encourage lower branches, ideal for climbing and reaching fruit. In winter, either cut it back lightly to keep it to a manageable size or prune it back hard, if necessary.

Harvesting

The tiny flowers are borne on separate male and female catkins, which then develop into the succulent fruit. Children have the right idea about picking the fruit off the tree — it doesn't store well.

Problems

The roots can get into broken drainage pipes and become a nuisance.

Above: White mulberry, 'Shahtoot'.

Left: Brambles growing among climbing roses.

Figs

Perhaps surprisingly, figs (*Ficus* sp.) are in the same family as mulberries. They also have tiny inconspicuous flowers, but these are actually inside the fruit, which is botanically known as a syconium. In many species it's pollinated by a wasp. Once opened, this round- or pear-shaped vessel reveals the pale pink or white flesh and a mass of hidden yet delicious blossom.

Figs are remarkable not only for their strange flowering habit, but also for their diversity as a genus. Some figs are strangling climbing plants that grow all over whatever host their seeds drop onto, often completely swallowing up and smothering the plant inside.

Some, like the banyan (*F. benghalensis*) — a sacred tree of Hinduism that is native to India — put down hundreds, sometimes thousands of trunks, forming a vast curtain-like structure up to 120 m (131 yd) wide and 12 m (39 ft) tall. Others, such as the rubber tree (*F. elastica*), are a source of

rubber or latex, known as 'caoutchouc', a commercial crop mostly grown in India and Bangladesh.

However, it is *Ficus carica*, the edible fig, that has left its mark in the food world. Figs are known to have been cultivated since before 3000 BCE in Western Asia and Asia Minor, where it is indigenous, but they also made their way via the Silk Road to the Mediterranean, where they have been cultivated for centuries.

A deciduous tree, small by comparison to its cousins — reaching about 10 x 9 m (33 x 30 ft) — in cultivation it's normally pruned back to keep it to a size that's manageable for harvesting the fruit.

Unlike many of the other tropical and subtropical species of the *Ficus* genus, *F. carica*, while happy in the warmth of the tropics, does not like the humidity, preferring a drier atmosphere. Too much summer rain can cause the fruit to split or sour if water gets into its 'eye' — the small opening at the end of the fig — so, while

Above left: Fig trees have dense foliage, so in summer they're ideal for screening out unsightly views.

Above: Young figs ripening on the tree.

Below: The 'eye', through which some species are pollinated by the fig wasp, can be seen at the base of the fruit.

the plant will grow very happily, you may not always get the best crop of fruit. On the other hand, this species is also quite cold-tolerant, withstanding frosts very well once it has been established for a couple of years.

Other edible species include Egyptian sycamore or mulberry fig (*F. sycomorus*). From the Arabian peninsula and the Sudan, it has sandpaper-like leaves and smaller, edible figs. There is also an Australian native sandpaper fig (*F. coronata*). Its small fruit appear sporadically throughout the year, so the harvest is a bit frustrating if you want to make jam but great if you're happy to graze. The tree itself is about 5 m (16 ft) tall and the fruit tastes like the larger figs, but is about the same size as a broad bean.

Cultivating figs

Figs are normally grown from cuttings, and are among the easiest plants to strike. Simply take pieces of one-year-old wood about 20 cm (8 in) long in late winter, dip them in hormone rooting powder and plant into pots of premium potting mix. Keep them moist and, the following winter, once the root system has established itself in the pot, plant them out.

Choose a well drained soil without any acidity. If you aren't sure, do a pH test (see page 15). It may be necessary to adjust the soil with lime in order to bring the pH up to neutral. Figs prefer a loamy soil with good access to summer water. Protect your tree from frosts for the first two years, but after that, it should cope with winter temperatures down to – 6°C (21°F).

Planting

Whether you're planting a nursery-grown fig tree or your own cutting, do so in winter when it's dormant.

1 Dig a large hole and ensure that its surfaces are rough, not smooth-sided, so that the roots can easily penetrate the sides.
2 Check that your specimen is not pot-bound, and cut away any tangled, circling or damaged roots before spreading the remainder out into a partially backfilled hole so they can establish themselves into loosened soil.
3 Backfill with more soil, firming down as you go, until you reach ground level.

Below: Fresh figs are delectable when served with nuts, cheeses or prosciutto, a cured ham.

Fig varieties

For the home gardener, it's important to choose a self-fertile fig so that you don't have to plant a number of different types for cross-pollination or rely on fig wasps to do the job. The most common figs are the Asiatic types, which include varieties such as 'Brown Turkey', 'Preston Prolific', 'Black Genoa', 'White Genoa' and 'Cape White', all of which are self-fertile.

'Black Genoa' is a regular heavy bearer with greenish purple skin and red flesh; 'Brown Turkey' has oval fruit, brown skin and pink flesh; and the smaller 'Preston Prolific', known for its rich flavour, has yellow skin and golden-coloured flesh. 'White Genoa', also known as 'White Adriatic' and 'Sugar Fig', bears green fruit with reddish flesh that is known for its sweetness. 'Cape White' is an early maturing fig with cream flesh and green skin that has a compact habit, so it's an ideal backyard variety. All can be dried, eaten fresh, cooked or glacéd.

'Brown Turkey' is an ideal variety for the home garden: it crops twice a year — once in spring and once in late summer.

4   Water in well to remove any air pockets and reduce transplant stress.

Feeding

Figs need feeding with a complete fertiliser, such as citrus food, at the end of each winter, before the leaves shoot. Citrus food has a N:P:K of about 10:4:6 and encourages leaf, fruit and root growth. Apply about 500 g (1 lb) around the root system (not the trunk) and water in thoroughly.

Pruning

Figs are very adaptable and can be trained easily into a wide range of shapes, including espalier, or 'flat-packed' trees. They bear fruit mostly on new wood, but can also produce some early crops on the older wood, so they're very forgiving of pruning mistakes. Generally, however, the main purpose of pruning should be to remove weak and rubbing branches, or to cut back old trees heavily to increase their vigour and hence crop size. For more on espaliering plants, see the box on page 156.

Harvesting

Figs don't continue to ripen once they're picked, so harvest them when they're mature or, if you're planning to dry them, when they're fully ripe. The fruit should be slightly soft, so avoid bruising by picking them carefully.

Problems

Figs are susceptible to the pests listed below. You may also spot ants on the fruit, but reconsider before getting rid of them, as they are pollinators.

- Birds: page 50.
- Dried fruit beetle: page 49.
- Fig bark beetle: page 49.
- Fig tree leaf beetle: page 49.
- Fruit fly: page 53.

tip

Store figs uncovered in the fridge for up to three days, but bring them back to room temperature before eating them.

Pomegranates

Some scholars believe the pomegranate, one of the oldest fruit trees in cultivation, was the forbidden fruit in the Bible's Garden of Eden. They were once thought to be from China, but were actually brought there from Persia in about 100 BCE by Jang Qian during the Han Dynasty. These days they are known to be native to the so-called 'Cradle of Civilisation', the eastern and southern parts of the Mediterranean region, although it was the Moors who brought them to Spain in about 800 CE.

Below and opposite: Botanically, pomegranates are true berries. This means that both the seeds and the pulp are produced by a single ovary. Other true berries include tomatoes, eggplants and grapes.

The genus contains only two species, but it is the common pomegranate (*Punica granatum*) that is most cultivated. It flowers in late spring and keeps blooming through to the end of autumn. Each bloom has prominent stamens and bright scarlet-red petals. There are double-flowered types: 'Wonderful' bears fruit that tastes of wine, and 'Flore Pleno' has double burnt orange flowers. The dwarf types, such as 'Nana', grow to 60 cm (2 ft) and produce inedible fruit, but they do make quite an attractive pot plant or hedging plant.

The pomegranate is a remarkable fruit. The orange-sized globe may turn from pale yellow or orange-red to purple, and the skin is quite tough and leathery, a bit like a passionfruit. Inside the flesh is coloured like an ember from a fire, with crimson-red jelly-like pulp around each pomegranate seed. These can be eaten fresh, juiced or used dried in cooking.

Each fruit has a 'crown' on top, which has given it another name — 'Royal Fruit'. (It was King Henry VIII of England who first brought the fruit to Britain.) Pomegranate seeds, or anardana, are used in Asian and Indian cooking in the same way as tamarind. They are normally dried, then steeped in hot water to reactivate them before cooking.

Pomegranates have glossy foliage, which starts off reddish green, then turns to mid-green in spring. As winter comes on, the display of yellows and reds develops. But as you might expect, the foliage of this 'forbidden fruit' can contain thorns.

Cultivating pomegranates

These trees need a hot, dry summer for the fruit to set properly; too much humidity can cause the fruit to split. They will also cope well with the cold, being deciduous, but are sensitive to spring frosts and also drying out in spring, so keep them well watered. Otherwise, however, they are drought-tolerant.

If in doubt, grow them in tubs, so you can bring them under cover in winter, or plant them in a glasshouse or against a sunny wall, which will help retain the heat of the day overnight.

Most pomegranates are either grown from cuttings from a reliable bearer, or from ordinary seedlings, sown in spring. Both grow into a small tree, which reaches about 8 m (26 ft) at maturity. Or, using 30-cm (1-ft) pieces, you can take hardwood cuttings in winter. Just cover these in potting mix so that the first couple of buds are exposed.

Feeding

This is normally done in winter, when a top dressing of citrus fertiliser (N:P:K of 10:4:6) can be applied.

Pruning

If you prefer a single-trunked specimen, prune your tree to remove suckers. Reduce crowding in the centre and encourage new spur growth from time to time, but remember that fruit-bearing spurs are produced on mature wood.

Harvesting

Harvest pomegranates through autumn, although you can also pick the fruit before it ripens and 'finish it off' in storage — just hang the stems with string and store in a cool, dry place for several months. This is particularly useful in areas that receive rain during harvest time, which can result in rotting and splitting. They usually take five years or so to start bearing.

Problem

• Fruit fly: page 53.

did you know? The ancient Romans used to tan the skins of pomegranates, or Punic apples, as they called them, and turn them into leather, which was sometimes used to make sandals for soldiers. These days, Greek Orthodox Christians spill pomegranate seeds and their juice on the ground at Easter to represent the blood of Christ. The word *'granatum'* means 'many seeds or grains'.

Tropical fruit

There is something exotic and mysterious about tropical fruit that entices us, like Eve to the forbidden apple in the Garden of Eden. Fruit from the tropics often comes from vastly different plant families and botanical parentage, so it can look like nothing we've ever seen before.

A taste of the exotic

Most of the Western world has been eating the same fruit and vegetables for hundreds of years, so it's no surprise that the weird and wonderful plants that are native to tropical climates — such as Central and South America, Africa and tropical Asia and Polynesia — hold such appeal.

Of course, this venturing into the unknown can be intimidating in a horticultural sense as well as a culinary one. Will they grow in our gardens? Will they perform? Do they have pests and problems we won't be able to deal with? These are all issues that may put us off experiencing some of the most delicious and easiest to grow fruits.

As you will discover, many of these plants grow well in areas that are subtropical, temperate or even where light frosts are experienced, so you might be able to find a place for one of them in your garden.

Above: Custard fruit (*Annona atemoya*).

Left: 'Lady's Finger' bananas.

Bananas

The banana (*Musa* sp.) is one of the most popular edible forms of starch in the world. Mostly native to Asia, the 40 or so species have varying cropping value, with some grown for fruit and others for their spectacular foliage and remarkable blooms. They are all suckering perennials, so they have an unusual care regimen (see pages 108–9).

Edible bananas are a cross between *Musa acuminata* and *Musa balbisiana*, with the relative strength of each parent determining whether it's a sweet-eating type or a starchier cooking variety, known as plantain.

In many parts of the world, where rice, potatoes and wheat are not grown, the banana — baked, fried or boiled — is the carbohydrate dished up with meals, although these normally have more *Musa balbisiana* in their parentage. *Musa acuminata*, the species usually sold as

eating bananas, has three main cultivars — 'Cavendish', 'Lady's Finger' and 'Williams'.

Like bamboo and grass, the banana 'tree' is actually a monocotyledon, so the actual 'stem' of the plant is underground in what's known as a rhizome or corm. The above-ground component of a banana 'tree' is the pseudostem, which contains the leaves, flowers and only growth point, and that's why, after you harvest a bunch of bananas, the rest of the 'tree' dies.

The flowers form a spike that, depending on the species, can either rocket skywards or hang like a bizarre chandelier. The spike starts off bearing female flowers, then, as it works its way down, the blooms change to hermaphrodites, then finally to males. The flowers are grouped in clusters, known as hands, each of which will bear a dozen or more flowers that produce

Above left: A banana flower in the process of developing into fruit.

Above: Green and ripe mangoes. Both can be eaten fresh.

Below: Red bananas have cream to pale pink flesh and a raspberry-banana flavour. Cultivars include 'Red Dacca'.

each 'finger' or individual banana. One bunch of bananas usually includes about 5 to 12 hands.

The leaves too can be extraordinary, with a large central midrib holding the fairly thin leaf together. This leaf can become quite straggly and ragged, especially if it's exposed to wind, which bananas don't like.

Cultivating bananas

Before you plant a banana in your garden, apply for a planting permit. Bananas are an important commercial crop, and in many areas of Australia you will need a permit from your state's governing agricultural body in order to grow them.

Select a warm, sunny site, preferably on a hillside with excellent drainage. Try to prepare the soil a few months before you plant out your sucker. Dig a large hole about 30 cm wide and 30 cm deep (1 x 1 ft), and add lots of organic matter, such as compost, rotted grass clippings or manure, then add about 1 kg (2 lb) of gypsum to the mix.

Bananas produce two types of suckers — water suckers (which are no good as propagation material) and spear-point suckers. The water suckers are easily recognised by their large, broad leaves, whereas the spear points have much smaller leaves but larger butts that taper to a point.

Top: A developed bunch of bananas, with the bell still attached to the end of the stem.

Far left and left: Some species of bananas with striking foliage are also valued as ornamentals. Abyssinian banana (*Ensete ventricosum*) is a stunning ornamental variety related to the edible banana. The maroon pink midrib on each leaf (far left) makes it a great feature in a temperate or tropical garden.

It is this spear-point sucker that is used as propagation material. Remove it carefully from its parent, cut off its head, remove the roots and plant it with the bud facing the direction in which you want the tree to grow — usually uphill. Backfill about 10 cm (4 in) of earth, which should leave a small depression around the sucker. As the sucker grows, gradually fill this with more soil and keep the whole plant watered sparingly but regularly.

Left: Commercially grown bananas are covered with blue plastic bags to protect them from birds and bats, and also to accelerate ripening. Each bag should have holes in the bottom to allow water to escape.

Feeding

After planting, don't feed your banana for 2 to 3 months. Then, every month while it's growing, use a nitrogen-rich organic fertiliser, but in winter apply dolomite and compost.

Pruning

Always let at least one or two suckers or 'daughters' remain on the parent plant, so they can replace the banana once it has fruited. Remove the others with a sharp, deep cut that removes the growing point. Also remove any old plants to reduce the likelihood of banana weevil borer.

Harvesting

Depending on the warmth of your climate, it takes 15 to 20 months from planting for bananas to reach the harvesting stage.

Harvest your bananas once the fruit has become completely rounded and lost its angular youthfulness. You can leave the whole bunch to ripen naturally on the tree, but if the weather is extremely hot, your bananas can spoil. If this is a risk, cut the bunch and hang it away from the sun in a well ventilated area. Alternatively, remove the bananas, one hand at a time, and ripen them in a plastic bag in a cool spot with another piece of ripe fruit.

Problems

In many areas, the law requires you to keep weeds away from the base of your bananas to help control weevil borer, which can leave you with undersized fruit and leaves that easily wither as the insect attacks the root system.

It is also best not to grow passionfruit or choko vines near bananas, as these plants can attract thrips and/or increase their numbers (see page 60). Watch out for aphids (page 58), armillaria root rot and snails (page 59).

A disease called banana bunchy top virus (BBTV), which is notifiable in Australia, causes the whole plant to have dark green streaks, a bit like Morse code, along the veins. Unfortunately, the whole plant will have to be destroyed.

Below: Bananas are great for baking in cakes, breads and muffins.

tropical fruit

1 'Lady's Finger' banana 2 Lychee 3 Feijoa 4 Jaboticaba 5 Wampee 6 Guava 7 Breadfruit
8 Jackfruit 9 Sapodilla 10 'Ruby Atkins' mango 11 Plantain 12 Prickly pear 13 Avocado
14 Tamarillo 15 Guava 16 Longan 17 Pink-fleshed pawpaw 18 Rose apple 19 White sapote

Above: Green mangoes are a popular ingredient in South-East Asian cuisines.

Below right: To cut a mango 'hedgehog' for eating, first remove the cheeks from the stone, then cut the flesh in a criss-cross pattern and invert the skin.

Mangoes

Few fruits can compare to mangoes (*Mangifera indica*), members of the Anacardiaceae family. They are known as the 'King of Fruits' for a very good reason — they are delectable. The mere sight of a mango tree is enough to make your mouth water, and their distinctive fragrance can make you swoon.

In ideal conditions, the glorious, full-figured tree grows to a grand size of about 12 m tall x 8 m wide (39 x 26 ft), but if your garden has poor soil or you're growing a less vigorous variety, your mango may only grow to about 6 m (20 ft), which is more suitable for backyards. For this reason, unless you can be absolutely sure about how specific types grow in your area, make sure you plant trees at least 10 m (33 ft) away from any buildings.

Mango's new growth is flushed red and pink, then matures to a mid- to dark green. The fruit itself hangs on the extremities of each branch, often on long pedicles, so the tree looks as if it has been decorated by the gods for we mortals to feast upon. Depending on the variety, each wonderful fruit ripens into a sunset palette of gold, amber, pink or rich ruby red and even deep purple and aubergine tones.

The most common varieties are Bowen types, including 'Kensington Pride', but others are useful for backyards because of their size or disease tolerance. For example, 'Irwin' is a small tree with quite good anthracnose tolerance, as is 'Tommy Atkins', which has a ruby-coloured skin.

Cultivating mangoes

Mangoes are native to areas of southern Asia down through northern India and into Malaysia. They will tolerate similar conditions to lychees, but they're true tropical plants and do not cope with

did you know? It took two attempts, and one of those was on HMS *Bounty*, but Captain William Bligh was responsible for successfully transplanting breadfruit plants from Tahiti to the West Indies, where the fruit was supposed to feed slaves. However, the slaves hated the breadfruit, and refused to eat it.

Mango ice cream

400 g (14 oz) fresh mango flesh
125 g (4¹/₂ oz/²/₃ cup) caster
    (superfine) sugar
3 tablespoons mango nectar
250 ml (9 fl oz/1 cup) pouring
    (whipping) cream
mango slices, extra, to serve

Put the mango in a food processor and process until smooth. Pour the mango purée into a bowl, and add the sugar and nectar. Stir until the sugar has dissolved. In a small bowl, beat the cream until stiff peaks form, then gently fold into the mango mixture. Spoon into a shallow loaf (bar) tin, cover and freeze for 1¹/₂ hours, or until frozen. Quickly spoon the mixture into a food processor and process for 30 seconds, or until smooth.

Return the mixture to the tin, then cover and freeze completely. About 15 minutes before serving, remove from the freezer, and serve with slices of fresh mango. Serves 6.

Above left: Flowers of the mango tree.

Above: Two mango cultivars — 'Irwin' (top) and 'Kensington Pride'.

anything more than the mere suggestion of a frost. If grown in a temperature range of 10 to 20°C (50 to 68°F) during their spring flowering season, they are likely to produce aborted fruit, known as nubbins, which don't develop properly. In cooler areas, choosing later flowering cultivars can help overcome this problem.

However, mangoes are often found growing in unsuitable areas with just

Jackfruit and breadfruit

Members of the family Moraceae, along with mulberries, are jackfruit (*Artocarpus heterophyllus*), from India and Malaysia, and breadfruit (*Artocarpus altilis*), from East Asia. Like mulberries, they both have tiny separate male and female flowers that join together to form a huge compound fruit, one of the staple foods in the tropics.

These flowers are cauliflorous, which means they're borne directly off the main trunk. Again, like the fig and the mulberry, they are big trees, reaching a height of up to 20 m (66 ft), with a spreading domed crown that's about 6 m (20 ft) wide. They also have milky white sap, like the figs, and glossy, somewhat leathery leaves.

Breadfruit are used as a source of starch in stews and curries throughout the tropics, while jackfruit are used in desserts, depending on the ripeness of the flesh. When it is very ripe, the flesh becomes yellowish pink and smells a bit like onion, banana and pineapple all in one. It has a smooth, glutinous texture and can be used in desserts.

The jackfruit can reach up to 90 cm (36 in) in length and 36 kg (80 lb) in weight, making it the largest tree-borne fruit in the world.

Sowing mango seeds

In order to sow mango seeds, first you need to remove the outer pip to reveal the polyembryonic seed inside.

1 Slice the fruit in half.

2 Using a short knife, peel off any remaining flesh.

3 Wash the seed under running water.

4 Using a dry cloth, such as an old towel, hold the seed down while you cut into it.

5 Pull the outer casing apart to reveal the seed.

6 Plant the fresh seed on edge with the curved side upwards, just below the surface of the seed-raising mix. Keep well watered for the first month or so until it germinates. Only keep the first seedling that germinates and discard the others.

the right microclimate. Here they'll fruit happily and reward their optimistic owner with their precious harvest each year, or every couple of years in cooler zones. Mangoes often start fruiting after three years — although this fruit should probably be removed to encourage more vegetative growth — and will keep on producing for decades.

Feeding

For the first few years of a mango's life, concentrate on encouraging leaf growth by feeding with a nitrogen-based fertiliser in spring and summer. As the tree matures, start feeding with a more balanced fertiliser that will stimulate flowers.

Pruning

Mangoes don't really need much pruning, especially in the home garden. When they are young, you can train them into about 4 to 5 main branches, each oriented evenly.

If desired, prune back any uneven growth after harvesting the fruit.

Harvesting

Mangoes can start to produce small crops from the age of 3 onwards, but may take a couple of decades to mature and reach full production. Harvest the fruit by cutting it from the tree; you can tell it's ready if it's coloured and, when cut, shows golden yellow by the seed. From that stage it will happily ripen off the tree in a cool place within 5 to 6 days.

Problems

Mangoes are prone to stem end rot, a fungal disease, and these problems.

- Anthracnose and bacterial black spot: treat both as for anthracnose, page 66.
- Fruit fly: page 53.
- Mango scale: page 58.
- Pink wax scale: page 58.
- Oriental fruit moth: page 55.

Chinese treasures

For centuries, China was responsible for the breeding and exportation of many fruits via the Silk Road — mulberries, citrus, apples, quinces, peaches, nectarines, persimmons, kiwi fruit and figs. Lesser known, however, are the members of the Sapindaceae family, which, being far less cold-tolerant, didn't survive in the Mediterranean and Far East, and so simply stayed put.

It wasn't until the nineteenth century, when tens of thousands of Chinese migrated to other warm countries such as the United States and Australia during the gold rush periods, that this fruit family began its world travels. Members of the Sapindaceae family, including the longan (*Euphoria longan*), the lychee (*Litchi chinensis*) and the rambutan (*Nephelium lappaceum*), have become more popular, and not just as tinned fruit in the Chinese supermarket.

Lychees

Lychees are probably the best known of all three. Their beautiful red-skinned fruits contain a sweet, whitish, translucent flesh similar to that of a grape. Within this is a dark, almost black seed. Lychees ripen over summer, which is over Christmas in the southern hemisphere, so it isn't surprising

Mangosteen

Although mangosteen (*Garcinia mangostana*) is also native to Malaysia and Indonesia, and is just as delicious as the mango, it's not a botanical relation. The fruit is about the same size as a tennis ball, with leathery purple skin, but you have to be patient and live in a warm climate to grow them: the trees take fifteen years to fruit, and the fruit can't cope with any frost.

Left: Persimmons (*Diospyros kaki*) are related to black sapote (see page 129) and ebony, from which black piano keys are made.

Below left: The outer casing of the lychee is easy to remove from the smooth white flesh.

did you know? Also in the same family as mangoes are poison ivy, rhus tree, smoke tree, hog plum, cashew, sumac, peppercorn and pistachio. Urushiol, an irritant found in many of the species, can cause violent reactions and anaphylactic responses. For this reason, wear gloves when picking plants such as cashews; rhus tree, while beautiful, is often best avoided in gardens.

Above: The lychee is an excellent source of vitamin C.

Opposite, top: Longans are called dragon eyes in Chinese, because the black seed can be seen through the translucent white flesh.

Opposite, bottom: Rambutans are better-tasting and longer-lasting when left on the branch after harvesting.

that in countries such as Australia they have become a favourite fruit in the festive season.

Unlike many other tropical fruits, lychees store well in the fridge, and there are several varieties that keep their season going throughout the summer, so they are quite economical buying for this time of the year.

The tree itself varies enormously in size, depending on the cultivar. Named varieties are available, but as a rule of thumb, the smaller the leaf size, the smaller the tree size so, when buying for your backyard, avoid large-leafed types, unless you have loads of space. Avoid large varieties, such as 'Tai So' or 'Kwai Mai', as they reach about 18 m (59 ft); smaller types — such as 'Wai Chee', 'Gee Kee' and 'Salathiel' — grow to only half this size.

Lychee trees also have a nasty tendency to lose limbs so, again, the smaller the tree, the less likely the tree will reach a size where this is likely to happen.

The glossy green leaves, flushed with pink and brown as the new growth develops, coupled with the beautiful fruit, make the lychee an ornamental tree. The fact that they are mostly self-fertile means that one tree will set fruit and you won't have to grow another sort in order to achieve cross-pollination. The flowers are actually a mix of male, female and hermaphrodites, having all sexes and combinations on the same panicle, so encouraging bees into the garden will help with pollination and fruit set.

Cultivating lychees

Lychees can tolerate temperatures down to 1 or 2°C (33.8 or 35.6°F), as well as survive light frosts, but the colder it is for any length of time, the less fruit will form. If winter temperatures in your area usually go below 5°C (41°F), then it's probably too cold to grow them.

They are also much less fussy about poor drainage than many other trees, and will even stand a day or two of total inundation, so they're worth considering if your garden occasionally suffers from flooding problems. In China, lychees are frequently grown along riverbanks, where they have good access to water — essential during fruit formation.

Longans

The most cold-tolerant of all these Chinese fruits is the longan, which follows seasonally after the lychee. The fruit is borne in similar clusters and the compound leaves also closely resemble those of the lychee; the main difference is the colour of the skin of the

fruit, which is golden to yellow-brown. Inside, the fruit is quite similar to the lychee, although longans have a stronger flavour, larger seeds and a shelf life of about six weeks in the fridge.

Longan trees are also more adaptable, coping with light frosts. They flower more consistently in this sort of marginal position. You can buy cultivars that are about 10 m (33 ft) high, with glossy foliage and new red growth that's attractive in its own right. They have similar cultural requirements to lychees, although they are more resilient climatically.

Rambutans

From Malaysia and Indonesia, rambutans are covered in remarkable curved hairs, or spinterns, and have a much milder flavour than lychees. They also don't keep as well and are better eaten fresh, although you can store them in the fridge for up to a week if you cover them in plastic wrap.

The rambutan is a truly tropical fruit that is unable to cope with temperatures lower than about 9°C (48.2°F) without dropping foliage. You can only grow a rambutan if the temperature in your area doesn't go below 15°C (59°F). Growing to about 12 m (39 ft) when grafted, this tree is one for enthusiasts who live in the tropics.

Look-alikes

Wampees (*Clausena lansium*), which are native to Vietnam and the south of China, have a compound leaf and oval grape-like fruit, borne on a panicle that is covered in a skin. In botanical terms, it's closer to an orange than a longan, as it belongs to the Rutaceae family.

The fruit is segmented (like a kumquat), the skin resinous and the fruit tastes like tangy citrus, slightly like a grapefruit. The fruit follows the lychee season in midsummer.

Wampee is a more suitable alternative for the home garden. The tree grows to only about 6 m (20 ft), and is much better at withstanding light frosts and tolerating a wide range of soils. The fertiliser and watering regimens are the same as for lychees.

The small grape-like fruit of the wampee tree.

Star fruit

Carambola (*Averrhoa carambola*) is one of the prettiest cropping trees for the backyard. With successive flower flushes of pink with red stems throughout spring, followed by angular, wax-coated golden fruit hanging down like baubles in late summer and into autumn, a star fruit tree looks as if it has been decorated by a fairy.

The fruit itself tastes a little like an apple; however, once you cut open a carambola, the spell is cast, as each cross-section looks like a star. They keep their colour well, and can be glacéd, pickled, cooked and even frozen.

The tree is a slow grower, taking about ten years to reach 8 m (26 ft). The leaves are mid-green, compound and look a bit like those of a honey locust (*Robinia pseudoacacia*). It is partly self-fertile, so if there's another tree, you'll get more fruit but won't need another tree to maintain reasonable amounts. Star fruit is also very adaptable to different soil types, although it prefers a slightly acid medium that drains well.

Star fruit will also stand light frosts, but may drop leaves, yellow slightly or not set as large a crop. Although they can tolerate a bit of gentle wind, on the whole they prefer a sheltered position. Closely related is the bilimbi (*A. bilimbi*), also known as pickle fruit, but it is not as sweet or as angular as the star fruit. Both species have light- and touch-sensitive leaves, and fold in the dark or when handled. They can be propagated by aerial layering or seed, and fed with an organic mulch annually.

Bounty from the Americas

It's hard to imagine how comparatively boring the diet of Europeans was before Christopher Columbus first sailed to the Americas. For instance, they had never seen or tasted pineapple, guava, blueberries or cranberries, passionfruit,

Below: Star fruit are ready to eat when the skin is firm and yellow, shaded with green.

Below right and opposite: European explorers coined the name 'pineapple' as they thought the fruit resembled a pine cone.

pawpaw or avocado, to say nothing of the less common fruit, such as custard apple, tamarillo, fruit salad plant, jaboticaba, sapodilla or casimiroa, or products such as coffee and chocolate, which have since taken the Western world by storm.

Pineapples

Pineapples (*Ananas comosus*) became the fruit superstars of the early 1700s when they were first brought back to Europe from their native Brazil. Nobody had ever seen anything like them before. Across Europe, on the estates of the very rich, special pineapple houses were built and heated at enormous expense to simulate the climatic conditions of Brazil. In fact, pineapples became a popular motif on buildings, landscape features, decorative items and even fabrics.

These days pineapples are mainly grown for canning and juicing, but the superior flavour and stylish appearance of fresh pineapple makes it worth growing at home. The whorled arrangement of leaves is very striking, and the silvery, slightly succulent leaves make it resilient to drought. A powdery bloom gives it a frosted appearance.

The fruit itself is actually formed by the fusion of the many flowers as they develop into the one fruiting body. In the pineapple's native habitat, each flower is pollinated by hummingbirds, but you'll probably have to hand-pollinate unless you live in the rainforests of Paraguay or Brazil! It takes two years in ideal conditions, and longer in cooler areas, for plants to crop.

Cultivating pineapples

Pineapples are actually a type of bromeliad and grow in any well drained, acidic soil. Although they are tropical plants, they will cope well with subtropical conditions and still fruit; they will also grow reasonably well in warm temperate climates, provided they are in a suitable microclimate — say, by the coast. Frosts adversely affect not only the plant, but also the fruit itself: chilling temperatures result in a condition known as blackheart, which can also occur

Planting pineapples

You can propagate pineapples from the crowns, or tops.

1 Using a sharp knife, cut off the top.

2 Cut away the rest of the flesh until you are left with the stub.

3 Pull off the lower leaves.

4 Allow it to dry off slightly, then plant the stub into a hole that's about 6 cm (2 in) deep.

to a lesser extent if you store them in a very cold fridge after harvest.

Before planting, make sure the soil is acid (in the range of 4.5 to 5), adding sulfur if necessary. Also add some organic matter. Choose a site that is protected from southerly and westerly winds. If you are planting a row, plants should be about 30 cm (1 ft) apart with 1-m (3-ft) spacings between rows.

Different parts of a pineapple are all suitable for planting. You can plant the tops of each fruit, known as crowns, by first removing all the flesh and then leaving a small 6-mm (¼-in) stub to plant about 6 cm (2 in) deep.

The leaves may yellow for many months but should green up and grow in their first spring. Remove some of the lower leaves and let the plant air so the base dries out slightly before planting. This will make rotting less likely. Alternatively, plant a pup or sucker from the side of your adult pineapple plant. Mulch with pinebark or wood chips, especially in cold areas, as it will keep the soil warm.

Feeding

Pineapples are heavy feeders and must be fed regularly with applications of complete fertiliser — each month from summer to late autumn, and a one-off application in spring. Apply it to both the leaf bases and the soil, and use extra liquid feed if your plants are still hungry, but be careful not to fertilise the growing top.

Pruning

Cut back any stalk bearing spent fruit right to the base, keeping only the most vigorous 2 to 3 suckers. While pineapple plants can continue to fruit for many years, each year the size of your pineapple will decrease, so encourage fresh suckers.

Harvesting

Pick pineapples when they're fully sized and showing at least some colour at the base. Leave a few centimetres of stalk on each plant, more in winter — at that time of year, the sugars won't continue to develop after harvest.

Problems

Overplanting pineapples can lead to infestations of sap-sucking insects such as scale and mealy bugs, which in turn can spread other diseases (see pages 57–9). It's therefore important to space plants adequately, so there is lots of air circulating around each plant. Every few years, rotate the position of your pineapple crop to avoid nematodes. If the drainage is not good, plants can also be prone to base rot and other fungal diseases. Rats and crows need to be controlled too, as both have a penchant for pineapples.

Right: The pineapple plant grows up to 1.5 m (5 ft).

Avocados

Although they are used as a salad vegetable, avocados (*Persea americana*) are actually fruit. Each piece is shaped like a large emerald green or black pear, and inside the flesh is creamy yellow-green with a large single seed. The flesh is great for a dip called guacamole, which can be used instead of butter as a spread, or you can slice it fresh for salads. Avocados are also pressed for oil, and are one of the staple foods of the Central Americas, its native habitat.

The avocado is a member of the Laurel family, Lauraceae, which also includes bay trees, camphor laurels and cinnamon trees.

Seedling trees can grow up to 20 m (66 ft) tall and just as wide, although you are much better off with a grafted tree that has a particular cultivar with known characteristics. These cultivars are normally smaller plants, growing to about 5 to 10 m (16 to 33 ft) tall by at least this wide. They also bear fruit in about three years rather than ten. Avocado trees are quite handsome, with dark glossy foliage and a broad, spreading canopy, but as their root system is not very vigorous, they may need extra summer water to compensate.

Cultivating avocados

It takes quite a bit of work just to keep the tree alive, let alone fruiting well. The key to growing avocados successfully is drainage. Choose a raised, sloping spot with porous soil. Avocados also like a moderately acid to neutral pH (5.5 to 7). They are frost-tender, and grow best in coastal, temperate climates in a sunny position, protected from wind. Under these conditions, they should produce enough fruit without being cross-pollinated.

The best varieties for the home gardener depend on the climate. 'Bacon', 'Sharwil' and 'Fuerte' (which can crop biennially) are the most cold-tolerant. 'Wurtz' and 'Rincon' are smaller trees but need the extra warmth. Planting more than one

Above left: An avocado cultivar called 'Fuerte'.

Above centre: An avocado tree in flower.

Above and below: 'Hass', a popular variety, has bumpy skin and a rich, buttery flavour.

wood chip over the surrounding soil, but not up to the trunk itself.

6 Place three stakes around your tree just beyond the root ball. Wrap these with hessian or shade cloth to give your establishing plant some protection from the cold, wind and sun.

Feeding

Avocados are quite big feeders, especially during their infancy. Apply 6 teaspoons of citrus fertiliser every six weeks or so during the warm weather for the first few years of growth, and then gradually reduce it to twice a year, in spring and then summer. You may also need to add lime or dolomite in winter if the pH gets too acid, which can happen with excessive fertilising. Use chicken manure instead.

Pruning

Avocados need minimal pruning. In the first few years, select a balanced branched tree, or tip prune to encourage even growth. Just keep an eye on the graft and remove any growth from below — this will be the understock.

Harvesting

Grafted avocados start producing small crops after only three years. They hold on the tree very well without spoiling and, in fact, only begin to ripen once picked, so you can pick them a few days before you need them. When the fruit is ripe, the stalk becomes yellow and the skin slightly dull.

Problems

Both fruit fly (see page 53) and scale (see page 58) can cause some grief, but the biggest problem with avocados is root rot (see page 69), so it's critical to pay careful attention to both drainage preparation and site selection.

Growing avocado from seed

You can plant an avocado seed in sawdust/potting mix for fun, but in order to ensure good quality fruit production, you'll need to graft.

1 Cut the avocado in half.

2 Peel away the flesh from the seed.

3 You should be left with the seed.

4 Plant in a pot with the conical point upwards and just showing.

variety that flowers at the same time will lead to heavier crops.

It's best to plant avocados during the warmer months of the year.

1 They don't have great root systems, so dig a hole that's only just larger than the rootball itself, so that the soil around it is still snug and stable.

2 Roughen the sides of the hole so that the roots won't hit a shiny surface and start to circle or spiral. Also make sure the tree's roots are straight and evenly oriented outwards in all directions.

3 Plant into the hole, then backfill, firming the soil as you fill.

4 Water well.

5 Clear all the ground around your tree of weeds, and mulch with leaf litter or

Custard apples

These fruit epitomise the weird and wonderful nature of the tropics. Custard apples (*Annona atemoya*), or atemoya as they are also known, are hybrids between *A. cherimola* and *A. squamosa* and are, quite simply, a bit odd. They are lumpy and bumpy, but once you get over their appearance and taste them, you'll probably be won over by their sweet, creamy texture and melting white flesh that's speckled throughout with large black seeds.

They don't like cold weather at all, preferring the humid, hot tropics, with shelter from wind. The best custard apple to grow in your backyard is one known as 'African Pride'. It grows to 9 m (29½ ft) and will produce fruit after 3 to 4 years. But there are other 'apples' worth noting. The cherimoya (*A. cherimola*), one of the custard apple's parents, is from Peru, so it is slightly more cold-tolerant. The fruit is similar, although a bit more acid in flavour.

The other parent, the sugar apple or sweetsop (*A. squamosa*), is inferior in quality. Its cousin, the soursop or guanabana (*A. muricata*), is a favourite in its native West Indies. This fruit is covered in soft curved spines, so it looks even stranger than the custard apple. Also common in Asia is the bullocks heart (*A. reticulata*).

In the same family as custard apples is the pawpaw (*Asimina triloba*), which is much more cold-tolerant, and even frost-hardy. This tree grows to a similar height, but the fruit are yellowish brown and have golden-orange flesh. Another plant also known as pawpaw is the papaya (*Carica papaya*; see page 132).

Yet another relation of the custard apple is rollinia (*Rollinia deliciosa* and *R. mucosa*), which tastes like lemon sherbet or lemon meringue pie. This tree is from the Amazon region of South America and grows to about 8 m (26 ft) in cultivation, fruiting after 3 to 4 years. It can only be grown in the tropics, however, needing not

Above left and centre: Custard apples can be eaten fresh, or puréed in a blender and used in fruit drinks and cocktails.

Above: Some young pawpaws (*Asimina triloba*) developing on the tree.

tip

If your avocado tree is far too big, you can cut it down to about 1 m (3 ft) along the main branches in spring. It will regenerate in a few months and start fruiting again in a couple of years.

did you know? Fresh custard apples should be eaten with a spoon, as the large black seeds in the flesh are toxic, and should not be ingested.

Japanese raisin tree

Hovenia dulcis, Rhamnaceae family

This incredible tree is grown not for its fruit, but for the swollen pedicels that develop towards the end of summer and into autumn. Once 'ripe', they have a sweet raisin-like flavour, but they are very high up in the tree, so actually reaching them is no mean feat.

Climate: Any temperate climate is perfect.

Culture: Their graceful habit, deciduous nature and heart-shaped leaves have made them popular as a shade tree throughout Asia.

Colours: The flowers are fairly small and yellowish green.

Height: Up to 9 m (29^1/$_2$ ft).

Planting time: Spring to autumn.

Soil: Well drained, reasonably fertile soil.

Position: Full sun with protection from hot dry winds.

Planting depth: 6 m (20 ft) apart.

Fertiliser: Once a year in spring with manure pellets is adequate.

Pests and diseases: None.

Propagation: Seed or semi-hardwood cuttings in summer.

Harvesting and storing: The stems become sweet after the first frosts and are best eaten fresh.

only warm temperatures but also high humidity to pollinate successfully. Even the fruit don't like being stored in the fridge.

Cultivating custard apples

The ideal site for growing custard apples is a warm, sheltered, frost-free position that is protected from cold winds. Space the trees 4 m (13 ft) or more apart. Keep them well watered, protected from extreme heat with shadecloth and weed-free while they establish through their first summer.

Feeding

Once they're established, you can feed them with a complete fertiliser throughout the growing seasons of spring and summer, even early autumn.

Pruning

Prune to create an open vase shape in summer. Custard apples produce fruit on both old and new wood, so many growers prune their tree in early summer to encourage new flowering growth that will bear fruit.

Harvesting

Patience is required for custard apples, as they can take many years to fruit, and even then be sporadic if the conditions are not right when flowering. Seven years is fairly standard. Depending on when your tree flowers, you will either have an autumn crop or a late winter/spring one. Clip fruit from your tree once it begins to change colour, then allow a few days for it to ripen indoors before eating.

Problems

While some sap-sucking insects can eat the leaves and fruit, the biggest problem is collar and root rot (see page 69), so make sure you select a well drained site.

Guavas

Guavas are popular for their fabulous juice, which is great fresh on its own or in cocktails. However, the fruit is very versatile, and can be made into jams and preserves and even turned into fruit leather. The plants themselves are also ideal for areas where the climate doesn't become too cold, as they can cope with very light frosts once established, but are best in the tropics and subtropics, such as the tropics of the Americas, to which they are native.

There are several species of guava (*Psidium* sp.), and many produce edible fruit. The most common is *P. guajava*, a small tree or tall shrub that grows to about 9 m (29¹/₂ ft) tall and half that wide. Its leaves are apple-green and have prominent veination. The fruit is about the same size and shape as a quince, with white or greenish (sometimes yellow) skin that has the dimpled look of cellulite. Inside, the flesh itself is skin-coloured to dark pinkish red, depending on the seedling variation.

Native guava

Bolwarra (*Eupomatia laurina*) is an Australian native guava that grows into a large shrub, up to 5 m (16 ft) tall, in the rainforests of the east coast and in some wetter bushland under gums. The fruit (pictured on page 224) can be made into jams and desserts and is used to spice other food. It needs protection from frosts, and prefers some shade and dappled sun.

The cherry or strawberry guava (*Psidium cattleianum*) is a slightly smaller plant with more ornamental red-toned bark, shinier leaves and smaller fruit that is rich in vitamin C. These only reach the same size as a cherry, and are mostly dark red both inside and out, although they can sometimes have yellow skin. It is quite a pretty shrub, with white blossom in spring.

The other guava, also a member of the Myrtaceae family, is known as pineapple guava (*Feijoa sellowiana*). Native to South America, it is a much tougher plant than the cherry guava, and is only mildly

Below, from left to right: Cherry guava, feijoa and a developing apple guava.

affected by frosts. It is also extremely salt- and wind-tolerant, so it's sometimes used as a coastal plant and/or windbreak.

The plant itself grows into a 4-m (13-ft) shrub with attractive mottled bark, a bit like a crepe myrtle. The flowers are strangely fleshy, with bright red stamens and silvery leaves. The fruit, which starts producing after about 3 to 4 years, is a joy. They look like small green eggs, but have white flesh that smells like a summer fruit salad. They can be juiced or eaten fresh and contain loads of vitamin C.

Cultivating guavas

Guavas will cope with virtually any soil type, periods of flood and even salty soils. They're easy to prune, fruit quickly and grow fast, especially if they're given adequate water and fertiliser when they're young and forming fruit.

Harvesting

Leave the fruit to fall on the ground rather than pick it off the tree, as it seems to be the bump itself that triggers the ripening process. This happens in autumn.

Problems

- Fruit fly: page 53.
- Ring-barking grub: page 56.

Other members of the Myrtaceae family

Botanically linked to the guavas by their flower parts (they have the same stamenous flowers) are lilly pillies, which also go by various names, such as rose apples and riberries, as well as an amazing plant from Brazil called jaboticaba (*Myciaria cauliflora*).

Top and left: Guavas — the apple guava (top) is the type most commonly cultivated.

Jaboticaba

The jaboticaba fruit looks a bit like an oversized blueberry or a round black grape, but it is the way it fruits that is unusual. This plant is cauliflorous, which means that the fruit grow right out of the stems and trunks themselves. Although this habit is reasonably common in the tropics, it's rare in cooler areas. Jaboticaba grows quite well in even temperate climates that get the occasional light frost.

The skin is fairly thick — again, a bit like a red wine grape. Put them whole into your mouth, pop them with your tongue, then spit out the seed and skin so you can enjoy the juicy white flesh, which has a sweet taste with a zesty overtone. Once you get going, it's hard to stop.

Jaboticaba grows into a rounded shrub or small tree to about 10 m (33 ft), but it does take some time to get that height. It will happily fruit at about the age of 10, or at 3 to 4 m (10 to 13 ft) in height. It can also be planted as a windbreak, and the fruit can be made into wine or marmalade. It crops throughout summer, when a child will happily hide within its canopy and suck and spit all day long.

Cultivating jaboticaba

This tree is ideal for the home garden. It's self-fertile, so one plant is enough for reliable, good cropping. Jaboticaba copes with a wide range of soils, including heavy clay and light sandy loams, and is not particularly fussy about pH. Its tolerance to wind and light frosts is well known.

Feeding

It doesn't need feeding, although applying fertiliser when it's young can help it to grow faster to maturity and, hence, fruiting age. There are no particular pruning techniques — a rare treat for the home fruit-grower.

Problems

The jaboticaba's only known pests are birds, which will have a go at the fruit. You can easily combat this by throwing a net over the whole tree when the fruit is approaching maturity.

Above left: A jaboticaba tree, netted to protect the fruit from birds.

Above: The fruit of the jaboticaba tree grows straight out of the trunk and stems.

tip

Straight after harvesting jaboticaba, store it in the fridge so it will retain its sweetness and flavour; if kept at room temperature, it may become bland.

Lilly pillies and rose apples

There are about 1000 members of the *Syzygium* genus, part of the Myrtle family. Many are huge evergreen trees from Australia, Asia and Africa, and are commonly known as lilly pillies, rose apples and jambos, depending on where you live. Undoubtedly one of the most beautiful plants is S. *jambos*, which is native to Malaysia and Indonesia. It has large glossy leaves, fluffy white flowers and pinkish fruit.

Below: The ethereal fruit of the rose apple (*Syzygium jambos*).

Also highly attractive is the small-leafed lilly pilly or riberry (S. *luehmannii*), a great hedging plant that is covered in beautiful pink foliage as it puts on new growth. The fruit is pink and pear-shaped, but not much bigger than a pea in size.

The giant water gum (S. *francisii*) is a fantastic tree for large gardens and parks, reaching about 20 x 20 m (66 x 66 ft). The bark is textural and flaky and the fruit violet-purple in colour, while the crown casts fantastic shade. (See also S. *formosa* and S. *australe* on page 224.)

Cultivating lilly pillies and rose apples

Lilly pillies are easy to grow in either full sun or partial shade. They can be hedged or left to mature into lawn specimen and park-like trees, depending on your situation. Either way, they will happily fruit and flower. An annual feed in spring will encourage new growth, which is a feature in itself due to their delightful colouring, but this may need protection if summer temperatures spike too high. Protection from frosts is also required. Pick berries when they are fully coloured.

Sapodillas or chicos

Even if you think you have never tried a sapodilla (*Manilkara zapota*, Sapotaceae family), chances are you have probably chewed a bit of it without realising: this plant used to be the main ingredient in chewing gum. Its sap is white and, like latex, tapped in much the same way as maple syrup is from sugar maples (*Acer saccharum*), or rubber from rubber trees (*Ficus elastica*).

In fact, every part of this plant, the fruit included, contains the sticky gum, so the neatest way to eat this fruit is like a boiled egg: slice the top off and eat it with a teaspoon, although it's worth noting that

Black and white sapote

Sapodilla and sapote, both black and white, sound as if they should be related, but in fact they belong to different plant families.

The casimiroa, or white sapote (*Casimiroa edulis*), is a member of the Rutaceae family and, like sapote, is native to Central America and Mexico. It is also a fine evergreen tree, attaining a weeping habit as it approaches its mature height of about 15 m (49 ft).

The three edible species are *Casimiroa edulis*, *C. sapota* and *C. tetrameria*, with the first being the most common. Both the buttery white flesh and seed are edible, although the seed must be roasted first. Make sure the fruit is yellow-skinned and soft-fleshed before eating it fresh. White sapote likes the same conditions as the avocado and is able to withstand the odd light frost.

Black sapote (*Diospyros digyna*) is actually a member of the Ebony family, Ebenaceae. Also known as the chocolate pudding tree, the soft fruit is dark-fleshed and tastes like chocolate, but doesn't carry the same number of kilojoules. This fruit — like persimmons (*Diospyros kaki*), to which it is related — is also in the same genus as the date plum (*Diospyros lotus*).

White sapote (*Casimiroa edulis*) is the size of a large grapefruit and has a banana-pear flavour.

many people squeeze some fresh lime juice over it to improve its flavour.

Sapodilla is native to Central America. The fruit is the size of a cricket ball and has brown powder on its skin, known as scurf, which gives it the appearance of an unwashed potato.

Inside this unattractive exterior is every child's dream fruit. You have to eat sapodillas when they're fully ripe so that any trace of the sliminess, evident when the fruit is green, is gone. The scurf will have disappeared and inside the light brown flesh will be very sweet, with no acid, just a slight chocolate flavour. Sapodillas also contain black and shiny seeds that look like flattened almonds.

In the Caribbean, children peel the outside of the fruit and gorge on the flesh while it is still warm from the tree.

Cultivating sapodillas

The sapodilla tree itself is very adaptable and hardy as well as extremely versatile. It's large and evergreen, growing to about 15 m tall by about 6 m wide (49 x 20 ft) and bearing small white bell-like flowers. It can cope with extremely salty and limey soils, strong winds, salt spray, very high temperatures and even cold snaps down to 1 or 2°C (33.8 to 35.6°F). Sapodilla is also self-fertile, bearing fruit that stores for 2 to 3 weeks once picked. The ripe fruit will be brown.

Relatively trouble-free, these plants are normally grafted or grown from aerial layering (also known as marcotting), in which case you can expect fruit after about 2 to 3 years, provided you fertilise and water your tree regularly to prompt strong growth.

Above: Sapodillas are delicious cool from the fridge or even frozen, like ice cream.

Above: Iceplant (*Aptenia cordifolia*).

Above centre: House leek (*Sempervivum tectorum*).

Above right: Sour fig (*Carpobrotus acinaciformis*).

Edible succulents

There are many plants native to desert environments around the world that are adapted to extremely low water requirements, and many have succulent foliage that holds water inside their fleshy leaves from one rainy day to another, a bit like camels holding fatty tissue in their humps. These plants are often armed with wickedly sharp spines to protect themselves against predators hoping for a moisture-rich feed themselves, in which case they are called cactus. Some of these succulents don't have edible foliage, but do have edible fruit, while others have edible flowers.

Iceplant
The heart-leafed iceplant (*Aptenia cordifolia*) is a succulent groundcover that grows quite flat to the ground, spreading about 1 m (3 ft) in diameter. It has apple-green foliage and pretty red daisy flowers, very much like pig face. The foliage, the edible part of this plant, has quite a nice texture when added to salads. Pick the young tender leaves. It's an ideal plant for rockeries in a sunny, well drained position.

House leek
The young tips of the common house leek (*Sempervivum tectorum*) are also edible and can be eaten fresh in salads or juiced. This plant is native to the mountain areas of Europe and, as its common name suggests, is used on roofs (both tiled and thatched) to stop leaks and protect against fire and lightening. It also grows happily in pots, rockeries and any well drained position.

Sour fig
Another groundcover is the sour fig (*Carpobrotus acinaciformis*), which has much broader, finger-like foliage. Its fruit, the edible component, has a similar texture to figs, and is made into jams in much the same way.

Bilberry cactus
The bilberry cactus (*Myrtillocactus* sp.) is another fruiting cactus grown for its edible

berries. From Guatemala and Mexico, the tree-like cactus flowers in summer, then bears either red (*M. cochal*) or blue (*M. geometrizans*) fruit about the same size as a blueberry. This cactus likes a position in full sun and will tolerate drought and short periods of frost, but good drainage is essential. Take cuttings in summer or sow seed in spring.

Yucca

One plant not generally known as edible is the yucca, which is usually grown for its striking architectural foliage. Dagger plant (*Yucca aloifolia*), as it is also known, bears edible flowers that can be eaten fresh in salads or dipped into batter and fried, as you would zucchini flowers.

Prickly pear

Part of the cactus family, prickly pear (*Opuntia* sp.) is native to various countries throughout the Americas. Its common name is due to its very prickly bristles, held in clumps all over the swollen, flattened stem segments. There are about 180 species, many of which produce edible fruit after flowering.

Two such species are the Indian fig (*O. ficus-indica*) and *O. vulgaris*. Their fruit are delicious if you're game to harvest them: the prickles are all over the fruit too and can cause pain and irritation if they get on your skin, so wear gloves when you're handling them. And try making this ingenious harvesting device: attach a tin can to the end of a long stake with a knife mounted on its tip, and use it to both cut the fruit and catch it. Before eating them, wear gloves as you remove all the spines.

Captain Phillip brought *O. vulgaris* to Australia with the First Fleet, hoping to set up a cochineal industry with the red dye-producing insects that feed on the pear. The dye was used to colour clothing, including the officers' uniforms.

By the nineteenth century, other species were imported into Australia. The species that became the most invasive pest was *O. stricta*, now a prohibited weed in Australia, but tiger pear (*O. aurantiaca*) is also a danger.

Right and below: The colour of pawpaw flesh varies, depending on the variety, from yellow to pink and orange tones.

Pawpaws or papayas and babacos

Pawpaws, or papayas (*Carica papaya*) as they are known throughout most of the world, are great home garden fruits for any frost-free position. They grow very quickly to about 4 m (13 ft), fruit from seed within about eighteen months, and produce vast quantities of fruit per plant, with two harvest periods (spring and autumn), for about five years.

They are not for everyone, however. The fruit, which varies in size from round (like a bowling ball) to large and oval (like a rugby ball) and even long and thin (more like a marrow), has a very distinctive flavour and smell that does not appeal to everyone. Then there is the babaco. This is a hybrid between the mountain pawpaw (*C. candamarcensis*) and *C. stipulata*. The sterile fruit obviously has no seed, just white flesh and bright yellow skin.

The varying shapes and colours of pawpaws relate not only to varietal differences but also to its sexual preferences: pawpaws can be female,

male or bisexual, and this varies from plant to plant, and from seed to seed.

The female plant produces the large round or oval fruit. Male plants, which only produce pollen, are needed to pollinate these trees. Bisexual plants, however, have both female and male (hermaphrodite) flowers, and the resulting fruit is elongated and extremely flavoursome, although it can become distorted, squat and ribbed if the temperature is too cold.

Pawpaw and babaco can be eaten when it's fresh and ripe (golden, red or pink inside) or cooked when it's green — in a similar way to how you would cook marrow — or when it's ripe, into chutneys, jams, pickles and even glacé fruit. Both the leaves and the fruit of pawpaw can also be used as a meat tenderiser: like Chinese gooseberries, pawpaw contains an enzyme called papain that breaks down protein. It's mostly derived from the white sap 'bled' from green fruit, and is used in a variety of products, including pawpaw ointment, for the treatment of scratches and nappy rash.

Cultivating pawpaws

Choose a cutting-grown bisexual plant that is certified disease-free. This will help to avoid diseases such as yellow crinkle, mosaic and ringspot virus.

Pawpaws prefer a deep, well drained friable loam with added organic matter and a soil pH of between 6 and 6.5. Any

did you know? Guajilote (*Parmentiera edulis*) is a tall tree, to 10 m (33 ft), which has thorns and beautiful bell-shaped greenish yellow flowers that are similar to the other members of its family, Bignoniaceae. The cucumber-like fruits that develop after flowering can be eaten fresh, pickled or cooked.

soil that can become waterlogged is a problem, as the plant can collapse under wet conditions. In fact, one of the best positions for pawpaws is facing north (in the southern hemisphere), beside a house under the partial cover of its eaves (but no closer than 1 m/3 ft), or near paving or a concrete slab.

This position will protect your tree from heavy rain, and the heat of the building — that is, its thermal mass — will keep it warmer throughout winter. The house will also provide a windbreak, protecting the pawpaw tree from both hot and cold winds.

About three months before you plant pawpaws, add some lime if your soil is very acid. Then dig a hole that's about 50 cm (20 in) deep, and add organic matter. Mix 30 g (1 oz) of citrus fertiliser with 60 g (2 oz) of superphosphate to make a complete fertiliser, then add this to the hole and mix it with the soil. Once you've planted the tree and backfilled, weed the area and add a thick layer of mulch. Don't dig over the soil, as pawpaws have many surface roots that are easily damaged. Water well in summer.

Feeding

Pawpaw trees are heavy feeders, so in late winter, late spring and late summer, feed with chicken manure or a complete plant food. Mulch well to help control weeds and the soil temperature.

Pruning

When the plant is too old to bear well, cut it back to the ground so it will reshoot vigorously and start to perform again.

Harvesting

Pawpaws are quick to fruit, generally producing only a year or so after planting.

Above: A pawpaw tree (*Carica papaya*), showing the wax-like flower as well as the developing and ripening fruit.

They have two seasons of cropping, depending on when they flower, so you could harvest in spring or summer. This is a simple matter of cutting the fruit off with a knife or just twisting it slightly once the fruit is yellow. To speed things along, the spring crop can be ripened indoors once it is just showing colour.

Problems

If you buy a certified virus-free plant, then your tree shouldn't experience any problems. The main problems associated with growing pawpaws — root and fruit rots (see pages 68–9) — result from bad drainage (for more information, see 'Cultivating pawpaws' opposite).

Stone fruit

As ornamental plants, stone fruit trees are very beautiful — spring blossom is followed by fresh foliage and wonderful, fragrant fruit with a captivating fragrance and flavour that makes you eagerly anticipate their short season. Many of these delicious fruits are eaten fresh, canned, dried, made into conserves, juiced and even turned into liqueurs.

Prunus species

Stone fruit are all members of the genus *Prunus*, part of the rose family, Rosaceae, to which most of the berries also belong. The species most widely cultivated for crops — plums, peaches, nectarines, cherries and apricots — were originally from Asia, but spread to the Middle East and the Mediterranean about 2000 years ago. Since then they have been extensively bred and selected.

Many other fruiting species — some from Africa and others from North America — also belong in this group, although often this fruit is either ornamental or used only for jams or animal fodder.

Apricots

Prunus armeniaca have been cultivated for more than 2000 years, spreading from China to Europe and the Middle East. Throughout summer, they produce round golden fruit covered in a soft, furry down among mid-green leaves.

Above and left: These small, slightly furry blushed fruit are delicious eaten fresh, but they can also be baked in cakes and puddings, or stewed and made into jams.

You can eat them fresh, and juice, dry or cook them in jams, desserts and cakes. This versatility, combined with the fact that most are self-fertile, make them ideal for the backyard. The trees can grow to 8 x 4.5 m (26 x 15 ft), although 4 m (13 ft) is typical for grafted specimens. Apricots are often trained as fans, or pruned to keep them smaller; root restriction is also an option for dwarfing them.

Apricots prefer well drained soil that is slightly alkaline, so liming may be necessary if your soil is very acid and, as they don't like heavy soils, it may be necessary to raise the ground slightly or improve its structure with gypsum and organic matter. The other tip is to buy an apricot that's been grafted onto plum rootstock, as plums are more adaptable to different soils.

To produce well, apricots need winter chill and summer heat. Frost-free areas with good air flow are ideal, although they will tolerate frosts provided they are not late — that is, during flowering time. The flowers are very pretty pink or white blossoms that appear on bare wood.

In frosty areas, apricots are sometimes grown in glasshouses. A proper cool period is needed to ensure full dormancy and leaf drop, so the glasshouse should be well ventilated to let in the cold winter air. However, once buds swell, the temperature should be maintained no lower than about 13°C (55.4°F), which will force flowers and

tip

If you live in an area that's prone to fruit fly, you can stew peaches with sugar while they're still green. When prepared this way, their tart flavour is delicious.

a crop to form. You can use a paintbrush to pollinate the blooms in this sort of closed environment because bees will be scarce. As summer comes on, open the vents again so that the temperature doesn't get too hot, and, once they are growing actively, spray with water.

Popular apricot varieties include 'Moorpark', whose rich flavour makes it one of the most popular home garden apricots; 'Caselin', the best variety for coastal areas; and 'Sungold' and 'Moongold', which are both self-sterile but will pollinate each other.

Plums

The domestic or European plum (*Prunus* x *domestica*) has been grown for centuries, although it's thought to be a very old hybrid, with sloe (*P. spinosa*) (see page 94) and *P. cerasifera* parentage. *Prunus cerasifera* is commonly known as the flowering plum, although it does produce small red fruit. The particular subspecies thought to be responsible is *diverticata*, which has small yellow flowers, not white.

On grafted rootstock, the European plum grows to about 4 x 4 m (13 x 13 ft). It flowers white, then bears soft-fleshed yellow-, purple- or red-skinned fruit. There are many well known cultivars,

Above: 'Santa Rosa', a plum cultivar.

New hybrids

Plant breeders continue to experiment with creating new types of fruit. The plumcot, for example, is an interspecific (or interspecies) hybrid between the apricot and the plum. It looks and feels like a plum, but the flavour encompasses the softness and aroma of the apricot; 'Plumcot' and 'Pluot' are popular cultivars. Another stone fruit hybrid is the nectacotum, a nectarine-apricot-plum hybrid with a very high sugar content. The bananange, a banana-orange cross, is currently in development.

such as 'Angelina Burdett', which tends to produce biennially and has purple skin; cross-pollinating 'President', which has dark purple skin with a wonderful bloom and large fruit; and also the Greengage group of plums (Reine Claude Group), used throughout Europe in wine-making.

The Greengages arrived in the United Kingdom from France in the early 1720s as an import to Sir William Gage of Bury St Edmunds, and thus became known as Green Gages Plums. The estate's gardener, Jervaise Coe, developed the 'Gold Drop' plum from this parentage and 'White Magnum Bonum', another heirloom variety. 'Damson' (*P.* x *domestica* subsp. *insititia*), a good bearing plum, is self-fertile, has a slightly tart flavour and dark reddish purple skin. Suitable for cooking and drying, it also makes an excellent jam.

The Japanese plum (*P. salicina*) is more suited to coastal and warmer areas. It grows to about 4 x 4 m (13 x 13 ft), has white blossom and yellow or red fruit that is yellow inside. 'Red Heart', one of the best eating cultivars, crops at an early age and is a smaller tree, making it more suitable for home gardens. 'Satsuma' is a very popular 'blood' plum — juicy and dark red from skin to stone. 'Santa Rosa' is a

Above left and centre: Unripe and ripe 'Angelina' plums, respectively.

Above: The blossom of *Prunus cerasifera*.

Below left: Sugar plums.

did you know? Oregon plum or oso berry (*Oemleria cerasiformis*), native to North America and another member of the Rosaceae family, is closely related to *Prunus*. A deciduous suckering shrub to 2.5 m (8 ft), it has dainty, almond-scented white flowers in spring, followed by plum-like fruit on the female plants in summer. If adequate water is maintained, it is suitable for growing in the shade of larger trees.

Prunes

Prunes are actually dried plums, but specific cultivars are used. The best of these is the cultivar 'd'Agen', which is very sweet and a good size for the home garden. It has oval-shaped purple fruit with a freestone, and should be allowed to fully mature on the tree so that the sugar content is maximised. It can be eaten fresh as well as dried. It does need cross-pollination, however, so you'll need to plant it with other plums such as 'Greengage', or other prunes, such as 'Imperial Epineuse', which is an 1870s French prune. The 'Italian Prune', which was actually bred in Germany, and is sometimes called 'Fellenberg', is one of the few self-fertile types with good flavour and sweetness. The fruit, which are purplish black, ripen in late to mid-season.

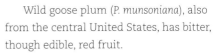

Wild goose plum (*P. munsoniana*), also from the central United States, has bitter, though edible, red fruit.

Plums can grow in a wide range of soils, although they love free-draining loamy soil. Most plums grow to about 5 x 4.5 m (16 x 15 ft), but again can be trained into a fan or espalier. Pick the fruit when it's slightly unripe, then ripen it indoors before eating it fresh or cooking it in stews, puddings and jams.

Nectarines and peaches

Peaches (*Prunus persica*) are categorised according to their stone and skin types into freestones and clingstones; white- or yellow-fleshed; and fuzzy- (peach) or smooth- (nectarine) skinned. They are very pretty small trees to about 6 x 2.5 m (20 x 8 ft), producing wonderful white or pink blossom in early spring, followed by tennis ball-sized fruit in late spring and into summer.

Both enjoy quite mild climates, and in cool areas will need to be grown under glass, or espaliered against sunny walls and protected with hessian over winter but, in a warm temperate zone, they are great backyard fruit trees, being self-fertile and a tree for all seasons. If you live in a tropical area, there are even cultivars that tolerate these conditions — for example, 'Florasun', a yellow-fleshed clingstone; 'Maravilha', with white flesh; 'Floraprince',

good choice for cross-pollination, but as it is self-fertile, you need only grow one tree — perfect if you have a small garden. The fruit is large and purplish crimson, with a pale blue bloom, while the flesh is yellow, with a red blush coming from just below the skin. It's slightly sweet, with some tartness near skin and stone. A good bearer, it's considered one of the best plums.

'Mariposa', with blood-red flesh, is another good choice for the home garden. It needs 'Santa Rosa' to pollinate it, however, so you'll need space for the two trees. Alternatively, you can buy a multigrafted specimen.

There are also other plums from North America. The hortulan plum (*P. hortulana*) is native to the central United States. It also has edible red or yellow fruit. Then there is the sand or beach plum (*P. maritima*), which is native to the eastern coast. It's only a small shrub, to about 1.5 m (5 ft), and in spring bears white blossom followed by purple, red or yellow fruit. Cultivars include 'Eastham' and 'Hancock'.

Above: A plum cultivar.

Opposite, clockwise from top left: Young peach fruit; the sweet blossom of a nectarine cultivar called 'Blue Boy'; nectarines developing on the tree; and peach blossom.

which has excellent large yellow semi-clingstone fruit; and 'Floragold', a compact tree that is great for coastal areas and home gardens.

For warm temperate zones, look for 'Double Jewel®', which has attractive bright pink double blossom and pleasant-tasting fruit. Its flesh is yellow and juicy with a freestone. Other popular yellow-fleshed peaches include 'Cresthaven' (freestone), 'Redhaven' (clingstone) and 'Sunred' (semi-freestone), the best variety for coastal areas.

Common nectarine cultivars include 'Goldmine', a white-fleshed freestone; 'Nectared No. 2', a yellow-fleshed semi-clingstone; and 'Nectared No. 4', a yellow-fleshed freestone. 'Peacherine' is a cross between peaches and nectarines. And there are also ornamental flowering peaches with tiny inedible fruit that are grown for their blossom alone, such as 'Klara Meyer', 'Versicolor' and 'Albo Plena'. Another species, known as David's peach (*Prunus davidiana*), is also from China. It grows to 9 m (29½ ft) and produces furry, edible yellow fruit.

Cherries

The main parent of fruiting cherries is the wild cherry (*Prunus avium*). Native to Asia Minor, it grows into a 15-m (49-ft) tree, the wood of which is very popular in cabinet making. The flowers are white and, as with all cherries, have a long flower stem known as the pedicel, which gives the fruit its characteristic look. The main drawbacks in cultivating these trees in the home garden are their height and the need to grow another variety for cross-pollination.

Below: 'Hale' peaches, an old variety.

Below centre: Peaches were once known as Persian apples, from the Latin *persicum malum*.

Opposite, left: Young fruit on a peach cultivar called 'Sherman Early'.

Opposite, right: A young peach tree in a spring garden. The fruit are very small at this stage.

Peach sorbet

400 ml (14 fl oz) peach-flavoured tea
300 g (10 1/2 oz/1 1/3 cups) caster (superfine) sugar
6 peaches, destoned and quartered
80 ml (2 1/2 fl oz/ 1/3 cup) rosewater

Pour half the tea into a small saucepan, then add the sugar and stir until it has dissolved. Bring to the boil and cook for 2 minutes, then remove from the heat and cool. Simmer peaches and remaining tea in a saucepan for 10 minutes. Remove fruit with a slotted spoon, reserving the liquid, and peel off the skins. Set the fruit aside.

Using a processor, purée the sugar syrup, peaches, poaching liquid and rosewater until smooth. To make sorbet, see the instructions for using an ice cream machine in the 'Strawberry sorbet' recipe, page 88. Makes 1 litre (35 fl oz/4 cups).

Dwarf peaches

You can buy dwarf peaches, known as 'Nectazee®' and 'Pixzee®', which are perfect if you want to grow a great-flavoured stone fruit in a small space. These are also ornamental, with a pretty show of bloom each year in spring before the new flush of foliage breaks. They're available on short standards, where the 'standard' is 1 m (3 ft) high before budding.

Sour cherries (*Prunus cerasus*), on the other hand, have similar-looking fruit but taste totally different. They are normally stewed or preserved; one example is 'Morello' cherries. Native to a region that covers south-eastern Europe to India, they grow to only about 5 m (16 ft) and are self-fertile, although they will also pollinate the wild cherries.

Hybrid cherries are now available. There's 'Starkrimson', which is heavy-bearing and self-pollinating, with firm, large, crimson-red, heart-shaped fruit with an excellent sweet flavour; and 'Sunburst', a partly self-fertile universal pollen donor (providing blossom coincides), which has

large heart-shaped cherries with a red to almost black skin. The dark red flesh is firm and juicy, with excellent flavour.

If size really is a problem, however, you could consider growing the ground cherry (*Prunus fruticosa*), a highly ornamental shrub from Europe and Siberia with a suckering habit. It's not usually grown for its fruit but rather for its delightful white frilly blossom, even though the dark red fruit is edible.

Alternatively, there is the sand cherry (*P. pumila*). Native to the north-eastern part of the United States, it has an unusual prostrate habit, growing to only 75 cm (30 in),

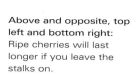

Above and opposite, top left and bottom right: Ripe cherries will last longer if you leave the stalks on.

Opposite, bottom left: A developing cherry cultivar, *Prunus avium* 'Starkrimson'.

Opposite, top right: In Japan, the blossoming of ornamental cherries is celebrated by festivals. While these flowering varieties are the best known, there are also fruiting species. The Japanese cherry tree (*Prunus cerasifera* 'Nigra') bears fragrant white blossom followed by edible red fruit.

Tropical cherries

From tropical America and the islands of the Carribean comes acerola, also known as Barbados cherry (*Malpighia glabra*). It is completely intolerant to cold, but looks quite similar to the fruit of the *Prunus* genus, despite being completely unrelated. The edible red drupes hang on the plant all summer and autumn, and are of a similar colour and size to those of *Prunus* species, although they have an apple-like texture; they are high in vitamin C.

A pretty shrub, it's adorned with rosy pink or red flowers that resemble fairy teacups from late spring into summer. The plant itself grows to about 3 m (10 ft), and responds well to pruning. If you keep it in check, acerola will form a nicely shaped, rounded bush with shiny mid-green leaves. If it has outgrown its spot, it won't mind being hacked back quite hard to a more manageable size. It will grow in any well drained soil, doesn't need feeding and will tolerate drought well.

Then there is the Surinam or Brazilian cherry (*Eugenia uniflora*), also known as pitanga. It's one of the many members of this genus that are very similar to lilly pillies and also bear edible fruit. This particular species grows to about 5 m (16 ft), has fragrant, fluffy white flowers and red, ribbed, cherry-like fruit.

The flower of the Barbados cherry.

but it still produces white blossom in spring followed by edible red fruit.

The other alternatives are the recently release dwarf hybrid varieties sold as 'White' or 'Black Cherree™ Trixzie Miniature Cherry'. These are miniature fruiting trees that bear delightful fruit. The flesh is medium to dark red — firm and juicy in the case of the black- and white-fleshed but, somewhat confusingly, blush-skinned in the case of the white.

Buying bare-rooted trees

Although you can pop a cherry pip or peach stone into the soil and watch it grow, raising plants by seed is not the best way to cultivate stone fruit, as anything could result. If you want a known cultivar, buy a plant that has been bud-grafted onto an understock or rootstock plant. It will not only be a more reliable bearer, producing quality fruit for your harvest, but also the rootstock will often be more vigorous than the ungrafted plant, as well as more likely to cope with disease and problem soils, such as those that don't drain well.

Choosing the right stone fruit will depend a lot on your climate, as the range of preferred weather extremes for these plants is quite broad, with some needing winter chilling and others growing happily in coastal areas. This variation applies to species within the genus as well as cultivars within each species. Thus you can choose from a range of stone fruit to suit your climate, from tropical peaches and nectarines, which can be grown in warm humid zones, to cherries, which cope happily in cold tableland areas.

Chances are you'll purchase your bare-rooted tree from a nursery in winter. A bare-rooted tree is usually about 2 to 3 years old when it is 'dug' in winter. This simply means it's been dug out of the ground, then root-pruned during the plant's winter dormancy so it can be transported and also to lessen the likelihood of transplant shock. The nursery may mail out pre-ordered trees, keeping the roots from drying out with either moistened hay or damp shredded newspaper.

These trees are budded to rootstocks that may be grown in the field from seeds. The rootstock is planted in spring then, in late winter the next year, a bud is grafted in. Once the bud has 'taken', the original tree is cut back, allowing the grafted scion to grow out. Thus the rootstock is about 6 to 12 months older than the scion (or top of the tree).

If you buy your stone fruit through a garden centre, it will be 'heeled in' for sale — that is, kept in a damp substance, such as sawdust or straw, to stop the roots from drying out before it's planted. This can only happen in winter for, as soon as the leaves begin to shoot, the plant should be in the ground or potted for sale.

The earlier you can plant your trees the better — even though the leaves may not be shooting, the roots will still grow and therefore establish themselves faster into your garden.

Cultivating stone fruit

Dig a hole that will accommodate all the roots. With bare-rooted specimens you may need to dig an irregularly shaped hole for a particularly good root without bending or cutting it. At this stage you can cut off any damaged or torn roots, or they might rot and let disease enter.

Once the hole is dug, hold the plant in place so that the graft is still well clear

Below: The flesh of nectarines can be either white or yellow.

Fruit salad tree

Multigrafted plants are now available in many garden centres or, bare-rooted in winter, by mail order through various nurseries. These have two, three and even more different cultivars budded onto the one parent plant, resulting in a veritable fruit salad tree.

These multigrafted fruit trees have a number of benefits for the home gardener, such as cross-pollination for those varieties that need it, and extended harvest from the one tree.

However, there is one problem: a weaker variety can be taken over by a vigorous one, so keep this in check with regular pruning. If you get the balance right, you'll have subsequent crops from each variety, spreading your stone fruit harvest over the season.

of the proposed ground level, and so that the soil level in the growing nursery is as close to the new soil level as possible. You can usually determine that by looking for a stain on the trunk from the soil in which it used to grow. Planting too deeply can result in rootstock reshooting constantly, while planting too high can expose the roots to heat, making them dry out.

Once it's at the correct height, you can backfill. Fill about half the hole first, then tamp down lightly with your foot to remove any air pockets. Add the remainder of the soil and gently tamp down again.

Water it in well and mulch, creating a moat as you do so to help trap and divert the water towards your young tree's root zone. Don't feed it now, as fertilisers can burn the developing new roots.

Pruning a plumcot

The basic principles of pruning are the same for all stone fruit.

1 This young plumcot needs a light prune.

2 Prune any inward growing branches.

3 Remove any branches that are rubbing together.

4 You should end up with an open, vase-like shape.

Left: The same tree in the following spring.

Feeding

Mulch annually with well rotted manure. Citrus fertiliser (with an N:P:K ratio of 10:4:6), or complete plant food around the drip line in late winter to early spring, will also encourage root development, growth and crop production. Apply any added fertiliser to moist earth, then water in well.

Pruning

The initial training of stone fruit is similar for all types. Basically, when you plant the young sapling in winter (in the case of cherries, plant just before leaf development in spring), you need to cut the whole plant back to a height of about 40 cm (16 in) to encourage it to branch. If you're buying a slightly more mature specimen, then this may have already been done. You'll know if this is the case because the branching of the basic framework into an open vase shape will be under way.

But that doesn't mean that you can just plant it and forget it. You'll still need to cut back the whole plant each winter by about a third all over to encourage strong new shoots to develop in the following

spring and summer. As this occurs, trim back shoots that may be growing more vigorously than others so that the overall growth is even, and pinch out completely any buds that will result in inward growth, spoiling the open framework you're trying to encourage. Be on the lookout for any growth that appears on the main trunk or below the graft too: these shoots will all need to be removed.

Apricots

Apricots produce fruit on the previous season's side shoots, or laterals. Thus the purpose of pruning is not to remove these completely, but to thin them out. This has two purposes: it promotes new growth that will bear the following season, and also prevents crowding, thereby producing a bigger, better disease-free crop this season. In winter, keep laterals about 20 cm (8 in) apart, and nip back water shoots to about 30 cm (1 ft) in length.

Cherries

Besides the initial training in early spring described above, cherries are not pruned

Below: An espaliered plum (*Prunus domestica*).

Below right: Peach leaf curl results in blistered and curling leaves.

Peach leaf curl

You must spray peach trees for peach leaf curl. At bud swell, either copper oxychloride or Bordeaux spray is a suitable fungicide, although the former washes off and needs to be applied more regularly. Alternatively, in winter, apply lime sulfur which, like Bordeaux spray, will burn off fungal spores as well as scale insects and mites on deciduous trees.

Lime sulfur spray

1 Fill a 2-L (3^1/2-pt) plastic spray bottle with water.

2 Add 10–50 ml/1 litre (^{1}/3–1^3/4 fl oz/1^3/4 pt) of lime sulfur to the water, and shake well.

3 Apply at bud swell, then repeat 10 days later.

Copper oxychloride

4 Fill a 2-L (3^1/2-pt) spray bottle with water.

5 Add 2 to 5 teaspoons of copper oxychloride, and shake well.

6 Spray the tree on a still day in winter, then repeat if rain falls within the next 24 hours.

---

any further, other than to remove diseased or damaged and rubbing branches and suckers because, after about three years, their framework is usually good enough to last their lifetime.

Nectarines and peaches

These trees fruit on the growth from last season as well as on young fruit spurs but, unlike apples and plums, these are only good for one season.

Each year in winter, to avoid crowding, thin out the growth so that each main limb has new growth at about 20-cm (8-in) spacings, and completely remove any inward-facing growth so the tree continues to grow in a single spreading layer. This will encourage healthier fruit and be easier to manage.

Plums

Plums produce fruit from wood that's older than two years. First remove any inward-growing branches or diseased and rubbing growth. Then thin out the laterals to help prevent overcrowding, keeping plenty of fruit-bearing spurs on the older wood. Trim the length of arms periodically.

Problems

See the 'The kitchen garden' section.
- Bacterial canker: page 70.
- Birds: page 50.
- Codling moth: pages 55 and 157.
- Fruit fly: page 53.
- Fruit tree borer: page 50.
- Pear and cherry slug: page 53.
- Scale: page 58.
- Oriental fruit moth: page 55.

tip

All stone fruit have a comparatively short season and spoil quickly if not harvested. Don't let your fruit rot on the ground, as the unhygienic conditions will attract pests and diseases.

Olives

One of the world's oldest cultivated fruits, the olive (*Olea europaea*) is also grown for oil production. The fruit must be pickled in brine before it can be eaten, or pressed to remove the oil. Green olives are not ripe when they're pickled, whereas black olives are, although different varieties are better for each purpose. For example, 'Manzanillo' and 'Verdale' can be picked when they are either green or black, but 'Sevillano' can only be harvested when it is green, and 'Kalamata' is best black.

Olive trees are beautiful ornamental trees. Their silver foliage waves in the wind, revealing an even paler underside to each leaf. The small cream flowers are fairly insignificant from a distance, but up close, each is packed with bright golden pollen.

Olives like a Mediterranean climate, with a cold winter and a long, hot summer. Their narrow grey leaves, which contain so much oil, make them very drought-tolerant once they're established.

Perhaps it's their longevity that makes olive trees so unusual: one tree may bear fruit for centuries. In fact, throughout southern Europe and around the Mediterranean, there are olive groves of sensational gnarled trees, hundreds of years old, still being cropped annually. Superb old specimens like these are also highly regarded as ornamental features: some have been used as centrepieces in landscapes at the Chelsea Flower Show.

Cultivating olives

Any time from autumn to spring, find an open, sunny position, dig a hole and plant your grafted or cutting-grown specimen. Water well, and don't allow it to dry out over the first summer. Once established, your olive will be drought-tolerant.

Feeding

Feed olive trees with citrus food (see page 178) in winter.

Pruning

Prune back your tree to encourage an open shape with lots of new growth, as the fruit are borne on these.

Harvesting

Once olives are about five years old they begin to fruit, and will keep this up for hundreds of years, although curiously they may bear a heavier crop every second year. Pick the fruit carefully to avoid bruising, as it can affect the pickling quality, or follow the traditional method: first, spread a sheet or tarpaulin on the ground around the tree, then shake the tree vigorously. The fruit will fall onto the sheet.

Problems

- Black scale: page 58.
- Olive lace bug can defoliate your tree: page 52.

Below: Olives are a traditional ingredient in Greek salad, which includes tomato, cucumber, red onion and feta cheese.

Opposite: In ancient Greece, the victors of the Olympic Games were crowned with garlands of olive leaves.

did you know? The olive branch is a symbol of peace. According to Genesis, the first book of the Bible, Noah built an ark to shelter his family and the animals of the world from the Great Flood. After the flood receded, Noah sent birds to find dry land. Eventually a dove brought back an olive branch, symbolising new life and that God had forgiven man.

Pome fruit

Pomes belong to a huge subgroup, Pomoideae, in the Rosaceae family, which includes apples, pears, loquats, quince, medlars and crabapples. Suitable for growing in a wide range of temperate climates, they have found their way into our lunchboxes, desserts, cakes, sauces, jams and chutneys.

Stars of the fruit world

Apples and pears are among the most popular fresh fruit in the world, while other ornamental members of the Pomoideae family — such as crabapples, cotoneaster, hawthorn (see page 94) and even rowans — are common in home gardens. Generally native to Asia and Europe, most members flower in spring, then develop into fruit over summer before ripening as the weather cools.

The seeds, held in the centre of the fruit, are surrounded by a five-sided casing, then the edible flesh. This is clearly seen when you cut an apple in half across the fruit to reveal this 'star inside', a characteristic that can be used to encourage children to eat fruit.

Apples

For more than 3000 years, modern apples (*Malus domestica*) have been selectively bred from wild *Malus pumila*, which often have a very bitter taste. Endemic to a vast area of

Above: 'New Gold' (left) and 'Earligold' (right) apple cultivars.

Left: Cut apples in half to show children the star-shaped seed casing.

Asia, from Western China and Central Asia to Europe, it's no wonder the species has such a wide range of characteristics.

Apples are very popular with home gardeners: they keep well and, although they are harvested in autumn, can be easily stored over winter. Children love to eat them fresh, but you can also dry, stew, poach, roast or juice them. There are many different types of rootstock, some of which have dwarfing effects, and many ways of pruning them, so you can grow apples in almost any garden, provided the climate is right.

Apples do have a down side, however: they are susceptible to various pests and diseases (see page 157), and also need another variety that flowers at the same time in order to be successfully pollinated, although multigrafted trees enjoy the same effect on the one tree. You'll also need bees around to 'work' the trees. Cold winters, warm sunny weather during blossom season and plenty of bees should result in good fruit-set for home gardeners.

Some of the best varieties for the backyard include 'Spartan' and 'Bonza', both of which have red skins, green-skinned 'Granny Smith' and 'Golden Delicious', which can be susceptible to fruit fly. All these varieties will cross-pollinate each other.

There are, of course, many different heirloom or old-fashioned apples as well as new varieties. The latter include 'Pink Lady' (also known as 'Cripps Pink'), 'Sundowner' or 'Cripps Red' and 'Fuji', all of which have become very popular of late. Heirloom types include 'Cox's Orange Pippin', one of the best-tasting old-fashioned cultivars still being grown.

To extend the season of apples in your backyard, planting early-season ('Pink Lady', 'Sundowner', 'Braeburn'), mid-season ('Jonathan', 'Granny Smith', 'Golden Delicious', 'Delicious', 'Lady Williams') and late-season ('Bonza', 'Fuji', 'Gala') types will ensure a continuous supply.

If you don't want to fill your backyard with apple trees, you can use crabapples

tip

Plant apples no more than 10 m (33 ft) apart to make sure they can cross-pollinate easily.

for cross-pollination instead. Studies have shown that bees will pollinate apples from crabapples reasonably successfully, especially if the blossoms of both types are of similar colours. Alternatively, growing multigrafted plants that have two or more cultivars grafted onto the same rootstock, each able to pollinate the other, can also save space.

Apples need a cold winter in order to drop their foliage properly, then blossom and leaf again promptly in spring. If the summers in your area are too hot or the winters too warm, your trees will have cropping problems. By the same token, blossom and frosts don't mix either, so you'll need to provide some form of shelter during this crucial period by either covering them with shadecloth or hessian, or creating fog with a misting system. In the old days, orchardists used to protect blossom with smoking pots.

Cultivating apples

Although apple trees are quite adaptable to different soils, they do prefer a slightly acid soil, with a pH of about 6, as well as good drainage and regular rainfall, especially in late summer and autumn when the crop is setting. They will also need protection from winds, particularly during the flowering stage. It usually takes about four years for apple trees to bear well.

To get your tree off to the best start, dig a hole that is about half as big again as the root ball. Prune away any damaged or twisted roots, and make sure they are oriented evenly in all directions. Refill the hole with the soil and added compost, if you have some. Prune back the upper part of your tree by about a third, again trying to orient its branches evenly so an open vase shape is the result. Finally, mulch well and water.

Feeding

Start feeding your apples at the end of their first winter in the ground. They need plenty of nitrogen, which can be supplied as manure, with compost as a mulch.

Pruning

Apples are mostly produced on wood that is at least two years old. Therefore, cutting back your apple all over will promote lots of new growth, but sacrifice fruit production. There are two common methods of pruning apples as garden trees. The first is the open vase shape, which is the same approach to pruning *Prunus* (see page 146), while the second method has gained popularity as it looks more 'natural' and results in less work later.

This other method involves making more of a candelabra or tiered shape. Start off with a young sapling and prune it to about 80 cm (31 in) above the ground. It should then branch and form some laterals, which can be encouraged outwards by clipping out unwanted ones and leaving about 4 to 5 evenly spaced

Opposite, clockwise from top left: Apple blossom; 'Granny Smith' and 'Golden Delicious'; 'Pinkabelle' blossom; and 'Topaz' (background) and 'Cox's Orange Pippin'.

Below: 'Granny Smith', a slightly tart variety that's suitable for cooking.

1 'Corella' pear 2 '20th Century' China pear 3 'Rouge d'Anjou' pear
4 'Beurre Bosc' pear 5 'Nijiseiki' China pear 6 'Shinsei' China pear
7 Unripe 'Purpurea' crabapples 8 'Kosui' China pear 9 'Splendour' apple
10 'Frosts Seedling' 11 'Smyrna' quince 12 'Coal' pear

pome
fruit

13 'Aromatic' apple   **14** 'Geeveston Fanny' apple   **15** 'Canadian Pippin' apple   **16** 'Bulmers Norman' apple
17 'Starks Blushing Gold' apple   **18** 'Winter Nervis' pear   **19** 'Ya Li' China pear   **20** 'Red Williams' pear
21 'Tsu Li' China pear   **22** 'Winter Banana' apple   **23** 'Pink Lady' apple   **24** 'McIntosh' apple   **25** 'Cox's
Orange Pippin' apple   **26** 'Canadian Spartan' apple   **27** 'Earligold' apple   **28** 'Twenty Ounce' apple

Maypole apples for small spaces

A new range of apples, sold under the registered name of Ballerina®, have a straight, pole-like growth habit and bear fruit on tiny side branches, so they're ideal for small gardens and tight places, such as against walls, along driveways or in tubs.

Cultivars include 'Bolero', a crisp and juicy red- over green-skinned apple; 'Flamenco', a late-season dessert apple; 'Polka', which has medium-sized fruit with green skin with some red touches; 'Charlotte', a red- over green-skinned mid-season apple; and 'Waltz', a solid red apple. All need cross-pollination, so make sure you also plant a pollinator so your trees actually bear crops, not just the pretty white, flushed pink blossom.

branches. The following winter, one of these will clearly be a stronger leader, which can then be nipped about 50 cm (20 in) above the previous tier so it will, in turn, start to develop more side branches, or laterals — your next tier.

Again, remove all but 4 to 5 of these, choosing the healthiest, most evenly spaced branches and nipping off the others cleanly at the stem. The following winter, shorten the leader again to about 50 cm (20 in) above the last tier, which by now is just short of a 2-m (6½-ft) tree. Keep the tiers shaped in this cake-stand manner by removing any branches crowding the centre as they sprout and by shortening any main branches. The lowest tiers will be the first to fruit, as their wood is oldest and 'ripe'.

Harvesting

Apple trees usually start producing in about 3 to 4 years, and can keep bearing good crops for some decades without experiencing any problems. Pick the fruit when the colour is showing well and they are mature — firm and juicy but not over-ripe. Apples will continue to sweeten after picking, so tart apples can improve in the fridge but, if you pick them too early, they'll quickly shrivel and be quite flavourless and astringent; on the other hand, if you pick them too late, they'll be starchy, soft and mealy.

To harvest apples, cup your hand under each fruit as you gently lift and twist it to remove it from the tree. Discard any bruised fruit before storing your harvest, as the old saying, 'A rotten apple spoils the cart', is very apt. Then wipe each apple with a cloth. Some apples, such as 'Fuji' and 'Goldrush', store better than others, and can be stored for 8 to 10 months without losing their flavour.

Apples keep best at temperatures lower than the average fridge, and like to be hydrated, so popping a damp cloth in the plastic bag with them will help keep them fresh. If you can't keep them in the fridge, wrap them in newspaper and store them in a well ventilated crate, shelf or seed tray.

Problems

Apples are susceptible to several pests and diseases.

Codling moth larvae

Codling moth larvae or grubs are a severe problem for apples, pears and quinces. The adult lays her eggs on the leaves of your apple tree, but it's the baby grubs that actually damage the fruit, usually tunnelling through the calyx (the stem end) undetected. Sometimes they'll leave behind them some frass, their sawdust-like

---

Traditional apple sauce

- 4 green apples, peeled, cored and chopped
- 2 teaspoons caster (superfine) sugar
- 2 cloves
- 1 cinnamon stick
- 125 ml (4 fl oz/1/2 cup) water
- 1–2 teaspoons lemon juice

Put the apple, sugar, cloves, cinnamon stick and water in a small saucepan. Cover and simmer over low heat for 10 minutes, or until the apple is soft. Remove from the heat and discard the cloves and cinnamon stick.

Mash the apple, or press through a sieve for a smooth-textured sauce. Stir in the lemon juice, to taste. Serve warm or cold with pork dishes such as roast pork. Will keep for 4 days if stored, covered, in the fridge. Serves 6 to 8.

droppings, but it's often not until you cut open the damaged fruit that you spot the telltale sign — brown trails in the flesh. Complete control is really only available from a penetrant spray that gets inside the fruit; withholding periods apply after use. Alternatively, cut your apples open before biting into them to make sure there are no unpleasant suprises.

Apple dimpling bugs

If your apples look as if they have a bad case of cellulite, chances are you have apple dimpling bugs lurking around. This tiny bug is only a couple of millimetres long and darts about quickly when approached. Active when your plant is blossoming and just beginning to form fruit, it usually causes problems with 'Granny Smith' and 'Delicious' apples, but the flesh below the bumps is fine to eat.

If your crop has become infested, tau-fluvalinate is probably the best spray available. It's a low-toxic, water-based chemical that is a low-hazard risk to bees, which is important as they will be foraging when apples are being attacked by this pest. It's a broad-spectrum synthetic pyrethroid that affects both the central and peripheral nervous systems of insects.

Some Australian pests

In Australia there are a couple of native pests that have adapted themselves to attacking apples.

Painted apple moth looks like a hairy toothbrush, and causes a very nasty sting if it lands on bare skin. The female is wingless, so these pests will stay where they are from year to year unless they migrate as larvae to another destination. If left undisturbed, they may build up their numbers and become an infestation, but they can be easily controlled by banding

around tree trunks (see page 62), being squashed at the larval stage or hand-picked off at the cocoon stage. This pest doesn't affect the fruit but damages the foliage, almost skeletonising the leaves.

Light brown apple moth is the other Australian native insect that now has a taste for many fruits, including grapes, citrus and all the pome fruit, but especially 'Jonathan' apples. They chew the leaves, often rolling them around themselves for protection, as well as the surface of fruit, especially around the stem. *Bacillus thuringiensis*, a naturally occurring bacteria that you can spray onto leaf surfaces, is registered for use with this moth. It's an organic spray that won't affect birds or bees. Sometimes pear and cherry slug can also attack apples (see page 53).

Apple scab

The disease most likely to ruin your fruit is apple scab, which starts on the foliage as black spots, similar in appearance to black spot on roses. As with roses, spraying with copper oxychloride can help destroy the spores of this fungus. Do this at half strength (5 g per litre of water/$1/5$ oz per $1/4$ gal) at the green tip stage when the shoots are just out.

If the weather is particularly favourable for black spot, with regular showers, it may spread to the fruit itself, especially on susceptible cultivars such as 'Granny Smith' and 'Delicious'. If this is the case, you may need to control it with a fungicide until conditions improve or the fruit is bigger and less susceptible.

Bitter rot

Raking up and getting rid of old leaves so reinfection doesn't occur is good hygiene for both apple scab and bitter rot, another fungus that causes much larger, brown

Opposite: When picking apples, choose firm-skinned fruit that feel heavy for their size. Mature fruit should detach easily.

Crabapples

Many of the apples we enjoy today are the result of breeding from crabapples (*Malus* sp.). While most of these hard little fruits are inedible raw, they can be made into wonderful jellies as well as provide beautiful flower and ornamental fruit colour in the garden. Popular cultivars include 'John Downie', which has large orange crabs blushed red; 'Golden Hornet', with lime-yellow fruit and a lovely pendulous habit; 'Gorgeous', with crimson-coloured fruit; and 'Wickson', which has edible red fruit.

rotten spots that have slight concentric circles in them. It particularly affects 'Granny Smith' and 'Gravenstein'.

Collecting and destroying leaves, old fruit (especially any mummified ones still on the tree), cutting the grass around trees and pruning to increase air flow are all steps that will help reduce this problem.

Smaller 3- to 6-mm (1/8- to 1/4-in) spots could be the result of a calcium deficiency, but are more likely to be a problem in very hot conditions or if watering has been irregular. It results in a disease called bitter pit, but fertiliser and adequate watering, especially in spring, can stop this happening.

Fireblight

This is a devastating disease that causes leaves to go bright reddish brown and then drop. It is not yet found in Australia, thanks to strict quarantine laws, but it's a serious bacterial problem in other countries.

Other problems

There are several other problems you should watch out for.

- Aphids, especially woolly aphids: pages 58–9.
- Fruit fly: page 53.
- San Jose scale: page 58.
- Mites: page 56.
- Plague thrips: page 61.
- Powdery mildew: page 69.

Pears

Pears, or *Pyrus* sp. as they are known botanically, grow to about 12 m (39 ft), so they are often considered too large for the home garden. They are beautiful plants, however, and their white blossom is a delight in spring.

There are two main species grown for fruit — the European pear (*Pyrus communis*) and the Asian or China pear (*Pyrus pyrifolia*). The European pear needs a similar cool climate to apples, and suffers if the winter chill is not long enough or if summers are too hot. Its fruit has the classic pear shape. The Asian pear, on the other hand, is much better suited to heat and coastal conditions throughout summer and to milder winters, and has rounded, apple-shaped fruit.

Some varieties of European pear include 'Beurre Bosc', which has dark, coffee-coloured skin, and yellow-skinned 'Williams' (also known as 'Bartlett', 'Williams Bon Chretien' or 'WBC'), which will cross-pollinate each other; the fruit is frequently canned or bottled. 'Packham's Triumph', an Australian variety, and 'Josephine', which has pale green skin, will also pollinate each other. 'Coal' is another yellow-skinned variety that needs to be eaten when soft in order to taste sweet, while 'Corella', named after the Corella parrot, has green skin with red-blushed cheeks and a lovely soft, curving neck.

Above: 'Corella' pears.

Below left: Pears are worth growing for their blossom alone.

Below centre: 'Nashi' pear, another China pear.

Below: 'Nashi Chojuro', one of the China pears (*Pyrus pyrifolia*).

Of the China pears, the varieties 'Nashi' and '20th Century', also known as Korean pears, are the most common. Eat these when they are crisp and juicy; they taste almost like a cross between apple and pear. Due to extensive breeding, some bear fruit the size of grapefruit and are given as gifts.

Quinces and Callery pears (*Pyrus calleryana*) are usually used as under-stock (see 'Cultivating pears' at right) for adaptability purposes or, in the case of quince, for dwarfing. Quince flowers will also pollinate many pears.

The other species of pear sometimes grown for cider include *Pyrus nivalis*, or snow pear, which has soft, greenish grey leaves and white flowers in spring. A pretty ornamental tree for home gardens that is also extremely hardy, tolerating very high or very low temperatures, it is smaller growing, to about 8 m (26 ft). The fruit has a sour taste.

Cultivating pears

Pears are usually bought in winter as bare-rooted trees, so follow the same procedure as outlined in 'Stone fruit' (see page 144). As they grow into such large trees, a deep soil is ideal. It should also be slightly acid, well drained and fertile although, once established, pears will cope with some water inundation. Do not add fertiliser at planting time.

The spacing will vary depending on the understock onto which your trees have been grafted, so specific information from the grower is probably your best guide. As a general rule, quince understocks result in a smaller tree, so 3-m (10-ft) spaces are suitable, whereas Asiatic pear understocks require 6-m (20-ft) spacings.

Feeding

Pears like lots of nitrogen, so an annual mulch of manure and/or compost will

Ornamental pears

Ornamental pears or Callery pears (*Pyrus calleryana*) have become very popular as street trees and ornamental garden plants due to their heavy set of white blossom and wonderful autumn-coloured foliage. Cultivars such as 'Bradford', which has no thorns, and 'Chanticleer', which is narrow in form, are the best known ones for gardens.

These very hardy trees are becoming the most popular street tree in North America, where birds spread their seeds. The small, 2.5-cm (1-in) fruit is even edible after frosts have sweetened it. Although not as tasty as a regular fruiting pear, you can still use it to make jams and sauces.

The silver pear (*Pyrus salicifolia*) is a graceful ornamental with a weeping habit.

Unusual pome fruit

Less commonly grown in the home garden are loquats and medlars.

Loquats

These evergreen trees (*Eriobotrya japonica*) grow to about 6 m (20 ft) and have very attractive foliage — dark green on one side and soft furry beige on the underside — which makes them popular for floral arrangements. 'Herd's Mammoth', one of the better known types, produces large fruit in spring. The fact that loquats ripen during winter is a double-edged sword…it's lovely to have fruit during this lean time in the garden, but they can also harbour fruit fly, so either only plant them in fruit fly-free areas, or be diligent about controlling this pest.

Cultivation

Native to Asia, loquats (pictured at right) are very tolerant of a wide range of climates, from tropical to cool, even cold, winters, although warm summers and milder winters are best for fruit production, as extremes and wind can cause some damage to the crop. Feed and water them regularly with a high-nitrogen fertiliser or, once established, mulch with chicken manure. Pruning is not necessary in the home garden, unless you wish to shape the tree or reduce overcrowded branches to increase fruit production. This is done after harvesting. Loquats can start producing fruit within only three years.

Medlars

Medlars (*Mespilus germanica*) were thought to have been cultivated by the Assyrians and Babylonians, then brought to Europe by the Romans. The trees certainly live a long time, ageing and fruiting for at least 300 years. The fruit itself is small and round, the colour of a 'Buerre Bosc' pear but the size of a loquat or plum, and has the very strange affliction of needing a frost or two to become edible. This is known as 'bletted', which translates to being slightly rotted. It can be eaten fresh, but is usually made into jelly, wine or sauces.

Cultivation

Grown principally for their beautiful autumn colour and great summer shade, medlars grow to about 6 m (20 ft), are not fussy about either climate or soil, flower in spring and require little or no pruning, as they fruit on old wood.

go a long way towards supplying this. Ensure all their nutrient needs are met by occasionally adding complete plant food, trace elements or blood and bone. This feeding regimen begins at the end of the winter after your tree has established (not the winter it was planted).

Pruning

Prune pears as you would apples (see 'Pruning', page 153).

Harvesting

Pears take about 4 to 5 years to start fruiting but, once they do, it's not unusual for a tree to continue to bear good crops for at least 50 years, and even to bear reasonably well for more than a century, hence the adage, 'Plant pears for your heirs.' 'Williams' is one of the earliest cultivars to ripen, with its season beginning in midsummer.

Unlike most fruit, pears shouldn't be left to ripen on the tree as this can make them develop a gritty texture within only a few days. Instead, pick them when they are fully sized and the colour is just changing — if you cut them open, they will be hard, with some juice, and taste slightly sweet.

Store pears at room temperature so they'll continue to sweeten, or keep them in the crisper of your fridge for up to three months. Once they have been picked, pears take about a week to ripen, but you can speed up this process by keeping them in a sealed plastic bag, where the trapped ethylene gas they produce will promote the ripening process.

Problems

Pears can fall victim to many of the same pests as apples, including fruit fly (see page 53), codling moth (pages 55 and 157) and light brown apple moth (page 158). They also attract pear and cherry slug, a slimy leach-like insect that damages the upper surface of foliage. If you see them, remove them by hand, or dust the leaves with flour or ash to help control them. They are also susceptible to San Jose scale (see page 58).

The most common disease is pear scab, which looks similar to apple scab even though it's a different fungus and therefore cannot cross-contaminate. Control it by using a registered fungicide during the few weeks from bud burst until late spring. Good hygiene can also ward off this disease, so keep leaves and clippings away and the grass cut.

Spraying lime sulfur in winter will also help control leaf blister mite, which attacks pear foliage.

Below: The contained shape of 'Bradford' pears, a variety of *Pyrus calleryana*, makes them suitable street trees.

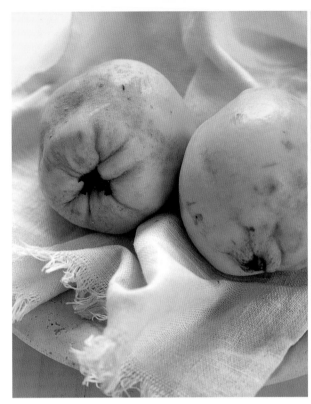

Above: Ripe quince will keep for up to three weeks in the fridge, or up to two weeks at a cool room temperature.

Above right: A young quince developing from its flower.

Below right: You can make jam out of the fruit of an ornamental quince.

Quinces

Native to Iran, Turkey and Armenia, the quince (*Cydonia oblonga*) has been grown for thousands of years, and can now be found throughout the Mediterranean and Europe. Once cooked, the fruit changes from a dreary-looking pear colour to a beautiful pinkish plum shade. In fact, the yellow fruit is virtually inedible raw, and it is only once it has been stewed or made into jam or paste that you can eat it.

Quinces are deciduous trees that grow to about 4 m (13 ft), and fruit after about five years. Like loquats (see page 164), the foliage is woolly or furry and paler on the underside, but the leaves are much smaller and rounded. They flower white or pink in spring, then mature in late summer or autumn. If grown in a cool enough area, the leaves also colour well in autumn, so it's a very ornamental tree for all seasons.

There is also a species of quince that is native to China, known as Chinese quince

(*C. sinensis*). It grows a little taller and has reddish pink flowers that are slightly smaller than the ordinary quince, as are the very aromatic fruit.

Cultivating quinces

Quinces are very adaptable, coping with anything from the subtropics to the cold highlands, but in colder areas they are

prone to frost damage (early spring frosts harm blossom, and early autumn frosts damage the fruit). In the high-humidity areas they are more prone to leaf spots and diseases. If your tree is deciduous, plant it in winter (see the instructions for planting stone fruit on page 144).

Quince trees are partly self-fertile, but growing different varieties — such as 'De Vranja', 'Portugal', 'Pineapple' and 'Champion' — in close proximity to each other does improve the pollination rate. They are so hardy and adaptable that they're sometimes used as rootstocks or to cross-pollinate pears.

Feeding

It's important to feed quinces annually with manure or blood and bone applications, and also to build up the soil with organic matter, as quinces like lots of nitrogen and fertile, deep, rich soils.

Pruning

Follow the same pruning method as for apples but, once the tree is in shape, remember to keep the new season's growth, as quinces produce on same-season growth. You can also espalier them (see page 156).

Harvesting

Quinces usually take about five years to produce decent crops. These mature in late summer and early autumn, depending on the variety, and are mature when golden. Use secateurs to remove them from the tree and handle them carefully as, like pears, they bruise easily.

Problems

The quince is prone to two main problems.
- Codling moth: pages 55 and 157.
- Fruit fly: page 53.

Ornamental quince

Also known as flowering quince (*Chaenomeles* sp.), this plant is recognised all over the world thanks to its iconic red flowers, which have been depicted in Japanese woodblock prints for centuries. There are actually three species — two native to China (*C. cathayensis* and *C. speciosa*), the other (*C. japonica*) to Japan, but they have been bred and hybridised to improve the colour range and flower size. The fruit is only a secondary concern, but it does make very aromatic jam and jelly.

Flowering quince grows naturally into a large shrub about 2 m (6½ ft) tall. It suckers into a 3-m (10-ft) round, impenetrable thicket with short, sharp spurs. You can tame it, however, by regularly removing canes that are at least three years old at the base, or by espaliering it against a wall. This technique is particularly useful in colder climates, where the warmth offered by the wall overnight can help it to withstand extreme weather conditions (see also page 168). It also makes a great hedge for keeping out intruders.

The flowers are a wonderful winter surprise, opening well before any other blossom. You can force it into opening early for cut flower arrangements — the blossom is popular in Ikebana, the Japanese art of flower arranging — by picking it in bud and placing it in a vase of warm water. The flowers are normally single and bright red, but there are also cultivars with prominent yellow stamens, pure white flowers, pink flowers and a delightful multiflowered one called 'Apple Blossom'.

Chaenomeles speciosa 'Apple Blossom' (left) and the typical red flowers of *C. japonica* (right).

Citrus

Nowadays it seems perfectly normal to drink a glass of orange juice, or peel an orange and eat it, but not so long ago, eating citrus fruit in the Western world was a treat so special it was reserved for special occasions such as Christmas and birthday celebrations.

For the home garden

Most citrus are warm-climate plants, tolerating only the lightest frosts. For this reason, the grand homes and palaces of the Renaissance period featured special garden annexes called *orangeries*, or orange houses, where enormous potted specimens were overwintered. One of the most famous of these *orangeries* was at Versailles, near Paris, where these sensitive plants were housed in Versailles planters — simple timber boxes with a turned finial on each corner.

Another tactic was to grow them against the sunniest wall (in the northern hemisphere this faced south), where the radiated heat enabled gardeners to grow citrus in cooler climates.

From Roman times and throughout the Middle Ages, citrus fruits spread around the world, from China and South-East Asia into Europe. But you don't need a palace to grow them; in warm temperate areas they are one of the most common backyard fruit trees. The versatility of

Above: Mandarins are easy to eat — the peel comes away without squirting juice.

Left: Blood oranges, varieties of *Citrus sinensis*, are stunning in drinks and salads.

lemons in particular is highly valued for its contribution to home cooking.

Their popularity is deserved. Growing to 2 to 5 m (6½ to 16 ft), depending on the type, citrus are very ornamental plants, with attractive evergreen foliage, scented white blossoms in abundance in spring, and then the highly decorative fruit, a delicious source of vitamin C, which hang on the tree like baubles of blazing colour all winter.

Varieties

There are whole books dedicated to citrus and their many varieties found across the world, but home growers use different selection criteria to orchardists. For example, they want to be able to pick fruit that's full of flavour over a long period, but it's not economically viable for commercial growers to cover extended harvests for fruit with a short shelf life.

In addition, home growers who live in a fruit fly-prone area will need to pick varieties that ripen in winter, not in summer and autumn.

Oranges

'Washington Navel' and 'Valencia' are the two most common orange (*Citrus sinensis*) varieties. The 'Navel' is a seedless orange characterised by the 'belly button' indentation on the skin. The fruit will hold on the tree for many months, and ripens in early winter. Ripening later in the season is the 'Valencia'. It has seeds, holds well and also has the advantage of not being

Above left: The scent of citrus blossom on a warm spring day will lift your spirits.

Above: A selection of limes, including rangpur, 'West Indian', 'Tahitian' and Indonesian.

Below left: Store lemons either in the fridge or at a cool room temperature.

Opposite, clockwise
from top left: Rangpur
lime; 'Verna' lemons
(cut and on the tree);
and 'Meyer' lemon.

so prone to fruit fly attacks. Growers in hot, dry areas may find the 'Leng' or 'Lane Late' navel orange is more suitable for their climate. 'Joppa' is a great mid-season orange that's perfect for juicing.

'Seville' oranges (*Citrus aurantium*) are commonly used for marmalade, liqueurs and shade, and are also a popular street tree throughout Spain. They have spines, sweetly perfumed flowers and very bitter fruit with thick flesh.

Lemons

'Eureka' is one of the best lemons (*Citrus limon*) for the backyard: it crops throughout the year, so you can usually find fruit on the tree. It isn't cold-tolerant, however, and does best in warm or coastal areas. Great vigour and few thorns are two other advantages for the home gardener.

If you live in cooler zones, the most cold-tolerant of the lemons is the 'Meyer', which produces juicy, orange-coloured fruit that is quite sweet (low in acid) throughout the year. This is also the best variety for growing in tubs.

'Lisbon' tends to have two main crops — a heavy one in autumn/winter and then a light one in spring.

Mandarins

Smaller than oranges, mandarins or tangerines (*Citrus reticulata*) are usually sweeter and easier to peel. Their season is shorter and the fruit

doesn't hold quite as well, but they are plentiful and delicious when in season and well worth planting in the backyard. The best two varieties are 'Imperia', which has small fruit with great flavour, and 'Emperor', which is easy to peel.

Grapefruit

Grapefruit (*Citrus x paradisi*) are larger, quite bitter citrus that ripen either yellow or pink, depending on the cultivar. A cross between pomelo (*C. maxima*) and sweet orange (*C. sinensis*), its name derives from the fact that the clusters of young fruit are reminiscent of grapes.

The most successful backyard tree is 'Marsh', as it crops yearly and is naturally resistant to fruit fly. 'Wheeny', the other common backyard variety, tends to crop heavily one year, then lightly the next. 'Thompson' has pink flesh, while 'Ruby' is much darker and sweeter, but does need a bit of cold to colour well.

Below: Before squeezing
a lemon, roll it on a bench
under your hand, so it will
produce more juice.

Growing citrus in small spaces

To the apartment or townhouse resident, having a lime handy for a gin and tonic or a lemon for cooking may seem like the impossible dream, but growing fruit in pots is much easier than you think.

Citrus have come a long way. Dwarfing rootstocks (known as 'Flying Dragon'), compact varieties such as the Australian native lime (*C. glauca*) and 'Lisbon' lemon, and new releases such as the intriguing 'Buddha's Hand' have made it practical for most people to grow attractive and portable edible pot plants.

These citrus varieties can be grown in large pots, using a quality premium standard mix, provided they are about 40 cm (16 in) across by about the same depth, or larger. An alternative to growing the natural tree shape is to espalier the plant flat against a wall. You can buy them trained this way, or you can do it yourself by simply pruning off any outward growing branches. Your reward will be scented white spring blossom, acid-coloured fruit in winter and, year-round, glossy green leaves.

While citrus can be grown from seed, it's easiest to buy a grafted three-year-old specimen that has been budded onto one of the various suitable understock plants. This way you are guaranteed a true-to-type plant, but you'll have the bonus of a hardy rootstock with its own qualities, such as vigour and disease resistance — especially tolerance to phytophora root rot in the case of trifoliata (*Poncirus trifoliata*), which is a popular rootstock in susceptible areas — or dwarfing ability, as with the 'Flying Dragon' rootstock, which naturally decreases the vigour of the variety grafted onto it by about a third.

Plants that are container grown can be planted out year-round in mild climates, but in areas where frosts are likely, it's best to wait until any chance of this has passed. Spring and autumn are ideal planting times, but summer is also suitable, provided you can keep the water up to them. As a rule, limes and lemons are more frost-sensitive than oranges and grapefruit, while mandarins vary, depending on the type.

Clockwise from above: Trifoliata or Japanese bitter orange rootstock; citrus blossom; and a close-up of a citrus graft on a mature tree.

Limes

Limes (*Citrus aurantifolia*), naturally smaller plants, grow quite well in pots. They tend to be harvested when they are still green, although they will turn yellowish if left on the tree.

The two most common varieties are 'Tahitian' and 'West Indian'; the latter's stronger lime flavour makes it more desirable. Both types do really well in the tropics and subtropics, but tend to suffer in the cold.

There is also an Australian native lime, *Citrus glauca*, known as desert lime. It has prickly branches, small leaves and juice cells that are not attached to each other as they are in traditional citrus, so they fall out like fish roe when the fruit is opened. These narrow and finger-like green fruit are sometimes flushed red.

The other popular lime is the kaffir lime (*Citrus hystrix*), a popular ingredient in Asian cuisines. The leaves are added to curries to flavour sauces, then removed before serving, in much the same way as bay leaves are used in French cooking. The fruit itself is wrinkled with little juice, and the thorns are wickedly sharp, so don't plant these next to a thoroughfare.

Lesser known limes include the rangpur lime (*Citrus limonia*), which looks like a mandarin and can also be broken into segments. The rangpur is actually a mandarin–lime cross with a strong acidic lime flavour, used for flavouring drinks. More cold-tolerant than other limes, it's a vigorous grower (to 5 m/16 ft) and produces lots of fruit from late autumn to spring. It can also be used as a rootstock.

The Indonesian lime (*Citrus aurantifolia* 'Engallis') is a small tree with dense, bushy, light green foliage. The fruit are small, like a kumquat, with a flattish shape. When ripe (usually in winter), they turn from green to yellow.

Above left: Kaffir limes are also known as makruts.

Above: Use the juice of the Indonesian lime for marinating meat.

Below: Pick limes while they're still green and full of flavour.

Other types

Calamondins (*Citrus madurensis*) look like a tiny mandarin, and are sometimes considered a hybrid between these and kumquats. They have the same easily peeled skin, but a much more bitter flavour that is better for making marmalade than eating fresh. Their most popular use is as an ornamental, as they look very pretty when both in flower or fruit. The variegated leaf form is also attractive.

Calamondins are frequently used as pot plants or symbols of fertility, as they flower and fruit together. Kumquats (*Fortunella* sp.) are also used in this manner, and for crystallising or liqueurs. 'Nagami' produces oval fruit that is sweet enough to eat off the tree, while 'Marumi' has round fruit that is extremely tart.

Chinotto (*Citrus myrtifolia*), which has round orange fruit and no thorns, is often used for crystallising too, as is citron (*Citrus medica*), with short spines and very bitter, thick-skinned, pulpy flesh. One of its cultivars is 'Buddha's Hand', which features many pointed apexes that make it look like a distorted clenched fist.

Native to South-East Asia, the pomelo, or shaddock (*Citrus maxima*), is the super fruit of the citrus family. Growing to 12 m (39 ft), its football-sized, yellow-green fruit, which have very thick rind and hardly any yellow or pale pink flesh, lend it an interesting novelty value.

Citrus hybrids

Tangors (*Citrus reticulata* x *C. sinensis* x *C. nobilis*) — hybrids between mandarins and oranges — are often large. One popular variety that is unsurpassed in sweetness and juiciness is 'Honey Murcott', with its deep reddish orange skin. It is late maturing, as is one of the other tangors, 'Ellendale'. Other citrus crosses include tangelos, mandarin and grapefruit hybrids that were developed in the 1930s.

Perhaps the most successful of these hybrids is the popular 'Lemonade' tree, a lemon and mandarin (tangerine) cross with the flavour of a sweet lemon, and rangpur lime, an orange-skinned lime–mandarin hybrid that's very juicy.

Cultivating citrus

If you live in a colder climate, grow citrus in a conservatory. All citrus love heat and water, as long as it drains away. Find a position that gets as much sun as possible; all day is best. Although citrus will cope with less sun, it will probably set less fruit. Avoid positions that expose your tree to strong salt-laden winds too, as this will also affect the ability of your tree to set fruit from blossom.

It's also worthwhile doing a pH test at this stage, as citrus prefer a soil that is neither too acid nor too alkaline — about 6 to 7.5. If your soil doesn't fall within this range, you can easily adjust it (for more information, see page 15).

Planting

The 'dig a hole and bung it in' routine may work for some citrus plants, but if you're growing them for their fruit, it's worth the effort to be extra careful with your planting technique. The hole itself is also important. Dig it about twice as wide as it is deep. Then do the water test to make sure it drains well (see page 17). If there are no problems, go ahead and plant, but if your soil fails the drainage test, build up the area so

Opposite, clockwise from top left: Grape-fruits; mandarins; lemon blossom; and blood oranges.

Below: Oranges fall into two groups: bitter oranges, which include 'Seville', are best used in cooking, whereas sweet oranges, such as 'Navel' and 'Valencia', can be eaten fresh.

Right: The 'Nagami' kumquat is a prolific bearer that does well in a pot.

Far right: Chinotto, which is used in a popular soft drink of the same name.

Below: Young pomelo fruit forming.

Opposite: Rangpur lime, perfect for juicing.

tip

Don't dig over the soil around citrus or you may damage the fibres of its surface roots, normally in the top 10 cm (4 in), which can lead to wood-rooting fungi taking hold.

that it is about 50 cm (20 in) higher than the surrounding area, then plant into the top of this mound; it should look a bit like the crater of a volcano.

Don't add any fertiliser to the planting hole, as this can cause burn. Remove the plant from its bag or pot and gently tease out the roots so they radiate in all directions. Cut off any that have started to spiral and are root bound, as this will severely affect the growth of your tree in years to come.

Backfill with soil to which you've added some organic matter, such as compost, but be careful not to bury the tree too deep, or to cover over the graft, as this can result in collar rot, to which citrus are very prone. The soil in the container should be the same level as the new ground level in the planting hole.

Firm down gently with your foot to create a slightly firmer, lower well around the tree, which will help the water stay long enough to penetrate into the root zone before it runs off the surface. Then water in really well, with at least a full 9-litre (4-gal) watering can, to help get rid of any air pockets.

Mulch to a depth of about 10 cm (4 in), being careful not to build up mulch around the trunk. Continue watering regularly — say, every week (more on windy or very sunny days) — until your citrus has reached the end of its first year. After this, it will have become sufficiently established to grow well with a 'once every three weeks if it hasn't rained' watering regimen.

Above: Citrus blossom.

Above right: Rough lemon (*Citrus jambhiri* 'Lush'), used as a hedge to a vegetable garden: it has thorns and strong-tasting foliage that keep out marauding stock.

Opposite: Collar rot.

tip

Don't build up grass clippings, mulch and weeds around the trunk of citrus, as the lack of air circulation can cause collar rot.

Feeding

Citrus are what's known as gross feeders, so they need regular applications of fertiliser, preferably every 3 to 4 months with blood and bone, or with well rotted animal manures, as well as a special citrus fertiliser in winter to help sustain the fruit. Spread the fertiliser evenly around the tree, water in well, and don't allow it to touch the trunk.

If you have citrus in tubs, use slow-release fertiliser regularly, as well as a pellitised manure every season.

Pruning

Sometimes citrus trees can grow too close to the ground, with low-lying branches reducing airflow and adding to the likelihood of collar rot. If you find this is happening with your citrus, lift up the crown by removing some of the lower branches. Besides removing suckers — that is, understock sprouting below the graft — and keeping your citrus trimmed if it's outgrowing its space, it will have a natural, neat habit without pruning.

Harvesting

Taste test citrus before harvesting. Some may have coloured well but not be sweet enough to eat. In any case, most citrus will store well on the tree. If you have a glut of fruit, make marmalade or lemonade, or squeeze the juice of lemons and limes into ice cubes and keep them in the freezer for cooking.

Problems

Citrus can be attacked by various pests. The most serious affect the viability of the fruit as well as the vigour of the plant.

Collar rot

One of the biggest problems associated with citrus is collar rot, a phytophora fungus that attacks both the roots and the lower section of the trunk, especially where

did you know? In India, branches of the citron tree (*Citrus medica*) are used as walking sticks. The wood is white, rather hard and heavy, and of fine grain.

Pruning an orange tree

Citrus trees don't need to be pruned to make them fruit — they do this naturally — but they do need help with pests and diseases. Increasing the air circulation around citrus trees by lifting their crown is a great strategy for keeping collar rot at bay. Taking out dead or damaged growth or rubbing branches, and removing any swollen stems that may contain a pest which causes this gall are all important parts of the pruning process, which can be done each winter.

1 This lush-looking orange tree needs a light prune to remove damaged branches and lift the crown.

2 Remove any small, diseased or damaged branches or twigs.

3 With its crown lifted, it now looks more like a tree, rather than a shrub.

it meets the ground. Poor drainage and lack of air circulation are the main causes of this disease, which eventually results in the tree's demise if it's not treated.

Make sure you remove or shorten the lower branches of your tree to encourage air flow all around it. If your soil doesn't drain well, plant in a raised bed initially, and keep mulch and any manure top dressings away from the trunk itself, as soil or even grass and weeds building up around the trunk can make the disease more prevalent.

If your tree does develop collar rot, cut away any diseased, soft and oozing bark until only healthy tissue remains, and also rectify any drainage and air flow problems, and your tree should recover. A soil drench of appropriate fungicide may also be needed in worst case scenarios.

Fruit drop

The most likely cause of fruit drop is irregular water supply when the young fruit are forming, straight after blossoming. This normally coincides with the first

Right: Try removing bronze orange bugs with a vacuum cleaner, but remember to protect your eyes from their spray.

Far right: Bronze orange bugs change colour during their life cycle, darkening from orange to dark brown. These are still at the nymph stage, when they are easier to control.

Below: In some areas, birds can be a problem. You may need to protect your fruit with netting.

Below right: Regularly clean up any fallen fruit.

bout of hot weather, at a time when your trees are particularly sensitive. The other problem can be pollution. Young buds don't like smog, so if the air quality is bad at this time, your crop can suffer.

Citrus leaf miner

This pest causes distortion in the new growth. It is actually a fly that lays its eggs in the leaf itself, and when they hatch, the larvae tunnel in between the layers of the leaf, leaving a mark like a snail's trail.

At this stage, all you can do is spray with a penetrant or systemic poison, or manually prune off all the affected growth. It is much better to use an oil spray, such as white oil or pest oil, during the growing season from late spring through to autumn: this will make the leaf surface slippery and discourage the fly from attacking in the first place.

Spraying white louse scale

First carefully read the safety instructions to identify withholding periods (see page 63) and other warnings about bees foraging, for example. These will also explain whether or not this poison can be mixed with oil successfully. Although the oil is safe to handle without gloves, always wear gloves and goggles when handling poisons.

1 White louse scale is a hard scale that looks very much like desiccated coconut, or a bad case of dandruff, all over the trunk of your plant. Like all scale, it's reasonably well anchored but will come off if you scrape it with your fingernail.

2 Following the manufacturer's instructions, measure the poison and add it to the correct amount of water already in the sprayer. That way, if any spills or splashes, it is diluted.

3 Next, measure out the white oil, and pour it into the spray bottle.

4 Agitate the bottle, then spray onto the foliage. Cover the affected area well with the spray, keeping it agitated to help it stay mixed. Wash out the sprayer carefully, then wash your hands thoroughly.

Aphids

These attack and distort new growth, and can result in sooty mould, which grows on the honeydew they excrete. It can stop leaves from photosynthesising properly. Treat the aphids themselves, and also wash off the mould with soapy water.

Bronze orange bugs

Also known as stink bugs due to their foul-smelling excretion, bronze orange bugs are a real problem. They feed by sticking their straw-like proboscis into the plant and sucking up the sap. The result is that dry, brown patches can disfigure the fruit itself, and the leaves become pocked. Use an oil treatment, especially during the nymph stages, and remove it manually.

Scale insects

These look like barnacles and suck sap from either leaves or fruit. There are many different types of scale that attack citrus, including white wax scale, red scale, soft brown scale and white louse scale. These are both hard and soft scales, so to kill them you need a combination of oil and contact pesticide. Also watch out for ants, which tend to 'farm' scales as they feed on their honeydew, a sugary excretion.

did you know? Tangerines, the other name for mandarins, derives from the fact that mandarins were first imported to Europe via the Moroccan port of Tangiers.

Vine fruit

Many climbing plants, often ornamental features in their own right, are not only colourful cover-ups for fences, pergolas and shade screens but also prolific producers of edible and delicious fruit.

Utilising fruiting climbers

Fruiting vines are very adaptable plants, using their climbing habit to make the most of competitive natural habitats. Use them to soften an architectural feature, such as a pergola or arbour, grow them in a pot or simply squeeze them into a spare space in the garden. Most of these plants have a natural inclination to climb over trees in a forest, or scramble along banks like a groundcover, but you can easily manipulate this flexibility to suit your garden. Imagine dining under the shade of a pergola smothered by a grapevine that's dripping with bunches of delicious fruit.

Vines use various methods to climb and, if you understand how they do this, you can provide the right sort of support. Some vines twine, turning like a corkscrew in either one direction or the other to head upwards. Others, such as passionfruit and grapes, have modified parts like tendrils and sucker pads, which help hold them onto a support. Some vines develop hooks, spines and thorns, even aerial roots, to hook and pull themselves up.

Above: Passionfruit (*Passiflora* sp.).

Left: Slices of cold watermelon make a refreshing snack on a hot day.

Melons

Melons are annuals, so you need to replant them each year. They are very fast growing, however, and if sown in a warm, frost-free environment, will grow quickly along the ground, spreading quite a distance, and producing large, sweet, water-filled fruit.

Melons are native to various hot spots around the world, including Africa, Arabia, Asia and Australia; the paddy melon (*Cucumis myriocarpus*), native to the deserts of southern Africa, is a poisonous weed.

The two main genera of melons are *Cucumis* — rockmelons and honeydew melons — and *Citrullus* — watermelons.

Watermelons

Citrullus lanatus, or watermelon, is native to Africa, but grows really well in tropical areas that have a wet and dry season but are always warm, such as northern Australia. They naturally scramble along the ground, but can be trained as a climber, although the fruit, with its green and white marbled skin, will need to be supported in net bags. For many, their sweet, juicy red flesh is the quintessential taste of summer. Seedless varieties and dwarf types of watermelon are also available.

There are some beautiful heirloom cultivars of watermelon. 'Moon and Stars' bears particularly pretty fruit, which has a dark green rind covered in golden dots and bright red flesh that stores well. The 'Cream of Saskatchewan', thought to have been brought to America by Russian immigrants, has very pale cream-coloured flesh and a very thin rind. Another watermelon with unusual rind tones is 'Sweet Siberian', which has orange flesh and only grows to 4 kg (9 lb). Other smaller fruits include the popular modern cultivar 'Sugar Baby'.

did you know? The serendipity berry (*Dioscoreophyllum cumminsii*), a trailing plant from Africa, has fruit so sweet, it can be used as a sugar substitute for diabetics.

vine fruit

1 Passionfruit — 'Panama Red' (above) and 'Ned Kelly' (below) **2** Honeydew melon and rockmelon
3 'Allsweet' watermelon **4** Banana melon **5** Grapes (from left to right) — 'Red Flame', 'Sultana' and
'Black Muscat' **6** Green and golden kiwi fruit **7** *Ampelopsis brevipedunculata* 'Elegans' **8** Jam melon

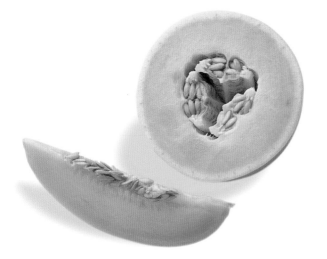

Above: The honeydew melon is so sweet that the rind can become sticky with sugar when the fruit is ripe.

Below: 'Sugar Baby', a watermelon cultivar that only produces small fruit.

Rockmelons and honeydew melons

Cucumis melo — a species that includes rockmelons (*C. melo reticulatus*, also known as cantaloupe and muskmelon), honeydew (*C. melo*, Inodorus Group) and golden or champagne melons (*C. melo cantalupensis*) — is closely related to cucumbers and prefers similar growing conditions. In cold climates you can raise them indoors in a glasshouse, or protect them in cloches and hotbeds in a similar fashion (see page 14).

Nowadays there are many different modern and heirloom cultivars of *Cucumis* sp. Of the heirloom types, the most popular are the cool-climate 'French Charentais', which has a light grey-green rind with darker green stripes and the aroma of wine; 'Sweet Granite', which has the usual orange flesh but with a wonderful sweetness; and 'Naples', with a dark green rind and pale yellow flesh that is extremely juicy and sweet.

From the Middle East come other beautiful contributions, such as 'Israeli' melon, which has cream- to apricot-coloured rind and cream-coloured, extremely sweet and aromatic flesh; 'Turkish Leopard', which grows to about 3 kg (7 lb), has spotted gold and green rind, copes very well with heat and stores well; and 'Persian Melon', with a strongly netted dark rind and a musky taste. This melon has a deeper root system than regular melons, so it's better at extracting moisture from the soil, and does not continue to ripen after picking like the other rockmelons.

Watermelon granita

250 g (9 oz/1 heaped cup) caster (superfine) sugar
250 ml (9 fl oz/1 cup) water
1.5 kg (3 lb 5 oz) watermelon, rind removed and cut into chunks
2 tablespoons chopped mint, optional

Put the sugar and water in a saucepan and stir over low heat, without boiling, until the sugar has dissolved. Bring to the boil, then reduce the heat and simmer, without stirring, for 5 minutes. Pour into a large bowl to cool.

Process watermelon in a food processor until a purée forms, then strain, discarding the seeds and fibre.

Mix together the purée and syrup, then pour into a shallow metal dish. Freeze for 1 hour, or until ice crystals start to form around the edges. Scrape these back into the mixture with a fork.

Repeat this process at least twice, or until the mixture has large, even-sized ice crystals. For extra flavour, add mint when freezing for the last time.

Serve immediately, or beat well with a fork and refreeze until ready to serve. Scrape the granita into serving dishes with a fork, or serve in scoops in tall glasses.

Serves 4.

Perhaps the most unusual of all, however, is the banana melon (pictured on page 184), which was originally bred in the United States more than 150 years ago. The fruit is about 40 cm (16 in) long and 10 cm (4 in) in diameter, with very little netting. It tapers like a banana and has salmon pink flesh.

Then there is the pineapple melon, a large oval melon with the aroma of a pineapple. Its orange-yellow skin is netted, and the flesh is either pale green or pale yellow. The US president Thomas Jefferson may have grown it on his Monticello estate in the late eighteenth century. It's now very popular, although it was not cultivated for many years.

Cultivating melons

Both genera — *Cucumis* and *Citrullus* — have very similar growing requirements: they like a frost-free, open sunny position with a long summer, loads of manure and a plentiful water supply while the fruit is forming. Raise them from seedlings, either planted directly into a mound or raised first in a protected seedling tray, and then plant them out in spring once all chance of frost has diminished, choosing only the strongest seedlings.

In order to spread and produce bountiful crops, melons need a position in full sun with plenty of space — say, about 2 m (6½ ft) for each plant. Water them regularly.

This page: The orange flesh (above), netted skin (below left), and flower (below right) of the rockmelon.

Drying melon seed

Melons can be regrown from one season to the next by saving seed. However, with home-grown plants there is no guarantee that the seed will be true to type, as it could have been pollinated by another variety in the field, and hence have either or both parents' DNA characteristics. Shop-bought melons, on the other hand, are often sterile hybrids that won't grow successfully from seed.

1 Soak the seeds in a bucket of water for a few days to loosen the pulp.

2 Pour the seeds onto a sieve. You'll need to do this a few times to get rid of all the pulp.

3 Rub the seeds against the sieve to remove any remaining pulp.

4 Leave to dry on some paper towel or a dry sieve, then store them in a jar in a cool, dark place.

Both genera may need help with pollination, which is simply a matter of using a paintbrush to distribute the pollen from the male flowers to the female ones, especially if bees are scarce or the melons are glasshouse-grown.

For both genera, protect the fruit from rotting where it touches the ground with either straw mulch or a flat rock. Once they start to ripen, ease off the water, as too much at this stage can cause rotting and splitting.

Feeding

Once the plants are established, apply complete plant food.

Pruning

Shorten the tendrils once to encourage side branching.

Harvesting

Once the watermelon's underside (the part touching the ground) turns yellow, it's time to start harvesting. For other melons, tap them: if they sound hollow, then they're ready. Pick rockmelons when the stem starts to break away from the main plant.

Problem

- Snails: page 59.

Kiwi fruit

The transparent green flesh of the kiwi fruit (*Actinidia deliciosa*) is so named because it underwent a lot of breeding work in New Zealand, although it is native to China. It's also known as Chinese gooseberry, as it is similar in colour and flavour to the English gooseberry.

Opposite: You can eat kiwi fruit fresh by scooping out the flesh with a spoon.

The fruit look a bit like furry brown goose eggs, and hang in clusters on the vine like oversized grapes. Inside, they are a wonderful chartreuse-green colour, finely specked with small, dark edible seeds.

Kiwi fruit is delicious in salads, juices and jams. But its most unusual attribute is as a meat tenderiser: the enzyme actinidia breaks down meat sinew in much the same way as papain in papaw. It also has a higher vitamin C content than citrus.

Maturing in late summer and into autumn, kiwi fruit also have excellent holding ability, lasting for weeks on the vine, provided temperatures don't spike too much. This attribute makes them popular between the stone fruit of summer and the pome fruit of autumn.

Kiwi fruit are also dioecious, which means they produce separate male and female plants, so you need to plant both sexes in order for the fruit to set; as in the animal kingdom, about 1 male to every 8 females is sufficient for successful pollination, but do try and keep them planted at least 5 m (16 ft) apart so they don't swap each other.

Take care that the varieties of male and female plants you choose both flower at the same time. Female cultivars go by the very unfeminine names of 'Haywood', 'Abbott', 'Bruno', 'Monty' and 'Dexter', while male varieties include 'McLean', 'Moona' and 'Matua'.

Cultivating kiwi fruit

The plant itself is a deciduous vine that becomes woody. A very vigorous plant, it can grow to at least 8 m (26 ft) on a support. It will cope happily with cold temperatures down to – 6°C (21°F) and, in fact, needs some winter chilling with temperatures below 7°C (45°F) in order to achieve an effective dormancy and leaf fall. Spring frosts when the leaves have already shot can cause damage, however, as will late frosts when the fruit is set.

These plants need well drained soil, although they're not particularly fussy about pH. Regular moisture throughout the growing and fruiting season is important, as is protection from the wind, otherwise the quality of the fruit is compromised.

Buy sexed, grafted plants from known varieties and plant them at any time of the year. As they will fruit for at least 30 years, you'll need a trellis that's strong enough to support them for their lifetime. Ideally, the support should face north or north-east (south in the northern hemisphere) to catch the maximum amount of sun.

Drainage is the critical factor, so do the drainage test (see page 17) and raise the beds if necessary. Adding organic matter to both sandy soils and clay soils is a good idea.

Keep the ground free of weeds during establishment, but don't cultivate the soil, as this can break the surface roots and allow soil-borne disease to take hold.

Other types of kiwi fruit

There are other species of *Actinidia* that also fruit. *Actinidia arguta*, known as cocktail kiwi or tara vine, has smaller, hairless fruit. 'Issai' is a self-pollinating form but it isn't a good producer. Then there is *A. chinensis*, which has golden fruit that looks just like the green, common type.

There are also two very pretty foliage types, which are not usually grown for their edible fruits even though they produce them. *Actinidia kolomikta*, from Asia, has pretty pink-tipped leaves; 'September Sun' is probably the best coloured form. There is also a metallic-leafed species (*A. polygama*), which has white flowers and either silver or gold leaves. In Asia the small fruit is salted and considered a delicacy.

Feeding

Mulch kiwi fruit with organic matter, as they have a shallow root system that can dry out easily. Apply fertiliser — with an N:P:K balance of 10:4:6 (see page 19) — 2 to 4 times between late winter and late summer. Well rotted poultry manure should do the trick.

Pruning

Train vines into a single strong stem up the post of a solid structure, such as a pergola. Once the lead shoot reaches the top of the post, pinch out the centre to trigger branching. You can then train these branches as permanent arms across the pergola's roof. The following season these will produce more side branches, known as fruiting arms.

Every 2 to 3 years, cut these back in winter to encourage replacement arms, as kiwis fruit on new wood. It may also be necessary to summer prune long, over-vigorous water shoots. Try to keep the plant open to the sun as well as stop branches tangling each other.

Harvesting

It takes about four years for kiwi plants to start producing fruit. Then they fruit in late autumn to early winter. The fruit holds on the vine very well and, in fact, you are likely to be disappointed by picking what look like ripe fruit too early. You can tell it's ready for picking if the seeds inside are well and truly black. They will continue to ripen in the fruit bowl, and will store well in the fridge for up to eight weeks.

Problems

Various pests are a problem for kiwi fruit.
- Caterpillars attacking leaves: page 55.
- Fruit fly: page 53.
- Rats ring-barking young vines: page 65.

Above: If stored at room temperature, kiwi fruit will keep for up to four weeks.

Left: An organic method of dealing with fruit fly is to hang a trap under the vines. For more ideas on organic solutions to this problem, see page 53.

Passionfruit

This vine's extremely vigorous habit makes it ideal for covering old sheds, paling fences and other eyesores. It's also one of the easiest fruits to grow in the home garden, provided you live in a warm climate. You can plant in one season and eat the fruit in the next, an attribute that's lacking in many fruiting plants.

The main edible species of passionfruit, also known as granadilla, is *Passiflora edulis*, which grows through trees in tropical Brazil. However, not all species are edible and, indeed, some are slightly poisonous. *Passiflora edulis* produces wrinkly purple fruit that are about 8 cm (3 in) long, but some hybrid forms — 'Panama Red' and 'Panama Gold' — have larger fruit that don't seem to wrinkle as much. The flowers are white with a purple-banded filament or 'skirt'. There are also grafted cultivars,

such as 'Ned Kelly', which are more resistant to mosaic virus (see page 71) and so worth paying a little extra for.

Giant granadilla (*P. quadrangularis*) has dusky pink flowers and bright yellow fruit that are 30 cm (1 ft) long. The other yellow-fruited species is the banana passionfruit (*P. mollissima*), which bears slightly elongated fruit, to 8 cm (3 in), after bright pink flowers. In warm climates it can become almost too vigorous and weedy, so choose with care and consult your local council's prohibited plants list.

Cultivating passionfruit

Plant passionfruit in spring, just when the soil temperatures are beginning to rise and the plants can establish themselves before any cold returns. Prepare the site properly a few months earlier with 100 g (3½ oz) of complete plant food and about 1 to 2 kg

(2 to 4¹/₂ lb) of well rotted animal manure. Space each vine about 3 m (10 ft) apart and mulch well after planting. And don't let them dry out at this stage: water your plants regularly and even shade them with a temporary hessian or shadecloth shelter until they establish themselves in their new position. Remove any weeds, as they will compete too strongly for the fertiliser and water.

Feeding

To keep up the fertiliser to this strong grower and plentiful bearer, you will need to feed it frequently. Use a liquid fertiliser every month, and mulch with compost or well rotted manure annually, always keeping the mulch at least 1 m (3 ft) away from the stem itself.

Pruning

Initially, choose a couple of the strongest leaders and train them as single stems until they are about 1 m (3 ft) tall, removing any side shoots as they grow and tying the stems securely to the support.

Once they are at this height, you can nip out the centre shoots, which will encourage side branching. The new growth produces fruit. Do any hard pruning in spring when the plant will recover quickly.

Harvesting

Passionfruit are very fast-bearing vines, producing about eight months after planting — even earlier with some of the hybrids. Collect the fruit regularly so it doesn't spoil on the ground, and remove the last of the crop before winter sets in, as it won't cope with cold.

Problems

Mosaic virus (see page 71) on passionfruit makes the leaves become mottled or streaky green and yellow. It can be avoided by growing grafted, certified plants.

Sometimes excess nitrogen-rich fertiliser can result in healthy plants but no fruit. Fruit set can also be adversely affected by wet or windy weather, low temperatures and dry or uneven watering. But the main problems are as follows.
- Fruit fly: page 53.
- Fusarium wilt (grafted disease-resistant plants will help): page 68.
- Root knot nematode: page 59.

Storing the pulp

Freeze passionfruit pulp to use another time, or use it to make syrup.

1 Use a teaspoon to scoop out the pulp.

2 Place the pulp in ice cube trays, then store them in the freezer.

Left: Eat passionfruit fresh, or add it to drinks, cakes, fruit salad and desserts, such as pavlova.

Grapes

The cultivation of grapes (*Vitis* sp.) goes back to ancient times, and viticulture, the science of growing grapes, is one of the oldest branches of horticulture. The plants themselves are vines, native to the northern hemisphere — in particular, Europe, Asia and America. It is the European species, *V. vinifera*, that has become one of the most popular fruit crops in the world, and not because they make such good eating, but because they are made into wine.

Grapes are broadly categorised into white (although they are actually green) and black or red grapes. Of the green grapes, the best known eating grape is 'Sultana', a seedless variety that's very popular with children. Other favourite varieties include 'Waltham Cross', with larger, more golden fruit, and 'Flame Seedless', which has firm fruit that stays that way.

Grapes do best in warm or hot areas with cool winters and less than 75 cm (30 in) of annual rainfall that doesn't occur when the berries are ripening. Some varieties are more tolerant to rainfall variations, which are outlined in 'Problems' (see page 198).

Grapes are also tolerant of a wide range of soil, provided they are well drained and aerated. These plants are surprisingly hardy, although they do prefer protection from wind and extreme temperatures.

Cultivating grapes

The easiest way to propagate grapes is to take hardwood cuttings in winter when the plant is bare. Choose pieces the thickness

Fruit salad plant

Monstera deliciosa, part of the Araceae family, which includes arum lilies, is native to southern Mexico and Panama. The fruit salad plant is commonly found in gardens where it's used as a shade-loving foliage plant, with highly ornamental leaves up to 1 m (3 ft) in length. The deep cut-outs on the leaves account for one of its other common names, Swiss cheese plant.

Monstera has a very adaptable nature, enabling it to withstand indoor positions. In the wild, it is a climbing plant, using its aerial roots to grow up quite tall trees, to at least 10 m (33 ft). These same roots can also prove themselves very adaptable by coping with poor soils and root competition under trees.

The fruit is long, with a honeycomb-like surface that stays green even when ripe. It opens up gradually from the base to indicate it's ready for eating, but there is quite a time lag between when the base and the top ripen. The fruit is quite astringent, and leaves a furry feeling on your tongue if it's not ready for eating. Its other common name is Mexican breadfruit, and the texture of both breadfruit (see page 113) and fruit salad plant is a bit similar.

of a pencil from the last season's growth. Each piece should be about 30 cm (1 ft) long and have about six buds. Trim each cutting just below the bottom bud and just above the top one. Then, making sure your cutting is the right way up, plant it with the top bud just above the soil level.

Feeding

Once the cuttings start to shoot in spring, you can apply a light side dressing of blood and bone, but nothing more. Grapes don't usually need added fertiliser, as they develop deep root systems that are adept at finding their own food.

If your vine lacks vigour, however, apply some well rotted chicken manure around the root zone, staying clear of the trunk. Alternatively, apply about 250 g (8 oz) of complete plant food with trace elements to a mature vine twice in spring — once early on, and again in late spring. Mulching also helps keep the soil moisture level constant, but added water may help to establish young plants or get them through periods of drought.

Pruning

Pruning grapes encourages balanced cropping and even ripening, so you won't have sour grapes, and also increases the vigour of your vine, helping it to produce for many decades to come. Pruning is a task best carried out a couple of weeks before bud burst in late winter.

In commercial vineyards, two methods are used to prune grapes. Spur pruning (see page 196) is used on heavy bearers such as muscatels, whereas less fruitful types, such as 'Sultana' and 'Iona', are usually cane pruned (see page 196). To help you decide what works best for your variety, especially if you're unsure what type it is, experiment with both methods.

Above: When picking grapes, give each bunch a gentle shake: if individual grapes fall off the vine, they are over-ripe.

The other appropriate pruning method for the home gardener is simply to choose a vigorous variety — such as 'Isabella', 'Ohanez', 'Waltham Cross' or 'Red Emperor' — and train it onto a pergola. Let the vine grow as vigorously as possible the first year in order to reach the correct height, but allow only one single shoot to grow by pinching off any lateral shoots as they appear. If your plant doesn't reach the correct height in the first year, cut it back hard in winter and have a go with the next season's growth.

did you know? Sultanas and raisins are dried grapes, but currants are the dried fruit of the 'Zante' grape. 'Currant' derives from the French *raisin de Corinthe*, which means Corinth grape.

Above: Hard young green grapes before the ripening process begins.

Opposite: Pick white grapes once they are a pale yellowish hue, an indication that they are sweet and ready to eat.

Once you have the right height, start to train your 'arms'; in this case, they should be about 50 cm (20 in) apart, with ten or so spurs of vine left from fruiting.

Spur pruning

To spur prune, which is the most common method, you need to install a tight, strong wire about 1 m (3 ft) off the ground. A second wire about 30 cm (1 ft) further up can also help support the grapes. Once your trunk reaches the first wire, train two main arms in opposite directions.

To get the grape up to the wire, choose the most vigorous shoot from the first season's growth and trim away any others.

The following spring, use a string to guide this shoot up to the wire. Once this happens, about late spring, cut this stem off, forcing it to shoot in two directions. In winter, prune these arms back to about 20 cm (8 in) long.

When the following season's growth occurs, twine this along the wires in opposite directions. Then, when you're pruning in winter, cut back to just above a bud on each arm. All shoots that occur in any other place — for instance, on the main trunk — should be rubbed back as soon as they appear (this is quite common in summer).

Cane pruning

This method is essential for producing decent crops on varieties such as 'Sultana' and 'Ohanez', as they produce their main crops on about the fourth bud onwards. To develop the trunk and two main arms, follow the same technique as spur pruning, but instead of cutting the plant back hard to a spur, allow about 3 to 4 tendrils from that season's growth to remain. Shorten one of them so that it has about twelve buds but is no longer than 75 cm (30 in), and wrap it along the wire. Shorten the others to two bud spurs. These will produce tendrils for the following year.

Harvesting

Don't harvest grapes or allow them to fruit for the first 2 to 3 years. They don't sweeten once picked, so they must ripen on the vine. Taste some first then, when you're happy with the flavour, cut off each bunch with secateurs.

Problems

Fruit fly can spoil fruit, but you can keep them off by individually bagging each bunch in a transparent fabric or in paper

---

Ampelopsis brevipedunculata 'Elegans'

Also known as porcelain berry (pictured on page 185), wild grape's blue fruit and variegated leaves make it a pretty garden plant, but in some areas it can become invasive, as wildlife like to eat (and then spread) the seeds. It's related to the pepper berry (see page 224), which is used as a spice substitute.

Above: The fruiting arms of these young plants have been trained onto strong supports.

Right: Both powdery mildew and heavy rain can cause the fruit to split.

bags. This will stop the flies laying their eggs and also keep birds from eating the fruit, while allowing the grapes to mature naturally in the sun.

Late-maturing varieties such as 'Ohanez' and 'Red Emperor' are more likely to be affected by fruit fly and powdery mildew, which is the other common grape problem. It looks very much like the white bloom that is naturally found on dark-skinned grapes, but it covers the leaves, fruit and stems. Unfortunately, it needs to be controlled, as it also affects the fruit itself, making it dry and often causing it to split. Keep it at bay by spraying with wettable sulfur every fortnight during spring, and even in early summer when growth is at its most susceptible.

After fruit set, you can use sulfur dust if the conditions are still prevalent. Applied as lime sulfur spray at bud swell, sulfur is also a good hygiene practice to help control not only fungal spores, but also mites, which can cause blistering on the upper surface of foliage, although it doesn't affect the grapes themselves (see page 147).

Whatever form of sulfur you spray, be careful not to do it on a hot day above 30°C (86°F), as it can cause burning. Copper oxychloride sprays are a good preventative for the other fungal problem that affects grapes — downy mildew. This appears as yellow spots on the leaves, which develop furry undersides.

If you live in a humid climate, even if it's on the coast, try growing American hybrids such as 'Iona', 'Carolina Black Rose' and 'Golden Muscat'.

Another problem is fruit splitting caused by heavy rain when the berries are already ripening — a particular problem for 'Cardinal' and 'Ohanez'; 'Concord' is a more tolerant variety where late rainfall is a problem.

Dragon fruit

Hylocereus sp., Cactaceae

Dragon fruit is a fast-growing climbing cactus that flowers in the evening. The flesh contains small edible black seeds but varies in colour, depending on the species. For example, *H. polyrhizus* is red-skinned with red flesh, while *H. megalanthus* has yellow skin, and spine-free pitaya (*H. undatus*) has red skin with white flesh that tastes like melon. It is grown as much for its large, scented white flowers as its delicious fruit.

Climate: Dragon fruit grows best in temperate to tropical climates but, once established, will tolerate light frosts.

Culture: Self-pollinating, but is also pollinated by bats.

Colours: Produces large white and yellow flowers at night in both summer and autumn. The blooms are followed by beautiful crimson- or yellow-skinned fruit that is sometimes spiny or scale-like.

Height: To 9 m (29 1/2 ft) tall on a suitable host.

Planting time: Any warm season.

Soil: Being a succulent, dragon fruit likes free-draining soil or potting mix with some added compost to help hold moisture.

Position: It prefers full sun, but will also tolerate light shade. Train it onto a post or trellis, and protect it from the wind.

Planting spacing: Grow one plant per tree or trellis panel (about 1.2 m/4 ft apart).

Fertiliser: Feed every three months with a slow-release fertiliser.

Pests and diseases: Dragon fruit is relatively pest-free; however, only water the plant while the fruit is developing, as excess moisture can inhibit flowering and cause rotting.

Propagation: Grow from cuttings, but allow to dry out slightly before planting so the wounds callous over.

Harvesting: Harvest dragon fruit when they turn red, or if the flesh feels soft when they're gently squeezed. Serve the fruit fresh, with a squeeze of lime juice.

Grapes can also suffer from sunburn, especially if they receive too much direct sun without the protection of some adequate foliage cover.

For more information on some of these problems, see the following pages in the 'The kitchen garden' section as well as the light brown apple moth on page 158.

- Birds: page 50.
- Downy mildew and powdery mildew: pages 66 and 69, respectively.
- Fruit fly: page 53.

Left: Sweet table grapes complement cheeses, especially blue cheeses.

Nuts

Botanically, nuts are dried fruits or kernels covered by a hard shell, which has evolved to protect their seeds from either animals or climatic extremes. We enjoy these delicious kernels either fresh off the tree or in a variety of dishes, from salads to bread and biscuits.

Almonds

An almond tree in flower is a very pretty sight, with the single or double, white or pink blossom — such as 'Alba Plena' and 'Roseoplena' — a late winter feature in itself. Native to the Mediterranean and North Africa, the almond (*Prunus dulcis*) is actually a stone fruit, except that it is the kernel inside the stone, not the flesh, that you eat. As with other stone fruit, the kernel can be poisonous, so if it tastes bitter, don't eat it.

And make sure you choose grafted, named cultivars rather than raise your own seedlings, as these can be variable and unreliable. The kernel is usually ripe in late summer and through autumn.

The almond's size is ideal for the average backyard, with grafted trees growing to only about 5 m tall x 3 m wide (16 x 10 ft). The only drawback is that they need to be cross-pollinated, so you'll have to plant another variety nearby for this to occur. Any two of 'Brandes Jordan', 'Chellaston', 'Early Jordan', 'Riverside' or 'Peerless' will do the trick or, alternatively,

Above: To remove their skins, place almonds in a bowl and cover with boiling water for about a minute. They should rub off easily.

Left: Most nuts are harvested in autumn.

you could look for a multigrafted plant with a piece of each of two varieties bud-grafted onto the one plant.

The exception is a self-pollinating type called 'Zaione', which bears heavy crops of soft-shelled almonds with a good, sweet flavour. This compact tree is also about 20 to 30 per cent smaller than a regular-sized almond tree.

Cultivating almonds

Almonds grow best in an area with a warm, dry summer, and in a soil with good drainage. Mounding or hilling your soil at planting time will help achieve this, although planting on a slope or hillside is ideal. Too much summer humidity and poor air circulation can lead to fungal problems, while inadequate moisture in the soil can cause the stones to shrivel. An area with winter rainfall is ideal. Avoid very cold areas, as the early blossom can be prone to frost.

Position your tree in an open, sunny spot, about 5 m (16 ft) away from buildings or other trees. Plant bare-rooted trees (see page 144) in early winter before bud break. Leave your tree unstaked so it can grow strong and sure without help. If you live in a very windy area, you may choose to tie it to three stakes with flexible tape, effectively creating a protective cage while your tree takes root. In spring, after your almond tree has shot, it may be necessary

Above left: Each almond is held in a furry husk.

Above: Almond blossom can be pale pink or white.

Desert almond

This shrub (*Prunus fasciculata*) is from the dry, arid regions of the south-western United States. Growing to only 3 m (10 ft) tall and a couple of metres (6½ ft) wide, it bears white blossom followed by fruit that is covered with brown felt. The leaves and seeds contain the toxin, hydrogen cyanide, which is responsible for the taste of almonds, but in this case the seeds are bitter and inedible.

nuts

1 Pecans **2** Almonds **3** Brazil nuts **4** Hazelnuts **5** Pistachios **6** Peanuts in the shell
7 Pecans **8** Walnuts **9** Macadamias **10** Pine nuts **11** Cashews **12** Nutmeg
13 Bunya nut pine kernels **14** Coconut **15** Tropical cashew

to remove any dieback and shorten the main branches to encourage an open vase shape.

Feeding

Once your almond has become established during its first spring, you can feed it with chicken manure at the end of summer and again at the beginning of winter, before the blossom appears. Apply it as a mulch about 5 cm (2 in) thick, avoiding the trunk, or as a pellitised manure in handfuls around the drip line of your tree. Apply ammonium sulfate (urea) in spring to encourage healthy growth.

Pruning

Prune in early winter, as you would for peaches and nectarines (see page 147).

Harvesting

Nuts ripen from the outside of the tree towards its centre. Once ripe, the shells or hulls begin to open. Be careful when harvesting almonds, as early removal may damage the fruiting spurs.

Problems

- Bacterial canker: page 70.
- Black and green peach aphids: page 58.
- Fungal problems, such as rust, and bacterial problems, such as shot hole (which causes fine holes in the foliage): pages 69 and 70, respectively.
- Mites: page 56.

Top: An almond tree in spring.

Far left: Use a nutcracker to remove the almond kernels from their shells, or carefully insert a knife where the shell halves join.

Left: Dieback is caused by a fungus or water stress at bud swell.

Opposite: Chestnuts are sweet and starchy.

Chestnuts

The sheer size of chestnuts (*Castanea* sp.) prohibits most people from having one in their backyard. However, if you do have a large garden or a long drive, they make a superb and beautiful specimen, growing to about 20 m (66 ft) tall and nearly the same width, and producing quite attractive yellowish green catkins, which then develop into the prickly round balls housing the nuts themselves.

The sweet chestnut (*C. sativa*) is native to North Africa, southern Europe and western Asia and, unlike many other nuts, contains more starch and water than oil. They are often made into marron glacé

(candied chestnuts) and other desserts, flour and soups, or are simply roasted on the fire.

The Chinese chestnut (*C. mollisima*) is a slightly smaller tree that is resistant to chestnut blight (not found in Australia); the Chinese love chestnuts and often use them in their traditional cuisine (see also water chestnuts on page 361).

Many hybrids between these two species (and some of the other ten in the genus) have resulted in heavier bearers. 'Colossal', 'Nevada', 'Schrader' and 'Skioka' — some of the most successful crosses — are useful for pollinating each other. Some variegated leaf forms, such as 'Albomarginata' and 'Variegata', are a good choice for those who like foliage contrast high in the canopy. There is also a weeping form known as 'Pendula'.

Cultivating chestnuts

Plant chestnuts just before bud break, in late winter or early spring. They like an acid, rich, deep soil, supplemented with organic matter and mulched. Regular and high rainfall is essential, as is regular watering through their first summer until they are established and a cold snap in

Planting bare-rooted almonds

Almonds are usually grafted onto the rootstock of either peaches or almonds, depending on their variety, so you can be sure your tree will produce good quality kernels. When planting your bare-rooted tree, make sure you identify the graft so you can keep it above ground level and therefore minimise the risk of the understock reshooting.

1 Dig a hole that's at least as wide as the root system, and position the tree upright. The roots should evenly radiate out from the centre.

2 Backfill with soil carefully, ensuring you remove all air pockets. Don't fertilise your tree at planting, as it can burn the tender new roots.

3 Firm down and mulch, and water in. Keep the area weed- and grass-free for about a 50-cm (20-in) radius while the tree establishes itself.

Right: The female flowers or catkins of the chestnut are pale green and hard to see among the leaves, while the larger male flowers are a buff colour.

Far right: Once chestnuts ripen, the green husks turn yellow-brown and fall to the ground.

winter. If your tree is well suited to your area, it may start to bear fruit within only three years.

Feeding

Use complete plant food at the end of each winter and also mulch annually with organic matter.

Pruning

Only prune to remove low-lying branches when the tree is young. Otherwise remove diseased or dead branches as the tree ages.

Harvesting

Chestnuts are incredibly prickly. The ripe nuts fall to the ground in autumn, but you must handle them with gloves as there are yellow spines all over the green husks to protect them from predators. Remove the husks and store the nuts in the fridge.

Problems

In the northern hemisphere, chestnuts are susceptible to black ink disease and chestnut blight, both of which are known to destroy whole stands. Under no circumstances should you take chestnuts into countries such as Australia, or you could be responsible for importing these terrible fungal spores and infecting quarantined trees.

Close cousins

Chestnuts are members of the beech family, Fagaceae, which also includes oaks and beech trees. The other lesser known members include *Nothofagus* or southern hemisphere beeches, and evergreen *Castanopsis*, which are native to warmer subtropical and temperate climates. They also bear edible nuts in autumn, although these are smaller, while the trees themselves grow into giants, at least 20 m (66 ft) tall. All genera are highly valued for their excellent timber.

tip

Cleaning up after the nuts fall is important, as rats and mice can become a problem, as can possums and even rabbits.

did you know? The seeds of the Moreton Bay chestnut (*Castanospermum australe*) were eaten by Australian Aboriginals, who would first crack them open, soak them in water, then pound them into flour for making cakes, or roast them. As with many native foods, soaking the nuts in water removes some of the soluble toxins, while roasting destroys other toxins.

Walnuts and butternuts

Deciduous trees native to south-eastern Europe, South-East Asia and parts of America, Mexico and Canada, walnuts (*Juglans* sp.) range in size from about 10 to 30 m (33 to 98 ft), depending on the species, so they're not your average backyard specimen.

Common walnut

The most commonly grown species is *Juglans regia*, a fine tree to about 20 x 15 m (66 x 49 ft). Walnuts can be eaten straight from the tree, baked in cakes, tossed through salads and even pickled. However, it takes 10 to 15 years for these trees to start producing decent crops and, even then, they tend to bear heavily every other year, so patience is required. Start them off with your children and by the time they're adults, they can pick the nuts themselves.

For the most part, walnuts like a deep, rich alluvial soil, and also enjoy protection from frosts. They do, however, like the cool, so providing you can regularly water them and give them shelter, even tableland areas are suitable. Walnuts like extra water in summer, so added organic matter and thick mulch helps in this regard.

Good drainage and plenty of room are two other keys to their success, so make sure there's a clearance of at least 7 m (23 ft) between them and buildings or other trees.

Other species

The other species of walnut grown for their nuts include the Japanese walnut (*J. ailantifolia*) and the American walnut (*J. nigra*). Two other species, called butternuts, also bear edible nuts. These are the Chinese butternut (*J. cathayensis*) and butternut or butternut walnut (*J. cinerea*). All are very valuable timber trees.

Walnut taratoor

250 g (9 oz/2^1/2 cups) shelled walnuts (or almonds, hazelnuts or pine nuts)
80 g (2^3/4 oz/1 cup) fresh white breadcrumbs
3 garlic cloves
60 ml (2 fl oz/^{1}/4 cup) white wine vinegar
250 ml (9 fl oz/1 cup) olive oil
fresh parsley, chopped, to garnish

Finely chop the walnuts in a blender or food processor. Set aside ^{1}/2 teaspoon of the walnuts for a garnish. Add the breadcrumbs, garlic, vinegar and 3 tablespoons water, and blend well. With the motor running, gradually add the olive oil in a thin, steady stream until smooth. If the sauce seems too thick, add a little more water. Season to taste, then transfer to a serving bowl and refrigerate. Combine the reserved walnuts and parsley, and sprinkle on top. Serve with seafood, salads, fried vegetables or bread.

Serves 8.

Pecans and hickories

Like walnuts, pecans (*Carya illinoinensis*) are in the Juglandaceae family, but they have some advantages over their cousins. For a start, they tend to bear fruit much earlier — after about five years. They are also slightly smaller trees, growing to about 10 x 7 m (33 x 23 ft), a slightly more manageable size; allow a 5-m (16-ft) clearance between them and buildings, services and other trees.

Of the 25 species belonging to this genus, most bear edible nuts, although some — such as the scrub pecan (*C. floridana*), pignut (*C. glabra*) and red hickory (*C. ovalis*) — are used as animal fodder. Other, better known species include the shagbark hickory (*C. ovata*) and nutmeg hickory (*C. myristiciformis*), which provides us with the famous spices, mace and nutmeg (see page 418). If the climate is cool enough, all species colour up very well in autumn, so your nut trees can also be beautiful ornamental features.

Mostly native to North America, pecans tend to be more adaptable to climate, coping with both coastal areas and inland positions as long as the maximum and minimum temperatures are not extreme. Their main requirement is soil, which has to be deep, fertile, well draining and slightly acid. Pecans also need regular summer water.

Pecans bear both male and female flowers on the same tree, but not all varieties flower at the same time. This is not usually a problem in an orchard, where rows of trees can pollinate each other, but for the home garden where there is only room for one tree, this could spell disaster. For this reason, make sure you select a cultivar that self-pollinates, such as 'Caspiana', 'Halbert', 'Moore', 'Texas Pacific' and 'Western Schley'.

Below and opposite: Pecans have a similar texture to walnuts but taste sweeter.

Below centre: As pecans ripen, the green husks turn brown and open.

Below right: A grove of young pecan trees.

Cultivating pecans and hickories

Plant out these nut trees during their winter dormancy, and keep them free of weeds and well watered while they establish. Until the canopy develops sufficiently, walnut trunks may need protection from sunburn; in fact, you'll often see walnut trunks painted white. A lime wash is a less permanent method of achieving the same end, and is only necessary during the first few years. Choose grafted cultivars for blight resistance (see the three cultivars listed in 'Problems', below).

Feeding

Throughout the year, mulch with organic matter (compost or well rotted animal manures are best) to both enrich the soil and build up its water-holding capacity and structure. Also use a high-nitrogen fertiliser each spring and autumn to encourage growth. This could be organic, such as chicken manure, or chemical, such as citrus food. Spread it evenly around the root area, then water in well.

Pruning

Select trees with one strong central leader, and prune off any secondary leaders that may develop. Also, as the tree grows, lift the crown for easier harvesting (so you don't bump your head) by removing lower branches until you have about a 1.5- to 2-m (5- to 6^1/$_2$-ft) clearance.

Harvesting

There is an old saying — 'A wife, a dog and a walnut tree, the more you beat them the better they be.' Clearly, you shouldn't beat anyone, but it is a curious fact that stress brings a nut tree into flower and, hence, into producing nuts. Any plant under threat will do anything it can to propagate, so it can reproduce its genes one last time.

When your walnut tree is ready, it should form nuts, provided it is mature and the weather has been cool and moist enough. Then you just have to wait for autumn for the hulls to split open and the nuts to fall to the ground. Laying sheets around the tree and shaking it will make collecting the nuts easier.

Problems

- With walnuts, bacterial blight is the biggest problem, although carefully selecting disease-resistant varieties such as 'Franquette', 'Eureka' and 'Wybaleena' will help.
- For both walnuts and pecans, large birds such as cockatoos can cause havoc in the tree — nets, bird scarers or fake hawks can help if you have a real problem: pages 44 and 50.
- Codling moth eat the ripening walnuts: pages 55 and 157.
- The longicorn beetle, auger beetle, weevil, fruit tree borer, scale and mite can all affect pecans, but none is a significant problem.

tip

As the husk of pecans is thin, gather fallen nuts regularly so rats, birds and the weather won't ruin your crop.

Hazelnuts

Providing you live in an area with cold winters, hazelnuts — also known as filberts and cobnuts — are probably one of the best nut trees to grow at home, as they are not only ornamental but also grow to only about 4 m (13 ft).

Related to birch trees (Betulaceae family), they like a similar, cool, moist position with a slightly acid soil and dependable rainfall. There are fifteen species native to Europe, Asia and North America, but the most commonly eaten type is the European hazelnut (*Corylus avellana*), which bears the smooth, amber-coloured nuts, rich in a delightfully fragrant oil that we enjoy fresh, roasted or in desserts.

The plant itself is a small suckering shrub that each winter bears beautiful yellow catkins (male flowers), sometimes known as lamb's tails, which hang all over the shrub like decorations. These are followed by the red female flowers.

This is the problem, as you will really need to plant a small wood or grove to achieve cross-pollination and a successful crop of nuts. To maximise the likelihood of male and female flowering times overlapping, buy or take cuttings from completely different parent stock, or buy named varieties that have different flowering times. Hazelnuts take about five years to start cropping.

Top: Hazelnuts go particularly well with chocolate in confectionery, cakes, desserts and biscuits.

Far left: Purple-leafed filbert (*Corylus maxima* 'Purpurea').

Left: Sheathed in a pale green husk, hazelnuts are borne in clusters. Their main problem is foraging squirrels and rodents.

Some of the cultivars of *Corylus avellana* are particularly beautiful. 'Contorta', as the name suggests, is very twisted and looks very similar to tortured willow. It is sometimes harvested for walking sticks. 'Aurea' has lime-coloured leaves — lovely for foliage contrast — and one of the American species, *C. maxima* 'Purpurea', has coppery purple foliage not unlike a beech or copper birch.

Cultivating hazelnuts

There are two ways of propagating hazelnuts. You can plant rooted cuttings in early winter to give the plants the opportunity for more root growth before spring foliage emerges. Shallow, mounded planting holes coupled with extra mulch help keep the roots cool.

Or, in winter, you can sometimes buy larger 'ball and burlapped' specimens, where the burlap or hessian protects the roots. These need to be planted before they shoot away in spring.

Feeding

Apply a complete plant food in late winter to encourage new spring growth, and mulch annually.

Pruning

When you plant your hazelnut, trim it down to a height of about 50 cm (20 in) to encourage lots of new shoots from the base. If your tree is a cutting-grown specimen, it will be true to type, but if it's been grafted, make sure you remove any suckers from below the graft. The following winter, choose about five of the healthiest stems and remove them cleanly with sharp secateurs at ground level. These will be your one-year-old ripe wood, which should flower and fruit.

Each season, trim away any tired old growth or diseased or rubbing branches at the base, again leaving five of the healthiest young shoots that, in turn, will be the next season's fruit-bearing wood.

Harvesting

Hazelnuts mature in late summer and early autumn. You can tell when they are ripe as the husks become brittle and deepen in colour. They will fall when they're ready, but you'll need to gather them quickly so they don't spoil. Hazelnuts take from 3 to 7 years to bear, depending on whether they've been grown from seeds or cuttings, or are grafted specimens.

Planting hazelnuts

Not only can hazelnut trees be damaged by severe frosts, but young trees can also be sunburnt. Provide protection by planting your hazelnut near other trees or shrubs or, if this is not possible, spray the sunniest side of the bare winter branches with a solution of half water and half white acrylic paint.

1 Position the shrub in a prepared hole that's at least as wide and as deep as the root you'll be moving.

2 Trim off any damaged roots.

3 Backfill, just covering the root ball with soil, then mulch heavily. This will keep the weeds at bay as well as help you locate the nuts when they drop.

Pistachios

Surprisingly, pistachios (*Pistacia vera*) belong to the same family as cashew nuts and mangoes, although the 'fruit' don't look at all alike; it's the flowers, which hide similarities, that have convinced botanists of their close relationship.

Pistachios originated in China but have spread to other parts of the world, especially the Mediterranean, where they are grown for their delicious green or yellowish seed. These are either dried fresh, or dipped in salted water, then dried, so the kernel develops a lovely salty crust.

The tree itself is a deciduous plant that grows to about 7 m (23 ft) tall, with a wide canopy to about 10 m (33 ft) across. Like the ornamental pistachio (*Pistacia chinensis*), to which it's related, it has pinnate leaves, panicles of flowers (either female or male, depending on the tree's sex) and red (not blue as with *P. chinensis*) fruit set on the females. Inside this fruit is a bony shell that contains the kernel.

Pistachios typically like a dry climate with a hot summer and a cold winter; it is often in almost desert-like conditions that you see them grow well. They are very drought-tolerant once established, and even cope with salty soil, but they won't tolerate damp, stagnant soil or summer coastal humidity: in these conditions they will fail to set nuts.

Cultivating pistachios

Pistachios like rocky hillsides and poor soils where they almost have to cling on to survive. Scorching sun and a 'treat them mean to keep them keen' strategy seems to work best, so if your site looks as if it's suitable only for goats, chances are pistachios will love it.

As these trees are dioecious, it's important to plant a tree of both sexes. The simplest way to ensure this is to buy grafted, known varieties. The best known female varieties are 'Bronte' and 'Alepp', while the most common male is 'Kaz'.

Plant pistachios during their winter dormancy. Spread out the root system, plant and water in.

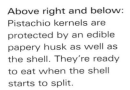

Above right and below: Pistachio kernels are protected by an edible papery husk as well as the shell. They're ready to eat when the shell starts to split.

Opposite: *Pistacia vera* is susceptible to root nematode, so pistachios are often grafted onto other species, such as *P. atlantica*, but only if verticillium wilt is not a problem in the area.

Feeding

If you want to encourage growth, you can feed pistachios with a complete plant food in late spring and again in late summer; however, because of their tolerance of poor soils, it's not really necessary to feed them.

Pruning

Pruning heavily will stop your pistachio from bearing, as the side branches from the previous year's growth are the fertile ones. If necessary, trim lightly after a heavy crop.

Harvesting

Pistachios should begin cropping in about five years, but it may take more than seven years before your tree is producing a significant crop. Also, bear in mind that they are biennial bearers, so you'll only get a good crop every other year. Shake the tree to make the nuts fall in autumn when they are ripe.

Odd nuts, saps and resins

Some edible parts of plants are more unusual than others. For example, the leaf of the sugar maple (*Acer saccharum*), the source of maple syrup, is the national symbol of Canada. And there are other, less known, but just as interesting nuts, berries and saps from various parts of the world that are used for culinary purposes.

Candle nut

Candle nuts (*Aleurites moluccana*), also known as kemiri kernels, are ground and used in Asian, especially Indonesian, curries as a thickening agent with a rich, nutty flavour. The nut has to be cooked first to remove a mild toxin that is only present in its raw state (this can cause stomach cramps and vomiting). Then it's usually roasted lightly in a pan before being shaved or cut into slivers. The oil levels are so high that the nut can burn easily; in fact, it was used by early Australian settlers as an oil substitute.

Mastic

Mastic 'tears' are the dried sap of a small Mediterranean tree that is closely related to the pistachio and cashew. Sometimes called masticha or mistki, *Pistachia lentiscus* grows to about 3.5 m (11½ ft) and has aromatic, leathery, dark green leaflets and small white flowers in spring, followed by black fruit. The dried sap is pounded, then added to bread, biscuits, ice cream, Turkish delight and other desserts.

Sumac

In the same family is sumac (*Rhus* sp.), known for the dried berries of some species which are ground to produce a tangy purple spice, often used on top of semi-dried tomatoes. Sumac (pictured) is popular in Middle Eastern cuisines and also in 'Indian Lemonade', which is made by soaking the berries in cool water, rubbing them to extract the essence, straining the liquid through a cotton cloth and sweetening it. Famous for their spectacular autumn colours, many of these trees also have foliage that can cause severe allergies, so be careful around *Rhus* trees if you think you'll be affected.

Warm-climate nuts

Peanuts and some nut trees, such as cashews and brazil nuts, can only be grown in warm and tropical climates. Although peanuts are in fact, legumes, with a papery shell over their underground nodules, we still call them nuts.

Cashews

These sweet, crescent-shaped nuts (*Anacardium occidentale*) are very popular, especially in the tropics, where they are often used in cooking. Their favourite climate is actually a monsoonal one with both a wet and a dry season, as they can develop fungal problems if they don't experience this dry period. Cashews are also very hardy to wind and salt spray.

What is particularly interesting about cashews is that the flesh surrounding the nut contains a toxic resin and must be handled with care. The stems are also edible, and often used as a sweet drink in India, where most commercial quantities of cashews are grown.

Also closely related is the oriental cashew (*Semecarpus anacardium*), known as bhallatak in India, its native habitat. It's a deciduous tree that's found in the outer Himalayas. The nut is smooth, lustrous and black, about 2.5 cm (1 in) long and oval-shaped. Another 'cashew' is the tropical cashew nut or shaving brush tree (*Pachira aquatica*), native to Mexico, which is roasted like chestnuts. Also known as saba nut, it has glossy mid-green leaves, shaped a bit like a hand, and tassel-like flowers — hence its other common name, shaving brush tree.

Brazil nuts

Brazil nuts (*Bertholletia excelsa*) are not really a garden plant, even if you happen to live in Brazil. They are simply too tall, reaching 30 m (98 ft) in height, and requiring pollination by an insect that lives in an epiphytic orchid growing in its branches. For this reason, world supplies are mostly harvested direct from the wild and, strangely, this mainly occurs in Bolivia, not Brazil, although Brazil is the second highest exporter of the nuts.

A deciduous tree that loses its leaves in the dry season, the brazil nut is the only species in the genus, although it's interesting to note that it's a distant relative of the magnolia.

Peanuts

Also native to Brazil, Peru and Bolivia is the legumous plant known as the peanut or groundnut (*Arachis hypogaea*), which was grown by the Incas. The pea plant has an extraordinary habit: it flowers, then plunges its seed head into the ground, where the pod develops a thin shell. It's later dug up and eaten as the nut we love to eat.

Peanuts can grow in any warm climate and, being an annual, can even stand some cool weather, as long as the growing season is long enough for flowering to occur. Dig up the nuts once the foliage yellows. You can use unroasted, fresh peanuts from the health food shop as a seed source. Sow them into well cultivated soil, mounded up into a small hillock.

Opposite, clockwise from top left: Cashews, brazil nuts and peanuts.

did you know? In Ayurvedic medicine, the fruit of the oriental cashew or bhallatak is considered a rasayana or 'essence' for longevity and rejuvenation. Recent studies have shown the fruit to be a good anti-inflammatory agent as well as effective in the treatment of arthritis and possibly various types of cancers.

Macadamias

Rich in oil, macadamia nuts have a smooth, creamy texture that has made them popular all over the world. The oil is used in cooking, and the nuts in both savoury and sweet dishes, or they are simply eaten fresh. The two main species of macadamia are *Macadamia tetraphylla* (rough-shelled) and *M. integrifolia* (smooth-shelled), but there are lots of hybrids and cultivars, including a pink-flowering type that is ornamental as well as productive.

Cultivating macadamias

The tree itself is native to the Australian rainforest, where it grows naturally in subtropical areas. In cultivation it should be grown in similar conditions — with regular rainfall; organically rich, well drained and friable soils; shelter from winds; and protection from frosts and hot sun. Macadamia trees vary in size and shape, depending on the cultivar, but they are all self-fertile, although how much and how often they bear varies; some are biennial.

The best cultivars for the home gardener are A16, as it has dwarfing tendencies that make it suitable for a small backyard; A268, as it copes with cooler areas well; and TMAC 1 (pink-flowered) and TMAC 2 (white-flowered), because they hold their crop well and have thick shells, making them rat- and possum-proof.

Before planting a macadamia, enrich the soil with organic matter and check that the pH is not too acid. If it is, adjust it with some dolomite, which will also add magnesium. Mulch the soil well to keep the roots cool and help keep weeds at bay.

Below: Macadamia trees are long-lived, and may bear nuts for more than 100 years.

Below right: The flower, produced on a long raceme, makes the macadamia a popular ornamental tree.

Feeding

Macadamias do best when fed regularly throughout the year. Start in spring with a dose of low-phosphorus fertiliser, and add light applications every couple of months throughout the warm weather. Mulching with organic matter is also beneficial.

Pruning

Macadamias shouldn't be pruned, as it will delay their nut production. Remember this before planting a tree in your garden, as plants will grow to 15 m (49 ft) tall. The exceptions to this rule are if the tree is still very young — say, under two years — and if the branches are coming off at too sharp an angle, causing the bark to wrinkle in the junctions, which can possibly develop into a cleft and cause the crotch to later split.

The other exception is to lift the crown once the tree is about 3 to 4 years old to encourage a clean, single trunk that will be less likely to split.

Harvesting

Macadamia nuts fall from the tree when they are ripe, so this is the easiest way to ensure you haven't picked them too early. They produce nuts after 3 to 4 years, but they are really difficult to remove from their husks, as the protective coat is very hard. You can buy special macadamia nut crackers, or use a hammer. Unless you're growing a thick-shelled variety such as TMAC 2, possums (in Australia) and rats can be a problem. Once dehusked, they can be stored in the shade for up to six months, often becoming sweeter during that time.

Problems

- Although, in Australia, native pests are a problem in commercial orchards, these don't seem to be a problem for isolated backyard trees.

Harvesting macadamias

Keeping the grass cut around your trees or mulching heavily will mean you won't waste time looking for the nuts. If you have more than a few trees, it may be worth investing in a roller. Otherwise, it's easy to do by hand, so simply give the children a basket.

1 Commercial growers use a small harvesting roller, the size of a lawn mower, which picks up the nuts.

2 The nuts are picked up by the harvester's bristles.

3 Use a special macadamia nut cracker to remove the husk.

4 Inside the husk is a delicious, crunchy nut.

- Macadamias are really susceptible to phytophera, so make sure you improve any poor drainage.
- Never use fertiliser that's high in phosphates: as macadamias are members of the Proteaceae family, their sensitive roots can easily burn off.

Right: Juniper berries are used as a spice in dishes such as gravlax.

Below right: Pine nuts, one of the traditional ingredients of baklava.

Conifers that 'fruit'

By definition, of course, conifers don't fruit; rather, they bear cones and have scale or 'needle' leaves, and the 'nut' is simply the seed within the cone. However, there are some that have long been used as food.

Juniper berry

Berries from *Juniperus communis* are used to flavour one of the most popular alcoholic beverages — gin. Traditionally, juniper berries also flavour game such as venison as well as aspic jellies. The tree has a few different forms; any will do for the berries, as only the height and size of the plant differs, with some growing horizontally and others reaching 8 m (26 ft) tall. Just make sure you plant a female.

Cultivating juniper berries

The plants themselves require some patience: they are slow to grow, and it

African walnuts

Schotia brachypetala is an African plant in the pea family that bears pods containing edible seeds. Also known as bean tree and tree fuchsia, it has a lovely habit, bears crimson flowers and is an ideal size for the home garden, reaching only 4.5 to 8 m (15 to 26 ft) in height.

African walnuts are extremely hardy, growing in semi-desert conditions and the subtropical woodland areas of Zimbabwe, Mozambique and South Africa.

takes three years for the berries to go from flower to blue berry then, finally, black. This is an advantage when it comes to container growing, as they last for decades without outgrowing their tubs, and look quite elegant as potted specimens. They don't attract many pests either, but can occasionally suffer from rust, which should be removed as soon as possible. Trim them if necessary, but be careful not to cut back into old woody growth, as they are unlikely to regrow from this.

Pine nuts

The other most commonly consumed conifer seed is the pine nut (*Pinus pinea*), also known as stone pine. Its sweet kernel is fabulous when toasted in a dry pan, then added to salads and pasta dishes.

Chilean hazelnut

Also known as avellano or Chile nut, the Chilean hazelnut (*Gevuina avellana*) is related to macadamias and grows into a similarly sized 12-m (39-ft) tall evergreen tree. The shiny divided leaves, which have serrated margins, emerge from buds covered in reddish purple felt. The coral-red fruit contains a hazel-tasting kernel. In summer, the white grevillea-like flowers smother the bush. Like many members of this family, the Chilean hazelnut needs very good drainage, otherwise it can succumb to phytophora root rot.

The bunya nut pine (*Araucaria bidwillii*), a close relative of the Norfolk Island pine (*Araucaria heterophylla*), was very popular in Australia in late colonial and early Victorian days, when it was often planted to highlight a property's location — its enormous height made it visible from great distances.

Once every four years it produces huge cones, which fall to the ground, split open and disgorge their sweet kernels. Many of these trees are now more than 100 years old, towering over country estates like huge sentinels. Their sharp foliage is cattle-proof, so on country properties the trees need no guard, which is an added bonus. They grow in full sun and part shade, but prefer a sheltered, frost-free position in free-draining soil.

Illawarra plum

Another Australian native is the Illawarra plum (*Podocarpus elatus*), which of course is not a plum but a berried drupe (where

Left: The cone-like fruit of the burrawang (*Macrozamia communis*), an ancient palm-like plant that's a member of the Cycad family. In evolutionary terms, it's an ancestor of flowering plants, such as palms, not a conifer. The raw seeds are poisonous, so they must be treated — the Aboriginals pounded the seeds, then soaked them in water for a week before cooking them.

the pit or stone is surrounded by flesh, as in the mango). Native to the east coast of Australia, it grows best in full sun or part shade and has beautiful deep green leaves. If you don't have room for a tree that is 15 m (49 ft) when it's fully grown, you can easily trim it; in fact, the Illawarra plum lends itself to bonsai, hedging and topiary.

Far left: The cone of the bunya nut pine, which can weigh up to 10 kg (22 lb), produces edible kernels that can be eaten fresh or cooked, or ground to make flour.

Left: The thorny foliage of the bunya nut pine.

Edible palms

Many palms and their close botanical relations have edible parts so, depending on your climate, you could consider growing some more unusual fruit.

Dates

Of course, the best known of all is the date palm (*Phoenix dactylifera*), which has been cultivated for at least 8000 years, leaving its place of origin a bit unclear, although North Africa and the Middle East seem likely candidates. It is known, however, that the Arabs introduced dates to South-East Asia and southern Europe.

The date palm is not the easiest plant for the home garden, as you'll need to grow both a male and a female plant in order to have date fruit, and both trees will grow to about 25 m (82 ft). But if you're still keen, consider that date palms take anywhere from 4 to 7 years to start bearing fruit, but once they do, they produce up to 120 kg (265 lb) of dates that ripen over a fairly long period, so you'll have to get out the ladders a few times to harvest them. Birds can also be a problem, and you may need to protect the developing dates by bagging them.

Coconut

Another palm whose origin is unclear is the coconut (*Cocos nucifera*). It too has been cultivated in the Pacific Islands, Asia and the Subcontinent for so long that its native habitat is much debated. The tree itself is self-fertile and copes with incredibly harsh

Below: If you store fresh dates in a sealed container in the fridge, they should keep for up to a year.

Below right: Eating coconut fresh from the shell requires some perseverance, as you have to remove the meat from the hard shell or endocarp.

conditions on poor, salty, sandy soils and in blazing sun and wind. It needs high humidity, however, for fruit to form, while frosts will usually result in the death of the plant. The seed, or nut as it is known, contains edible flesh as well as water, and the husk is made up of coir, sometimes used instead of sphagnum or peat moss.

Other palm fruit

Also from the tropical Pacific region is the betel palm (*Areca catechu*), which bears yellow to orange-red fruit up to 8 cm (3 in) long. Known as betel nut, this fruit is chewed throughout India and Papua New Guinea, where it grows naturally in rainforest areas.

The assai palm (*Euterpe oleracea*), from the tropical Amazon, produces edible berries that contain a large single seed. It has a very dark purple, almost black skin, with a little dark purple juice with a rich chocolate flavour. The Amazonians turned it into a wine called *acai*, but nowadays it is sometimes sold as a 'rich man's' health drink, as it has such high levels of antioxidants; in fact, it may be the most nutritious fruit of all.

This 10-m (33-ft) tree is also the main source of palm hearts for the canning industry, although many say the palmito (*E. edulis*) bears sweeter ones.

Other unusual edible palms can be found in the Pandanus and Cycad families; many produce cones that can be eaten after various treatments, such as being soaked in water and roasted. Others, such as the common screw pine (*Pandanus utilis*), can be eaten when the fruit are ripe.

Sago palm is actually two different plants that share the same common name. The first is a palm (*Metroxylon sagu*) from

did you know? The date palm is a very useful plant. Its seeds are burnt to make charcoal for silversmiths, and are also used as a coffee substitute. Fruit clusters are stripped and used as brooms, and palm leaves are used for everything from basket-weaving to thatching roofs.

Above: Canned palm hearts are usually available in supermarkets.

the Pacific Islands. Growing naturally in swampy areas, its fibrous stems are harvested for tapioca, or sago, made by scraping the inside, making a paste with water, putting it through a sieve and then drying the remainder into a flour, from which desserts and flat breads are made.

The other sago is actually a cycad (*Cycas cicinalia* and *C. revoluta*), not a true palm at all. Many cycads are used for food, but they also contain some very strong toxins, so they need to be processed in just the right way to make them edible. The seeds and pith from the trunks are then made into flour, which can be used for flat breads.

Wild food

Gathering and tasting wild food isn't a simple matter of picking and eating fruit off the tree or bush: to be palatable or even safe to eat, some of these foods need to undergo some form of processing, so exercise caution when collecting them. In Australia wild food is regarded as a gourmet ingredient and is exported all over the world.

Pioneering days

In 1861, three famous Australian explorers — Burke, Wills and King — tried to eat a water plant known as nardoo (*Marsilea drummondii*), which the Aboriginals traditionally grind into flour. But they didn't realise it had to be soaked to remove a poison; eventually, both Burke and Wills died on the banks of Coopers Creek in June 1861 from a combination of starvation, exhaustion and poison. King, on the other hand, lived with the Aboriginals, who showed him how to live off the land. He was rescued three months later.

There have been more successful moments in Australia's history, however, such as when Captain James Cook landed on the shores of Botany Bay in New South Wales and ordered his crew to search for edible greens that could protect them from scurvy. They found warrigal greens (*Tetragonia tetragonoides*) — still one of the more popular wild foods, although it must be cooked first in boiling water to remove oxalic acid. Then it's either eaten hot, or plunged into cold water to be then eaten as a salad vegetable.

Left: The foliage of Davidson plum (*Davidsonia pruriens*).

Throughout the eighteenth and nineteenth centuries, Europeans settling in Australia experimented with various other greens, using them as spices, and also tried using wild fruit to make sauces and jams. Considering these early culinary trials, it's extraordinary that, of all the thousands of species of plants in Australia, only one native plant has really rocketed to popularity around the world as an edible crop, and that's the macadamia nut (see page 217).

Modern trends

Since the late twentieth century, attitudes have gradually changed, and there is now a definite trend towards using wild food ingredients in mainstream cooking, particularly in innovative restaurants frequented by tourists. Native plants such as finger limes (*Microcitrus* sp.) and quandongs, also known as native peach (*Santalum acuminatum*), are now farmed

for their fruit, and lemon myrtle and other plants are grown for their essential oils.

Many of us unwittingly grow wild food in our gardens, unaware that it is edible. For example, the *Backhousia* species have scented leaves that can be used for flavouring. Lemon myrtle (*B. citriodora*) is more intense than lemon grass and can be used as its substitute in marinades or as a skewer for seafood. Also worth trying are

Above left: The blue quandong (*Elaeocarpus angustifolius*) bears fruit that tastes a bit like olives.

Above: Native peach or sweet quandong (*Santalum acuminatum*).

Bush limes

Although most of the limes known as bush limes belong to the genus *Microcitrus*, from the coastal areas of Australia, there is a different genus, *Eremocitrus*, which is also called native kumquat. It's from dry inland areas and has glaucous blue foliage.

1 Native guava 2 Bunya nut cone 3 Various lilly pillies, including
riberry (*Syzygium luehmannii*), *S. formosa, S. australe, S. francisii*
4 Native freeze-dried pepperberries 5 Wombat berry vine
6 Native bush tomato 7 Cycad nuts 8 Crosier of tree fern

wild food

9 Lemon myrtle **10** Finger limes **11** Native blueberries **12** *Dendrobium speciosum* **13** Blue quandong berries **14** Sandpaper fig **15** Aniseed myrtle **16** Wattle seed **17** Lemon-scented tea tree **18** Midgen berries **19** Warrigal greens, nardoo and ferny azola **20** *Lomandra* sp.

The bush tomato is related to the usual garden tomato, both being members of the Solanum family. It is a fast-growing shrub that fruits prolifically the year after fire or good rains. The tiny tomatoes are collected dry off the plant, mostly by the women in traditional Aboriginal families, then ground up before being laid out to dry yet again.

aniseed myrtle (*Backhousia anisata*), cut leaf mint bush (*Prostanthera incisa*) and Dorrigo pepper (*Tasmannia insipida*), which are all usually dried before they're used.

Since the turn of the century, various lilly pillies have been very popular as ornamental screening trees and hedging plants. Many fruit beautifully each year, providing bats and birds with some fruit, but often just spoiling on the ground. But these berries can be made into delicious sauces, jams or jellies. Midgen or midyim berry (*Austromyrtus dulcis*) is another small shrub suitable for hedging or a pretty border that also happens to produce lovely speckled berries, a bit like tiny eggshells.

The Davidson plum (*Davidsonia pruriens*) is an ideal tree for home gardens, growing to only 4 to 6 m (13 to 20 ft) with a straight, upright habit — perfect for small backyards. The fruit is formed directly off the trunk, making it easy to pick, and it's so sour that possums won't eat it.

Another unique flavour comes from the intensely flavoured bush tomato (*Solanum centrale*), which dries easily. Wrapping fish, such as salmon, in paperbark (*Melaleuca* sp.) instead of foil and then baking it is a delicious way of adding flavour and keeping the fish moist. Wattle seeds (*Acacia victoriae*) have a hazelnut/mocha coffee taste that is delicious in baked goods, custards and ice cream. It's also very good for you, having a very low glycaemic index. And the seed head of *Lomandra* sp. contains a kernel that's ground for damper bread.

Top: Lemon myrtle (*Backhousia citriodora*), the 'Queen of the lemon herbs'.

Far left: Midgen berry (*Austromyrtus dulcis*).

Left: The seed heed of *Lomandra* sp.

Opposite: Warrigal greens.

Wholesome freshness.

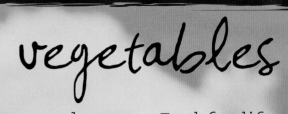

vegetables

Nourishing yield.   Crisp, earthy goodness.   Fuel for life.

Contents

good health

Growing organic vegetables in your own garden is a very satisfying way to supply your family with a wide variety of delicious produce. Recent studies have shown that eating at least five serves of vegetables a day reduces the risk of developing serious health problems, such as diabetes and heart disease. And we also know that digging and weeding in the garden burns energy and releases stress and tension — another health benefit of growing your own.

There are many other advantages too. Starting your own vegetable patch means you can be a lot more adventurous with the range of vegetables you eat, as you can grow unusual cultivars as well as heirloom varieties. Once you have tasted a fragrant, sun-ripened, organically grown heirloom tomato, you'll never buy supermarket tomatoes again. And you can pick homegrown vegetables straight from the garden and eat them within minutes. With tomatoes, for instance, this means that their sugar content is naturally higher, as sugar starts to be converted into starch the longer it is stored.

Similarly, the flavours of freshly picked asparagus and 'Sugar Snap' peas, or carrots, beetroot and potatoes that have just been dug up are all a joy.

So try delving into the world of vegetables. They are just as colourful and interesting as fruit.

Leafy greens

There's a wonderfully wide range of leafy greens available, and eating these vegetables provides you with antioxidants, vitamins and minerals such as magnesium. Leafy greens such as spinach and cabbage, which are high in fibre, are two of the many plant sources of zinc.

Growing a year-round supply

One of the tricks to having a year-round supply of leafy greens is to understand their life cycles and also their seasonality. Some greens are spring, summer, autumn or winter vegetables, depending on the variety and also the time of sowing. Others are perennial, perpetual or very long season — such as beet greens and chard — and so grow over at least one season.

The most heat-tolerant of all greens is probably purslane (see page 398), which has succulent foliage that copes with extreme temperatures. Other greens — amaranth, Egyptian spinach, warrigal greens and many Asian vegetables as well as certain cultivars of lettuce — also cope well with hot weather. (It's worth noting that so much breeding has gone into lettuces over the centuries that there are types suitable for all seasons and almost all climates.)

Of the cold-tolerant greens, you can choose from many cultivars of lettuce as well as radicchio, endive, kale, spinach,

Above: Butter lettuce, a hearting lettuce.

Left: Harvesting Asian vegetables, including purple-leafed shiso or purple perilla.

chicory and rocket, even dandelions. And many Asian greens, such as mizuna and mustard, are cold-tolerant too.

Naturally, using cloches will extend your greens' adaptability to both climatic extremes, as the shade will protect them from the sun in summer and keep the frost at bay in winter. But whatever vegetables you grow, sowing every four weeks into a bed with added manure will spread the harvest and result in a continuous healthy supply for your dinner table.

Lettuces

The best known salad vegetable is probably lettuce (*Lactuca sativa*), of which there are dozens of different cultivars. A member of the daisy family, Asteraceae, it is just one of about 75 species, some of which are weeds. The wild lettuce originated in the Mediterranean, with the 'Cos' lettuce supposedly harking from the Greek island of Cos.

There are a couple of ways to classify lettuce. One is to categorise them as

crisphead, butter types, 'Cos' ('Romaine') or leaf, but each cultivar has a slightly different colour or hearting quality, so they can be separated into hearting and non-hearting, or continuous picking types.

Hearting lettuces

The most popular of all hearting lettuces is undoubtedly the 'Iceberg', which was bred in the United States in the 1930s to travel well from garden to store. Its dark green outer leaves protect its crisp white heart.

Above left: Radicchio, a red-leafed chicory, is rather bitter but a pretty addition to salads and pizza toppings.

Above: Silver beet is best eaten straightaway, as it doesn't store well.

Below left: Popular 'Iceberg', a crisp but mild-tasting lettuce.

tip

Spread your harvest times by planting a variety of lettuces with different maturing times.

Other hearting lettuces commonly grown include the 'Lake' strains, such as 'Great Lakes' and 'Pennlake', which are resistant to hot weather and can be sown in summer; the large-headed 'Greenway', which has been specially bred for warm summer climates; mignonettes, which have either red or green cultivars; and butter lettuces, which have a slightly waxy feeling and soft hearts. Butter types include varieties such as 'Buttercrunch' (good in warm climates) and 'Cos' types, including the semi-'Cos' lettuce, 'Romany'.

Non-hearting lettuces

Non-hearting lettuces or 'loose leafs' include the 'Oak Leaf' types, which have a wavy leaf margin very similar to that of an oak leaf, and come in red and green cultivars. Of these, 'Coral' has an extremely frilly margin, and 'Salad Bowl', popular in the United States, is fairly heat-resistant.

Other types of lettuce include celtuce (*L. sativa* var. *augustana*), which grows on a tall stem that can be used like celery once you have finished picking the foliage. Sometimes known as asparagus lettuce or even Chinese lettuce (syn. *L. sativa asparagensis* and *L. angustata*), or stem lettuce, they are all actually the same plant. Alfacinha (*Lactuca watsoniana*) from the Canary Islands, however, is a totally different species. Larger than most species, it grows to about 30 to 60 cm (1 to 2 ft) in diameter, with mid-green foliage featuring prominent veins.

Cultivating lettuces

Lettuce seeds are generally sown in spring to summer in cool and cold climates, while in warmer climates they can be sown from autumn to spring. You can extend their season by providing partial shade in summer in warmer climates, and winter protection with cloches in cold climates. They enjoy well drained but moist, rich soil with a neutral or slightly acid pH in a sunny position.

You can easily raise lettuce seeds in germination kits. Simply sow seeds into seed-raising mix, then top it with vermiculite, but don't sow any deeper

Above right: Germinating lettuce seedlings. Keep them moist but, if you overwater them, they'll develop fungal problems.

Below, from left to right: 'Cos', 'Mignonette', 'Red Coral' and 'Green Oak'.

Opposite, clockwise from top left: A 'Cos' lettuce called 'Red Romaine'; red and green 'Coral' varieties; a young 'Iceberg' lettuce; and Chinese lettuce.

than 1 cm ($^1/_2$ in) or germination will be unlikely to occur. The vermiculite helps keep the surface area from drying out and saves the germinating seedlings from suffering any water stress, significantly increasing germination rates. When the seedlings all bear their true leaves, transplant them into the garden or pots.

Feeding

Always grow leafy greens quickly so they keep their fresh flavour: slow-growing, poorly fed lettuce may be coarse and even taste bitter. Side-dress your lettuce plants with complete plant food, or use liquid feed every couple of weeks, but make sure you wash your plants down afterwards so fertiliser burns or marks aren't left on their delicate foliage. Alternatively, dig in poultry manure a few weeks before planting.

Harvesting

To harvest hearting lettuces, cut them at the base with a sharp knife in the cool of the morning, or pull the whole plant out, removing the roots. Harvest non-hearting lettuces by taking several leaves at a time.

Problems

Lettuce can be attacked by leaf miners, which is the grub stage of a fly. After laying eggs on the leaves, the leaf miner will tunnel into the leaf itself. Pest oil, a form of white oil, is quite useful in deterring the fly from laying eggs in the first place, so apply this in late spring and early summer when this bug is most prevalent.

Other problems to watch out for include the following.
- Anthracnose: page 66.
- Downy mildew: page 66.
- Earth mites: page 56.
- Rutherglen bug: page 52.

Spinach

Iron-rich spinach was celebrated by the American cartoon character Popeye, who used to tip a can into his mouth every time he needed some 'superhuman' strength.

English spinach (*Spinacia oleracea*), the most commonly used 'spinach', has arrow-shaped foliage and grows to about 25 cm (10 in). There are also summer cultivars, which have round seeds, not prickly ones,

Forming a heart

To help hearting lettuces form a heart, tie the tops together with raffia.

1 This 'Cos' needs some assistance to form a heart, and also to stop the outer leaves from splaying outwards.

2 Gently gather the leaves together with one hand and tie a length of raffia around the leaves with the other.

Far left: Harvesting 'cut and come again' lettuce leaves.

Left: A lettuce plant in flower, about to go to seed.

Below: English spinach.

like those on the winter varieties. These include 'Forkhook' and 'King of Denmark', which cope with warmer weather, but tend to bolt if they dry out. 'Medania' is a modern variety with rounded leaves and excellent flavour that is also slow to bolt.

Cultivating spinach

Spinach prefers damp, rich but well drained soil. Protect seedlings with a cloche if you live in an area that's prone to frost, and sow every three weeks for continuous cropping.

Sow spinach seeds about 1 cm (1/2 in) deep in rows spaced 30 cm (1 ft) apart in autumn and winter. As the seedlings germinate, take out (and eat) them as baby leaves until you restore the original spacings of about 30 cm (1 ft). Plant summer spinach in a shady position to help it stay moist, or between rows of taller plants such as beans and corn.

Harvesting

When eaten young, spinach is very tender and can be eaten fresh or lightly steamed. After about 8 to 10 weeks, when the leaves mature, pick the largest leaves first, being careful not to pull them, or you'll dislodge the whole plant. Instead, cut up to half the leaves on each plant at a time.

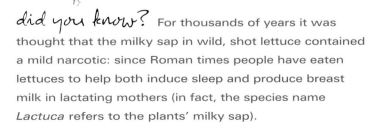

did you know? For thousands of years it was thought that the milky sap in wild, shot lettuce contained a mild narcotic: since Roman times people have eaten lettuces to help both induce sleep and produce breast milk in lactating mothers (in fact, the species name *Lactuca* refers to the plants' milky sap).

Other types of 'spinach'

Depending on where you live, you may be a little confused about the naming of spinach varieties. For example, generations of Australian children grew up calling silver beet spinach, but it's actually a different species altogether.

Silver beet

Spinach beet or silver beet (*Beta vulgaris* var. *cicla*) is another really useful, long-lasting crop. It has crinkly, dark green leaves and a white mid-rib that can be cooked in a similar way to celery or asparagus. Also known as seakale beet and Swiss chard, it is a relative of beetroot, but rather than develop swollen roots, it bears leaves with white stalks to 60 cm (2 ft).

There are also rainbow-coloured versions that have gold, red or green stalks, giving a vegetable patch a bejewelled look. Plant seedlings in mid- to late spring about 30 cm (1 ft) apart, and harvest continuously from the outer leaves so there is always new growth. The seeds themselves have a distinctive, angular shape and can be sown from autumn to spring.

Ceylon spinach

Alternatively, try Ceylon or Malabar spinach (*Basella alba*), a summer climbing or trailing 'spinach' to 1.5 m (5 ft). Its thick, glossy green leaves have a similar taste to silver beet, and can be used in salads and cooked dishes. Sow Ceylon spinach in both spring and summer.

Egyptian spinach

Another unusual plant used as a substitute for spinach is Egyptian spinach or West African sorrel (*Corchorus olitorius*). It's a very hardy, fast-growing annual to 1 m (3 ft), and is used in the same way as sorrel, with young foliage being eaten as a salad green, while the older tips and leaves are cooked like spinach. It's reputed to be high in protein and very suitable for subtropical and tropical areas. You'll need to watch it, however, as it self-sows readily. Plant seeds in spring and summer.

Above right: The small leaves of Chinese spinach are tinged with red.

Right: Before using silver beet, check that the leaves are firm and the stems crisp.

Opposite, clockwise from top left: Harvesting yellow-stemmed chard; silver beet; amaranth flowers; and Swiss chard.

did you know? The name 'amaranth' comes from the Greek word *amaranth*, meaning 'to not fade', referring to the colourful tassels that last well after the plant itself has faded.

Amaranth

Amaranth (*Amaranthus gangeticus*), or Chinese or Indian spinach, is a suitable annual for warm climates. It grows to 1.5 m (5 ft), and both the leaves and stems are used. A striking plant to grow, 'Princes Feather' or red amaranth (*A. cruentus*) has red tassels, red seeds and purplish red leaves, and can be used as a leaf vegetable.

Like the other leafy greens, amaranths are high in protein, vitamins and minerals. Sow seed in spring or early summer, and harvest through late summer and autumn.

New Zealand spinach

Another option is New Zealand spinach (*Tetragonia tetragonoides*), which is native to New Zealand and Australia, where the Aboriginals call it warrigal greens (see also page 222).

It is a low-spreading vegetable that grows to about 1 m (3 ft) in diameter over a very long growing season, continuing even into dry summers. You can encourage it to branch with regular picking.

Cultivating spinach look-alikes

To grow these nutritious greens well, dig manure through a light soil a month before planting. Sow seeds 2 cm (¾ in) deep in spring, either direct into rows spaced 50 cm (20 in) apart or, if conditions are frosty, into seed-raising mix, to be planted out once frosts have finished.

Once these greens are established, encourage fresh growth with a side dressing of complete plant food.

The leaves are best eaten lightly cooked, but only use the new growth, as the older leaves can become tough.

Bitter greens

Chicory, radicchio, escarole and endive are actually all members of the same genus, *Cichorium*, but represent different species, each with its own unique flavour. Collectively, they are known for their cold tolerance, making them all excellent winter crops.

Chicory

Chicory (*Cichorium intybus*) is a very hardy biannual with a white taproot that is sometimes dried and roasted as a coffee substitute. Very popular for this purpose in the eighteenth century, it is now available in health food shops. The slightly bitter green leaves can be used in salads, typically served with citrus fruit.

A popular cultivar for salads is 'Catalogna', while another beautiful form with red ribs is known as 'Red-ribbed Catalogna' or 'Red Dandelion'. Its deeply cut, frilly deep green leaves are streaked with red and, once cooked, it's one of the few leafy vegetables that retains the crimson colour; however, it becomes very bitter if harvested too late.

Chicory leaves are commonly baked, stir-fried or poached, especially in the case of the most widely grown cultivar, 'Whitloof'. Sometimes known as witlof, which means 'white leaf', this chicory is generally grown for what are known as 'chicons' — the creamy white-hearted centres, similar in appearance to miniature

'White gold'

According to one theory, the technique for growing white chicory leaves was accidentally discovered in the 1830s by a Belgian farmer named Jan Lammers. The story goes that, while he was away at war, he stored his chicory roots in his cellar. Upon his return, he found that they had shot in the damp environment, but had pale white and cream leaves that tasted quite sweet and crisp. Another theory credits M. Brezier, the head of the Brussels Botanical Gardens, with developing this discovery during the same period, before releasing this new vegetable in Paris. Such was its popularity in the markets of Europe that it was called 'white gold'.

Chinese cabbages, which are achieved when the plant is grown in darkness.

You can raise chicons by blanching and forcing shoots over winter — whether you're growing them indoors or out, simply place an upturned pot over the new shoots. This treatment removes some of the bitterness, and the paler the chicon, the sweeter it will be. Serve them fresh in winter salads, or lightly braise them.

To force chicons, lift the roots, trim the leaves, plant in pots or light garden soil, cover with pots and, when they are about 15 cm (6 in) high, harvest them with a knife at ground level. As they reshoot, you can cover them again to produce a second crop.

Although chicory can be sown year round, it can run to seed in summer if not cooled with some shade; also, cool weather helps remove some of the bitterness from the leaves. Ideally, sow plants in late summer and autumn into well manured, rich soil that drains freely. The leaves should be ready to harvest about 10 to 12 weeks later, but will last well over winter. In areas that are severely affected by frost, cover the plants.

Harvest by cutting just above soil level so they will reshoot and give you further crops — that's why they are sometimes called 'cut and come again'.

Radicchio

Red-leafed chicory or radicchio is a variety of wild chicory that looks a lot like a red cabbage, with a rotund shape and deep red wine-coloured leaves. It's frequently used in Mediterranean cuisine, even as a pizza topping after it's been cooked with leeks in oil. However, radicchio is mostly used in salads as both a flavour (the leaves are bitter) and colour contrast to green leaves. Once cooked, the leaves lose their colour and revert back to green.

Left: To store chicory, wrap it in some paper towel, place it in a plastic bag and store it in the fridge, where it will keep for a day or so.

Endive

Endive (*Cichorium endivia*) and escarole or broad-leafed endive (*Cichorium endivia* 'Frisée') are mainly used in salads to give other greens a real bite. They both have serrated curly leaves, but endive is frizzier at the tips and shorter in growth than very cold-tolerant escarole, which has a slightly broader leaf and taller growth.

To use endive and escarole in salads, remove the leaves from the stalk. Rinse them carefully in cold water before wrapping them in a tea towel and popping them in a plastic bag. Then place the bag in the fridge to crisp up the leaves. You can also blanch the leaves with an upturned flowerpot, which takes about a week in warm weather or up to a month in winter.

Below left: Radicchio is sometimes called Italian chicory.

Below: Harvested endive.

Asian greens

Full of flavour and easy to grow, more and more Asian greens are becoming available in mainstream supermarkets. Plant them in your kitchen garden, or even dot the very pretty red mustard greens around the garden for some foliage contrast. They all like to be grown quickly, and enjoy fertile, rich soil that also needs to be limed if the pH is below 6.5.

Below: Choy sum.

Opposite, clockwise from top left: A mizuna flower; Asian greens, including perilla and water spinach; red mustard; and a collection of freshly harvested leafy greens.

Chinese mustard greens

Kai tsoi, known in English as Chinese mustard greens or Chinese celery (*Brassica juncea*), is an annual native to China, where it has long been grown for both its leaves and its seed. This plant grows to 60 cm (2 ft) with large, slightly puckered, spicy leaves that have a wide, prominent mid-rib. The young foliage can be eaten fresh in salads, while old leaves are cooked in stir-fries or fried with onion and garlic and used as a side dish.

did you know? Chinese celery is closely related to wild celery, or smallage, and has a stronger taste than European celery. Looking more like a herb than a vegetable, it is reminiscent of parsley in both taste and appearance. In China, where it is a popular ingredient in soups, stews and stir-fries, the whole plant is used.

Chop suey

Chop suey (*Chrysanthemum coronarium*) — or shungiki, kikuna or tung hao — is a pretty annual that grows to 1.5 m (5 ft). The leaves are eaten raw or cooked while young, but if left to bolt, they produce very pretty yellow daisy flowers. Sow seeds at any time into a sunny, well drained position, and harvest two months later. Pinching out flower buds will help prolong the crop and induce more fresh foliage that's perfect for picking.

'Red Giant', a cultivar of red mustard (*B. juncea rugosa*), has red-purple leaves and a peppery flavour, while 'Osaka Purple' has a darker red edge. All lose their intense flavour when cooked, with the purple colour of the leaves reverting to dark green. Sow the seeds direct into the soil about 5 mm ($1/5$ in) deep and thinned to 20 cm (8 in) apart.

Wrapped heart mustard, which is also known as dai gai choy (*B. juncea* subsp. *integrifolia*), has 'Cos'-like leaves and a very strong flavour. It's one of the ingredients in kimchee, the Korean side dish of pickled vegetables.

Mizuna

Mizuna (*Brassica juncea* var. *japonica*) is a quick-growing Japanese salad plant with a mild mustard flavour. Sow it directly into the soil, about 5 mm ($1/5$ in) deep, at any time except during the hottest or coldest months, then thin the seedlings to 30 cm (1 ft) apart.

You can either pick and eat the young, raw leaves, or salt and pickle them.

Opposite: Harvesting Asian greens.

Far left: Bok choy.

Left: Tatsoi.

Below: Gai larn or Chinese broccoli.

Bok choy

Bok choy or pak choy (*Brassica rapa* var. *chinensis*) or Chinese celery cabbage, is compact and fast-growing, with spoon-shaped green leaves atop thick, succulent stalks. It forms a dense, loose clump, but there are also cultivars with shorter stems and a rosette form called tatsoi; a Japanese rosette form of bok choy is *B. rapa* var. *rosularis*. They can be used fresh or in stir-fries, or as a substitute for spinach. Sow seeds in situ in autumn to spring, and thin to about 20 cm (8 in) apart.

Chinese cabbage

Wong bok, pe-tsai or Chinese cabbage (*Brassica rapa* var. *pekinensis*), as it is known in English, is also sometimes called napa cabbage. It looks like a traditional cabbage, but has a more elongated, rugby ball-like shape, and is very adaptable and tolerant of semi-shade, with a good resistance to bolting. Chinese cabbage is very crunchy — fabulous for salad — and holds its shape well even when stir-fried. Like 'Cos' lettuce, it can sometimes fall open, so you may need to loosely tie some raffia around the head to help it form a heart (see page 236).

Chinese broccoli

Gai larn or Chinese broccoli (*Brassica oleracea* var. *alboglabra*) produces multiple mini heads, each about the size of a golf ball and crowned with yellow flowers. It has foliage right up the stem, and the whole plant can be eaten once it has been trimmed of any thick, woody stalks. Choy sum (*Brassica parachinensis*) is a more mellow version of the Italian favourite, rabe (see page 249).

did you know? In Cantonese, *bok choy* means 'white vegetable', which describes the white stems of Chinese celery cabbage.

asian vegetables

1 Bok choy **2** Mizuna (top) and coriander **3** Chinese cabbage **4** Vietnamese mint
5 Chinese lettuce **6** Tatsoi **7** White pak choy **8** Chop suey **9** Snow pea **10** Mustard
11 Young white onions **12** Spring onions **13** Garlic chives **14** Chinese broccoli

Brassicas

This family contains many of the vegetables we eat — root crops, greens and even seeds. Sometimes known as cruciferous vegetables because of the cross-shaped flowers they bear, brassicas have great cold tolerance, making them wonderful staples for winter meals.

Common brassicas

Cultivated for more than 3000 years, members of the Brassica family contain a wide range of antioxidants and phytochemicals (including carotenoids, vitamin C and indoles), which are said to keep cancer at bay. They also contain fibre and complex carbohydrates. Once you discover how many edible plants belong to this group, you'll realise the world could go hungry without them.

There are about 30 species in the biggest genus, *Brassica*, but within this there are many subgroups and cultivars. Broadly speaking, *B. juncea* contains the Asian mustard group, *B. nupus* contains swedes, *B. oleracea* is the cabbage and broccoli parent, and *B. rapa* contains many Chinese vegetables and turnips.

Two basic requirements for the Brassica family are limed soil, so that the pH is not acid, and adequate calcium. Grow these vegetables fast in cool weather to bring out their best flavour and prevent them from bolting, or going to seed.

Above: Broccolini, also known as green-sprouting broccoli.

Left: The edible part of cauliflower is actually a cluster of tiny florets.

Brassicas are so common that you can almost be forgiven for dismissing them, especially if your mother instructed you to 'Eat your broccoli' or 'Finish your cabbage' when you were a child. However, not only do brassicas feed millions of people in less than hospitable climates, but they are also easy to grow and store well.

Broccoli

It probably won't surprise you to learn that broccoli and cauliflower are closely related — after all, they look very similar — but did you know that before broccoli was green, it was purple? Known as purple-sprouting broccoli, it had small heads that were about the size of the individual florets of today's heads, with much longer shoots and a faint asparagus flavour.

Today, the green version of sprouting broccoli is quite common, and often goes by the name broccolini. All versions of broccoli (*Brassica oleracea* 'Italica') are rich in calcium, vitamins and minerals, and you can eat the stalks, leaves and heads.

Although the seeds can be planted all year round, the heads of broccoli will form best in cool weather. Cultivars include 'Albert', 'Green Sprouting', 'Purple Sprouting' and 'Calabrese'.

Very similar in appearance is the Sicilian broccoli or rabe (*Brassica rapa*), also known as broccoletto, rapini and raab. Some say it is the equivalent of rocket compared to an 'Iceberg' lettuce — in other

Above left: Store brussels sprouts in the vegetable crisper of the fridge. Their flavour intensifies the longer you keep them.

Above: Broccolini (left) and broccoli.

Below: A young head of broccoli developing.

words, while the head may not amount to much, the flavour is more intense, peppery and assertive. The leaves, stems and small florets are all eaten; usually parboiled first, they are then sautéed in butter and garlic and eaten as a side dish. Sicilian broccoli is high in potassium, folic acid and vitamins A, C and K.

After you have harvested the main head, further smaller heads, leaves and sprouts, all of which can be harvested and eaten, will continue to grow for some months.

Cauliflower

Cauliflower (*B. oleracea*, Botrytis Group) is actually the flower head in bud, and the part of the plant traditionally eaten. Unlike broccoli, cauliflower has one head per plant, so repeat harvesting is out of the question. Instead, stagger the planting times, planting out half a dozen plants every fortnight so that your crop matures at different times.

Cauliflowers also come in colours other than white: breeding has resulted in green-, purple- and orange-headed varieties that have become popular novelty vegetables.

Brussels sprouts

Bearing their tiny cabbage-like hearts on the stem, brussels sprouts (*B. oleracea*, Gemmifera Group) can also be harvested continually. This vegetable is the great divider, with people tending to either love or hate it vehemently; perhaps the latter group grew up eating frozen vegetables that had been boiled for hours. Try picking them fresh from the garden, then lightly stir-frying them with garlic and oil. There is also a purple variety called 'Ruby'.

Above: Brussels sprouts.

Opposite, clockwise from top left: Purple-headed Sicilian broccoli; young cauliflower before the head has formed; white-headed cauliflowers; and a broccoli flower.

Separating broccoli seedlings

Once your broccoli seeds have germinated, lift and separate them, making sure that each one is spaced correctly.

1 Carefully dig up a clump of seedlings with a sharp spade and separate them.

2 Dig a hole for each seedling and plant it, then mulch well with organic matter and water in.

Kale

Kale (*B. oleracea*, Acephala Group) is commonly sold as an ornamental cabbage, but there are also edible iron-rich kales favoured for their cold and salt tolerance. The most common variety, known as 'Tuscan Black', has beautiful, crinkly dark green foliage. Some people swear by kale as the ultimate vitamin pill, not only boiling the leaves and eating them but also drinking the liquid as a tonic.

Salad brassicas

These days you can buy interesting salad mixes or mesclun that might include different varieties of lettuce as well as greens such as baby spinach leaves and rocket. Very versatile, rocket can also be used in cooked dishes.

Rocket

Rocket (*Eruca sativa*), arugula, roquette or Italian cress has shot to popularity around the world from its Mediterranean homeland. Another member of the Brassica family, with the same characteristic four-petalled flowers, this slightly peppery green is delicious, especially when eaten young.

Sow rocket seeds into open ground in a sunny position, only just covering them with a few millimetres of earth, sand or vermiculite. Once germinated, which takes about two weeks, you can thin them out and eat some of the 'baby' leaves. They are really tender and delicious eaten this way, so sowing them successively every fortnight can keep up a good supply.

Leave the remaining seedlings to mature at about 30-cm (1-ft) intervals, but keep them growing rapidly so they stay full of flavour. Hardened, mature plants can be bitter and too strong-tasting, so regularly cut the plants back to the ground once they are full-sized, about

Left: A young 'Tuscan Black' kale plant.

Opposite, clockwise from top left: 'Tuscan Black' kale; 'Thousand Head' kale; harvesting rocket; and ornamental kale.

seven weeks from sowing. They will then regenerate with new shoots, and grow vigorously if you feed them with some liquid fertiliser.

Snails can be a problem, while hot summer weather can cause them to bolt to seed if they're not kept shaded, but otherwise they are trouble-free and not fussy about the soil.

Sand rocket

There is also a salad brassica from the Mediterranean called wild rocket (*Diplotaxis tenuifolia*), which has naturalised and become weedy in many areas of the world, including Australia, where it is called sand rocket, due to its ability to grow on very poor, sandy soils.

This plant can grow 'between a rock and a hard place' and is very adaptable. It's not recommended that you plant it, but you can gather new leaves for salads where you find it growing. With finer, deeply divided leaves and a stronger, more complex flavour than rocket, it also grows taller.

Below: Fresh rocket adds a peppery bite to salads.

Cabbages

These brassicas (*B. oleracea*, Capitata Group) look beautiful in the garden. Their splendid leaves even inspired Wedgwood potters to model their majolica plates on them. The most beautiful of all is 'Savoy', so named because of its popularity in the French alpine region of the same name. It has wonderful glaucous green foliage with a marvellous crinkled texture.

Another cabbage with ornamental value is the sensational red cabbage, which brings rich colour to the garden in winter. 'Sugar Loaf' is a popular cultivar, and the typical ingredient of coleslaw. In fact, cabbages have been made into many dishes, from sauerkraut to the pickled Korean dish, kimchee, and it is this versatility and hardiness that has earned them a place in cuisines around the world.

Cultivating brassicas

Brassicas are generally winter vegetables. They are normally sown in late summer or autumn then grown over winter, taking 4 to 5 months to mature. Raising plants from seed is trouble-free, but you should prepare the soil well with compost, lime and complete plant food about one month in advance.

Once a few true leaves appear, when the plant is about 7 cm (2¾ in) tall, you may have to separate the seedlings in order to space them correctly. After transplanting, use a weak solution of liquid seaweed to encourage healthy root growth and reduce shock, as well as encourage new growth.

Top: 'Sugar Bowl' cabbage.

Left: 'Red Empress', a cabbage cultivar.

Feeding

Provided you have prepared the soil well initially, you shouldn't need to feed your plants again.

Harvesting

Most common brassicas are not repeat harvest, so once you cut the plant for picking, that's it. The exceptions are the many Asian vegetables, which tend to be continual croppers, and broccoli, as after you cut the main head it will branch and send out smaller side heads that are just as delicious.

Problems

Young plants may be very susceptible to snails, so be vigilant about setting snail traps (see page 59).

All the brassicas are susceptible to club root rot, which results in abnormally large and misshapen roots. The affected plants will also wilt easily on hot days and grow slowly. This disease is best treated by crop rotating: don't grow any members of this family in the same section of the garden for three or more years, otherwise fungal spores may build up. Other contributing factors are moist soil, temperatures around 18 to 25°C (64.4 to 77°F) and soil pH. If the soil is acid, diseases such as club root are more likely, so make sure your soil is neutral to only slightly alkaline.

Whiptail, which results in distorted, puckered and small leaves, is the result of molybdenum deficiency, which in turn is usually due to acid soil. You can rectify the problem by liming the soil. Weed control

Above: A brassica that has gone to seed.

Below left: The leaves of 'Savoy' cabbage.

Below: The densely packed, crisp leaves of white cabbage, sometimes called Dutch cabbage.

is also very important in helping to deter pests and diseases.

The biggest problem for members of this family is the caterpillar from both the cabbage moth (*Plutella xylostella*) and the cabbage butterfly (*Pieris rapae*). The adults lay their eggs on the outside of brassicas then, as they hatch, the young larvae start to eat away at the leaves, the outer ones first, gradually making their way into the hearts of the plants themselves.

There are two types of spray suitable for use on brassicas. Neither has disastrous effects on the birds that might eat them or the environment. One is a product called *Bacillus thuringiensis*, a bio-insecticide that only affects certain caterpillars, eating away at their stomachs, but has no effect on other insects, birds or warm-blooded animals. In fact, after washing, you can eat the sprayed vegetables without observing a withholding period. As soon as you see any grub activity, use this every week or two.

The other product you can use was awarded a major environmental science prize when it was released in 1999. It's a natural insect control that contains spinosad, derived from a soil bacteria that occurs naturally. Once sprayed, it moves into the leaf itself, making it effective on bugs ingesting the leaves, even those inside the heart. Grubs stop feeding immediately but take about three days to die. This chemical is broken down with soil and sunlight, and doesn't build up in the soil so, again, it's safe to use on vegetables.

Opposite: A collection of brassica flowers and foliage, showing their subtle colours.

Top: The magnificent 'Savoy' cabbage.

Right: The cabbage moth on broad beans.

Far right: The cabbage moth caterpillar at work on a cabbage leaf.

roots

Many plants are grown for their underground edible parts rather than their leaves or fruits above ground. These tubers, bulbs and rhizomes are known collectively as 'root crops', and include plants such as potatoes, beets, carrots, turnips, sweet potatoes, yams, cassava and parsnips.

Storage systems

Tubers are underground storage systems that are actually modified stems, not roots, and they help plants cope with adverse conditions, such as a winter period or a dry spell. Generally, they are starchy stores, and many of them are edible. The best known of all tubers is the common or Irish potato (*Solanum tuberosum*), which sends rhizomes (also modified stems) down into the ground in the same way as roots, but develops swollen or enlarged tips that form tubers, the part of potato we eat.

When you dig up a potato, you can identify all parts of the stem, including the shoots (lateral eyes) and terminal growth point, which is the terminal eye opposite the scar where the tuber was removed from the rhizome. The principle food stored in potatoes is starch, but there are also small quantities of protein and sugar.

Other modified stems, such as bulbs (see page 286), are also called root crops, even though botanically they are stems, not roots. Included in this group are

Above: Kohlrabi, a member of the Brassica family, is a descendant of wild cabbage.

Left: Chits, otherwise known as seed potatoes, ready for planting.

onions and garlic. With true root crops, the principle root becomes swollen, as with carrots and parsnips.

Brassicas grown for their roots

The huge Brassicaceae family includes vegetables grown for their roots, not for their foliage, as well as some that can be eaten as both root and leaf crops. Like their foliaged cousins, the popularity of these root vegetables has waxed and waned, but their heartiness, reliability and hardiness has kept them on our plates.

Turnips

Popular vegetables throughout the Middle Ages, particularly in cold areas such as Scotland (where they are still called neeps), turnips (*Brassica rapa* var. *rapifera*) are tapered white roots, about 5 cm (2 in) in diameter, with a crown of edible leaves

that are sought after when they are fresh in spring. The French serve baby turnips and call them *navets*, but there are also more carrot-looking shapes known in France as *vertus*. They can be used fresh or cooked, and the tops can also be steamed and eaten.

Sow them from seed from early spring to midsummer in drills 1 cm (1/2 in) deep, then thin them to 40 cm (16 in) apart. They should be ready for harvesting within three months — earlier in warmer areas.

This page: Trim off the green tops of radishes (above left), then store them in the fridge, where they'll keep for about ten days. Carrots (above), on the other hand, will last for several weeks if stored in the fridge, and turnips (below) even longer.

roots

1 Beetroot **2** Kohlrabi **3** White radish **4** Long black Spanish radish **5** Pink radish
6 Turnip **7** Parsnip **8** Salsify **9** Swede **10** Round black Spanish radish **11** Red radish
12 Sugar beet **13** 'Daikon' radish **14** 'Roly Poly' carrot **15** Carrot **16** Young white carrot

Swedes

Sometimes called rutabagas, swedes (*Brassica napobrassica*) can be used exclusively as stock fodder or welcomed, roasted and caramelised, to the dinner table. Sow this round, purple-topped root vegetable in autumn to spring and it'll be ready to harvest in 60 days.

Kohlrabi

If you have shallow soil, kohlrabi or turnip-rooted cabbage (*Brassica oleracea*, Gongylodes Group) is a good alternative to the turnip. The bulbous part of the plant, a swollen stem, actually grows just above the soil, and is ready for harvesting when it reaches the size of a cricket ball. There are white and purple varieties, and all have a flavour similar to turnips or, some say, water chestnuts. They can be eaten raw (peeled and thinly sliced) or cooked. The leaves are edible too and can be lightly cooked in oil, garlic and chilli.

Radishes

Radishes (*Raphanus sativus*), which have a peppery flavour and a very crisp texture, are usually eaten raw, adding a zest to salads. There are four main types — the small, rounded, red cherry types; the French white and red; the slightly larger, more elongated ones ('French Breakfast'); and the long white Japanese type known as 'Daikon' or 'Mooli'.

Another interesting heirloom type is the black Spanish radish, which is round or long, large and quite strong-smelling. It keeps well, and is best sown in autumn.

Red radishes are mostly served fresh in salads or finely sliced with bread and butter as a sandwich hors d'oeuvre. The long white radish is often used in stir-fries, but can also be eaten fresh and grated, or pickled.

Useful for breaking up the soil, radishes grow all year. The best method is to sow them directly into the ground any time

Above and below: Swedes, also known as Swedish turnips and turnip-rooted cabbages, taste better when young.

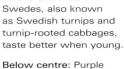

Below centre: Purple kohlrabi. The name *kohlrabi* is German for 'cabbage turnip'.

Below right: Freshly dug radishes.

from autumn to spring. You can also buy seed tapes, where the fine seeds are already impregnated, correctly spaced, into the tissue, which saves you the trouble of thinning out the seedlings. After about 3 to 5 weeks, try a radish to see if it has reached maturity; if you leave radishes too long in the ground, they become tough.

Apiaceae family

You can identify members of the Apiaceae family — which includes celery, fennel and parsnip — by their umbel-shaped flower clusters, which are extremely successful in attracting beneficial insects such as lacewings and hoverflies into the garden.

Carrots

One of the most popular vegetables, carrots (*Daucus carota*) are actually biennial plants, but they're treated as annuals because the edible root is formed during the first year of their two-year life cycle.

Flowering occurs in the second year, but flavour can be robbed back from the root to produce seeds, and they become woody and bitter as a result.

The roots store extremely well and travel easily, which is why carrots have become one of the world's best-selling vegetables. They are sweet, full of beta-carotenes and versatile, as you can eat them raw or cooked or pickled, in sweet or savoury dishes. In fact, they are so sweet that children love eating them raw.

The thing that sets carrots apart from any other vegetable is their colour — such a brightly golden orange that one might assume it inspired the carat, the measure of gold's fineness. However, carrots were actually red, yellow, purple and golden hues until the sixteenth century, when Dutch horticulturalists bred only orange ones in honour of their royal family.

Regardless of their colour, carrots are very good for you. Red carrots have more

Below, from left to right: Fennel's umbel-shaped flower, which is typical of the Apiaceae family; fennel bulbs, ready for harvest; and pulling a 'Daikon' radish.

Above: If the soil in your carrot patch isn't friable and open-textured, you'll probably end up with stunted carrots like this.

of the antioxidant lycopene (the same chemical found in tomatoes), while the purple ones contain anthocyanin. This antioxidant is also found in cranberries, ripe olives and even ornamentals such as purple-leafed *Prunus* and bromeliads.

Part of the subfamily Umbelliferae, common carrot types include 'Chantenay Red Cored' (12-cm/5-in roots, so it's good for shallow soils); 'King West' (20-cm/8-in or more orange roots); and 'Western Red' (long, tapering, deep orange root, 60 days to maturity); while the more exotic or heirloom varieties include yellow 'Austrian Lobbericher' and 'Belgium White'.

Cultivating carrots

Carrots can be sown all year, but they prefer cool weather, not frost. Most important is the soil texture, which has to be open-textured so they don't 'fork'. Soddy or stony soils won't do, neither will freshly manured soil or fertilised earth, as this can also cause forking or hairy roots. A regular water supply is important during both germination and growth, as drying out will cause the roots to crack.

Carrots don't like being transplanted, so sow thickly direct into the soil, then thin out the baby carrots to leave bigger spaces between the plants rather than sow sparsely in the first place. Also, don't hill the soil as you do for many other root crops (see page 281).

Harvesting

About four months after planting, your carrots will be ready for harvesting. You can also lift them with a gardening fork when they're young and sweet.

Problems

In countries where carrot fly (see page 53) is prevalent, plant garlic, sage or any other fiercely aromatic plant in between the rows to put these pests off the scent. Also watch out for the following problems.

- Aphids: page 58.
- Leaf spot: page 68.
- Root knot nematodes: page 59.
- Weevils: page 62.

Above: Rows of carrot seedlings.

Opposite, clockwise from top left: Pulling up white carrots, which are too young to eat; 'Chantenay Red Cored'; freshly harvested carrots; and a 'Roly Poly' carrot, one of the stump-rooted cultivars.

did you know? During World War II, when there was a glut of carrots, Britain's 'Dig for Victory' campaign promoted the carrot, claiming it improved night vision. It has been suggested that this may have led the Germans to believe that the British became better at spotting enemy aircraft thanks to carotene (a source of vitamin A found in carrots), and not to radar on land and in the air.

Celery

With a wonderful flavour that is particularly good in soups, celery (*Apium graveolens* var. *dulce*) can be used either raw or cooked. Cultivars include hardy 'Tendercrisp', a smooth, stringless green type whose stalks have a slightly nutty flavour, and 'Red Stalked', an ancient form with reddish stems and leaves that retain their colour when cooked. Low in kilojoules (calories), celery grows 40 to 60 cm (16 to 24 in) and contains potassium and calcium.

It can be rather cumbersome to grow, however, especially if it's the white heart you're after. This is traditionally achieved by growing it in a trench and gradually earthing up around the stems — or burying them, if you like — so they blanch. This trench should be about 40 cm (16 in) wide and 30 cm (1 ft) deep, so it requires some digging. Plant seedlings into it and, as they grow, tie the tops together to help stop the earth from polluting the stems, then backfill the soil into the trench.

Thankfully, self-blanching cultivars, which are much easier to handle, are now available. These are usually planted in clusters, 20 to 25 cm (8 to 10 in) apart, and then, once the plants are reasonably mature, mulched heavily up the stem with straw. You can box in the whole cluster to contain the soil, or simply mound it around each plant. As an added precaution in this case, it's worth wrapping each plant with newspaper and plastic, allowing the tops to peek out. This not only helps to block out the light but also keeps the plant fairly clean.

Celery doesn't like very cold or windy conditions, and certainly doesn't like to dry out. In fact, with so much of the stem's content being water, you must give it an ample supply while it is growing or it will become stringy and unappetising.

Sow the seeds in autumn into well drained soil with a neutral pH and good structure so that it will hold moisture but also have good air-filled porosity.

Below, from left to right: Blanching celery by wrapping it in newspaper and plastic; celery tops; and bunches of celery.

Parsnips

Parsnips (*Pastinaca sativa*) also belong to the carrot family. They have long, edible, creamy white taproots with a sweet, slightly earthy, nutty flavour. These cold-hardy vegetables will tolerate frosts; indeed, it's said that you shouldn't eat parsnips until after the first frost, as it makes them sweeter still.

Containing vitamins A, B and C, and calcium, iron and potassium, parsnips are delicious baked, and can also be used in beer, wines, jams and desserts. The Romans liked to use parsnips in broths, and introduced them to Britain. In fact, until the potato arrived in Europe from the Americas, parsnips were one of the main sources of edible starch.

The seed, which is very fine, needs to be fresh. Sow it in an open-textured soil, but take care to dig the soil well beforehand and check that it has a neutral pH. Only lightly cover it (no more than 12 mm/$\frac{1}{2}$ in) and be patient, as it is slow to germinate, taking three weeks to come up. Parsnips can be sown at any time, apart from winter, and take about eighteen weeks to mature. Spring sowings result in autumn crops. If you haven't harvested them by the following summer, greenish yellow flowers will appear.

As parsnips take 4 to 5 months to grow, you can make use of the space between their rows by sowing other, faster crops, such as lettuces, radishes or spring onions. This has a two-pronged effect: not only will this increase the productivity of your patch, it will also help to keep down the weeds — after all, they'll grow wherever there is bare earth.

Celeriac

Celeriac (*Apium graveolens* var. *rapaceum*) is actually a form of celery that develops a swollen rootstock. The leaves are much shorter than traditional celery, although they're still edible, and the root is swollen to about the same size as a turnip. Like celery, celeriac prefers cool temperatures, tending to bolt to seed if the weather warms. It doesn't like to have its roots disturbed, so weed the area carefully before planting and, as the plants develop, hand-weed judiciously. Sow seeds early in autumn to give your plants the

Above left and below: You can leave parsnips in the ground for up to three months after they reach maturity.

Above centre: Parsnips, with their celery-like leaves, with cabbages.

Above: Remove the leaves, then store celeriac in the crisper of the fridge for up to one week.

maximum period of cool weather in which to form the swollen root.

Once you've harvested celeriac, treat them like potatoes and boil them for soups and salads. You can also eat them grated and raw for a crunchy texture in salads; however, because the flesh discolours very quickly on exposure to air, plunge them into water with a squeeze of lemon juice to help them maintain their colour.

Fennel

Florence fennel (*Foeniculum vulgare* var. *azoricum*) — the root form of fennel, not the foliage herb — is not at all fussy. In fact, it can be weedy, often springing up in degraded and abandoned areas such as alongside railway tracks and expressways. A perennial that smells distinctly of aniseed, it's called *finnicchio* in Italy.

Plant fennel in spring in colder areas, but in autumn in warm and tropical climates. For a white heart, mulch over with straw, or hill with earth, then lift it in spring.

Hamburg parsley

Hamburg parsley (*Petroselinum crispum*) is actually the same genus and species as regular parsley, but it also produces a taproot, much like a small parsnip.

Sow seeds in spring into fairly rich soil, then thin the seedlings to 15 cm (6 in) apart. You can dig the crop throughout autumn, when the roots reach about 15 cm (6 in) long, but you don't have to take them all out — you can leave them in the ground throughout winter (unless your soil freezes, in which case store them in peat or wood shavings) and just dig them up as you need them. Alternatively, leave them for another season, and they will still taste all right. Pests seldom affect them, and they will also cope with a bit of shade.

tip

Celeriac and fennel are both sweetest when the bulbs are small. They can be stored in the fridge for at least a week.

Top and right: Florence fennel has a distinct aniseed flavour.

Salsify and scorzonera

With roots similar to a dandelion's are two other little known plants, salsify and scorzonera. Purple salsify (*Tragopogon porrifolius*) has white or pale brown skin, a bit like parsnip, and is supposed to be the more flavoursome of the two. Its root has a slight taste of oyster, which led to its common names of oyster plant or vegetable oyster. It is native to the Mediterranean and also associated with herbal remedies.

Salsify has been cultivated for at least 700 years, but was particularly popular in seventeenth century Europe. It produces long fleshy roots that can be baked, boiled, fried or stewed; you can even cook the leaves as you would spinach. Alternatively, blanch the leaves in spring by covering them with straw — you'll end up with chards that are similar to asparagus in flavour.

To grow salsify, find fresh seed and sow them 1 cm (1/2 in) deep in spring,

thinning to 30 cm (1 ft) apart, so it has the longest period to grow before you harvest the roots in autumn. It is, however, a biennial, and sowing later just means you can produce spring crops. The plant itself grows to about 1 m (3 ft), likes a pH of 6 or above (so your soil may need liming) and will need stone-free, well dug soil.

Scorzonera (*Scorzonera hispanica*), sometimes called black salsify, has purplish brown skin. It's sown from seed in the same manner but, unlike salsify, is a perennial, so it can be left in the ground for a couple of seasons. The root will simply grow larger, without becoming coarse or stringy. If you live in a cold zone, protect it from frost by covering it with straw in winter.

Prepare both salsify and scorzonera in the same way: either scrub the roots, and peel after cooking, or peel and place into water with a squeeze of lemon juice immediately as, like sweet potatoes, they discolour immediately. Try sautéing them lightly with butter and serve, once cooled, with a vinaigrette dressing.

Digging up salsify

Salsify roots are nutritious, containing vitamins, minerals, protein and fats.

1 Use a sharp-edged spade to dig under the roots.

2 Salsify roots grow up to 1 m (3 ft) long.

Left: Native to the Mediterranean, scorzonera is also grown for its daisy-like purple flower.

did you know? The name *scorzon* may derive from the Old French word for 'snake'. Until the sixteenth century, scorzonera was considered an effective remedy for snake bites and the bubonic plague.

The daisy family

You wouldn't think that daisies and dinner go hand in hand, but some members of this enormous family do have edible roots.

Dandelion

The dandelion (*Taraxacum officinale*), which is considered either a weed or, at most, a salad green, is one such member of the Asteraceae family. The name 'dandelion' is a corruption of the French *dent de lion*, or 'lion's tooth', which refers to its coarsely toothed edible leaves.

Use the thick taproot finely sliced in salads or, roasted, as a coffee substitute. It is also said to be a mild laxative and has been used since at least the eleventh century, when the Arabs promoted its medicinal qualities.

You probably don't need instructions on how to grow dandelions, but bear in mind that any part of the root will reshoot. Dig up the root and dry it in autumn.

Jerusalem artichoke

Jerusalem artichoke (*Helianthus tuberosus*), or sunchoke as it is often called in North America, is a tuberous perennial with yellow daisy flowers. Discovered in

Nova Scotia by the French in the early seventeenth century, it grows to 3 x 1.5 m (10 x 5 ft) and flowers in autumn, with the same sunflower-type blooms for which the rest of this genus is well known. These flowers are usually 'nipped in the bud' to stop the plant from flowering and taking nutrients out of the tuber, which is dug up in autumn. There is also a purple-skinned cultivar called 'Fuseau'.

Because of their size, Jerusalem artichokes are usually only grown outside the vegetable garden, but sometimes they're used inside the patch as a wind barrier, protecting sensitive crops such as beans and tomatoes from breezes, or greens from the strong summer sun. Harvest the creamy white tubers once the stems have withered in late autumn. They have a slightly nutty flavour; eat them raw or cooked, in soups, or sliced and cooked au gratin with smoked salmon.

Plant tubers quite deeply in spring, or leave some in the ground after harvest to reproduce for next year's crop. There is no need to apply fertiliser, as they make their own nitrogenous fertiliser, using nitrogen-fixing nodules on their roots to extract nitrogen from the soil; however, you do need to lime the soil in order to stimulate good tuber production. The average plant

Planting Jerusalem artichokes

Like potatoes, Jerusalem artichokes will grow easily from tubers as long as there is a dormant bud, known as an eye, attached. The same rules apply (see page 281 for more information). Plant unblemished tubers when they are fresh, and don't let them dry out before you plant them.

1 Cut the tuber into pieces, making sure each section has an eye. It's easier to recognise these if the tuber has started to sprout, or chit, as it is known.

2 Dig a trench 20 cm (8 in) deep, then place the sections of sprouted artichokes inside. Backfill with a fine, crumbly soil, then mulch to help stop them drying out.

will produce about 1.5 kg (3 lb) of tubers — which is a fantastic yield — so take care when removing them that they don't overrun the vegetable patch. Any small piece of tuber left behind will reshoot, so before you plant them, decide whether you want them to be permanent members of your vegetable garden.

Yacon

Even though it's in a different genus, yacon (*Smallanthus sonchifolius*) has very similar flowers to a sunflower. The tubers, however, are much larger than Jerusalem artichokes, growing to the size of a sweet potato. Their texture, crispness and internal colour is much the same as apples, giving them their other common name, 'apple of the earth'. Almost kilojoule- (calorie-) free, they can be eaten raw (they taste a bit like a honeydew melon) or stir-fried, made into chips, pickles or even baked like potatoes.

Each season, the plant itself grows to about 1.5 m (5 ft) tall, dying back to

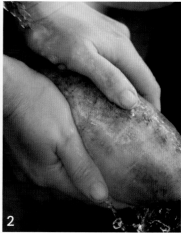

its perennial rootstock during winter, after it has flowered. Yacon likes a sunny position and is tolerant of heat, poor soil and even drought.

To harvest the tubers, lift the root ball carefully to expose its roots, then carefully unearth the larger tubers, which are quite fragile. Divide the smaller offsets and store them in pots of sand over winter in wet or cold areas or, if your soil has excellent drainage and you live in a mild climate, replant them into the soil.

Digging and washing yacon

To harvest your yacon tubers, gently reveal them, as if you were on an archaeological dig, so that the soft, juicy tubers remain intact.

1 Dig them out slowly and carefully so they're not damaged in the process. The large tubers are the ones to remove and use.

2 Wash their skins carefully to remove the dirt before eating the white flesh.

Opposite, top: Jerusalem artichokes can be left in the ground until you're ready to harvest them.

Far left: The flower of the yacon plant.

Left: Any smaller yacon tubers can be stored in moistened sawdust in terracotta pots, ready to plant the following spring. Half-fill some small terracotta pots with sawdust, then place a yacon tuber in each one. Top up each pot with sawdust, and then water.

roots

1 Chicory **2** Oca **3** Arrowroot (*Maranta arundinacea*) **4** Florence fennel **5** Dandelion
6 Coriander **7** Carrot **8** Hamburg parsley **9** Turmeric **10** Ginger **11** Peruvian
parsnip **12** Duck potato **13** Chinese artichoke **14** Arrowroot (*Canna edulis*) **15** Galangal

Other root crops

Despite most of the root crops belonging to two major families, there are also other root crops. Some are important economically, while others are staple food crops in the tropics or simply make interesting culinary additions to both the garden and the dinner table.

Beetroot

Beetroot (*Beta vulgaris*) is a stunning plant to grow and an amazing plant to consume. Even if you don't think you like them, chances are you've only tried the canned type, but once you've eaten them fresh, you'll appreciate the difference in flavour.

The ruby-veined, crinkly emerald foliage adds a royal flush to a kitchen garden, so it's worth adding for its ornamental qualities alone. The leaves are edible, and taste especially delicious when picked young and eaten fresh, but you can also fry them in a little olive oil, chilli and garlic for a tasty, spicy alternative to spinach. Of course, it's the root they're renowned for, especially the common round globe type, but there are others too, such as the rainbow selections, which have red, orange, gold and yellow roots, and also the long-rooted, cylinder types.

Whatever your selection, beetroot are quite easy to grow. They prefer a light, friable, fertile soil that has a neutral or slightly acid pH; in alkaline soils, they may suffer boron deficiency. The seeds are a strange angular, slightly spaceship-like configuration but, once they've been soaked in water for an hour or so to soften the outer layer, they germinate readily in any

This page and opposite: Beetroot mature in about 3 to 4 months. Dig one up to check its size before harvesting (left). You can also grow heirloom varieties such as 'Burpees Golden' beetroot (below).

damp ground. A cluster of plants is the result, which can be carefully teased apart and separated into plants at about 10-cm (4-in) spacings.

The trick is to grow beetroot quickly so the root is neither tough nor susceptible to beet nematode. To achieve this, apply complete fertiliser — not manure, as it can make the roots fork — once the young seedlings have rooted. Remove any dead or spotty leaves as they grow to help control leaf spot (see page 68) and beet rust (see page 69).

Climbers with edible roots

Many tropical plants have adapted to growing in wet climates and rainforest conditions by climbing towards sunlight. Some of these climbing plants bear rather extraordinary fruit, while others produce tubers that are invaluable sources of starch in the tropics.

Yams

Yams (*Dioscorea* sp.) are an enormous genus containing over 850 species, many of which have become the staple carbohydrate food in various regions, especially Africa, where the boiled flesh is pounded to make a dough that is served with stew. Yams are native to Asia, but have spread around the world due to their ability to grow in subtropical conditions, making their way to the Americas in the sixteenth century via the slave trade. The exception is cush cush or Indian yam (*D. trifida*), which is indigenous to America.

The most common yam is the greater yam (*D. alata*), also known as white or water yam and guyana arrowroot. The vine grows to 2.5 m (8 ft) wide and 3 m (10 ft) tall, and has heart-shaped foliage as well as enormous tubers with either white or red flesh, covered in coarse brown skin. The record holder is a tuber weighing 62 kg (137 lb).

Potato or Chinese yam (*D. esculenta*), sometimes called lesser yam or cinnamon vine, due to its scented flowers, has smaller oval-shaped tubers covered in fine whiskers. Some species of yam are poisonous, however, so it's probably best to eat only the well documented ones that are popular in Africa and Asia as a food source. Also, there is a poison under their skin called dioscorine, so it's best to peel them wearing gloves and cook them well in salted water.

Both species can be easily raised from tubers. Plant them about 10 cm (4 in) deep once frosts have finished and the soil has warmed up a bit in spring. A position in either full sun or semi-shade is suitable. Plants usually grow to about 3 m (10 ft) tall, so they'll need a trellis or support of

Below: The vine of the African yam, which must be cooked before it can be eaten.

Below centre: Jicama has a very crisp flesh that tastes rather bland.

Below right: Plant chokos with their narrow end facing up.

some sort. They die back each year and can be divided and harvested in late autumn. For maximum yield, water well when the plants are growing over summer. Yams can become invasive so, if you're worried that your climate may be too suitable, keep them in a large tub.

Sweet potatoes

Sweet potatoes (*Ipomoea batatas*) belong to the same genus as many ornamental climbers and even weeds, such as morning glory vine. This trailing plant from tropical America develops tubers over summer, and usually sprawls all over the ground to a diameter of 3 m (10 ft). Some ornamental foliage forms are available, including 'Blackie', which has deep purple leaves.

Sweet potatoes like full sun, frost-free conditions and plenty of water during the growing period. Plant tubers in spring or early summer, then harvest the tubers at the end of autumn by digging them up.

The skin of sweet potato tubers can be white, red or orange-brown, while the flesh itself can be orange or white. Sweet potatoes vary in shape and size, and discolour very quickly after peeling unless you sit them in water with a squeeze of lemon or vinegar.

Sweet potatoes need a warm climate with no more than three months of frosty weather; warmer weather will result in better yields, although the cultivar 'Beauregard' is more adaptable and can cope in temperate zones. These plants are happy to sprawl over the ground, but can also be trained up a support. A position in full sun, in a free-draining soil, is best.

Yam bean

Native to tropical South America and Mexico, yam bean or jicama (*Pachyrhizus tuberosus*) is also sometimes referred to as the Mexican potato or turnip. Depending on its host, this vine can grow to 6 m (20 ft) tall and 2 m (6½ ft) wide. The whole plant is poisonous, except for the tuber, which is brown-skinned with white flesh. Each tuber can weigh up to 23 kg (51 lb), has a crunchy texture and a slight nutty taste, and can be eaten either raw in salads or cooked like potatoes.

Yam beans are in the same family as peas, and have purple or violet to white flowers, followed by flattened green pods up to 20 cm (8 in) long. Most of these should be removed to concentrate growth into the tuber, which should be harvested before the first frosts. Allow a few flowers to develop for seeds, then sow them in spring into a warm, sunny spot that has good drainage.

Choko vines

Although mainly known for their fruit, choko vines (*Sechium edule*) also have edible tubers that are considered a delicacy in some parts of the world. Known variously as chayote and christophene, they are native to South America but do well in any warm climate, growing to about 6 m (20 ft) across on a support. They are disease-resistant, grow in hardy to poor soils and just need a sunny fence on which to grow. (For information on how to grow chokos for their fruit, see page 317.)

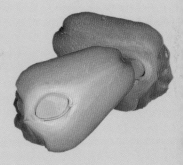

Above: Sweet potatoes are popular in both African and Caribbean cuisines.

Below: The fruit of the choko vine. The edible tuber is similar in texture to a potato.

did you know? Sweet potatoes were introduced to Spain via Christopher Columbus, then to England, where it is said that Henry VIII liked them to be cooked into what he considered an aphrodisiac pie. They were also known to be grown in South America before the Incas, and in Polynesia and New Zealand during the fourteenth century.

Elephant's ears

Elephant's ears or giant taro (*Alocasia macrorrhiza*) are native to tropical Asia, India and Sri Lanka. They are also enormously important to the Pacific Islands, where they have become one of the starchy food staples of the diet. In the Caribbean they are sometimes called eddo or dasheen.

Members of the Arum family, which also includes many poisonous members, they grow to about 2 m (6½ ft) tall and enjoy a shady position with lots of moisture. There is also a golden cultivar that is edible and very pretty.

The swollen rootstock is the part that is usually eaten, but you can also eat the heart-shaped broad leaves, known as callaloo, which are usually chopped up and boiled in coconut milk and lime juice, then served as a soup — a very popular dish in both the Caribbean and Asia. The leaves can also be used to wrap food before it's cooked.

The root itself contains a poison just under the skin that can give you a skin allergy, so it's prudent to either wear gloves while peeling them, or cook them in their skins, which eliminates the toxins and leaves you with a skin that's easy to peel.

Above: Taro can be stored for several months in a cool, dark place.

Above right: Golden taro, an edible cultivar of *Alocasia macrorrhiza*.

Right: Oca, also known as New Zealand yam.

Cassava

Cassava or bitter cassava (*Manihot esculenta*) is a member of the Euphorbiaceae family, which is famous for its poisonous milky white sap. It's popular as a vegetable in the West Indies but is actually native to South America, where it's known as mandioc and used to make tapioca and liquor. It grows easily in warm areas, where it reaches about 1 m (3 ft). After 8 to 10 months it produces tubers that you can eat like a potato. Replant fresh tuber sections each spring for a new crop.

Oca

Native to the Columbian region, oca is a tuberous perennial species of a genus many loathe — the *Oxalis* or wood sorrel group. While many of these have troublesome bulbs that make them a weed, others are collectors' items, needing alpine conditions in which to grow. The edible species, *O. tuberosa*, is referred to by a swag of names, including New Zealand yam.

Oca was introduced to New Zealand from South America in 1860, and to Europe 30 years earlier, as an alternative to potatoes. While the potato remained the king of root vegetables, oca is still a sentimental favourite in New Zealand, where it is known as yam and eaten boiled or fried. It has a sweet yet slightly tangier taste than the common potato. The tubers are used as pig forage.

This low clumping perennial, which grows to about 20 cm (8 in), has characteristic clover-like foliage that can be used like sorrel. It likes mild climates, preferably above freezing and below 28°C (82°F), as very hot temperatures can cause wilting. Its yellow flowers are typical of the rest of the genus but, unlike its relatives, it develops knobbled edible tubers that are red, yellow or white.

Plant oca in spring, in well drained soil about 5 cm (2 in) deep and 30 cm (1 ft) apart. About six months after planting, the tubers should be ready for harvesting. You can encourage them to form by mounding them with earth as they grow. Store next year's crop in dry sand or sawdust in a cool, dark place.

Chinese artichoke

Chinese artichoke (*Stachys affinis* syn. *S. tuberifera* syn. *S. sieboldii*) is a little known, easy to grow perennial closely related to sage and lamb's tongue. It likes any temperate climate, and produces edible white tubers that often have a contorted knob-like appearance. The plant itself has upright stems with mauve or white flowers and crinkly foliage that grows to 60 cm (2 ft) and spreads to about 1 m (3 ft) in diameter.

They don't produce a huge yield, but if you want to try them, plant tubers in winter or spring into an open, sunny position with reasonably fertile, well drained soil. Top-dress with manure, and water in dry spells. Harvest in late autumn when 5 to 7 cm (2 to 2¾ in) in diameter, replanting a few for the following season and protecting these from frosts if necessary. Store them in sand, peat or a peat substitute throughout winter for eating at a later stage.

Above: In Mexico, oca tubers are served with salt, lime and chilli as a refreshing 'fruit' snack.

Cunjevoi

Australia also has a native species, called cunjevoi or spoon lily (*Alocasia brisbanensis*), which has very large, mid-green, heart-shaped leaves. Native to the rainforest and wetter areas of eastern Australia, it's a smaller grower, usually to only 1.5 m (5 ft) or less, and likes a similar moist position. Its architectural form makes it a splendid ornamental plant in the garden. In summer, it also bears cream-green flowers that look like an arum lily. Other species known for their striking foliage, such as *A.* x *amazonica* 'Magnifica', can be used exclusively for ornamental purposes: if you eat the leaves, they tend to have an unpleasant effect on your tongue.

The large, ribbed foliage of cunjevoi.

Potatoes

The versatile potato (*Solanum tuberosum*) has come a long way since it was 'discovered' in the New World in the sixteenth century. Whether boiled, roasted, fried or mashed, the potato is now the most popular vegetable in First World countries, and is certainly of enormous economical value around the world.

However, such popularity does have its drawbacks. The humble potato is in danger of being so generic that its inherent value as an individual could be lost, as it nearly was during the Great Famine of the nineteenth century (see box, at left). All the stock at that time was from the same gene pool. Today some of the rarer varieties, which have been rediscovered, are replacing some of the 'mainstream' ones.

To the backyard gardener, however, potatoes enjoy a unique status. For a start, they take up quite a lot of space, and are not expensive to buy, so you have to be motivated to grow them in order to be bothered with allocating the space and putting in the effort. It might be more rewarding to grow the 'gourmet' types

Historical background

In 1536, when Spain conquered Peru and plundered the region for gold and other treasures, they also brought home to Europe the potato, a starchy lump cultivated by the Incas. The humble potato has helped cooler-climate countries such as Ireland, Russia and Germany produce enough to feed themselves: before the advent of the potato, these countries had relied strongly on grain imported from southern Europe, or on a rye, which is far less productive per area.

It's no wonder then that these countries celebrate the potato with national dishes. But a study of the history of the potato reveals a lesson — that relying exclusively on one crop results in reduced resistance to disease and an inability to adapt to new environmental challenges. Thus, when the potato succumbed to blight during Ireland's Great Famine in the 1840s, millions either starved to death, or fled to other countries such as the United States. Potatoes still suffer from this and other diseases, so commercial crops are often sprayed with huge amounts of pesticides and fungicides. This makes organically growing as many different varieties as you can an attractive alternative.

Above left: Potato plants.

Above: 'Purple Congo' potatoes.

Opposite: Potato flowers, which are typical of the nightshade family.

Planting spring potatoes

The thin skins and delicate flavour of chats or spring potatoes make growing them worth the effort.

1 Mark your trench with a string line.

2 Dig the trench about 10 cm (4 in) deep, heaping the removed soil to one side.

3 Cut your sprouted potato 'chits', as they are known, into pieces. Each should have an 'eye'.

4 Place the pieces into the trench about 20 cm (8 in) apart and in rows spaced at about 75-cm (30-in) intervals.

5 Place 30 g (1 oz) or so of potato fertiliser (N:P:K) on either side of the pieces. Backfill with soil, taking care to remove the lumps and break up any sods. You should now have raised rows. Mulch well, water and label.

6 Harvest baby chats about one month after sowing, or larger potatoes after three months.

that are difficult to buy, such as 'King Edward', 'Nicola', 'Otway Red', 'Ruby Lou', 'Pink Fir Apple', 'Purple Congo' and 'Toolangi Delight'. And, of course, as with so many other vegetables, the flavour of freshly dug 'new' or 'chat' potatoes, the first of the season, is much better than that of shop-bought potatoes.

Cultivating potatoes

Potatoes are susceptible to a number of diseases, so the first step in growing a healthy crop is to buy seed potatoes that are certified, or guaranteed to be free from viral and other problems.

The next step is to choose a suitable position. Potatoes need an open, sunny spot, and a frost-free, sheltered position with lots of available water during the growing season. For this reason, they usually prefer slightly heavier soils, as long as they have good structure and still drain well.

Potatoes are renowned for breaking up the soil, so they are sometimes planted into new beds in an establishing kitchen garden, as the process of growing potatoes is good soil preparation for future crops, whatever they might be.

As your crop grows, continue to mound the soil or apply some rich organic mulch around the plants to help trigger the formation of tubers. This should be done when the shoots are about 25 cm (10 in) tall; bury about two-thirds of this growth. In about three weeks, once the shoots are a further 25 cm (10 in) taller than the raised ground level, repeat again, and so on.

Potatoes planted in winter in frost-free areas will produce delicious spring chats, but if you live in a colder area, delay the process by a few months.

edible tubers

1 Yacon 2 'Pinkeye' 3 'Pontiac' 4 Jerusalem artichoke 5 'Purple Congo' 6 'Nicola'
7 'Russet Burbank' 8, 9, 10 Sweet potato (orange, white, red) 11 Yacon 12 'King Edward'
13 'Royal Blue' 14 'Kipfler' 15 'Desirée' 16 'Sebago' 17 'Coliban' 18 'Dutch Cream'

Feeding

Potatoes need lots of fertiliser, particularly potassium, so take care not to give them too much nitrogen in case you encourage leafy top growth instead of roots. Regularly apply fertilisers evenly across the soil to not only keep up their vigour, but also to help prevent a problem called 'hollow heart', where cracks and hollows occur inside the potatoes themselves. You can also use wood ash to supply the potash they need, but make sure you add this some months before sowing.

Harvesting

You can harvest tubers in spring by collecting small potatoes from under the mound, a technique known as bandicooting. If small tomato-like fruits appear on your plants after flowering, remove them, as they are not edible. Harvest the majority of potatoes, however, at the end of the season, once the foliage

Growing potatoes in containers

Tubs and tyre stacks (or wire cages lined with straw) are also suitable for growing small quantities of potatoes. Start with only a couple of tyres, stacked on the ground and filled with soil. Plant your 'seeds', then continue stacking tyres and soil as the plant develops (see the instructions for mounding the soil in 'Cultivating potatoes', page 281). When the potatoes are ready to harvest in about three months, simply remove the stack.

Alternatively, use a pot about 30 cm (1 ft) in diameter and put a small quantity of potting mix in the bottom, then plant your sprouted seed potato. As the plant grows, use more potting mix on top, and so on, until you have nearly reached the top. After three months, you can gently prize the plant out of the pot and harvest some tubers from the base, then put the plant back in the pot and continue growing and harvesting throughout summer.

Both methods require regular food and water (for more information, see 'Feeding', above).

has died down. Be careful not to damage the skins when you harvest the tubers, as cuts and bruises can cause gangrene. A large sieve can help with the cleaning process. Discard any green-skinned potatoes, as these contain a toxin called solanine, which can cause stomach aches, cramps, fever and headache; however, the flesh underneath the skin, if it's not discoloured, is safe to eat.

Problems

Choosing certified disease-free plants is essential for successful potato growing. Also, crop-rotating members of this family into new garden beds will help control disease. Try not to grow potatoes in the same soil more than twice in the same decade. In wet weather, copper oxychloride sprays can help control fungal outbreaks.

Potatoes hate frosts, and can be killed off by a late frost if they have already shot. In addition, irregular watering can cause problems — brown fleck and potato scab (page 70) in dry conditions, and bacterial soft rots (page 70) in wet conditions.

Potatoes can be prone to a number of sap-sucking insects, and also potato beetle, which is a pest in the United States. Try using a soap spray every week to keep them at bay, and also see the following pages for further information.

- Aphids: page 58.
- Weevils: page 62.

Opposite, top: It's better to cook potatoes with their skins on, as the most nutritious part is just under the skin.

Above left: 'Kipfler' potatoes are waxy, with cream-coloured flesh — ideal for potato salad.

Above: After harvesting, store your home-grown potatoes in a cool, dark place so they don't sprout or turn green.

Left: Labelling your potatoes at planting time will help you keep track of when you should harvest them.

Bulbs

Like tubers, bulbs are specialised storage systems that have been modified to enable a plant to hibernate when conditions are less than ideal. This may occur during extended periods of drought, or in a cold winter spell, as with many northern hemisphere bulbs, ornamental and edible.

Self-contained packages

The exquisite biology of the bulb is perfect in its form. The centre point of each bulb is actually the leaf's terminal bud (sometimes the flower bud is there too), and the many rings inside each other are leaves, layer upon layer, waiting to unfurl. Just above the root is a hardened disc, which is actually a compressed stem. In this way, each bulb is a perfect plant— stem, flower and food — within one protected package.

Onions

Onions (*Allium cepa*) have been used for culinary purposes for thousands of years. In ancient Egypt, the concentric rings inside each bulb symbolised eternal life, and there are said to be inscriptions singing their praises in the Great Pyramid. By the Middle Ages, onions were believed to absorb the effect of the plague, and were hung in bunches by the door in the hope that they would save the occupants from almost certain death.

Above: Golden shallots have a delicate onion-like flavour.

Left: Alliums include onions, shallots, chives, spring onions and leeks.

While the exact origin of today's modern onion is unknown (some think it may be Asia), the theory is that it spread from the Middle East to Europe and Britain with the Romans. Various alliums — native to Asia, Africa, Europe and North America (the Pilgrim ship *Mayflower* even carried onions on board) — are staple foods in almost every culture and cuisine.

Allium subgroups

The species is divided into three subgroups, each with its own characteristics.

The most common is the Cepa Group (*Allium cepa*), to which the common onion belongs. The onions in this group are sometimes called maincrop onions. There are the better known types — such as red, yellow (golden brown skins), brown, white and Spanish — but there are also other non-storage types that are harder to find in the shops but a delight to grow in the home garden.

These fresh onions, including cultivars such as 'Calred' and 'Golden Globe', have a higher water content, which is why they don't store well, but they compensate for this shortcoming with a generally milder, sweeter flavour. Depending on the variety, the onions in the Cepa Group can be grown throughout the season, from spring-sown to late-summer types.

The Aggregatum Group (*Allium cepa aggregatum*) includes spring onions or scallions, which are sometimes called bunching or clustered onions. Those who don't like digging might prefer to cultivate the third group, tree onions or Proliferum

did you know? It's a volatile acid below the onion skin that causes your eyes to water. Its high sulfur content acts as a natural disinfectant, antibiotic and antispasmodic, and it has been used medicinally for everything from gastroenteritis to the common cold.

alliums

1 Golden brown onion **2** 'Italian White' garlic **3** 'Hunter River Brown' onion **4** 'Giant Russian' garlic **5** Chive flowers **6** Garlic **7** Leek **8** Blue onion sprouts **9** Spring onions **10** 'Australian Brown' onion **11** 'Printanor' garlic **12** Golden shallots **13** Rocambole garlic **14** Spanish onion

(*Allium cepa proliferum*), which are also
known as Egyptian, top set and walking
onions. These produce 1.5-m (5-ft) stems
that need staking, and produce clusters
of bulbils (the crop) instead of flowers.
To propagate, simply reserve a few of these
to replant or, as this type is perennial, lift
the clump itself and divide it in winter
every three years or so. They are best
eaten pickled, but can also be eaten as
a leafy onion.

Cultivating onions

All onions like a soil with plenty of well
aged manure, but this is usually added a
few months prior to planting so that the
soil is firm when planting time arrives.
The pH also needs to be higher than

neutral (6.5), so if necessary add lime at
this stage to compensate. Use a complete
fertiliser in midsummer to encourage the
formation of healthy plants and bulbs.

Sow onion seeds in very shallow
drills, just covering the seeds with sand
and thinning them out to 15 cm (6 in)
apart after germination. They won't
push through hard, crusty soil 'skins',
so just dust them very lightly with sand.
Alternatively, sow them in seed trays, or
buy seedlings, and then plant them out.

Onions usually take six months to
develop fully, although you can pick
them when they're younger than this and
pickle them in brine. Traditionally, they're
planted on the shortest day of the year,
then harvested on the longest, but planting

Planting onion seeds

Onions can also be sown from seed and
raised under glass for planting out once
they're at the seedling stage. Use seedling
trays filled with a mix of propagating sand
and peat moss (or a peat substitute) in a
ratio of 3:1. Once the seedlings are about
3 to 4 weeks old and about 3 to 4 cm (1 to
1¹/₂ in) tall, transplant them into drills in situ.

1 Moisten the peat moss so that it's holding
water well, then mix with moistened
propagation sand in a ratio of 1:4. Spread
this mix evenly onto a seed tray, and gently
press some drills with a stick or stake.

2 Sprinkle the onion seeds into the drills,
trying to keep an even spacing between
each seed.

3 Carefully replace the small amount of mix
on either side of the drill over the onion
seeds. Don't overdo it, or the seedlings will
find it difficult to push through.

4 Spray lightly with an atomiser of water,
and cover with a sheet of glass until the
seeds germinate.

successive crops can lengthen the season significantly. Weed control is important during the growing season, as onions don't compete well with weeds, especially when they're young. In addition, weeds tend to harbour significant onion pests (see below).

Harvesting

Onions need their bulbs exposed to the sun to help them 'ripen'. Do this when the foliage begins to bend over by unearthing a bit of the bulb. Once the foliage has withered completely, lift the bulbs with a gardening fork so that the air can flow all around the bulbs and the soil can dry out. Once the soil is completely dry, remove any soil and hang the onions in string bags or stockings. As long as the air is able to circulate around them, they can be stored this way in a dry, dark place all winter.

Problems

- Over-fertilised or rich soil is likely to encourage foliage growth at the expense of bulb development, or open necks, which can lead to fungal infections.

- One of the major pests is onion thrip (see page 61), which often builds up in weeds, so keep your onion patch free of them.
- Onion crops need to be rotated at least every three years to stop the build-up of fungal problems.
- Irregular watering may cause onion bulbs to split.
- Onion maggot is the larval stage of a 5-mm (1/5-in) greyish brown fly, which lays its eggs in decaying organic matter and even seedlings. If this is a problem where you live, then use a non-organic fertiliser, or complete plant food, instead of manure and blood and bone.

Above, from left to right: An onion crown; blue onion sprouts; and harvested red onions.

Below: Red, white and brown onions.

Opposite, clockwise from top left: Young, developing garlic bulbs; 'Sperling Toga' Welsh onions; golden shallots; and spring onions.

Other onion species

Depending on your climate and the varieties you grow, there may be a gap between the seasons when your supply of onion bulbs run out. Fill the gap by growing leafy onion crops, which have a milder flavour, and shallots.

Spring onions

Spring onions or scallions, members of the Aggregatum Group of A. *cepa*, are sometimes incorrectly called Japanese shallots (*Allium fistulosum*). There are a few different types, including some lovely red-stemmed ones that look ornamental and also taste great.

These straight-leafed perennials, which grow to about 50 cm (20 in) and form clumps, are ideal for salads and stir-fries. 'Toga', a beautiful purple-stemmed spring onion with a superb flavour for salads and stir-fries, is also available.

As the name suggests, spring onions are sown from early spring onwards, usually in successive sowings about four weeks apart to keep up a continuous supply over the year. Sow them 5 mm (1/5 in) deep and 5 mm (1/5 in) apart in rows 15 cm (6 in) apart. Sow direct into drills and they should germinate in about two weeks and mature in 2 to 3 months.

Golden shallots

Golden or French shallots (A. *ascalonicum*) look like small onions but are, in fact, a separate species. The size of a walnut, their delicate flavour is perfect for dishes where a light touch is required. They can also be used pickled or raw in salads. Varieties include 'Giant Yellow' and 'Giant Red'.

Traditionally planted from bulbs on the day of the winter solstice, shallots take six months to mature before they're lifted on the day of the summer solstice. You can tell when they're ripe, as the leaves yellow and flop.

Before lifting, remove some of the soil from the bulbs to expose them to sunshine, as this helps the bulbs to 'ripen'. Then clean off any soil, separate the cluster and dry them thoroughly before storing them in net bags, where the good airflow should keep them for months. You can grow shallots in full sun or part shade.

Planting golden shallots

Shallots are extremely hardy, thriving in most soils and conditions.

1   A few weeks before planting, add a little lime to your soil and then cultivate it to a fine tilth.
2   Plant the bulbs into a hole 5 to 7 cm (2 to 2 3/4 in) deep and 15 cm (6 in) apart, with the points up and the roots down.
3   Backfill with soil, top with mulch and then label.
4   Feed with some complete plant food when they start to shoot in spring.
5   As the plants develop, push some more soil and mulch around their stems to blanch them. These paler stems can be used in the same way as spring onions or chives.

Wild onion species

As is often the way with common names, Welsh onions — sometimes known as cibouls or onion greens (A. *fistulosum*) — have nothing to do with Wales, but are actually from the Far East. Their foliage and stems are harvested and used in both cooking and salads.

There are other wild species of edible onions too, many from North America — hooker's or pink wild onion (A. *acuminatum*); ladies leek or nodding onion (A. *cernuum*); and the aptly named crater onion (A. *cratericola*), which can be found in volcanic screes in California.

Harvesting chives

During warm weather, the plants will keep producing both flowers and foliage, but in winter they'll slow down somewhat. To encourage the production of leaves, remove the flowers during the growing season. If your clump is big enough, you may prefer to leave the flowers, as they are not only pretty but also edible.

1 Using a sharp pair of scissors, harvest chives by starting at the outside of your plant and working inwards, so that the new leaves, which come up at the centre of each clump, have room to grow.

2 Tie the bunches together with string, and freeze any spares (chopped into pieces) in ice cube trays for later use.

Chives

Chives and Chinese or garlic chives are actually two different species, and are quite easy to tell apart, as traditional chives or onion chives (A. schoenoprasum) have a more rounded, tubular leaf and very pretty mauve flowers, although there are also some dark purple- and white-flowered cultivars. Garlic chives or Chinese chives (A. tuberosum), on the other hand, have flatter foliage, more bluish green leaves and larger, white flowers in summer. They are native to South-East Asia and are used a lot in Asian cuisine. Chives are very adaptable to different soil types and cope with semi-shade, but prefer manured, well drained soil in a full sun position.

Chives are perennials but they can get tired and even die out in the centre if not refreshed every three years. You can do this by dividing up the clumps in either spring or autumn. Simply dig up the clump then separate it into smaller clumps. Replant into freshened up, composted or manured soil, and prune the foliage back to about 2.5 cm (1 in) off the ground.

Opposite: With their mauve flowers, onion chives make a pretty border in the garden.

Left: Dividing chives before planting them out.

did you know? Chives are a natural insect repellent and also inhibit mildew. They are sometimes added to soap sprays and used as a 'tea' for organic pest control.

Garlic

Although it is thought to have originated in India and Central Asia, garlic (*Allium sativum*) is now virtually unknown as a wild plant, even though it is cultivated all over the world. Featured in myths and legends — whether deterring vampires or stopping the witch Circe from turning Ulysses into a pig — garlic is also a useful medicinal herb. Studies have shown that it can reduce blood pressure and help control blood sugar. It is also an effective antiseptic: in World War I, soldiers' wounds were dressed with a sphagnum moss poultice or dressing soaked in garlic juice to prevent gangrene.

Sometimes known as 'softneck' garlic, the clove is used in cuisines all over the world, but you can also use the leaves as you would chives. A variety known as rocambole or serpent garlic (*A. sativum* var. *ophioscorodon*), which has looping stems, is sometimes sold. It is a 'hardneck' garlic.

The '-neck' classification refers to the stalk that grows up from the bulb. If garlic is pliable at maturity, it's classified as a softneck. This is the type that's usually sold at the shops, as it stores best. Hardnecks are milder tasting, with a shorter shelf life, due to the diminished number of layers of skin around the bulb.

Cultivating garlic

To grow traditional Italian garlic, you need to plant the annual each season. In spring, separate the individual cloves and put them into free-draining soil in a sunny position, about 2.5 cm (1 in) deep and

Above right: The word 'garlic' comes from *gar*, old English for 'spear', and *leak* (for 'leek').

Below left and right: If any of your cloves are soft, like this one, don't use them.

did you know? **Society garlic is so named because it's supposed to leave you with less 'bad breath' than real garlic.**

Aïoli

4 egg yolks
8 garlic cloves, crushed
1/2 teaspoon salt
2 tablespoons lemon juice
500 ml (17 fl oz/2 cups) olive oil

Put the egg yolks, garlic, salt and half the lemon juice in a mortar, or food processor, and pound with a pestle, or mix, until light and creamy. Add the oil, drop by drop, from the tip of a teaspoon, whisking constantly until it begins to thicken, then add the oil in a very thin stream. (If you're using a food processor, pour in the oil in a thin stream with the motor running.) Season with sea salt and freshly ground black pepper, add the remaining lemon juice and, if necessary, thin with a little warm water.

Serve the aïoli in a bowl as a dipping sauce. You can keep it sealed in a sterilised jar in the fridge for up to three weeks. It's delicious served with poached fish, chicken or seafood. Try it with a selection of crudités — carrots, celery, blanched asparagus, beans, cauliflower — as an appetiser, or spooned beside barbecued or roast beef fillet or as an accompaniment to whole baked potatoes.

Makes 525 g (1 lb 3 oz/3 cups).

Above: Dry harvested garlic in the sun for a few days, then plait the stems and hang them in a cool, dark place.

Far left: A clove of traditional Italian garlic.

Left: A variety of garlic called 'Giant Russian'.

Other types of garlic

Spanish or giant garlic (*A. scorodoprasum*) is another so-called edible garlic, with shorter flower stalks and fewer cloves within each knob, covered in a dark violet bulb wrapper. Sometimes called sand leek, it is native to the coast of southern Europe and to western Asia. It should not be confused with rocambole or Levant garlic (*A. sativum* var. *ophioscorodon*), which may also be called elephant garlic due to the size of its bulb.
Sometimes it's incorrectly sold as Spanish garlic, but it is a subgroup of this species.

Society garlic (*Tulbaghia violacea*) is not a garlic at all, although its edible leaves do have a similar strong pungent smell. It can be used fresh or cooked as a garlic substitute. There is also a pretty variegated form called 'Silver Lace' (right).

15 cm (6 in) apart. Try to keep each clove as well wrapped in its skin as possible, and make sure it is firm to touch, as if it feels squishy, it's probably going off.

Using a dibbler, punch 5-cm (2-in) holes about 10 cm (4 in) apart and then backfill with soil before watering well. When the leaves start to lose their greenness in late summer, gently lift them to reveal the knob, then dry them in the sun for a few days to prepare them for storing. Either hang them in string bags or plait the stems and hang them like a rope.

If you separate the cloves, you can keep garlic in a plastic bag in the freezer for up to three months.

Many gardeners follow the tradition of planting the cloves on the shortest day of the year and harvesting them on the longest, but as garlic doesn't really like the cold, avoid this if you live in an area that receives frost or snow.

Planting garlic seedlings

People in cooler areas like to raise cloves of garlic in pots until they're of reasonable size before planting them out, but if you live in a mild climate, you can sow directly into the soil. If you are raising them in pots first, you'll need to separate them at planting time.

Garlic can be planted in rows or simply in a clump. Dig a hole about 5 cm (2 in) deep and, for five bulbs, about 25 cm (10 in) in diameter.

1 Plant each seedling using the backfilled soil, mounding the bed slightly to increase drainage.

2 Hold each seedling upright while you backfill.

Leeks

Leeks (*Allium ampeloprasum*) are wild to areas of Iran and North Africa as well as southern England, Ireland and Wales — in fact, they are the national floral emblem of Wales.

The modern plant, which is in the Porrum Group, includes named cultivars such as 'Unique', 'Colossal', 'Elephant' and 'Autumn Giant'. As their names suggest, these are larger, longer-stemmed varieties that are useful for baking. Leeks have a superb flavour, which is delicious in pies, stir-fries, soufflés and soups such as vichysoisse.

The plant itself grows to about 50 cm (18 in), producing pinkish red flowers, but it's the white stem that's used for cooking. You can accentuate this by wrapping the stems in paper and gradually hilling earth around them as the plant grows.

Sow seeds in autumn into the bottom of a trench about 20 cm (8 in) deep and then, when the stem is about pencil thick and the plants are separated, trim the top third of the growth. As they grow in winter, slowly build up the soil to help keep the stem white. The whole process usually takes about five months.

Alternatively, sow seed 1 cm (1/2 in) deep into a tray of seed-raising mix. Once the seedlings are pencil-thick, separate them, then remove the top third of the seedling leaves and half their roots. Plant them 2 cm (3/4 in) deep and 8 cm (3 in) apart into a trench. Water in well.

Leeks cope with cold and frost, and like plenty of water when they are in their growth spurt, but they don't like weeds crowding their stems, so make sure you weed them regularly, and also feed them weekly with liquid fertiliser during their growth period. Harvest leeks by pulling whole plants from the ground.

Left: Mound the soil around leeks to keep the stems white.

Below: To prepare leeks for cooking, remove the coarser green part, then cut lengthwise through the white stems and then wash thoroughly to remove the dirt between the layers.

Pods and pulses

Legumes — to which peas and beans belong — are among the most versatile food crops. They can be eaten fresh, as sprouts and as dried produce, making them as much a part of each season as any other vegetable. Pulses are the edible seeds of these plants, which are generally low in fat and high in fibre, making them very good for you.

Replenishing the soil

There are well over 1000 different legumes, many of which are either edible, or useful as stock fodder. They are characterised by their nitrogen-fixing roots that, working in tandem with a soil bacteria found in their root nodules, take nitrogen from the air and turn it into food for the plants.

Peas

Peas (*Pisum sativum*) are a sweet and tasty winter vegetable that can be eaten fresh (cooked or raw) or dried, but they can also be frozen very effectively, so they're popular all over the world. With soft grey-green foliage and tendrils for climbing, peas bear flowers that are typical of the family Fabaceae, to which the species belongs. The developing fruit are pods — many of which can be eaten whole — that contain edible seeds.

Traditional shelling peas include 'Greenfast', 'Telephone' and 'Purple Podded', which, as the name suggests,

Above: Snow peas can be eaten whole.

Left: Butter beans have a delicate flavour, so just steam them lightly or eat them raw.

has not only purple pods but also mauve flowers. If you prefer to eat the whole pod, choose one of the varieties that have sweeter edible pods, such as 'Sugar Pod', 'Snow Pea' and 'Sugar Snap' (known in France as *mangetout*).

Cultivating peas

Sow peas in the cooler seasons, from autumn to spring although, in cold climates, the dwarf types do better over winter. To grow peas, you'll need to provide a support — use either twiggy sticks or netting so they'll have something on

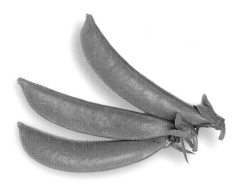

which to hook their tendrils. You can plant peas in rows, or train them up tripods or wigwams. Most varieties start to produce their crops within two months.

Peas are the vegetable equivalent of Goldilocks, needing soil that's not too acid nor too alkaline, but just right, with loads of added organic matter and a crumbly, well drained texture. Pea seeds are quite prone to rotting off, so they're normally sown into moist soil, then not watered again until they germinate. In fact, some people sow them into seed-raising mix first, in little pots or even polystyrene cups punctured with drainage holes. Once the seedlings are about 5 cm (2 in) tall, carefully transplant them into the ground.

Feeding

As peas make their own nitrogen, you won't need to feed them. In fact, if the seeds come into contact with fertiliser, the rate of germination may be poor.

Above left: Borlotti beans, also known as roman or romano beans, were bred in Italy.

Above: Pea flowers.

Below left: Ripe pea pods that are ready to eat should be fat and bright green in colour.

Right: If you shell peas straight after picking them, you can store them in sealed bags and freeze them for use at a later stage.

Harvesting

Don't be shy about collecting peas from your garden, because the more you pick, the more you get. Also, if you leave pods on the vine to grow old, you'll hasten the ageing process of the vine.

Problems

Peas are beset with several problems.

- Budworms are difficult to control once they're inside the pods, but regular applications of *Bacillus thuringiensis*, a soil-dwelling bacterium, are a safe option, especially as the weather warms and the budworms become more prevalent. It is a bio-insecticide

that affects the moth larvae but has no effect on bees, birds or mammals. It also has no withholding period on fruit and vegetables.

- Green vegetable bug (see page 51) overwinters in plant litter, so regular weeding and an annual clean-up will help remove the adult bug and reduce the likelihood of young nymphs feeding on your peas in spring.
- Lucerne flea: page 56.
- Pea weevil: page 62.
- Crop rotation for peas is also recommended: pages 33–5.

Broad beans

The broad bean (*Vicia faba*), also known as tic pea, is a hardy vegetable growing to about 1 m (3 ft). High in protein, the beans store well in their dried form, and are great eaten fresh when in season. This legume hates the tropics, enjoying temperatures a little over 20°C (68°F), and even withstanding severe frosts.

Below, from left to right: Peas need to be grown on a support; 'Purple Podded' peas; and developing purple peas.

Opposite: Fresh peas don't store well, so keep them in the fridge and try to eat them within a few days.

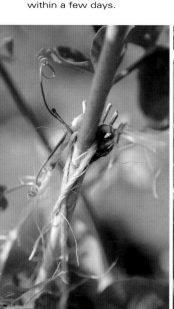

There are a couple of different types of broad bean — those with long pods that are heavy-yielding; hardy types with white and green seeds; and the sweeter 'Windsor', which has round white or green pods. There is also a red-flowered broad bean called 'Crimson'.

Cultivating broad beans

Sow broad beans in autumn or winter, then harvest in late spring and early summer, but adjust this in temperate zones to ensure that as much as possible of their 20-week growing season is spent at the coolest time of the year. All but the shortest types (60 cm/2 ft) need some support, so use canes and strings.

Plant in rows 20 cm (8 in) apart and staggered in the gaps between each row. If you're planting more than two rows, leave 60 cm (2 ft) again before another pair of rows. This will both allow sun penetration and affect a windbreak. Then wait a few weeks before planting again to stagger the cropping.

Don't overdo nitrogen-based fertiliser, as this will promote leaves instead of pods. When your beans start to flower, pinch out the new growth. The tops of the plants can be cooked and eaten like spinach. Cook young beans in pods, but shell the older ones, as the pods will be too tough to eat.

At the end of the season, dig the plants back into the soil, as they are a rich form of green manure.

This page: Beans need to grow on a support such as a trellis, or even on strings tied to stakes. To minimise the risk of spreading bacterial blight, check that the beans are completely dry before picking.

Other peas

After peas and beans, chickpeas (*Cicer arietinum*) are the third most important pulse crop in the world. Native to North Africa and central and western Asia, they are very popular in Middle Eastern and Indian cuisines. They grow best in light, well drained soil, and need dryish weather to grow properly. For this reason they are sown to coincide with the dry season in monsoonal areas, and in late spring in other areas.

Pigeon pea (*Cajanus cajun*) is considered one of the oldest food crops. Also known as dal, red gram, poor man's bean and catjang pea, it's a major food source in tropical regions. It can be eaten fresh or dried, and is said to have seven times the protein of other legumes.

Other species of pea include the asparagus pea (*Lotus tetragonologus*), which bears asparagus-flavoured pods. Also known as the winged pea, it is cooked and eaten whole. The cowpea (*Vigna unguiculata*), which spreads to 1.5 m (5 ft), has mauve flowers and can be eaten as pods when young, but it's usually grown for its black seeds, which can be harvested and cooked as pulses. Each plant produces 1 kg (2 lb) of seeds. This is a warm-season (spring/summer) vegetable that's also grown, like all the legumes, as a soil improver.

Asparagus peas should be lightly steamed.

French beans

French beans or string beans (*Phaseolus vulgaris*) are small growers, not climbers, with pea-shaped white flowers. When picked young, they need only topping and tailing, not stringing. These high-yielding crops, which are rich in protein, are native to the Americas, not France.

Cultivars include dwarf 'Brown Beauty', which is an old French, disease-resistant selection; 'Butter Bush', a compact grower to 45 cm (18 in), with black seeds and yellow pods that are stringless when young; and dwarf 'Hawkesbury Wonder', a popular stringless type with 15-cm (6-in) green pods, which produces over a long period.

Other heirloom types include 'Prestons', a very old stringless and long-cropping variety; 'Redland Pioneer', another type that bears a stringless, but flatter bean; and 'Windsor Long Pod', known for its red seeds contained in flat, 20-cm (8-in) stringless pods (when young).

Cultivating French beans

A warm-season crop that is planted out every month, French beans are sown directly into the soil after the last frost. To provide a continuous supply, start sowing in early spring and keep going throughout summer. They take about ten weeks to

did you know? There is archaeological evidence that humans ate broad beans in the Neolithic Era, and we also know they were a major part of the European diet throughout the Dark and Middle Ages. French, lima and climbing beans are a staple part of the diet in the North and South of America, but have only been part of the Western diet since the discovery of the New World.

produce from seed, so they bear earlier than runner beans by about two weeks, but aren't as plentiful.

You must plant them in a sunny position into well manured, well drained soil, with a pH of 6.5; otherwise, add some lime prior to planting. These beans prefer warm and dryish soil; if it's too wet, the seeds will rot. In marginal or cold areas, erect cloches, or sow in seed trays.

Climbing beans

Climbing beans (*Phaseolus multiflorus*), with their trifoliate, mid-green foliage, need a trellis, tripod/wigwam or a double row of crossing stakes for support. These plants can grow to 2.5 m (8 ft) on really rich soil, although the typical height is about 1.8 m (6 ft). Tie stems as they grow (they twine anticlockwise) and mulch with manure, taking care not to let your plants dry out.

These are also a spring/summer crop, being even more cold-sensitive than the bush types but three times more productive. They will crop throughout summer and autumn about three months after seeding, and are well suited to tropical or warm temperate areas, where their yield per plant makes them worth growing in the home garden.

There are quite a few varieties of climbing bean, but the most prolific is 'Lazy Housewife', an old variety that dates from 1810 and produces masses

Below: Developing 'Purple King' beans.

Borlotti beans

Native to North America, borlotti beans (a cultivar of *Phaseolus vulgaris*) have been well and truly adapted by the Italians, who use them extensively as a dried, or 'cooker' bean. The beans should be left on the vine to mature and ripen before being picked, shelled and stored for winter.

of easy to harvest beans, hence its name. 'Purple King' is a lovely purple-flowered and podded variety, although these turn green when cooked. 'Delago Black Mexican' grows to 2 m (6½ ft), has green pods and black seeds, and can be used dried or fresh. It is also a useful black dye. 'Blue Lake', the most popular stringless type, is known for its good flavour.

Runner beans

The runner bean (*Phaseolus coccineus*) from Mexico is sometimes called Dutch case knife bean. It's a red-flowered type, with cultivars such as 'Scarlet Runner', which looks beautiful in bloom, and 'Painted Lady', an heirloom white- and red-bicoloured bean. It is also beautiful, bearing lovely succulent beans with brown markings on them.

Runner beans differ in that they are perennial, dying down in winter, then reshooting in spring. They need a milder climate than most beans and won't set if the temperature gets too hot.

No matter what bean you choose to grow, don't leave pods of old beans on the vine, or they'll stop producing. Once your beans are 15 cm (6 in) long, pick them every couple of days. The more you pick, the more your plant will produce.

Watch out for snails and slugs, and keep your beds well manured. At the end of the season, leave the roots in the soil as organic green manures.

Cultivating beans

Make sure the soil pH is alkaline and, if necessary, add lime. The soil under the seeds should be firm, while the seeds need 3 cm (1 in) of soil and light mulching to stop it forming a crust, which can inhibit the emergence of seedlings. Beans can develop collar and stem rot, so don't grow

Above: Butter beans with green string beans.

them in the same ground for more than three years.

Hill the plants when the seedlings are about two weeks old, and then again when they are larger. This technique helps support the plants and also reduces the likelihood of them developing lower stem damage from bean fly (see page 52). Take care not to damage the stems or shallow roots when weeding.

Harvesting

It takes about three months for beans to reach the harvesting stage. The stems are brittle, so be careful when picking them. The pods should be firm and full-sized, but pick them before they get tough, which happens when the seeds mature, by regularly harvesting the young pods.

Problems

Beans are susceptible to these problems.

- If the soil pH is too strongly acid, your beans will be subject to manganese toxicity. This shows up as a lack of flowers, stunted growth and scorched leaf edges and even yellow areas between the veins, but it can be rectified by liming your crop (see 'Cultivating beans', page 307).
- Beans also have a low salt tolerance, so never fertilise at planting or allow your seeds to come in contact with any fertiliser. They also hate windy conditions and waterlogged soils, but do require regular water, especially from flowering time onwards.
- Rotating your crops will help control fungal problems.
- Very hot weather can result in spots on pods or poor pod set, but a light overhead watering to cool plants down will increase the humidity, and also help to deter thrips (see page 60).
- Controlling thrips will help prevent the spreading of viral and bacterial diseases. However, killing all bugs will also kill off the mites' predators and can result in severe outbreaks of red spider damage.
- When weeding, take care not to disturb the roots.
- Beans are very susceptible to stem and collar rots (see page 69).

  Other pests to watch out for include the following.

- Green vegetable bug: page 51.
- Harlequin bug: page 51.
- Pod borer: page 50.
- Red spider/two-spotted mite: page 56.
- Rutherglen bug: page 52.

Opposite: A tripod made from trimmed branches or bamboo poles provides an excellent support for growing beans.

Unusual beans

Adzuki (*Vigna angularis*) is a Japanese variety of bushy bean with red seeds that are high in protein and can be used fresh, dried or sprouted. Sow them in spring and they will crop throughout summer. Soya (*Glycine max*) is another popular Asian bean that's used for tofu and other vegetarian dishes, milk substitutes and soy sauce.

Lentils (*Lens culinaris*) are an important legume that's native to western Asia and Africa, where they love the hot, dry climates and can cope with arid, infertile soils. They have been found in archaeological sites more than 9000 years old, making them one of our most ancient food sources. Sow them direct into the ground in late spring, then harvest them once the plant withers in summer. *Lens culinaris* is a sprawling plant that grows to about 60 cm (2 ft) wide by 45 cm (18 in) tall.

Snake beans (*Vigna sesquipedalis*) are sometimes called asparagus beans, as they have a similar delicate flavour and pencil-like thickness. They too hate cold weather and need a support, growing to about 1.8 m (6 ft) tall, but take much longer to bear from seed — about four months from planting out. Fresh or cooked, the pods, which grow up to 45 cm (18 in) long, are popular in Asian cuisines.

Adzuki beans (top) with soya beans (above left) and sinuous snake beans (above right), also known as yardlong beans.

Fruits

After flowering, many 'vegetable' plants develop sensational edible fruit, including such stars as the cucumber, pumpkin and zucchini. While the cultural requirements for these flowering plants are included below, remember that most of these will need full sun in order to promote flowering in the first place.

The cucurbits

This is a large group of warm-season vegetables (and fruit, see page 183) that includes marrows, zucchini, squash, pumpkins, gourds, cucumbers and even chokos. There are many different genera as well as species within this family, but most are short-lived trailing or climbing plants grown for their fruit, and they finish their life cycle within one year.

Cucumbers

Cucumbers (*Cucumis sativus*) are cylindrical water-filled vegetables with green skins and white flesh that are eaten raw as a refreshing salad vegetable, made into dips or pickled. They like rich, well drained soil in full sun and can grow as trailing vines or along the ground, whichever habit suits the position.

Cultivars vary in colour and size, and include fresh-eating types and pickling varieties, or gherkins. These include 'Giant

Above: Three varieties of cucumber: telegraph (top), common (middle) and Lebanese (bottom).

Left: 'Japanese' pumpkin and 'Butternut', a type of squash.

Above left: A developing grey zucchini.

Above: Harvest young white squash before the skin hardens.

Russian', 'Green Gem', 'Lebanese', 'Long White' and 'White Spine', although the most common type is 'Burpless'. Other unusual types include West Indian gherkin (*Cucumis anguria*), which produces 5-cm (2-in) diameter fruits with soft spines on the outside. Sweet and juicy when young, it can be used for pickling or eaten fresh. It's available by mail order from heritage seed companies.

'African Horned' (*Cucumis metuliferus*) is another weird type with 15-cm (6-in) spiny fruit with orange skin protecting jelly-like green flesh. It is alleged to contain four times more vitamin C than oranges.

To grow cucumbers, sow them from seed in groups of threes and fours direct into the soil in spring. One of their benefits is that they fruit after only two months, and will continue to bear throughout summer and autumn.

Cucumber relish

4 tablespoons rice vinegar
125 g (4 oz/$\frac{1}{2}$ cup) sugar
1 small red chilli, seeded and chopped
1 teaspoon fish sauce
80 g (2$\frac{3}{4}$ oz/$\frac{1}{2}$ cup) peanuts, lightly roasted and chopped
1 Lebanese cucumber, unpeeled, seeded and finely diced

Put the vinegar and sugar in a small saucepan with 125 ml (4 fl oz/$\frac{1}{2}$ cup of water). Bring to the boil, then reduce the heat and simmer for 5 minutes.

Allow to cool before stirring in the chilli, fish sauce, peanuts and cucumber.

Makes 185 g ($\frac{3}{4}$ cup).

did you know? In ancient Rome, married women wishing to conceive wore cucumbers around their waists.

Cucurbita pepo and its cultivars

Within this species there are many different cultivars, each with different colours and shapes. They include zucchini (also known as baby marrow or courgette) and winter squash. Each plant starts off with delicately flavoured flesh and soft skin, but with age matures into a harder-skinned, more floury vegetable that keeps better but needs longer cooking times.

Zucchini

Perhaps one of the most popular zucchini (C. pepo var. melopepo) is the prolific 'Black Beauty', with dark green, nearly black skin. It's very easy to grow and takes about three months to reach maturity.

There is also 'Gold Rush', an abundant producer with a lovely yellow skin and, of course, the popular white or grey Italian zucchini. Another golden form is the 'Crookneck', which, as the name suggests, has a bent top. It has slightly warty skin, and can be eaten young when it is 15-cm (6-in) long, or allowed to grow to maturity, when it's attractive enough to be used as a table centrepiece.

Other heirloom types that are also fast-growing include 'Spaghetti' — when cooked, it has flesh that looks like spaghetti — and pale lime 'Tromboncino', which can grow up to 1 m (3 ft) long, although it is best when it's eaten at 25 cm (10 in).

Winter squashes

These frost-tender, thick-skinned fruits grow as a vigorous groundcover with large leaves, and you can store the fruit for use in winter. It's interesting to note that winter squashes are often called pumpkins. They include 'Delicata', a beautiful hybrid with ribbed green and cream skin protecting buttery yellow, sweet flesh. It can be picked small or allowed to develop into an impressive 450-g (1-lb) vegetable that copes well with hot weather.

'Butternut', which is thin-skinned and sweet-tasting, and 'Gold Nugget', which produces 1-kg (2-lb) fruit on a compact bush, are actually both winter-ripening versions of Cucurbita pepo, not pumpkins. This makes sense botanically because, apart from growing into long, oval shapes, squashes can also be scalloped, round fruits, such as the popular cultivar known as pattypan squash.

Other varieties include 'Custard White' and the lesser known green-fruited 'Scallopini', but whatever varieties you choose, plant them all in spring.

---

tip

The tender young leaves and shoots of nearly all cucurbits are edible, so rather than trim the vigorous growers back to keep them under control, lightly fry the new shoots in some olive oil and garlic.

Above: A young cucumber developing from its flower.

Right: 'Black Beauty', a zucchini cultivar.

Opposite: The flower and developing fruit of grey zucchini.

did you know? Zucca is the Italian word for 'gourd', hence zucchini means 'little gourd'.

Pumpkins

Pumpkins (sometimes also known as winter squash, depending on the variety) are cultivars of *Cucurbita maxima*. They are used in soups, baking and, of course, for Halloween jack-o-lanterns. Many types are available, such as 'Baby Blue', which bears 15-cm (6-in) fruit; 'Gramma', a trombone-shaped vegetable used in sweets; 'Jap', a squat fruit with yellow-orange flesh; 'Queensland Blue', a good keeper with orange flesh; 'Triamble', which has grey skin and a distinctive, three-lobed shape; and 'Walham Butternut', which bears 2-kg (4¹⁄₂-lb) pear-shaped fruit with dry, tasty flesh and a small seed cavity at one end.

Gourds

Gourds (*Lagenaria siceraria*) can be eaten when young (as with squash) or grown into their dried fruit form for use as musical instruments, bowls and even pots. 'Ancient' bears trombone-shaped fruit on a vine that's large enough to climb. The 'Miniature' vine, which grows to 2 m (6¹⁄₂ ft), bears 8-cm (3-in) tapering fruit that's green-yellow drying to brown.

Snake gourd (*Trichosanthes anguina*) is a vigorous annual that produces 1-m (3-ft) fruit with a hard shell. It has extremely long fruit that are up to 2 m (6¹⁄₂ ft) in length, yet only about 10 cm (4 in) thick. Inside each gourd is red pulp that can be used as a substitute for tomatoes. The flesh itself is popular in curries, and the leaves and shoots are also edible.

Snake gourds grow best in a frost-free climate with regular summer water and well drained soil.

did you know? In the United States, the tradition of eating pumpkin at Thanksgiving started when the pilgrims, who had settled in New England, celebrated their first harvest. They cut open the top of a pumpkin, removed the seeds and filled the cavity with spices, honey and milk for baking. While the recipes have changed over the centuries, the pumpkin is still celebrated.

Above and left: Gourds are so ornamental that you can use them as table decorations.

Opposite, clockwise from top left: Pumpkin varieties — 'Japanese', 'Triamble', 'Queensland Blue' and 'Golden Nugget'.

Okra

Abelmoschus esculentus, Malvaceae family

Okra (*Abelmoschus esculentus*) is closely related to hibiscus and members of the same family, Malvaceae. Unlike rosella, another member of this family, it is the okra's seed pods or immature fruits that are usually eaten once they have been steamed or cooked in stews but, once cooked, the leaves are also edible and have a taste similar to asparagus. Native to Africa, they made their way to the Americas with the slave trade, and have become popular in many southern areas of the United States and also in the Caribbean, where they are cooked in a traditional stew called gumbo. A quick-growing summer crop, it's planted out each year in spring after frosts. It grows to 1 m (3 ft), at which stage it flowers and produces the pods. About four plants should supply a family.

Climate: Warm conditions for about four months are needed for germination and to produce fruit and heavy crops.

Culture: Okra have a similar growth pattern and life cycle to capsicums (see page 328).

Colours: The flowers are yellow, like hibiscus flowers, with red centres.

Height: 1 m (3 ft) tall.

Planting time: Plant out raised seedlings in late spring or early summer.

Soil: Well drained soil with plenty of added manure and compost is ideal.

Position: Full sun, sheltered from the wind.

Planting depth and spacing: 30 cm (1 ft) apart, 60 cm (2 ft) between rows.

Fertiliser: Regularly apply either liquid manure or nitrogen-based fertiliser from the time the plant is about 30 cm (1 ft) high until the first few flowers start to appear.

Pests and diseases: They can be attacked by caterpillars, white fly and bronze orange bugs.

Propagation: To increase germination rates, first soak the seed in tepid water for a few hours. Sow into trays in spring, then plant out once all chance of frost has passed.

Harvesting: Pick when the pods are tender and the seeds immature (about five days after flowering), as the longer they stay on the plant, the tougher and stringier they become. Daily picking is necessary to promote continual cropping. Store okra in a paper bag in the warmest part of the fridge for 2 to 3 days.

did you know? Also known as lady's fingers, okra is normally green-podded, but there is now also a red-podded type that reverts to green when it's cooked.

Chokos

The oval, slightly warty green fruit of the choko vine (*Sechium edule*) is best eaten when it's about the size of an egg, but if you leave it to grow, it will eventually reach the size of a football. Each plant can produce many hundreds of fruits in two seasons, the first in spring and the second in summer. The plant also develops edible tubers that are considered a delicacy in some parts of the world (see page 277).

Culturally, these vines are as tough as old boots, growing into a vigorous climber about 6 m (20 ft) across — ideal for a backyard fence in a sunny spot. They cope with any soil, but do like a warm climate and won't tolerate frosts. Unless they are protected when reshooting, they will not fruit unless the temperature is warm enough. Each winter, cut the vine back to the ground.

This unusual pear-shaped fruit is one of the easiest plants to grow in a mild climate, provided you have the space and taste for it. They need temperatures between 15 and 35°C (59 and 95°F) to germinate successfully, so wait until the soil has warmed up in spring before planting. Make sure the pointed end is upright, and if you are unsure of the drainage, plant your vine on a slope. Each fruit contains one seed and, if you prefer, you can wait until this has sprouted before planting. Backfill with soil to just below the top of the choko so that it is slightly exposed.

Above: Chokos will keep well in the fridge for up to two weeks.

tip

With their high water content, cucurbits need lots of water: drying out can lead to fruit drop, blossom end rot and poor fruit set.

did you know? Chokos are also known as chayote, sayote, tayota, chow-chow, chocho, custard apple, mango squash, vegetable pear, christophene and pipinella.

Asian melons

There are also lots of Asian melons, known variously as bitter melons or bitter cucumbers. They have either warty or hairy skins, and grow into quite large vegetables about 40 cm (16 in) long, which are usually boiled to take some of the bitterness out of the flesh before stir-frying. For advice on cultivating Asian melons, see 'Cultivating cucurbits' below.

Cultivating cucurbits

Sow seeds direct into a small mound in threes or fours, then remove the weakest seedlings, leaving the strongest ones to mature. For the best germination rate, sow cucurbits when the soil temperature is about 20°C (68°F) so, if you live in a marginal area, you may need to raise seedlings in cold frames or indoors. As they grow, pinch out the growing points of each shoot when they are about 60 cm (2 ft) long to encourage side branching.

As they flower, encourage fruit set by using a paintbrush to transfer male pollen onto the female flower (you can identify it by the swelling behind it).

Feeding

All cucurbits are adaptable to various soils, as long as there is good drainage with added organic matter and a slightly acid pH. Prepare the soil prior to planting as, once they're planted, they don't like root disturbance.

Harvesting

Pick these fruits regularly to encourage more cropping. Store thick-skinned marrow and pumpkins for months in a dry, well ventilated place at 10 to 15°C (50 to 59°F).

Problems

Soils that are too acid can lead to molybdenum deficiency (page 21), which results in mottled yellow leaves, especially around the edges.

Above: A warty bitter or Asian melon.

Opposite: A selection of cucurbits — yellow squash, green and yellow zucchini, and marrow.

Above: A variety of bitter or Asian melons.

did you know? Loofahs are cucurbits, and, while they're usually grown as a body/bath scrubber, they too can be eaten when young — just fry them in garlic and butter.

Fungi

The fruiting bodies of fungi evoke magical associations, and not just because some are hallucinogenic: they can appear 'out of nowhere' as fairy rings and on forest floors. But growing them at home is extremely safe and easy...unlike collecting them in the wild, which can result in accidental poisoning if you don't know what you're doing.

Right: The part of the mushroom that you pick and see is the fruiting body, which produces the spores. These are like primitive seeds. The rest grows either on a host plant or underground.

Opposite: Mushrooms are often used as the key ingredient in vegetarian recipes, as they are rich in protein and B group vitamins. Clockwise, from top left: Shiitake mushrooms; cultivated buttons; Swiss browns; and shimeji.

Types of mushroom

Mushrooms are highly unusual: they are actually fungi, and, unlike the green plants we normally grow and harvest, these organisms do not photosynthesise, transforming the sun's energy into food. Instead, they rely on being 'fed' a diet of complex carbohydrates and microbial proteins from organic matter.

Not all fungi are edible, however. Many contain toxins that can cause mind-altering states and even death, so sticking to the known species is much more sensible than collecting them in the wild, unless you're accompanied by an expert. Common names for deadly fungi include 'The Destroying Angel', so beware.

Below: Enoki mushrooms have a sweet flavour but are very delicate, so add them to dishes such as soups at the last moment.

Wild mushrooms

The most commonly collected mushrooms are the field mushroom or meadow mushroom (*Agaricus campestris*). These start off as small white caps, or button mushrooms, but, as they mature, they open up to reveal a darker underside of gills, which are full of flavour. Woodland mushrooms or porcini (*cépes*) (*Boletus edulis*) are also commonly gathered. These have a gill-like appearance when fresh, but are usually sold dried for an even more intense flavour. They can be reconstituted in warm water — simply soak them for 30 minutes.

Cultivated mushrooms

Of the cultivated mushrooms, the most common is *A. bisporus*. Many other cultivated mushrooms — including button, Swiss brown, chestnut and portobello — are various stages of this species when picked; buttons are the first stage. Cups are the buttons that grow until you can just see the gills, while the flats have all their gills visible. All are low in kilojoules (calories) and rich in vitamin K.

Exotic mushrooms

The popularity of Asian home cooking around the world has resulted in the increased availability of Japanese mushrooms such as oyster (*Pleurotus* sp.), shiitake (*Lentinus edodes*) and enokitaki (*Flammulina velutipes*). Many of these are available either fresh or dried.

Japanese mushrooms traditionally grow on wood; in fact, the name 'shiitake' derives from *shii*, the Japanese word for 'mushroom', where *shii* means the hardwood tree that sprouts these gems.

did you know? In Ancient Egypt, mushrooms were documented as being rare and, as one pharaoh declared, 'too fine to be eaten by the common people'. They were also served at feasts in ancient Greece and Rome.

mushrooms

1 Shimeji white cap   **2** Swiss brown   **3** Oyster   **4** Button   **5** King trumpet
and king brown   **6** Chestnut   **7** Nameko   **8** Enoki   **9** Enokitaki

Cultivating mushrooms

Mushrooms may seem exotic, but there's no reason why you can't grow them at home. The ideal areas are sheds, garages, under houses or in cellars — in fact, any position that is well ventilated but fairly dark. Mushrooms live off rotting organic matter, so they're not fussy eaters, but they do like fairly constant humidity.

You can buy mushroom kits, complete with spawn and sterile growing media. After only a few weeks, your mushrooms will be ready for cropping. Alternatively, place the spawn in a pile of well composted animal manure. Whichever method you use, they should keep cropping for several months as long as you keep them moist and harvest them regularly.

Commercial growers make their substrate out of a variety of sources, including straw, poultry manure and stable waste. These are mixed together to provide the nutrients required by the mushrooms, and can be recycled back to the garden as a mulch and soil conditioner when the mushrooms are finished with it. The spawn

Above: Oysters range in colour from white and yellow to pinkish orange and even purple-brown.

tip

Always store mushrooms in a paper bag in the fridge; storing them in a plastic bag will make them sweat.

Truffles

These extremely valuable fungi grow in association with the roots of certain trees. Different types of truffle are associated with specific trees, and the best known are those that grow on the roots of hazelnut bushes and oak trees in Europe, but there are also truffles that are native to some paperbarks and eucalypts in Australia. These too are highly aromatic, and native animals often search for them in the same way as truffle-hunting pigs and dogs do in Europe, especially after bushfires.

Mushroom plant

Mushroom plant (*Rungia kiossii*), a perennial that grows to 1 m (3 ft), can be used in salads and cooked dishes to impart a similar earthy flavour to real mushrooms. Mushroom plants like a shady, moist position, where they develop shiny, coin-sized dark green leaves, which contain vitamins A and C, calcium and iron, as well as protein.

is added to this, then usually covered with a mixture of peat and lime, which is called casing. Unless it's stored at very low temperatures, the spawn should be planted quickly, as it is subject to temperature changes and can dry out.

The ideal air temperature for growing mushrooms successfully is between 15 and 18°C (59 and 64.4°F), which is why they are not grown in warmer climates over summer. They like a very humid atmosphere, about 85 to 90 per cent, especially at picking time.

Mushrooms also need a constant source of fresh air so they can stay disease-free and their growth isn't inhibited by a build-up of carbon dioxide.

Harvesting

Fruits appear in about six weeks and continue to flush, usually three times in all. Harvest them at the base of their stems with a sharp knife.

Above: Fan-shaped oyster mushrooms, with a field mushroom and some buttons.

Above right: Shimeji mushrooms.

Right: Button mushrooms, their little caps fitting against their stems, are delicious either raw or cooked.

Nightshade family

There are many toxic plants in this family, hence its name — Deadly Nightshade. However, its edible members — including eggplants, capsicums, chillis and tomatoes — are among the most delicious and flavoursome of edible plants.

Eggplants

Grown in India and China for at least 2500 years, eggplants or aubergines (*Solanum melongena*) made their way to the Middle East, then to Spain and Italy via the Moors about 1200 years ago. The plant itself is a very pretty annual shrub with mauve flowers and usually large oval black fruit. They are very cold-sensitive and need good drainage as well as plenty of water during their growth season.

Sometimes called guinea squash, eggplants generally grow to about 1 m (3 ft), so they may need staking in more exposed conditions. These plants are the chameleons of the vegetable world, with the fruit varying in size and shape — some are like cherry tomatoes but in colours of yellow, white or purple, while others, such as 'Ping Tung', look like purple bananas. There are even much larger, football-shaped purple and near black fruit.

Some of the smaller eggplants have beautiful variegations, with white, pink and lavender shades in speckles and

Above: 'Listada de Gandia', a beautiful bi-coloured eggplant cultivar.

Left: Both Thai and pea eggplants are popular in Thai cuisine for pickles, soups and curries.

stripes. They include 'Rosa Bianca', 'Violetta de Firenze', 'Listada de Gandia' and 'Turkish Orange'. But whatever the variety, regular picking will encourage your plants to crop longer.

Cultivating eggplants

Good drainage is essential for eggplants, as they can develop verticillium wilt, and will therefore also need to be rotated annually around the vegetable garden.

These vegetables flourish in hot, humid weather, but struggle in anything lower than about 25°C (77°F). If you do have the right climate, however, they are well worth growing, not only because they taste great and look lovely, but also because they produce heavily — up to 8 kg (17½ lb) of fruit on a single plant, although less on the smaller-fruited types.

To give eggplants a head start, sow seeds in pots or trays about eight weeks before planting, then plant out seedlings in spring into warm, acid soil once temperatures surpass 18°C (64°F). They will respond well to regular applications of fertiliser.

It takes at least ten weeks for eggplants to grow from seedling to cropping stage; the fruit should be in full colour as well as firm and unwrinkled. Store eggplants in the fridge for about a week, or pickle them to serve on an antipasto plate.

Above left: A developing globe eggplant.

Above: Japanese, Thai and pea eggplants.

Below: Japanese eggplants are slightly sweeter than globe eggplants, the most common type.

did you know? Capsicums are first green-coloured, then ripen to red, becoming sweeter as they do so.

Capsicums and chillis

Capsicums or bell peppers, long peppers and chillis (all cultivars of *Capsicum annuum*, a species that is native to South America) are another colourful group of plants worth growing for their ornamental attributes as well as the kilo or so (2 lb) of fruit that each plant can yield. The species is divided into groups according to shape — cherry-shaped (Cerasiform), cone-shaped (Coniodes), elongated cones (Fasciculatum), sweet peppers (Grossum) and long hot peppers (Longum).

The distinguishing feature that separates chillis from capsicums is a compound called capsaicin, which is responsible for the heat in chillis. Most of the capsaicin is contained in the seeds and septae, the white ribs inside the fruit, and the heat is measured on the Scoville scale, which ranges from 0 to 10: capsicums or bell peppers have a rating of 0, while the 'Habanero' chilli scores 10. As a rule, the larger the fruit, the less intense the heat and the greater the sweetness of the flesh.

Cultivars of the small-fruited types commonly known as chillis include the famous 'Jalapeno', an 8-cm (3-in) thick-fleshed Mexican chilli with red and green fruit; the beautiful yellow banana pepper; tiny, round chocolate-coloured mini peppers; and the traditional red bell capsicums.

Cultivating capsicums and chillis

It takes about three months for each plant to develop from a spring seedling into a shrubby bush that will produce over summer and autumn, even over winter in warm areas. Capsicums and chillis need very similar conditions to tomatoes — regular feeding and watering as well as protection from the cold. Sow seeds in spring when the temperature reaches 21°C (70°F) then, when all chance of frost has passed, plant outside about 50 cm (20 in) apart. It's not usually necessary to prune and stake these plants, unless the conditions are windy.

Opposite, clockwise from top left: Chilli flowers; capsicum or bell peppers; 'Masquerade', a variety of chilli; and green and red chillis with red capsicums.

did you know? Capsaicin is an adaptation that protects chilli plants from marauding mammals, so it's interesting to note that birds are unaffected – just as well, as they are attracted to the bright colours of the fruit and spread the seeds.

Pepino

Pepino (*Solanum muricatum*) has a beautiful creamy skin that ripens to a wonderful soft gold, developing lavender-coloured stripes in the process, although some cultivars are completely golden. The apricot-coloured flesh is reminiscent of rockmelons, both in look and taste. The fruit is ripe when it is striped (if it is a striped cultivar), fragrant and slightly soft to touch. While they don't ripen once picked, some say their flavour is improved by a few days' refrigeration. The sweet, juicy fruit can be served in fruit salad, juiced and even dried. The plant grows to about 1 m (3 ft) tall and can also be trained on a trellis, as the stems are quite pliable. Easily propagated from cuttings or layering, pepinos can be attacked by snails. They can also rot if left to hang on the ground, are susceptible to fruit fly (see page 53) and need regular water during hot weather.

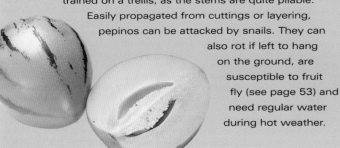

Tomatoes

Arguably the most popular vegetable in the home garden, tomatoes have only been grown in the West for about 400 years. After Hernando Cortez conquered the Aztec Empire in sixteenth-century Mexico, he returned to Spain with gold as well as the plants that bore 'golden apples'. These yellow-skinned tomatoes were first used in Spanish cooking before the Italians made them part of their cuisine. The red-skinned versions are thought to have been introduced to Europe from the Americas by Jesuit priests in the eighteenth century.

The tomatoes we buy in supermarkets have all been bred for their tough skins and solid flesh, which help to minimise bruising during transport as well as prolong their shelf life; however, their taste has suffered in the process. But you can grow delicious heirloom varieties to use in cooking, or just to eat fresh off the vine.

Tomatoes (*Solanum lycopersicum*) are all frost-sensitive, and need to be raised either outdoors in frost-free areas or indoors where there is no chance of frosts, then transplanted outside once the soil temperature is at least 20°C (68°F) in

Above: Tomato seedlings.

Below left: A variety of heirloom tomatoes.

Opposite: Cherry tomatoes are a sweet-tasting variety.

spring. They fruit throughout summer, usually once the weather is warmer.

The fruit can vary enormously in shape and colour, from the charcoal-fleshed, apricot-sized 'Black Russian', the marble-sized cherry tomatoes and the pear-shaped, yellow minis up to the enormous 'Mortgage Lifter'. Bred from beefsteak tomatoes in the United States in the 1930s by 'Radiator Charlie', it produces an amazing 6.4 kg (14 lb) of fruit per plant.

As a general guide to flavour, orange and yellow tomatoes have less acid, followed by pink and purple. The sweetest are white fruits. Striped tomatoes come in a variety of flavours and sweetness, while reds are obviously the classic high-acid, fully flavoured varieties.

Cultivating tomatoes

Plant tomatoes in an area that's protected from frosts and strong winds. Areas with temperatures between 15 and 38°C (59 and 100°F) are ideal, but outside this range they will have difficulty setting fruit.

Any soil will suffice, as long as it's not alkaline and has good drainage and high organic matter content. Rotate the planting position each year, as pests can build up if you have planted potatoes, tomatoes,

tip

Even when part of a plant is edible, another part may be poisonous. For example, the leaves of tomatoes and the green skins of unripe potatoes are both toxic.

tip

Watering evenly will control blossom end rot and sclerotium stem rot, but the opposite will encourage it, so be vigilant in this regard.

chillis, capsicums or eggplants (all members of the Solanaceae family) in that area before (see page 333). If you live in an area that's prone to bacterial problems, buy certified seeds, as these will have undergone the appropriate seed treatment (such as heat).

Feeding

Keep up a good supply of fertiliser, but not too much nitrogen, as it will cause leaf growth at the expense of fruit. Traditionally, a light dressing of poultry manure is applied a few weeks before planting, then liquid manure can be applied once the fruit starts to appear.

Pruning

Many people like to prune their tomato plants in order to reduce the overall size of the plant and therefore increase the size of the fruits themselves. The common practice is to remove laterals, or side branches, as soon as they appear. Keep the main leader or leaders intact, and the main side branches to a well spaced, even

distance, and then pinch out any other shoots from the stem as they appear. Prune with clean hands to reduce the risk of spreading viruses such as yellow mosaic.

Harvesting

Tomatoes are best picked when ripe off the vine, and should never be allowed to

Above: Some yellow pear tomatoes.

Above right: Pinch out laterals as they appear.

Right: Heirloom varieties of tomato.

Tomato sauce

125 g (4¹/₂ oz) roma (plum)
tomatoes
3 basil leaves
2 garlic cloves, crushed
1 tablespoon tomato passata
(purée)
2 tablespoons extra virgin olive oil

Core the tomatoes and purée in a food
processor with the basil leaves (or chop
the tomatoes and basil very finely and
stir together).

Stir in the garlic, tomato passata and
olive oil, and season well. Leave for at
least 30 minutes to allow the flavours to
blend. Use on pizzas, toss through pasta
or serve as a sauce with arancini.

Makes 200 ml (7 fl oz).

over-ripen, as they quickly become floury
and lose their sweetness. If there is fruit
fly in your area, cover them with bags to
protect them, or pick them when they are
just turning colour, then ripen them inside
on a sunny windowsill.

Problems

Crop rotation in the same bed — that
is, alternating with members of other
plant families (not Solanaceae) — is an
important aspect of growing tomatoes:
try not to repeat a crop for 3 to 4 years.
Select varieties that are resistant to
verticillium wilt, fusarium wilt and root
knot nematode, depending on which is
a problem in your district. Staking your
tomatoes will reduce the incidence of
anthracnose and soil rots.

Control aphids and thrips to reduce
the incidence of viruses. The best organic
approach to these pests is to use an
insecticidal (potassium) soap spray
every 5 to 7 days.

Fruit fly (see page 53) is also a major
problem with soft fruit. Spinosad, a new
chemical that's very low in toxicity, can
be bought mixed with a protein and sugar
to attract fruit flies, thereby confining
its effect on the insect population quite
effectively. Do not spray it on the fruit
itself, but use it as either a band or spot
spray to the trunk or lower foliage of about
six bushes per patch. Repeat weekly, but reapply it more often if there has been rain.

Other problems with cultivating
tomatoes include the following.

- Leaf-eating ladybirds: page 44.
- Rutherglen bug: page 52.
- Tomato grub (corn earworm): page 56.
- Tomato russet mite: page 56.
- White fly: page 54.

Saving tomato seeds

It's easy to save the seeds
of your favourite varieties.

1 Quarter your tomatoes
then, using a teaspoon,
scoop the seeds into a
tea strainer.

2 Use the teaspoon to
separate the seeds from
the flesh.

3 Pour water over the
seeds to wash away
the juice.

4 Lay the seeds on some
paper towel to dry.

tomatoes

1 'Jaune Flammee' 2 'Red Fig' 3 'Gold Nugget' 4 'Siberian' 5 'Wapsipinicon'
6 'Black Russian' 7 'Green Zebra' 8 'Martino Roma Red' 9 'Black Koim'
10 'Sugar Lump' 11 'Green Sausage' 12 'Cream Sausage' 13 'Tigrella'

Shoots and stems

The sweet new growth or shoots of many plants from around the world are also edible. Asparagus, rhubarb and sugar cane are some of the more familiar ones, but you can also eat exotic shoots and stems such as bamboo shoots and cardoons, even fern shoots.

Botanical background

Shoots and stems are sometimes confused with each other, so it's worth distinguishing between the two.

Shoots are the tender new growth on mature plants and can include flowers, stems and leaves; they may be the new growth on a herbaceous plant or the new stem and/or flower growth on a woody plant. They are sweeter and easier to eat because the cells have not yet developed the mature walls that make them harder and much less enticing to foraging animals.

Stems, on the other hand, provide the structural support of a plant — for smaller stems and flowers and leaves. Some stems are important commercial crops — for example, sugar cane stems provide us with sugar.

Asparagus

Asparagus (*Asparagus officinalis*) is a semi-climbing perennial plant that grows to 2 m (6½ ft). Native to Europe, Asia and North Africa, it's popular around the world for its delicate spears, which can be eaten

Above: Native to Asia, rhubarb was once an important medicinal crop in China.

Left: Eat young, tender asparagus spears as soon as possible after harvesting.

raw, steamed, lightly boiled or baked. It's a tuberous rhizome that is herbaceous — in other words, it dies down each winter to a permanent rootstock, then reshoots in spring. It is these new shoots or 'spears' that we enjoy.

'Mary Washington' cultivars are the most common varieties used today, mostly because they are resistant to rust. 'Larac' is a white French form that is very adaptable, and 'Sweet Purple', naturally, is a purple variety. There are also male and female asparagus plants. Both produce edible spears, although the male produces more spears and thicker stems than the female.

Related to asparagus fern (*Asparagus densiflorus*), asparagus is also very pretty as an ornamental plant. Its needle-like foliage looks similar to the scale foliage on a conifer, and the female plants bear white flowers, followed by red berries.

Cultivating asparagus

Asparagus needs plenty of room to grow and prefers a position in full to filtered sun,

with protection from wind. You may need to provide supporting canes or cradles if your plants are too exposed. Asparagus likes rich, moist soils that are slightly acid or neutral, with added manure and a thick layer of mulch.

If drainage is an issue, grow asparagus in raised beds, as wet feet can cause rotting off, especially when the plants are dormant in winter. Also, remove any weeds, as perennial weeds will be a real problem if they remain in the soil with asparagus, which will last for some years.

Sow seed 1 cm (1/2 in) deep into seed-raising trays in spring and summer, but first soak them in tepid water a few hours prior to planting. When they are 15 cm (6 in) tall, prick them out and plant them into individual pots. Once they are well rooted, they'll be ready for planting in the ground.

Better still, in winter purchase crowns from a nursery or mail order company. Make sure they are healthy and fresh, and have neither dried out nor succumbed

tip

Blanching or mounding asparagus when the spears appear creates the highly desirable white asparagus.

Right: A healthy crown of asparagus.

Below: A standard variety of asparagus called 'Mary Washington'.

Opposite, top: Harvest spears that are firm and brightly coloured.

to fungal contamination. If you're growing asparagus as a serious crop and not just for novelty value, plant it in a trench about 20 cm (8 in) deep. Into this add some sharp sand, mixed with the existing soil, and mound it so that the crowns are slightly raised. Cover the crowns immediately with about 8 cm (3 in) of soil so they won't dry out. You will end up with excess earth, but this should be added gradually back onto your plants as they grow, and by the end of the next autumn, they should be completely covered.

Space asparagus 1.5 m (5 ft) apart. If you're growing asparagus from crowns, it will take two years before you'll be able to harvest the spears without damaging the plant (as they are the new shoots); if you're growing from seed, add an extra year. You will need twelve plants to feed a family, but even one will give you the luxurious taste of really fresh spears.

To plant a single crown, ensure your hole is weed-free and free-draining. Add some pellitised manure and then, to stop any fertiliser burn, some more soil. Next, place your crown onto this soil and backfill with more soil to create a slightly raised mound. Mulch and label.

Feeding

Each spring, apply both complete plant food and a side dressing of manure or compost as a mulch. In autumn/winter, when you prune the plant down, apply a thick layer of mulch.

tip

Don't let asparagus dry out during the growing season.

Asparagus lettuce

Asparagus lettuce or stem lettuce or celtuce (*Lactuca sativa* var. *augustana*) is a great alternative for those who want the taste of asparagus without the long-term commitment. Sow it in autumn or spring, and grow it in the same way as any other annual lettuce (see page 234), then pick off the leaves and use them as you would a regular loose-leaf type. Cook the stems left at the end of harvest as you would asparagus.

Pruning

Pick off the berries to stop unwanted seedlings from germinating and choking your asparagus bed. Cut the whole plant back to just above ground level when the foliage yellows in autumn, then mulch heavily with manure or compost.

Harvesting

Don't cut any spears for the first year, and only a few during the second. Cut off spears just below ground level when they are about 20 cm (8 in) tall. Stop cutting after 6 to 7 weeks so the plants can develop into ferns and the crowns can build up some strength for the following year. These plants will produce for at least a decade and even as long as 25 years.

Problems

- Asparagus beetles can attack your plants, so be vigilant: page 49.
- Some fungus problems, principally rust and violet root rot, can also occur, so ensure good air circulation and drainage. See page 69.
- Watch out for slugs and snails: page 59.

Unusual leaf shoots and stems

Wombat berry (*Eustrephus latifolius*) is an Australian native vine with edible new shoots. Pick them when they are about 5 cm (2 in) long and eat them as you would asparagus spears. Choko vine (*Sechium edule*) from South America is another plant that has edible new growth, which is sometimes called poor man's asparagus. Choose fresh, succulent stems about 10 cm (4 in) in length. Similarly, the young leaves of okra (*Abelmoschus esculentus*), a quick-growing summer vegetable normally grown for its fruit, can also be eaten as a shoot (see page 316), as can the new shoots of sweet potato.

Udo (*Aralia cordata*), from Japan, has young shoots that are used like celery. Also in the same family as celery is the herb sometimes known as wild celery, or angelica. It's used for both its root and shoots, and is known for its candied stems (see also page 386).

Then there are the ferns, whose new shoots or crosiers, as they are known botanically, are often edible. The crosiers of interrupted fern (*Osmunda claytonia*), tree ferns (*Cyathea* sp.) and *Blechnum indicum* can all be cooked and eaten. The tuberous root of *Blechnum indicum*, which grows in swampy areas in many parts of Northern Australia, was traditionally soaked, roasted and ground by Aboriginals to make flour.

Licorice fern (*Polypodium glycyrrhiza*), a deciduous epiphytic fern that is a different species to true licorice (*Glycyrrhiza glabra*), has rhizomatous roots that were used by native Americans for flavouring food and medicinal purposes. Palm hearts (see page 221) are the edible new shoots of a palm tree, but harvesting these kills the palm, as they only have one growth point. They are reminiscent of artichokes.

Clockwise from above: Wombat berry; crosiers of oyster or ostrich fern (*Osmunda cinnamomea*); and licorice fern.

Blanching the stems of cardoons

To block the light from the young stems, wrap thick cardboard around the emerging shoots, then gradually fill the tube with chopped dry straw. The young shoots will grow through the straw, becoming blanched and tender in the process. After the midsummer harvest, allow the remaining shoots to grow as usual.

1 Holding the plants together, surround them with a dismantled cardboard box.

2 You should now have a cardboard tube with the plants inside. Secure it with tape or string.

3 Push the tube into the soil and fill it with straw.

Cardoons

Like globe artichokes, their close relatives, cardoons (*Cynara cardunculus*) like a moist, fertile soil. However, it is the stem of the beautiful cardoon that is used for culinary purposes, not the flower. Just as beautiful, these deeply divided, silvery grey leaves form a rosette that makes a handsome whorl, befitting both the ornamental and the edible garden.

Cultivating cardoons

Native to the Mediterranean, cardoons need a full sun position with shelter from strong winds. Plant cardoons in spring into well manured and mulched soil with a high organic component. To encourage the blanched edible stems, you will need to plant them in a trench as you would celery (see page 266), or cut off the light in another manner, either by wrapping or by mulching with straw.

These frost-sensitive plants will take about five months to mature, so patience is required.

Rhubarb

The broad leaves and rich red stems of rhubarb are an attractive sight in the garden. Rhubarb (*Rheum rhabarbarum*) looks very much like *Gunnera* sp., the famous water plant, crossed with ruby chard. Its umbrella-like foliage, which reaches about 75 cm (30 in), is held aloft on crimson stems; when ready for harvest, these should be about 2.5 cm (1 in) thick.

The stems are the only edible part of this plant, and they vary in colour from green to deep burgundy, depending on the variety. Although rhubarb is a vegetable, it is usually treated as a fruit, and served as a dessert in fruit pies and crumbles, for example. The foliage itself, while handsome to look at, is poisonous due to its oxalic acid content. Snails don't seem to notice this, however, and often have a go at the leaves.

Opposite: Cardoons can grow to 2.4 m (8 ft), so they make ideal accent plants in the vegetable garden.

Above: The simplest way to grow rhubarb is to plant a crown.

Below right: The red stalks of rhubarb are usually sweeter. Remove the leaves, wrap the stems in plastic wrap and store them in the fridge for up to one week.

Cultivating rhubarb

As it is very adaptable to soil and climate, rhubarb is easy to grow. However, it prefers a moist soil that's rich with manure, and requires regular watering during its growth period as well as protection from hot winds. These conditions will produce the best quality stems.

There are two ways to grow rhubarb — the hard way, and the easy way.

The hard way is to raise seeds (sown from spring to autumn) or buy seedling plants. These will take an extra year to become plants that are worthy of harvesting, and can also be variable in type (green- or crimson-stemmed), as rhubarb reproduces sexually.

The easy way, on the other hand, is to buy rhubarb crowns, although these are only available in winter when the plants are dormant. Plant these out any time during winter or early spring into manure-enriched soil, allowing about 1-m (3-ft) spacings.

Edible grasses

As a food source, grasses are invaluable for the world's quadrupeds, but are sometimes overlooked by humans. The beauty of growing edible grasses is that they are multi-harvest crops, replacing themselves quickly. They range in height from the giant bamboos, which grow up to 25 m (82 ft), right down to the rather ornamental lemon grass bushes (about 1 m/3 ft), which are used as flavouring in Asian cuisines and in teas (see page 405).

Bamboo shoots

Bamboo shoots are the edible culms or stems that emerge from the ground from either of two main species — *Bambusa vulgaris* or *Phyllostachys edulis*. These shoots are used in many Asian dishes and soups,

and are available in cans. Fresh bamboo shoots are hard to come by, however, unless you come from Asia, where they are commonplace. Bamboo is easily grown, but there is a fundamental problem — keeping the plant in check.

Phyllostachys edulis or mousou, as it is also known, grows to 6 to 20 m (20 to 66 ft) tall and at least that wide. The cultivars, which are often golden or variegated, are smaller, but they are all still sizable plants that are also used for timber. The slightly smaller species, *P. dulcis*, known as sweetshoot bamboo, is regarded as the best and sweetest of all.

The common or yellow-stemmed bamboo (*Bambusa vulgaris*) is a slightly smaller bamboo, growing to 15 m (49 ft) tall by about half that wide. It is also used for both shoot production and timber supply.

Cultivating bamboo

Both species like deep, friable soil with lots of summer water and shelter from strong winds and frost. Most require at least a subtropical climate although, if protected when young, as adults they can often withstand light frosts and lack of water, but this is not ideal.

Sugar cane

Perhaps the biggest grass crop in the world is sugar cane (*Saccharum officinarum*). Although it was first used in Polynesia, it's believed to be native to New Guinea. The journey to Europe occurred in 520 BCE when the Emperor Darius of Persia (now Iran) invaded India, where he found 'the reed which gives honey without bees'.

The Arabs distributed sugar cane throughout their expanding empire, and in the eleventh century Christian Crusaders talked of this 'new spice' when they returned to Europe. Subsequent centuries saw a major expansion of this trade, but it was a luxury item for many hundreds of years.

Cultivating sugar cane

Sugar cane grows in any suitable frost-free climate as long as it receives strong sunlight and abundant water as it does in its natural habitat, the tropics.

It grows up to 5 m (16 ft) tall and, with its segmented stems, looks very similar to bamboo. The cane stem, where the sucrose is stored, contains about 10 per cent by weight of a mature plant, producing about 10 tonnes (10 tons) per hectare annually from stems that are cut down to the ground, ready to grow again.

Above: The edible flesh inside a bamboo shoot.

Below left: Bamboo shoots retain their crispy texture after cooking.

Below centre and right: The cellulose in sugar cane is used to manufacture several products, including paper.

Seeds and grains

Seeds and grains are among the oldest plants ever cultivated. Many remain some of our staple foods, while others have all but disappeared. Today some are popular with those who have allergies to gluten or an intolerance to wheat, or perhaps just prefer a varied diet.

Staple crops

Each region of the world has a native grain on which it has depended at some stage in its history. For example, wheat is native to countries around the Mediterranean; rye comes from the colder northern European and Scandinavian countries; rice from Asia; corn from Central America; buckwheat from North America; and grain amaranth from South America. These are supplemented by many other grains and seeds, which are popular today for both snacks and producing oil.

Although most of today's home gardeners wouldn't bother growing their own cereal crops, they can use them to make great sprouts and healthy shoots in juices.

Barley

Barley (*Hordeum vulgare*), a member of the Poaceae family, is an annual cereal crop from the northern hemisphere, coming up in spring, then forming its precious grain over summer for autumn harvest. It was used by the ancient Egyptians to

Above: Barley makes a hearty and nutritious addition to soups and stews.

Left: Corn can be steamed, boiled, roasted, barbecued or cooked in a microwave.

Above left: Young sprouts of sorrel (*Rumex* sp.).

Above: Wheat contains more than 12 per cent protein. Unfortunately, many people are unable to tolerate gluten, one of its proteins.

make bread and beer, and to this day is a staple food of Tibet, where it is made into a flour product called *tsampa*. Tibetans eat it by mixing it with a little buttered tea in a drinking bowl until it resembles a dumpling — sort of a traditional Tibetan convenience food.

In the Western world, barley is still used to make various products, including bread, beer and whisky.

Buckwheat

Buckwheat (*Eriogonum* sp.), from North America, is actually not a cereal crop but a flower whose seed is used in a similar way. The most commonly grown species (*E. strictum*) is ground into a flour that is used in buckwheat pancakes, noodles and tortillas. The plant itself is adaptable to a wide range of situations, from shade to sun, and from rocky, dry areas to richer media, while the flowers are quite attractive and well suited to growing as ornamentals in rockeries. Harvest the seed after flowering in summer.

Chia

Chia (*Salvia rhyacophila*) is native to South America, where it was once considered the ideal travelling food, providing a man with enough sustenance for 24 hours' travel, provided he had plenty of water: the crunchy seeds, which contain omega-3 fatty acids, protein and vitamins, are a good source of energy.

Like all the salvias, chia is very hardy and copes with a wide range of soils and conditions. This species is an annual, growing to about 1.5 m (5 ft), with very pretty blue flowers in autumn. The leaves can also be eaten in salads, or the seeds used for sprouts. Sow seeds in spring once the cold weather has finished, then harvest throughout late autumn.

seeds and grains

1 Wild rice **2** Linseed **3** Cracked wheat **4** Sunflower seeds **5** Wheat grass **6** Wild rice **7** Baby corn
8 Dried corn **9** Rice **10** Wheat **11** Sago **12** Barley **13** Chia **14** Pepitas **15** White sesame seeds
16 Sunflower **17** Buckwheat **18** Grain amaranth **19** Black sesame seeds **20** Poppy seeds (white and black)

Corn

From the New World came many wonderful seeds and grains, but none more important than maize or sweet corn (*Zea mays*). The yellow or white kernels are borne on a cob, which is sheathed in a green husk. Now one of the most popular crops in the world, it varies in colour, from the dark-grained cultivars such as 'Blue Popping', 'Black Aztec' and 'Blue Jade', through to 'Indian Summer', which is a mixture of red, yellow, purple and white kernels.

Corn takes about three months to ripen, but the flavour of homegrown corn is much sweeter than its shop-bought equivalent, so it's worth a go if you have the space. Also available are mini cob and coloured cob varieties such as 'Mini Blue Popcorn' (a small grower — to 1.2 m (4 ft) — that produces several cobs per plant); 'Golden Bantam', which takes only 70 to 80 days to mature and produces two cobs per plant; 'Hawaiian', a sweet, compact grower to 1.5 m (5 ft); and 'Jolly Roger', which is both heavy bearing and very sweet.

Cultivating corn

Easy to grow, corn reaches 1.2 to 2 m (4 to 6½ ft) and likes fertile, well drained soil in a sunny position. Dig over the site well, adding plenty of manure and some compost or complete plant food. The soil

did you know? Corn, the Aztecs' principal crop, is indicated on the famous Aztec Calendar, an agricultural/ritual calendar in the form of a relief sculpture that was discovered under the site of Mexico City. Centeotl, one of the Aztec deities, was the god of corn.

Pollinating corn

It's easy to pollinate corn by hand.

1 Using a small paint-brush, pick up pollen from the male flowers.

2 Transfer the pollen to the female flowers.

should be slightly acid or neutral in pH (see page 15), so a soil test may be necessary. Warm days are needed for sweet corn to grow, so plant out raised seedlings or sow direct in full sun in spring or summer after all chance of frost is over. Keep the soil moist, and mulch well.

The pollination of corn 'ears' is one of the most crucial factors with corn. In the home garden, it's best to plant in small blocks rather than rows so that the wind will spread the male pollen evenly, or it may be necessary to hand-pollinate plants: simply use a paintbrush to transfer pollen from the feathery male tassels onto the silk of the female flowers (see the step by step sequence opposite).

You can also use corn as a companion plant for growing beans. Native Americans use the Three Sisters method, whereby corn provides a support for the beans, which also return nitrogen to the soil; the third 'sister' is squash, which covers the ground, controlling weeds and deterring pests. For more information on companion planting, see page 46.

Feeding

Corn needs lots of fertiliser, such as poultry manure, which is usually applied at planting time. Nitrogen is essential for promoting vegetative growth to about 1.8 m (6 ft).

Harvesting

Corn is ready for picking when the kernels are plump and full of milky fluid; if this is clear, the cobs are not yet ripe.

Problems

Corn is affected by various problems.
- Many caterpillars and chewing bugs affect corn, so keep a lookout for these: pages 55–6.

Above left: A young cob of corn developing.

Above: You can use corn as a support for growing beans.

- Make sure the pH is correct — that is, slightly acid — so that your plants don't develop zinc deficiency, which results in the death of seedlings and stunted, cream-striped growth in more mature plants. Spray with zinc sulfate if this is a problem in your region.
- Inadequate food and water supply or frost damage are the other likely reasons for distress and tissue damage.
- Corn can also fail to form kernels properly down the whole length of the cob. This is caused by inadequate fertilisation, which can be aided by block planting rather than planting in rows, or by hand-pollinating cobs (see the step by step sequence opposite).

did you know? When Christopher Columbus landed on the island of Cuba in 1492, the Indians presented him with two gifts. One was corn, the other tobacco. The gift of corn indicated the status this grain enjoyed in both North and South America, where it is known as the 'source of life; the first mother and father'.

Flax

Linseed or flax (*Linum usitatissimum*) has been grown for its oil content for about 6000 years. When pressed, the seeds themselves produce a very fine oil, popular for varnish and paints but also for medicine. The fibre obtained from the stems is made into linen, and the plant itself can become a bit of a weed, easily naturalising itself in stony places. The blue flowers are quite pretty, held aloft by wiry stems about 1 m (3 ft) tall throughout summer. Sow the seeds in spring into a well drained, full sun position.

Linseed oil contains many vitamins and minerals, as well as some highly valued omega-3 fatty acids. The seeds themselves can also be used, and have a slightly nutty flavour, but are usually ground first (or sold as meal) to make a flour for baking into breads. Sow seeds in autumn and winter.

Grain amaranth

Also from South America is grain amaranth (*Amaranthus hypochondriacus*), which has white seeds that are high in protein and can be popped like corn. To grow it, find a warm, sunny spot with good drainage and sow the seeds directly in spring so they can grow during the warm weather. Known commonly as love-lies-bleeding, the leaves can be eaten and cooked or used raw in salads; in summer, after flowering, you can also harvest the seeds.

Inca wheat

Inca wheat or quinoa (*Chenopodium quinoa*), from South America, is an ancient grain crop high in protein that reaches 1.8 m (6 ft) in full sun. The seeds are used cooked in dishes or for oil, and the new leaf shoots can be eaten too (it is related to Good King Henry; see page 396). The seed is red, yellow, black or white.

did you know? In the fifth century BCE, the Greek physician Hippocrates, the 'father of medicine', prescribed ground flax seed to treat digestive ailments.

Nigella

Love-in-a-mist (*Nigella* sp.) is a pretty annual with sweet pink, white or blue flowers surrounded by thread-like leaves that give the plant a most unusual 'misty' veil, especially as they dry off at the end of their life cycle. One species, *N. sativa*, however, is used as a food source, with the seeds eaten like peppery poppy seeds in India and the Middle East. It is also known as kalonji or black cumin, and goes well with pulses and vegetable dishes, curries and even salads once the seeds have been dry-roasted to release their fragrance.

Oats and rye

Oats (*Avena sativa*) and rye (*Secale cereale*), which both grow to 1 m (3 ft), are sown into cultivated ground in spring, and are ready for harvesting in 6 to 8 months. Sow about 100 g (3 1/2 oz) of seed per 7 m (23 ft) square.

Rye is particularly popular in northern Europe, as it ripens despite the shorter growing season. This is why black bread and pumpernickel are staples in these cold climates: there simply isn't a long enough summer in which to grow crops such as wheat. In warmer climates, rye is sown in autumn and treated as a cool-season crop, being harvested in late spring and early summer.

did you know? The association of the poppy's drooping head with fallen soldiers can be traced back to the Greek poet Homer in the eighth century BCE.

Opposite, clockwise from bottom left: *Nigella damascena*, whose seeds are not edible, growing among the yellow flowers of *Sedum aizoon*; flax or linseed flowers; and the feathery seed pods of *Nigella sativa*.

Above: A crop of rye.

Below left: Eat pepitas on their own or add them to muesli and dried fruit and nut mixes.

Below: Poppy seeds.

Pepitas

Another seed common in North America is the pepita, the edible green seed of pumpkins and squash. Once the hulls or shells are removed, pepitas can be pressed for oil or roasted. Used in cooking by the Aztecs, they are one of the essential ingredients in *mole*, a traditional but complicated Mexican stew.

Poppy seeds

Poppy seeds, from the opium poppy (*Papaver somniferum*), native to the Mediterranean region, are used all over the world as a decorative and flavoursome topping for bread; their bluish black tones provide not only visual contrast and interest, but also a delicious nutty flavour. Growing opium poppies is illegal in most countries, but there are some cultivars with very low levels of opium that are cultivated commercially.

tip

Sunflowers are ready to harvest when the seeds are plump and most of the petals have fallen. Cut off the heads and rub the seeds out by hand.

Rapeseed

Rapeseed or canola (*Brassica napus* subsp. *oleifera*) is now one of the most important oil-producing plants worldwide, and an essential ingredient in many margarine spreads. It is another member of the cabbage family (Brassicaceae), and likes similar cold conditions. In Scandinavia, rapeseed has been grown since at least mediaeval times.

Sesame seeds

Sesame seeds are produced by an annual plant (*Sesamum orientale*), which is native to Africa. It's one of about fifteen other species in this genus that have been cultivated for thousands of years. The famous password, 'open sesame', derives from the pods that split open and dry, casting out the seeds in a mini explosion. The white or pink flowers themselves grow on the leaf axils of the plant, which is about 1.5 m tall x 50 cm wide (5 x 1¹/₂ ft). Sesame likes rich, well drained but moist soil, and is grown from seed.

These days, sesame is grown as a food staple in many tropical and subtropical areas of the world. The seeds are collected before the pods open and then pressed for oil or made into the popular paste called

Above right: Sunflowers are members of the daisy family (Asteraceae).

Below: Black and white sesame seeds.

tahini. Eaten whole, they are popular as black (or unhulled seeds), white (hulled) or cream brown (toasted) and used as a topping in baking, desserts such as halva, and in Middle Eastern and Asian dishes.

Sunflower seeds

Sunflowers (*Helianthus* sp.) are from North America. The species most grown today for oil production is *H. annuus*, an annual growing up to 3 m (10 ft). The flowers turn their large daisy heads in the direction of the sun, and each blossom is centred with a mass of the edible oil-rich seeds, surrounded by golden ray florets.

Sown in spring, these frost-sensitive plants like full sun and a warm position in free-draining soil as well as protection from frost and snails. Feed with blood and bone or another organic fertiliser as they grow. They can look very pretty in the vegetable garden at the rear of the patch. Dwarf (40 cm/16 in) and double forms are available, although these are less productive.

Wheat

Wheat is, of course, one of the biggest crops in the world, as it is made into flour for bread, cakes, biscuits and many other products. The wheat grown for these purposes is *Triticum aestivum*, but durum wheat (*Triticum durum*) is also very popular as the flour component in pasta.

One of the ancient forerunners of modern wheat is spelt wheat (*Triticum spelta*), which can still be grown today. Its hard grain is used in health foods such as pasta and bread, as the gluten, the protein found in wheat, is not as reactive for those with some gluten intolerance.

Wheat needs an open, sunny position in order to grow well, with regular water during germination and growth periods, but dry spells during the harvest, as rain can spoil the crop.

It grows to about 1 m (3 ft), including the flowering heads, which contain the grain, and is ready for harvesting in about 110 to 130 days, depending on the climate. It can also be used to feed chickens.

Wild rice

Wild rice (*Zizania aquatica*) is an aquatic plant that grows naturally in the lakes of Northern Canada. It has a long, thin grain that tastes earthier and nuttier than traditional Asian rice. There are many different types of regular rice (*Oryza sativa*), depending on whether it is from Asia or India, with the grain varying in length from place to place.

Rice has been cultivated as a food source since the beginning of recorded history, but is thought to be originally from South-East Asia. It too needs a flooded area (even a pond) to grow effectively, and can look quite ornamental. It is the drooping seed heads that carry the grain.

Above left and below: The flowering heads of wheat.

Above: Wild rice heads, plump with grain.

did you know? The roots of sunflowers can also be roasted and eaten as a vegetable. They have a similar nutty flavour to Jerusalem artichokes.

Sprouts

Seeds are the beginning of life, containing everything that's needed for a plant to survive, except water. Traditionally eaten in many cultures and cuisines, but once regarded in the Western world as 'hippie food', nature's own vitamin pills are now likely to be available in the juice bar at your local shopping centre.

Nutrient-rich food

Alfalfa probably started the Western sprout 'movement'. Snow peas, soya beans, mung beans, adzuki beans, chickpeas (which are full of protein and fibre), fenugreek, wheat, buckwheat, sunflowers, chia and lentils are the most common nowadays, but almost any legume or cereal crop can be eaten in this way. Even radishes, broccoli, celery, cabbages and spinach can be eaten as sprouts or young seedlings.

Sprouts also contain every essential amino acid and many vitamins, including C, B_1, B_2, B_3, B_6 and B_{12}. Special mixes are

available so you can grow your own salad, sandwich or stir-fry mixes. One of their great attractions is that they can be sown all year round.

Sprouts generally take 3 to 6 days to germinate in a jar, or 10 to 14 days if sown in seedling trays so they can be harvested as seedlings with scissors. Place them on a windowsill out of direct sun and keep them

This page: You can grow your own sprouts either by sowing seeds in trays or by letting them germinate in a jar. If sprouting them in a jar, you'll need to rinse them twice a day and keep them away from direct sunlight.

Opposite, top right: Alfalfa, snow pea and mung bean sprouts.

moist. When their first true leaves appear (not the seed leaves), they are ready for harvest. Use them straightaway, while they are still full of nutrients.

Alfalfa

Alfalfa is just lucerne, the hay that's eaten as stock fodder by animals and also used by gardeners to mulch their gardens. It's high in antioxidants and a great source of minerals.

Alfalfa tastes like nutty peas and, if grown in a jar, will sprout and be ready to eat in only three days. Grown in a tray, they'll be ready for harvest in ten days.

did you know? In China watercress is used as a tonic but it is actually an exotic there, having been imported from Western Europe in the Middle Ages. Its Chinese name translates to 'overseas vegetable'.

Growing sprouts

You can easily grow your own sprouts at home. All you need is a collection of small clear containers with lids that will serve as mini hothouses. Empty strawberry punnets are ideal.

1 Place some seed-raising mix in each punnet.

2 Level it with a fork or a small weeding tool.

3 Moisten it with water. A spray bottle is best so that you don't dislodge the soil surface.

4 Sow a different type of seed in each punnet, and cover lightly with more mix or vermiculite.

5 Spray lightly with some water again.

6 Place the top back on, and wait for your little plants to sprout.

Beans and pulses

Adzuki beans (*Vigna angularis*) take about five days to sprout, and are often blanched before they're eaten, as are mung beans, which can take up to a week to shoot. Chickpeas and lentils are faster — ready in about three days, they can be eaten raw or cooked.

Right: Adzuki beans.

Far right: Fenugreek seeds and fenugreek powder.

Fenugreek

Fenugreek (*Trigonella foenum-graecum*) has a spicy flavour and a pungent smell that makes it great in stir-fries and perfect as a garnish. Its sprouts too can be grown in a jar or on a tray, but the shoots are best when only 2.5 cm (1 in) long, as they will still have their intense, curry-like flavour. If growing them in a jar, be sure to rinse them twice a day.

Cress

Cress (*Lepidium sativum*) contains high levels of vitamins A, B complex and C, and is perhaps the easiest of sprouts to grow. It's often grown in combination with mustard, but should be sown 4 to 5 days earlier in order to be harvested at the same time.

Other types of cress

Upland cress or American land cress (*Barbarea verna*) and bittercress (*B. vulgaris*) are two other cresses that can be substituted for watercress. Both are perennials to 60 cm (2 ft), bear yellow flowers and love lots of water and sunshine. The leaves can be used in salads, soups and stir-fries.

Lebanese cress (*Aethionema cordifolium*), which is sometimes known as fools watercress, is actually native to Ireland. It is a celery-flavoured spreading perennial to 20 cm (8 in) that loves living in damp conditions, where it can romp slightly out of control if not kept in check by regular use or pruning.

The less vigorous *Oenanthe javanica* 'Flamingo', a tricolour cress, makes a very pretty alternative, and, like Lebanese cress and watercress, loves lying in a wet spot. It is a member of the carrot family, Apiaceae, and in both India and Japan it is commonly grown as a leaf crop.

Lebanese cress can be easily grown from cuttings.

Grains

Buckwheat (*Eriogonum strictum*) will grow in either a jar or on a tray, and can be harvested in about four days. If grown in a warm place, traditional wheat takes about the same length of time, as do sunflower seed shoots, which taste delicious when young but can be overpowering if left too long.

Snow peas

Snow pea sprouts are used in Asian cuisine as a garnish or tossed through stir-fries at the last minute. They are rich in calcium and niacin, and also perfect raw in salads. Sow them in seed trays and harvest when about 7 cm (2¾ in) tall.

White mustard

White mustard (*Sinapsis alba*), a member of the huge Brassicaceae family, grows to about 30 cm (1 ft) tall, forming a rosette, from which grow tallish flower stems with bright yellow flowers — so typical for this family. Usually, however, mustard is grown as a salad vegetable and harvested long before the flowers form, when the seedlings are only two weeks old, or about 5 cm (2 in) high. Sown in seed trays, they can also be grown outdoors in the garden on a bed of fine sand in full sun. Cut them with scissors then cook them with eggs — just delicious.

did you know? Cress has been grown since the days of the ancient Persians, who would always eat cress before they baked bread. This may be because it stimulates the appetite, but some scholars have attributed garden cress's reputation in the Middle East to the fact that it was recommended by Muhammad, the prophet of Islam.

Above: The garnet-coloured sprouts of red amaranth look pretty in a salad.

Left: Snow pea sprouts taste a bit like spinach.

Aquatics

Each country has its own versions of edible aquatics, be it samphire and watercress in Europe or wild rice in North America. In Australia, Aboriginals have been harvesting waterlilies and nardoo, a clover-like aquatic, for thousands of years.

The benefits of growing aquatics

Growing plants in aquatic or marine environments is becoming more and more popular, especially as Western chefs now have a more comprehensive understanding of Asian cuisines.

Many of these ingredients, such as rice, are grown in water or damp areas, but so are less common vegetables, such as water spinach, seaweed and water chestnut. However, there are other reasons for growing plants in water: with a shortage of arable land in some countries, growing these plants in a controlled, intensive hydroponic system provides much greater control of nutrients and growth.

Moving aquatic plants out of their natural habitat into another one has inherent risks — in the right conditions, many will spread very quickly, becoming invasive. For this reason, take extra care when planting your water crop that it does not become a water weed. An effective safeguard is to grow these plants in a container of some sort.

Above: The seed pod of the lotus.

Left: Growing aquatics in a water feature such as a tub or bath rather than a dam or pond makes harvest time much easier.

Arrowhead

From Asia, arrowhead (*Sagittaria graminea*) bears 2-cm (³/4-in) wide sweet tubers, sometimes known as duck potatoes, which can be baked, fried or boiled; even the young shoots are edible.

Arrowhead is a weed in Australia, as it spreads too easily, but you can buy non-flowering forms that pose no danger when planted into ponds and tubs. It grows to 30 cm (1 ft), likes full sun and only needs about 10 to 30 cm (4 to 12 in) of soil cover. Plant tubers into a mix that is 70 per cent soil and 30 per cent manure.

Indian shot

Indian shot or arrowroot (*Canna indica* syn. *C. edulis*) is a beautiful ornamental with stunning bright foliage in amazing colours and combinations, complemented by yellow, tangerine, pink, red and orange flowers. The tuber or rhizome of the straight species, which has green leaves and smaller, red flowers, can be eaten either cooked (like potatoes, or ground into flour) or raw. It contains protein, calcium, phosphorus, iron, potassium and vitamins A, B and C. The small tubers are the tastiest. The young leaf shoots can also be eaten as a vegetable, after they've been cooked.

Indian shot is native to tropical Peru and Equador, in South America, where it was one of the first domesticated plants of the region and, indeed, one of the food staples of the Incas. It grows to about 2 m (6½ ft) in sun and part shade, and loves water, coping well with damp positions. It is also very fast growing, so you can harvest it after six months. Plant tubers 30 cm (1 ft) apart.

Indian shot is bothered by few pests, but may attract some rust (see page 69), which can be identified by the orange spots on the plant's leaves. The only thing it doesn't like is frost so, if this is likely in your area, protect it or dig up the tubers for overwintering.

Above left: The young tubers of Indian shot are sweet-tasting.

Above: You can eat the seeds and stems of waterlily — just peel the stems first, as you would celery; however, before eating the roots, you must bake them.

Sacred lotus

Native to Australia are various edible water plants, including waterlilies, which have stems that are eaten like celery; nardoo, which is ground into flour after treatment (see page 222); and warrigal greens, which grow in both damp and shady situations (page 222).

Perhaps the most versatile, however, is the sacred lotus (*Nelumbo nucifera*), which is native to the Northern Territory of Australia and further north as far as India. It is extremely vigorous and can easily take over a dam or pond, but it can be contained in an old bathtub or pot, as long as it is no smaller than about 30 cm (1 ft) across and 20 cm (8 in) deep.

The plant grows to about 1 m (3 ft), and all parts are edible: the leaves, which can be used to wrap fish; the young shoots; the roots, which can be stir-fried or roasted; the seeds, which can also be pan-roasted; and the flowers, whose petals are edible and can be eaten in salads.

Samphire

In nineteenth century London, where samphire (*Crithmum maritimum*) was sold as crest marine, it was popular as a pickling herb, but these days it is usually cooked as a vegetable and regarded as a delicacy. Its aromatic succulent leaves have been described by the herbalist Culpeper as having a 'pleasant, hot and spicy taste'. The stems, leaves and seed pods are all edible.

Top: Unlike the waterlily, the lotus has a prominent seed pod that stands proud of the petals and stamens.

Left: In still or slow-moving water, waterlilies can quickly become weeds.

If you can get hold of some seeds, you don't have to grow it by the seaside either — any light soil will do. It is frequently confused with marsh samphire (*Salicornia europaea*), which is also edible, either cooked or raw, with a similar texture to asparagus after steaming.

Taro

In the tropics, taro is often grown for its edible tubers (see page 278), but this particular one — the celery-stemmed taro, Tahitian spinach or cocoyam (*Colocasia esculenta*) — is also grown for its stalks, which are eaten, as one of its common names suggests, like celery.

It can grow in most soils, as long as it's kept moist or wet, or well watered and mulched if dry conditions are expected. Plant the tubers just below the soil surface into warm soil, and harvest the stems year round once the clump is a decent size.

Water chestnut

A Chinese aquatic vegetable, the water chestnut (*Eleocharis dulcis*) is a reed-like plant with 'nuts' or root nodules, which can be eaten either raw or cooked. The plant is very productive for its size, with one bulb producing up to 1 kg (2 lb) of food, and each 'chestnut', or edible corm, growing to about 4 cm (1½ in) across.

Water chestnuts grow to about 1 m (3 ft), and are harvested when the foliage dies down at the end of autumn. This is easily done if you are growing them in a container — it's simply a matter of lifting out the mass, hosing it off to remove the soil, harvesting the corms and replanting a few good ones back into the mix, about

Left: Celery-stemmed taro is sometimes called elephant's ears.

Sea kale

A perennial in the cabbage family (Brassicaceae), sea kale (*Crambe maritima*) grows about 70 cm (28 in) tall and at least the same wide. It grows naturally in shingle along the coasts of Europe, so it's ideal for coastal positions. With sprays of honey-scented white and orange flowers to about 1 m (3 ft) and fleshy, blue-green leaves, it also produces delicious, nutty-tasting blanched shoots. Cut these shoots when they are 15 to 20 cm (6 to 8 in) long throughout winter and spring.

The best way to grow sea kale is from offsets, which appear at the base of the plant in spring and again in autumn. These can be separated when they're about 20 cm (8 in) tall. Use a sharp knife to remove them, making sure you retain some roots from the mother plant. Keep the plants well watered until they have taken root.

Don't let your plants flower, or the crowns will suffer. Cut any flower buds off at the base, and these will be your supply for the following year. A small dose of salt, applied in autumn, regular manure and water is all sea kale requires.

did you know? Marsh samphire is also known as glasswort, as its ashes were used to make soda-based glass until the nineteenth century.

50 cm (20 in) apart, for the next season. Keep your water chestnuts covered with about 5 cm (2 in) of water, especially during the growing season.

The corms are ready for harvesting when the stem tops have turned brown and died down. Even after cooking, the corms remain crunchy.

Watercress

Watercress (*Nasturtium officinale*) needs to be grown in a wet situation in the garden or in a pot in a pond. It will tolerate both sun and shade, as long as the moisture level is constant.

To start it off, just buy some from the greengrocer and plant the bunch into some potting mix, mulched with gravel then sunk into your pond, where it will quickly strike roots (see the step by step sequence opposite). Use it in sandwiches, salads and herb butters.

did you know? Many Chinese will only eat small amounts of water spinach, and only if they are fit and well, as the stems are hollow and they don't want to take on the 'weakness' of such a plant themselves, especially if they are elderly and frail.

Planting watercress

You can plant watercress in a pot, then use it as a centrepiece in a water feature like this one.

1 Mix together some premium potting mix and garden soil. If your soil has a high clay content, so much the better, as the heavier soil will help to anchor the plant when it's submerged.

2 Take a large bunch of watercress that you've bought or grown yourself, and place it in a plastic pot that's about 25 cm (10 in) in diameter. Then add the soil mix and water in well.

3 The roots will continue to grow from the bottom node, shown here.

4 Finish off with some decorative gravel.

5 If you're adding the pot of watercress to a large pot or bowl, test the height of the pot, and add some bricks if necessary so that when the water feature is full, the plant will sit above the surface.

6 Fill the water feature with water.

Water spinach

Water spinach (*Ipomoea aquatica*) is a vigorous plant that should be planted with caution. It is, in fact, a declared weed in parts of the United States, particularly the warmer states such as Florida and Texas, where it has become an environmental menace. Growing 2 to 3 m (6½ to 10 ft) or more, and liking a moist, even wet soil, it has found its way into waterways where, depending on whether or not it's being harvested as a crop, it is either an invasive pest or a handy cut-and-come-again perennial vegetable.

The leaves are used in many Asian cuisines, particularly in the eastern and south-eastern ones such as Malay and Vietnamese. Its other names are water cabbage, water convolvulus, kangkong,

eng chai and ong choy, depending on where you live. Usually it's stir-fried and served as a green vegetable with garlic and chilli, or oyster sauce and shrimp paste. It can be eaten raw with green papaya salad, a Thai dish known as *lao*.

Left: Water spinach is a popular ingredient in Thai cooking.

Opposite, clockwise from top: Some water chestnuts growing in a fish tank; a sprig of watercress, which has a strong peppery flavour; watercress growing; and a water chestnut corm.

Intense flavours.   Fragrance.

herbs and spices

Tantalising tastes of the world. Memories and aroma.

Contents

plants for the senses

In many cultures, the history of herbs and spices and their uses is a long and fascinating one. The Romans distributed their knowledge of Mediterranean herbs as well as the plants themselves as they conquered nations in Western Europe and Britain; in fact, since the fall of the Roman Empire, this has been one of their great legacies.

Asian herbs travelled to Europe via the Spice Road, as did many spices from the subcontinent, such as pepper and cardamom. Today herbs and spices enrich many dishes, making both dining and gardening more exciting.

A culinary herb is any plant with edible parts — leaves, flowers, stems, bark or roots — that is eaten cooked or raw, as a delicious garnish or on its own, while spices are the dried edible parts. Most common herbs fall into the leafy 'green' category — that is, we use the leaves themselves; the four classic herbs 'parsley, sage, rosemary and thyme', which are often grown in the home garden, fall into this group.

There are also root herbs, such as turmeric and ginger; buds and flowers, like globe artichokes; and even edible weeds, such as dandelion and purslane. And there are some unusual herbs, once collected in the wild, which are used to flavour and preserve meat, poultry and fish.

Lamiaceae herbs

The Lamiaceae family includes sage, lemon balm, mint, basil, rosemary, thyme, marjoram and oregano. All members have the characteristic square stems, oil-rich, fragrant foliage and flowers with a tongue, or insect 'landing pad'.

Growing Lamiaceae herbs

With the exception of perilla, summer savory and basil, which need to be replanted each year in spring, all these herbs are perennials and, if grown in a well drained position in lots of sun, will thrive for many years.

Many members of this family — such as marjoram, oregano and mint — are quite vigorous spreaders, so it may be wise to plant them into large containers in order to prevent their runners spreading into surrounding beds.

For the majority of these herbs (except basil), a chalky soil is the norm so, in acidic soils, you may need to apply lime to bring the pH up to neutral.

Sage, rosemary, mint and basil can benefit from tip pruning all summer and autumn to remove the flowers and promote new, bushy growth. The fragrant foliage of Lamiaceae herbs means most pests leave them alone, so they remain generally trouble-free.

Above: Salad burnet, a member of the Rosaceae family, can be used in summer drinks and salads (see box, page 379).

Left: Before buying herbs, always check that the plants are healthy, with green leaves and balanced growth.

Basil

Basil (*Ocimum basilicum*), a wonderful herb for summer, complements any tomato dish. Indeed, it's also a good companion plant for tomatoes, helping to keep them free of certain pests, such as fruit fly.

Native to India, the Middle East and some Pacific Islands, it is now universally popular in many cuisines. If you have a glut of basil in season, make some pesto that you can serve with pasta (see the recipe on page 370).

As well as the common or sweet basil, there are many different types, colours and flavours. The best eating types are Greek basil (*O. basilicum* var. *minimum* 'Greek'), lemon basil (*O. basilicum* var. *citriodorum*) and bush basil (*O. basilicum* var. *minimum*), which has much smaller leaves. 'Thai Basil' or 'Siam Basil' (*O. basilicum* 'Siam Queen') is great in Asian cuisine, but the purple-leafed type (*O. basilicum* 'Purple Ruffles'), while pretty in the garden, is not as tasty.

Cultivating basil

Basil hates the cold, and the seeds will not germinate if temperatures are too low, although you can raise them early in mini glasshouses or cold frames, or even on the kitchen windowsill if it's bright enough.

Not all basils die off in winter. In fact, there are more than 60 species and many are perennials, including 'Sacred Basil' or 'Holy Basil' (*O. tenuiflorum* syn. *O. sanctum*). This variety grows into a 1-m (3-ft) shrub, and will still hold and flower throughout mild winters, giving you a continual supply of leaves that have a similar — but not as sweet — taste and fragrance.

Above left: 'Siam Queen'.

Above: 'Holy Basil', which has a mild spicy scent, can be either purple-leafed (shown here) or green-leafed.

Below: Cut sprigs of basil after the flower buds have formed but before they open, otherwise the plant will become woody.

Below right: Add fresh basil leaves to dishes at the last moment, as cooking destroys the flavour.

Opposite, clockwise from top left: Purple basil; 'Thai Basil'; golden lemon balm; and lemon balm.

Regardless of the types you grow, pick the new, young leaves for best flavour, and also to encourage branching and new growth. When freezing fresh leaves, brush both sides with olive oil to help retain their flavour and keep them apart, then store them in the freezer double-wrapped (once in foil, once in plastic wrap) or, alternatively, use them in pesto, which can also be frozen.

Fusarium wilt (see page 68) can also be a recurring problem, especially if basil is grown in the same place each year, so rotate the position of this herb annually.

Lemon balm

Closely related in appearance and habit to mint is lemon balm (*Melissa officinalis*). This intensely lemony herb has a ground-covering habit and mid-green foliage, and will also cope with similar conditions, although it will tolerate more sun. Its botanical name, *Melissa*, which means 'honey bee' in Greek, alludes to one of its main features — it attracts bees. Lemon balm is used in teas and vinegars.

There is also a pretty golden cultivar called 'All Gold' and a variegated form, 'Aurea'. The flowers of all cultivars are white or pale yellow, and appear throughout summer on spikes held about 15 cm (6 in) above the bush, which grows to about 75 cm (30 in). Cut back old flowers to stop them going to seed.

Cultivating lemon balm

Lemon balm likes a moist spot and shelter from the heat of the midday sun, although it copes well with early morning or late afternoon sun. Keep it in shape by pruning it in spring.

To harvest fresh leaves, pick new growth and use it as soon as possible in salads, sauces, teas and summer drinks. Although the leaves can be dried, much of their fragrance is lost this way.

did you know? In India, where it is called *tulsi*, basil is sacred, and dedicated to the gods Vishnu and Krishna in a special Hindu ceremony. It is also used in the Greek Orthodox Church in the preparation of holy water, as it is said to have been found growing around Christ's tomb after Easter Sunday.

Pesto

2 garlic cloves, crushed
50 g (1³/4 oz/¹/3 cup) pine nuts
2¹/2 large handfuls basil leaves
75 g (2¹/2 oz/³/4 cup) grated parmesan cheese

Put the garlic in a large mortar or food processor; add a pinch of salt and the pine nuts. Pound to a paste using a pestle, or process. Gradually add the basil leaves and pound them against the side of the bowl, or continue to process. Stir in the grated parmesan cheese, then gradually add olive oil.

Use the pesto immediately, or store covered in the fridge for one week. If storing, cover the pesto surface with a thin layer of olive oil.

Makes 250 ml (9 fl oz/1 cup).

Mint

Like rosemary, mint (*Mentha* sp.) made a name for itself in England, mainly because of its culinary associations with lamb, but it has been used for thousands of years in other cultures — Japanese, Egyptian, Roman and Greek. As the herbalist John Gerard wrote in 1633, 'the smell of mint doth stir up the minde and the taste to a greedy desire of meate'.

Popular in Asian foods as a fresh ingredient, mint is another extremely versatile herb that can be used in desserts, drinks (both teas and alcoholic beverages; see pages 426–9), salads and stir-fries.

There are dozens of different types of mint and their various cultivars. Some have completely prostrate habits, while others reach about 60 cm (2 ft) in height, but they all love moisture.

The better known mints include peppermint (*M.* x *piperita*), spearmint (*M. spicata*), apple mint (*M. suaveolens*) and eau de cologne mint (*M. piperita* x *citrata*), but three others also worth growing are chocolate mint (*M. piperita* 'Chocolate'), ginger mint (*M.* x *gracilis*) and basil mint (*M.* x *piperita citrata* 'Basil'), which is fantastic as a basil substitute in winter, when basil is unavailable.

Cultivating mint

If your mint is growing in a spot it likes, it will romp uncontrollably if it's not restrained. One way around this problem is to plant it in its plastic pot, with the base cut out and the rim proud of ground level. Or simply plant mint in a pot above ground so there is no chance of it getting away. Mints also hybridise together easily, so growing them in containers will limit their ability to do so.

Corsican mint (*M. requienii*) and pennyroyal (*M. pulegium*) are also mints,

although they are used more often as scented groundcovers that double as insect repellents (see page 47) in moist areas rather than as culinary herbs.

Mint has purplish mauve flowers in late summer and autumn. Cut the stems right back to the ground after flowering, and divide the plant at this stage if you want more plants from root cuttings or any rooted piece. Harvest mint before flowering. It's better frozen in ice cube trays than dried (see above).

Problems

Pick any rust-affected leaves off mint bushes as soon as you notice them, as the disease can spread through the patch quickly. Although rust is a very seasonal problem, and more prevalent when

Freezing mint

You can preserve mint by freezing the chopped leaves in ice cube trays.

1 Remove the leaves from the stems.

2 Chop the leaves.

3 Pour water into the tray. Add the chopped mint and freeze.

4 Use your mint ice cubes in refreshing summer drinks or add them to curries.

Opposite, clockwise from top left: Peppermint, a small-leafed type; Korean mint; variegated apple mint; and apple mint.

Masquerading mints

Native to North America, mountain mint (*Pycnanthemum pilosom*) is a small shrub, with a wonderful mint scent, which likes a sunny position. Wild hyssop (*P. virginianum*), the other species, is also very pretty. Both are sometimes used for flavouring teas.

The Australian native mint (*Prostanthera* sp.) is another highly pungent shrub, with a strong mint-like scent and delightful white, pink or mauve flowers. Dry the leaves and use them as a spice substitute for common mint. Like mountain mint, it's also a Lamiaceae herb.

A member of the Polygonaceae family, Vietnamese coriander or Vietnamese mint (*Persicaria odorata* syn. *Polygonum odoratum*) is a highly fragrant plant with dark stems and smooth leaves with brown markings. It likes warm climates, and can sometimes become a bit too invasive, but it does make a lovely, slightly coriander-like addition to Asian dishes. The plant grows to about 50 x 50 cm (20 x 20 in), and can be cut back hard after the summer and autumn pink flower flushes finish.

Vietnamese mint tastes a bit like curry.

Bottom right: Marjoram tastes like mild oregano.

Opposite, clockwise from top: Golden oregano; common oregano; and oregano in flower.

tip

Don't plant voracious spreaders such as mint next to less vigorous herbs, or they may be overrun.

conditions are humid, it can help to move mint from one spot to another every few years; in that way you may help your plant stay ahead of the spores. You can try sterilising the roots of plants by placing them in hot water (40 to 46°C/104 to 115°F) for 10 minutes to kill the spores, then rinse them immediately in cold water before planting them into fresh soil or mix.

Oregano and marjoram

Oregano and marjoram are both different species of the same genus, *Origanum*, from the Greek words *oros* or 'mountain', and *ganos*, meaning 'joy' or 'beauty', so it's not surprising that its native habitat, in the case of oregano (*O. vulgare*), is the hills of southern Europe. Marjoram (*O. majorana*), on the other hand, is from North Africa, and it's an essential ingredient of the spice mix za'atar (see page 42). Its leaves are pale green and not as hairy.

Both herbs are hardy, although they can suffer frost damage during harsh cold spells. They make excellent groundcovers, growing to about 30 cm (1 ft), and will spread over quite a distance if they like the position. Marjoram has white flowers, oregano pink, and there are also some very pretty ornamental varieties. Some, such as the *Origanum* hybrid 'Kent Beauty', bear larger, showier flowers, and others have golden foliage (*O. vulgare* subsp. *vulgare* 'Aureum'), or variegated foliage (*O. vulgare* 'Country Cream').

Cultivating oregano and marjoram

Plant out these herbs either by seed or as rooted cuttings or divisions, which can be dug in spring after flowering. Pick fresh leaves throughout the growing season, or harvest them for drying in a cool, dry place. Cut back after flowering. Thanks to their oil-rich leaves, both herbs are disease-free.

Perilla

Another herb from India and Asia is perilla, also known as wild sesame or Chinese basil or beefsteak plant (*Perilla frutescens*). There are green-leafed varieties among the six species, including the most common species, shiso (*Perilla frutescens* var. *japonica*), which is mainly grown in India and East Asia and used a lot in Japanese cuisine.

The leaves of shiso are lightly fragrant, reminiscent of cinnamon and filled with strong-tasting essential oils that are rich in vitamins and minerals.

The dark, beetroot-coloured foliage form (*P. frutescens* var. *crispa*; pictured on page 243, top right) resembles opal or purple basil (*O. basilicum* 'Purple Ruffles'), but with crinkly edges that look a bit like stinging nettles.

Cultivating perilla

In mild climates the plant re-seeds itself, but you can easily prevent it from doing this by regularly trimming off the flowers before they go to seed. The seeds themselves are also edible and can be ground with chilli and tomatoes to make a savoury dip/side dish.

Plants grow to about 60 cm (2 ft) and look great in both kitchen and ornamental gardens. Sow seeds in spring, once the soil has warmed up, into a well drained, open sunny position. Pick the fresh growth when it is young.

Rosemary

Rosemary (*Rosmarinus officinalis*) is another significant Lamiaceae herb that's versatile and popular, especially with lamb. This small shrub, about 1 x 1 m (3 x 3 ft), is well steeped in history, being used over the ages to protect against infection and plague, and to aid memory.

Rosemary is covered in beautiful blue flowers from spring to autumn. The thin, needle-like leaves, streaked white on one side, are so packed with oil that you just have to touch them to feel the oil on your skin. There are also prostrate, white-flowered, dark blue- and pink-flowered forms; all have fragrant, oil-rich leaves.

Cultivating rosemary

Trim the plants after flowering to promote new growth and feed them at the same time. Liming once a year can also help rosemary growing in acid soils, as it is native to the Mediterranean, where the soil is quite chalky and alkaline.

Rosemary likes a well drained position in full sun, and will cope with frosts once established. In very cold areas, however, it may be better to grow rosemary either in front of a sunny wall, so it receives the radiant heat at night, or in pots that can be moved to a protected place over winter.

If you want to grow cuttings of rosemary — a much cheaper option if you're planting a hedge — take heeled semi-hardwood cuttings in late summer/autumn or, alternatively, layer from the mother plant to produce true-to-type offsets. Replace rosemary about every five years so it doesn't get too woody or lanky.

did you know? In Europe in the Middle Ages, when herbs were used in perfumes and cosmetics, rosemary leaves were boiled in white wine and used as a face wash.

Top: 'Blue Lagoon', a rosemary cultivar.

Bottom: White-flowering rosemary.

Opposite, bottom: A sprig of common sage.

Being evergreen, rosemary can be harvested year round. Longer, straight stalks make great skewers for the barbecue, while the leaves complement meat, fish and vegetable dishes as well as savoury breads. And it's easy to dry: simply hang bunches in a cool, dry place. You can also wrap it in foil and freeze it for some weeks.

Sage

The largest genus in this family is *Salvia*, of which sage is one of about 900 species. The botanical name comes from the Latin *salveo*, which means 'to save or heal', and in many cultures — including Chinese, ancient Greek and Roman — it has been held in the highest regard for its healing properties and culinary virtues.

Common sage (*Salvia officinalis*) is an evergreen perennial, with soft grey-green leaves, which grows to about 60 cm (2 ft). The pungent foliage is highly valued, and can be collected all year round in all but very cold areas, where you'll have to protect the plant with fleece, or something similar. In early summer, it bears tongued, mauve flowers.

Pineapple sage (*Salvia elegans*) is usually grown for its fragrant foliage and beautiful edible scarlet flowers rather than for culinary use, although it can be added to dried fruit for pork stuffing. The leaves can also be used in cool summer drinks.

Propagating rosemary

Take semi-hardwood cuttings in late summer or early autumn. Plant them out when they have put on new growth, indicating they have put down roots.

1 Trim short lengths.

2 Remove the soft tip.

3 Then remove all the lower leaves.

4 Take a thin layer off the stem to reveal the cambium layer.

5 Dip the stem in some rooting powder.

6 Dampen some peat moss, then squeeze out the excess water and mix it with some propagating sand. Place some in each small pot.

7 In each pot, make a hole with a stick, and plant the cutting in the hole.

8 Water each pot.

did you know? Rosemary has long been used as a hair tonic, especially for dandruff, and can also be added to the bath to promote healthy skin. Sage is said to help stop hair from greying, mint makes a good rinse for oily hair, and chamomile brightens blonde highlights.

Above, from left to right: The attractive foliage of golden variegated sage (*Salvia officinalis* 'Icterina'); purple sage (*S. officinalis* 'Purpurea'); sage flowers, typical of the Lamiaceae family; and summer savory (*Satureja hortensis*). Both summer and winter savory can be grown in hanging baskets, gaps in paving and rockeries.

Sage can be made into a tea, or used in fatty or buttery foods to aid digestion. Traditionally it's been used as an antiseptic in sausages and other meats because of its preservative qualities.

Cultivating sage

Sage can be grown from seeds sown in spring or, in mild areas, in autumn. Plant them out when the seedlings are about 10 cm (4 in) high, and water well until established. Alternatively, take soft-tip cuttings in late spring and early summer; this is usually done at the same time as cutting established plants back after flowering in order to encourage healthy new growth. This is particularly important if you're growing one of the beautiful coloured-leaf forms of sage, as they may not grow true to type otherwise. These include 'Purpurea', a purple form; 'Icterina', a golden one; and 'Tricolor', a pink, cream and purple form.

Pick sage fresh whenever possible. Dry the leaves carefully so they don't go musty, freeze them in ice cube trays with some water, or chop them into butter, then freeze the butter in chunks.

Savory

These days savory (*Satureja* sp.) is a lesser known member of the Lamiaceae family, but over the ages it has been used in vinegars and sauces, even love potions.

There are two main species — the annual *S. hortensis*, or summer savory, and *S. montana*, winter savory, which is a perennial subshrub. Both grow to about 30 cm tall x 15 cm wide (12 x 6 in), but summer savory has light green foliage, while winter savory has darker and shinier leaves.

Both types make a pretty edging plant; in fact, winter savory was a favourite plant in English knot gardens in the sixteenth century, as it can be clipped into various decorative shapes.

Use these herbs in vegetable or meat dishes, or serve them with pulses, as savory is said to reduce flatulence. Its other, delightful, characteristic is that it attracts both bees and butterflies, so it's great for aiding pollination in the garden.

Cultivating savory

Sow savory seeds in spring — about 20 cm (8 in) apart for hedges, but twice that if you're growing it as a sprawling plant. Savory can be grown from cuttings that are taken as soft-tip segments about 10 cm (4 in) long in spring. Full sun with a well drained, gritty soil and no fertiliser is the best spot for savory. Protect winter savory from extreme cold over winter.

Savory can be dried, but a simpler method is to make a herb butter with the chopped leaves, then freeze this into ready-to-use chunks.

did you know? Next time you're stung by a bee, remove the stinger, then rub the wound with savory — an old-fashioned remedy.

Unusual salad herbs

Some herbs taste so fresh and delicious that they are natural salad ingredients. These herbs are members of the Rosaceae family, to which strawberries and roses belong.

Salad burnet

Native to North America, salad burnet (*Sanguisorba minor*) is a beautiful herb that prefers growing in the shade, especially in moist spots, as it doesn't like drying out over summer. A member of the rose family, Rosaceae, it bears delicate greyish green leaves and tiny green flowers on slender stalks to 45 cm (18 in). The leaves add a cucumber flavour to salads, vinegars and sauces. The leaves of greater burnet (*S. officinalis*), sometimes called bloodwort because it was traditionally used to stop bleeding, are edible when young. Its natural habitat is damp meadows, so follow nature's lead and mass plant salad burnet in any position that is poorly drained.

Lady's mantle

Another member of the rose family is a wonderful plant for cool, moist shade — lady's mantle (*Alchemilla* sp.). It is a very pretty grey-leafed ground-covering plant that has delightful golden-coloured flowers and edible young leaves that can be added to salads. Its scientific name derives from the mediaeval science of alchemy, as it was once thought that the silvery drops of dew collecting in the centre of each leaf in the morning could be part of a recipe for making gold.

Stimulate new growth in salad burnet by pruning the flower stalks.

Thyme

Thyme (*Thymus* sp.) makes a lovely small border plant or pot plant, as long as the pot has good drainage and is in a sunny spot. Or you can grow the groundcover varieties as rockery plants or a fragrant herb carpet between stepping stones and around paths.

Thymes love the drainage in this sort of position, and when you step on them, bruising their leaves, they release their scent into the air. Thyme's small leaves, pretty flowers and heavenly scent are always welcome.

The best eating thyme is garden thyme (*Thymus vulgaris*), an ingredient in bouquet garni (see page 421), which has long been used in stuffings, stocks and stews. The leaves can be dried easily, and are also used in vinegars and oil.

There are various cultivars, including the golden-leafed 'Aureus' and the silver-edged 'Silver Posie'. Lemon- and orange-scented thymes are crosses of *T. x citriodorus*. Other ground-covering types — such as 'Pink Chintz', 'Annie Hall', 'Snowdrift' and 'Goldstream' or woolly thyme (*T. pseudolanuginosis*) — are more likely to be cultivars of mother of thyme (*T. serpyllum*).

Cultivating thyme

Thyme hates good, rich soil, preferring — as in its native habitat in Southern Europe and Asia — an impoverished gravel or well drained, sandy soil. A perennial, thyme can be harvested all year round in all but the very coldest areas, where it can die off in winter unless given shelter; alternatively, pot it up and bring it under cover.

Keep your thyme plants healthy by lightly trimming them back after flowering, reducing watering in winter and layering them in spring by lightly top-dressing with gravel to encourage vigorous new growth. Spring is also the time to divide your plants if necessary, before they produce their sweet pink or white flowers.

Pick thyme in the morning and before flowering, and use it fresh in butters, teas, stuffings and vinegars. You can also freeze or dry it for later use.

feature plant

Bay laurel

Laurus nobilis, Lauraceae

This slightly peppery-flavoured herb was held in high esteem by the Romans, who used it to crown their poets and victors; indeed, the Latin word *nobilis* means 'famous'. One of the essential ingredients of bouquet garni (see page 421), its upright growth habit makes it ideal for growing as a potted standard or topiarised specimen.

Climate: Cool to warm temperate.

Culture: Popular as a standard, in hedging and as a feature plant.

Colours: Gold form and dark green-leafed forms.

Height: 12 m (39 ft).

Planting time: Autumn.

Soil: Bay likes a well drained soil enriched with manure or compost and mulch to protect its shallow roots.

Position: Full sun or half shade, and shelter from the cold when establishing.

Planting spacing: 3 m (10 ft).

Fertiliser: Feed with liquid fertiliser in spring, and mulch annually with manure.

Pests and diseases: Pink wax and brown scales can be a problem, as is sooty mould which grows on their honeydew (see page 58).

Propagation: Cuttings root easily from semi-hardwood pieces, about 10 cm (4 in) long, taken in summer.

Harvesting and storing:
Pick leaves fresh at any time, or pick them in the early morning, hang them in a cool, airy place until dry, then store them in an airtight container.

Asteraceae herbs

One of the largest plant families in the world, with more than 23,000 species, the daisy family includes useful herbs such as wormwood as well as some famous culinary herbs, such as tarragon, curry plant and mace.

Curry plant

Curry plant (*Helichrysum italicum*) smells just like a superb, freshly made curry paste, ready to use. The sad truth, however, is that the leaves, once cooked, lose a lot of their flavour and intensity. But they can be added to stuffing for chickens or to vegetable and rice dishes that require a mild curry flavour, or tossed in at the last minute to already cooked dishes so they still keep their fragrance.

In the garden, the yellow button flowers are pretty, while the soft grey, needle-like foliage gives off its wonderful aroma whenever the sun comes out or someone brushes past.

Cultivating curry plant

To help curry plant maintain its shape, lightly trim it back after flowering, especially in summer. Curry plant is also suitable for growing in containers. A full sun position with good drainage is essential, especially over winter.

Above: A sprig of yarrow.

Left: Curry plant grows to about 60 cm (2 ft) and is perfect as a low-growing hedge in the garden.

Mace

Garden mace (*Achillea decolorans* syn. *A. ageratum*) is an extremely hardy plant. Like its relative, yarrow (*Achillea millefolium*), if left to its own devices it will conquer an abandoned space, such as a railway siding, or your garden.

These days most people grow mace for both this adaptability and its lovely flowers, and don't realise it has any other qualities. Mace is not the outer casing of nutmeg (*Myristica fragrans*; see page 418), but a totally unrelated plant that has a similar aromatic flavour. The leaves can be used in stuffings, stews, soups, salads and rice dishes.

Cultivating mace

Also known as sweet Nancy or sweet yarrow, mace grows easily from cutting and division, likes full sun, and is very adaptable to different soils. It also rarely suffers from any pests or diseases.

Tarragon

Tarragon (*Artemisia* sp.) is regarded by many as the 'king of herbs', especially in French cuisine where it is held in high esteem for all sorts of foods, from salads to stuffing, but mainly for béarnaise sauce. It's a member of the same genus as wormwood, a herb so bitter that just touching the leaves, then touching your tongue, can make you grimace.

There are two culinary varieties of this herb — French and Russian. French tarragon (*A. dracunculus*) is a perennial herb with a wonderful perfume and an anise-like flavour. It goes with white meats such as chicken and fish, makes superb vinegars and was once even used as an appetite stimulant for royalty.

did you know? In Russia and the Ukraine, tarragon is used to make a popular bright green soft drink called *Tarkhun*, which is the Russian word for tarragon.

Russian tarragon (*A. dracunculoides*) can grow in the most difficult conditions, and may be native to Siberia, but you would have to be hard up to eat it, as it tastes not much better than grass.

Winter or Mexican tarragon (*Tagetes lucida*), which is also known as sweet mace, is a member of the marigold family. While none of the other tarragons are edible, this perennial from Mexico has aromatic foliage that can also be used as a substitute for French tarragon.

Cultivating tarragon

All types of tarragon grow to about 1 m (3 ft), spreading by rhizomes, or underground stems, and liking a position in full sun. French tarragon dies back in winter, but in very frosty areas it will need some protection, such as a straw mulch. It also needs good drainage and summer moisture, and can be divided in early spring to freshen the clump.

Russian tarragon is a vigorous grower that can also be propagated by seed, but its bitter flavour makes it hardly worth growing for culinary purposes; however, it can improve in flavour as it matures.

Pick new shoots as they appear in spring to use in vinegars, and continue harvesting the youngest leaves for cooking throughout the season. You can also pinch back flower heads to promote new growth. Freeze slightly hardened off foliage for use in winter when the plant is bare.

Left: *Dracunculus* is Latin for 'little dragon'. French tarragon (*Artemisia dracunculus*), known as *herbe au dragon* by the French, was once used to treat snake bites.

Opposite, top: *Petasites hybridus*, a species of butterbur, in flower.

Sweet things

Stevia (*Stevia rebaudiana*), another member of the Asteraceae family, is at least 300 times sweeter than table sugar, so for decades it has been used as an alternative to sucrose in everything from cola drinks to artificial sweeteners.

It grows easily to about 1 m (3 ft) in any warm climate out in the open and, once established, is quite drought-hardy. Also known as sweetleaf, stevia is herbaceous, dying back each winter when it is cut back to the ground so that new growth can come up in spring. Use either the fresh or dried leaves.

Although used in place of artificial sweeteners in Japan and approved as a sweetener in Australia, its use is banned in many other countries.

Stevia is also known as sugarleaf.

did you know? Butterbur (*Petasites* sp.), also known as sweet colts foot, is used to make a condiment in Japan, although it contains toxic alkaloids. These plants have underground rhizomes and huge leaves that look a bit like rhubarb. They grow best in cool, moist areas, such as on riverbanks, and even in poorly drained areas.

Béarnaise sauce

80 ml (2¹/₂ fl oz/¹/₃ cup) white wine vinegar
2 green onions (scallions), roughly chopped
2 teaspoons chopped tarragon
2 egg yolks
125 g (4¹/₂ oz) butter, cut into cubes

Put the vinegar, green onion and tarragon in a small saucepan. Bring to the boil, then reduce the heat slightly and simmer until the mixture has reduced by a third. Set aside to cool completely.

Strain the vinegar into a heatproof bowl, and add the egg yolks. Place the bowl over a saucepan of barely simmering water and whisk until the mixture is thick and pale.

Add the butter, one cube at a time, and whisk after each addition until the mixture is thick and smooth. Season to taste, and serve immediately. Serve with roast beef or lamb, or pan-fried steaks of poached salmon.

Serves 4.

Apiaceae herbs

This family contains many edible herbs and plants, including some of the most toxic, so gathering wild herbs is an occupation best left to experts. Luckily, many of the culinary members of this family are also easy to grow.

Angelica

Angelica (*Angelica archangelica*) is quite a tall herb, growing to more than 1 m (3 ft). When topped with flowers, it can shoot up another 30 cm (1 ft). The stems can be crystallised and used for decorating cakes and desserts, while the leaves add natural sweetness to stewed tart fruits, such as rhubarb.

Cultivating angelica

It will grow in a half-sun to half-shaded position and needs well watered, heavily compost-enriched soils to support its growth. Angelica, like many other members of this family, is a biennial, dying after flowering and seeding in its second year. Removing the flowering head and stopping it from seeding can extend its lifespan by at least another few years.

Anise

Anise or aniseed (*Pimpinella anisum*) is used mainly for its dried seeds, which add a licorice flavour to many drinks, such as pastis and ouzo, and also to sweets, such as

Above: The toothed leaves of angelica.

Left: With an aroma that has been likened to musk, angelica has distinctive red stems and umbels of tiny flowers.

Above left: The pale green fruits of angelica are oblong and fluted.

Above: Caraway has ferny leaves and grows to about 60 cm (2 ft).

bullseyes. Native to the Mediterranean and the Middle East, it has the characteristic finely cut leaflets of the daisy family and broad, umbrella-like flower heads, which become covered in tiny yellow or white flowers before forming seeds. The plant is an annual, about 50 x 50 cm (20 x 20 in).

Cultivating anise

Sow anise in spring and it will flower in summer, before producing seeds. Anise is not at all fussy about soil, coping with any type, from boggy to dry and even alkaline soils. It does, however, like a full sun position. Pick the seeds once they are ripe, then hang them by their stems to dry. Tie a brown paper bag around the flowering head to catch the seeds if they drop.

Caraway

Caraway (*Carum carvi*) has been used for at least 5000 years in both savoury and sweet dishes. It bears heads of small white flowers, followed by dark brown seeds.

While it is the seeds that are usually used in cooking, the finely cut leaves can also be used in salads and stews and, in its second year, the root can be dug in autumn and cooked as a vegetable, in much the same way as other biennial members of this family, such as carrots and parsnips, which also have edible roots.

Cultivating caraway

To grow caraway, simply sow seed directly into well weeded and cleared, free-draining soil in full sun. Thin out any excess plants so that seedlings are about 20 cm (8 in) apart. When overwintering caraway from its first to second year, cover it with mulch to protect it from the cold, then discard and replant it after the second autumn, or dig up and use the roots.

did you know? Angelica's botanical name allegedly comes from the archangel Raphael, who is said to have told a monk that the plant could cure the plague.

Right: Coriander seeds and powder are popular spices, especially in Asian cuisines.

Below: A coriander sprig.

Opposite, clockwise from top left: Coriander flowers; coriander leaves; dried coriander seed heads; and chervil.

Collect the seeds in brown paper bags by tying them around the flowering stems just as they ripen and are about to begin dropping in summer. You can then either cut them and bring them inside or, if the weather is dry, leave them outside. Once all the seeds have fallen, store the dry seeds in an airtight container.

Celery herb

The wild leaf version of celery (see page 266), celery herb (*Apium graveolens* var. *secalinum*) can be grown as a herb. Harvest the leaves when necessary and use them in much the same way as parsley to give a celery flavour to soups and stews.

Cultivating celery herb

Like the modern version of celery, this old form needs regular watering to stop it from becoming bitter. Sow seeds into enriched soil with lots of compost, which should help hold moisture in the soil as well as supply a steady flow of nutrients. A position in full sun with protection from wind is ideal, but this plant is frost-hardy.

Chervil

Chervil or French parsley (*Anthriscus cerefolium*) is native to the Middle East, South Russia and the Caucasus. It's an annual or biennial, depending on the climate, but is particularly cold-tolerant and can be a problem to maintain in summer, when the heat can cause it to bolt. It's often grown in semi-shade or at least out of the midday sun, or under deciduous trees.

A popular herb in French cuisine because of its delicate aniseed flavour, it's one of the ingredients of the classic herb mix, *fines herbes* (see page 421). Toss the fresh leaves — rich in vitamin C, carotene, iron and magnesium — through salads, or add them to cooked meals.

Cultivating chervil

From spring onwards, sow seeds over three weeks or so into lightly raked, well drained soil. Germination usually takes about three weeks, and the plants are ready for harvesting about a month later. Chervil can become slightly invasive and has a habit of self-sowing, so keep it in check by harvesting it regularly.

Coriander

Coriander or cilantro (*Coriandrum sativum*) is also known as Chinese parsley but is actually native to southern Europe; it made its way to the Middle East, India, Asia and South America as the great trade routes opened up. All parts of the plant are edible and, indeed, useful, from the fragrant foliage to the roots and seeds.

Mint and coriander chutney

30 g (1 1/2 cups) mint leaves
30 g (1 cup) coriander (cilantro) leaves
1 green chilli
1 tablespoon tamarind purée
1/2 teaspoon salt
1 1/2 teaspoons sugar
3 tablespoons thick plain yoghurt

Wash the herb leaves, keeping the young soft stalks. Blend all the ingredients together in a blender or food processor, or chop everything finely and pound it together in a mortar and pestle. Add more salt to taste. Stir in the yoghurt. Serves 4.

The lemony fragrance of the fresh young leaves has made it particularly popular in Asian cuisine, especially Thai. There are at least two cultivars, but for foliage the best variety is 'Cilantro', which is slower to bolt into seed. It grows to about 60 cm (2 ft).

Cultivating coriander

Coriander doesn't like growing near fennel, or rather, fennel doesn't like coriander, but otherwise any light, well drained soil in a sunny position is ideal, with more shade required over summer. Freshly washed leaves, wrapped in foil and frozen, will keep well for some weeks.

Dill

Dill (*Anethum graveolens*) is an annual with feathery foliage that is not only delicious, with a taste similar to parsley and anise, but also very attractive, and its lovely soft leaves can be picked at any time. The golden yellow flowers, well known for their butterfly-attracting abilities, can also be added to pickled gherkins and cucumbers to make the popular condiment known as dill pickles. The seeds themselves have a stronger flavour than both the leaves and flowers, so they are more likely to be used in slow-cooked meals such as soups and stews. Dill is also used for curing salmon in gravlax, the traditional Scandinavian dish.

Cultivating dill

It takes about eight weeks for dill to grow to maturity from seed, and it is this speed that frustrates many cooks who want to use the foliage, not just the seeds, as the leaves then become bitter and less palatable or plentiful.

To combat this, repeat sowings throughout the year are a good option, and, in very warm climates, you may need to skip summer altogether as it will bolt so quickly to seed, especially if the plants are allowed to dry out, and it may not be worth growing.

Picking leaves from the centre of the plant rather than the outside also delays flowering. Regular feeding with liquid fertiliser and trimming back any flower heads as they form will slow down this process, however. Dill leaves can also be frozen in water in ice cubes, or wrapped in foil, then frozen.

Fennel

The foliage of fennel the herb (*Foeniculum vulgare*) is very similar to dill but has a strong aniseed taste, while Florence fennel (*F. vulgare* subsp. *vulgare* var. *dulce*) is the subspecies of fennel that is grown for its swollen aniseed-flavoured leaf bases and seeds (see page 268). Of particular beauty in the garden is the bronze fennel (*F. vulgare* 'Purpureum'). Its soft, feathery, burgundy-coloured foliage is also edible.

Right: You can freeze or dry dill leaves but, even stored in the fridge, the fresh leaves will not last more than a few days before losing their flavour.

Cultivating fennel

Foeniculum vulgare can become a weed, so keep its flower heads trimmed if it's a problem in your area. If you're growing the bulb type, or *finnochio*, as they call it in Italy, make sure you buy Florence fennel.

To keep the bulb white and sweet, earth up over the bulbs once they reach the size of a golf ball, and continue to do so every few weeks, until the bulb is ready to harvest. Fennel does well in any sunny, well drained spot. The seeds can be sown in spring, but Florence fennel is usually sown in autumn for spring harvest.

Lovage

Lovage (*Levisticum officinale*) looks very much like a paler version of flat-leaf parsley that has tripled in size after taking a course of steroids.

Traditionally prescribed as a love potion or aphrodisiac in Europe, lovage sometimes goes by the delightful name of love parsley. Its success in that department remains unclear, but one thing is certain — the celery-flavoured leaves are quite tasty and can be used as a substitute for celery in soups, or fresh in a salad. They can even be boiled and added to white sauce as you would spinach. All parts of this herb are edible and can be candied like angelica (see page 386).

Cultivating lovage

Lovage likes a rich, moist soil and a shady position. Propagate by sowing seed into trays in spring, then planting them out 60 cm (2 ft) apart after they have reached about 10 cm (4 in). They are ready to start harvesting about two months later and, if kept regularly trimmed, will continue to produce foliage for another four years.

Pick fresh leaves as required, or dry them quickly in a cool, airy place.

Above: Bronze fennel is a wonderful contrast plant in the garden.

Left: Lovage can grow to 2 m (6½ ft) with ribbed stems that look and taste like celery.

Parsley

Parsley (*Petroselinum crispum*) is the best known species in the genus *Petroselinum*. There are three types of parsley: curly (*P. crispum* var. *crispum*), often used for garnishing; French (*P. crispum* var. *neapolitanum*), which is said to have the best flavour; and Hamburg parsley or turnip-rooted parsley (*P. crispum* var. *tuberosum*). (For more information on Hamburg parsley, see page 268.)

The curly-leafed cultivars of parsley include popular 'Afro' parsley, 'Triple Curl' and 'Darky', which is one of the most cold-tolerant forms.

French parsley — also known as flat-leafed, broad-leafed, Italian or continental parsley — is thought to be from Sardinia. This species of parsley has bright green, curled edges and a mild taste. French parsley is an ingredient in *fines herbes* as well as bouquet garni (see page 421).

Cultivating parsley

All parsleys grow easily in full sun, provided they receive adequate water over summer, and will reach about 45 cm (18 in). The soil should be deep and have a neutral pH (see page 15), and will benefit from added organic matter.

Parsley is a biennial, which means it lasts for two years, but self-seeds so readily where it grows that you can almost count on it being there for years, as long as the conditions are suitable. Prolong leaf growth by removing flower heads as soon as they appear, and keep this up for two

Above right: A sprig of curly-leafed parsley.

Right: Flat-leafed parsley.

Far right: If you're happy for your parsley plants to self-seed, just leave the seed heads, which will also attract beneficial insects, such as bees.

years before allowing the plant to seed. Then remove it, as the foliage is bitter and unusable after seeding unless you are trying to encourage beneficial insects, such as parasitic wasps, in which case let some plants flower, as it is their nectar that attracts the wasps into your garden.

Pick parsley foliage from the outside of the plant, as the new growth is produced in the centre. Rich in vitamin C, it can be dried easily in an oven preheated to 130°C (266°F). Spread the parsley out evenly on trays, then turn off the oven and place the trays in the cooling oven. Turn them occasionally. Once dry, store them in an airtight container in a cool, dark place.

Left: 'Triple Curl', one of the curly-leafed types of parsley.

Sweet cicely

Sweet cicely is a beautiful herbaceous plant that grows to about 1.5 m (5 ft) and bears delicate ferny foliage and tiny white flowers throughout summer. The leaves, roots and seeds of sweet cicely (*Myrrhis odorata*) are all edible. Use the sweet, anise-scented foliage in salads or egg dishes, and even with stewed fruit as a part substitute for sugar.

Sweet cicely is particularly popular in colder climates, as it's one of the first young herbs to come up after winter, and one of the last to die down. However, it does suffer in warm, humid areas, as it likes a short period of winter dormancy, when it is cut down to the ground.

Cultivating sweet cicely

Like many members of this family, sweet cicely is easy to grow; the problem is stopping them from becoming weeds, as they can easily self-sow. The foliage and seeds are usually picked and used fresh, but the roots can be dug in late autumn when the plant is preparing for its winter dormancy, then dried for later use.

Some toxic family members

In the Apiaceae family, there are a few dangerous plants you should take care to avoid.

The first is cow parsley (*Anthriscus sylvestris*), which has made it onto the invasive plant 'watch list' in many areas of the United States, but in its native habitat of Europe, the Mediterranean and western Asia, it grows happily in hedgerows and woodlands.

Another poor relative of this family is fool's parsley or poison parsley (*Aethusa cynapium*), which has such an unpleasant smell even rabbits won't go for it. Fool's parsley is poisonous and can prove fatal. It too gets out of hand in parts of the world, and is best eradicated as soon as you notice it.

Finally, the real black sheep of the family is hemlock (*Conium maculatum*), famous in literature and history. Its leaves look like parsley and the root looks like parsnip, but the smell of both is so unpleasant that it should be warning enough. Hemlock contains alkaloids, the most toxic of which is coniine, a neurotoxin that disrupts the workings of the nervous system. It is toxic to both humans and livestock, causing muscular paralysis and eventually paralysis of the respiratory muscles, which results in death due to lack of oxygen to the heart and brain.

Edible weeds

Cultivating weeds to eat may seem odd, but there are many that taste great and, after all, a weed is simply an unwanted plant that is easy to grow. Just don't allow these plants to spread where they are not welcome, and check that they are legal in your area.

Bugle weed

Bugle weed (*Ajuga reptans*) may seem an unlikely salad green, but it can be eaten as fresh new growth. Better known as a groundcover in shady areas, bugle has delightful spurs of blue flowers in spring, and many of its cultivars have wonderfully ornamental foliage.

To grow bugle successfully, you need to have consistently moist (even damp or boggy) soil, but that's about it. It will happily grow in sun or shade, cope with frost and quite severe cold, and even grow with root competition from large trees. Keep young plants weed-free until the seedlings or runners establish themselves.

Corn salad

Corn salad (*Valerianella locusta*) is in the same family as valerian. It is native to Eurasia and Africa, where it grows wild in cornfields, hence its common name. Also known as *mache* in France, it has been used as a salad vegetable for centuries; in fact, it was said to have been introduced to the British Isles by the Huguenots.

Above: Stinging nettle.

Left: Bugle weed has the square stalk and tongued flowers that are characteristic of members of the Lamiaceae family.

This delicious green has become popular in mixed leaf assortments for its slightly nutty, earthy flavour. The leaves can also be blanched by tying the outer leaves together with raffia and inverting a flowerpot over the whole plant. Block the drainage hole, then wait for the darkness to sweeten the inner leaves and turn them pale. After a few weeks, they should be creamy and ready to eat.

Sow corn salad at any time from early spring to autumn, depending on when you want to harvest; it will take three months to reach maturity.

Particularly known for its cold tolerance, if sheltered with cloches corn salad can continue to grow right through winter in even very cold zones. The spoon-shaped foliage grows from a rosette in a very similar style and size to dandelion leaves, but with smooth edges that are more like sorrel leaves. Various forms are available, including a golden-leafed form called 'Blonde Shell'.

Dandelion

Dandelion (*Taraxacum officinale*) is one of the most common garden weeds, but also a favourite with children. Who cannot remember blowing the round papilionate seed heads and sending the aeronautical seeds into the wind, or picking the juicy leaves to feed pet birds and rabbits? And how many adults have had to fork them out of the lawn?

Well, rather than just curse them, why not eat them? If picked in spring and early summer when they are young, the leaves make delicious salad greens, but can also be lightly sautéed and used as a cooked vegetable. Some cooks advise

Above left: You can eat the fresh leaves of red orache (*Atriplex hortensis* var. *rubra*).

Above: The children's game of blowing the seeds off dandelion seed heads accounts for some of its other common names — clocks and watches, fairy clock and old man's clock.

Below: Dandelion has diuretic qualities, which give it the French name *piss en lit* (piss-a-bed).

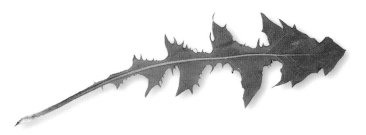

Above: Sunny dandelion flowers attract bees and other beneficial insects.

Below right and opposite: Nasturtium flowers are great for brightening up a salad.

adding the sweet flavour of caramelised onion to temper their bitterness. Later in the season they tend to become too intense and coarse to be eaten fresh. You can also blanch the leaves by covering them with upturned flowerpots and blocking out the light. This should be done in early spring. Once the foliage is pale, pick these leaves and let the remaining plant recover through summer. The root can also be eaten as a vegetable (see page 270).

Good King Henry

Good King Henry or mercury (*Chenopodium bonus-henricus*) is originally from Europe and Asia, but has managed to naturalise itself in the United Kingdom and the United States. The leaves have an arrow shape, like spinach leaves, and can be cooked in a similar manner, but the tender new shoots are prepared like asparagus.

did you know? The herbalist Culpeper declared that Good King Henry is 'preferred to Spinach and is much superior in firmness and flavour'. It's still eaten as a spinach substitute in parts of the United Kingdom.

Good King Henry is drought-tolerant, but the more water and better soil you can give your plants, the better the flavour and the more prolific the growth. It can become a weed, so check with your local council before planting it. Another edible relative is fat hen (*C. album*), which has a milder flavour.

Nasturtium

In warm, temperate zones, nasturtium (*Tropaeolum majus*) is sometimes an urban escape artist, running away into bushland areas. However, in other regions, it's a beautiful sprawling plant that covers the ground to about a 3-m (10-ft) radius, but it will also climb if given support.

Both the flowers and buds are edible, but it is usually the young leaves that are picked to add a peppery taste to salad, or a spicy touch to a tomato sandwich. You can pickle the buds of nasturtium, and eat them as you would capers.

There are some very pretty cultivars that can be grown either in the kitchen garden (although these must be contained) or in hanging baskets and pots. The leaves are orbicular and grey-green, and look marvellous after dew when the drops settle like jewels in the rounded centres. The leaves of 'Alaska' and the 'Jewel' series

Above: Harvest sorrel by cutting the leaves at the base with a sharp knife.

Above right: In late spring or early summer, sorrel produces spikes of tiny reddish green flowers.

Below right: Purslane, shown here, and sorrel are traditional ingredients in the French vegetable soup *bonne femme*.

have very pretty clotted cream markings, which bring out the autumn-toned flowers even more. 'Empress of India' is another worthy cultivar — its foliage is decidedly blue and its flowers are bright red.

Nasturtiums can grow in full sun or part shade, like well drained soil and can be frost-sensitive.

Orache

In the same family as Good King Henry is orache or salt bush (*Atriplex* sp.). There are about 300 species in the genus and they are native to all continents, except Antarctica. Orache have an extraordinary ability to adapt to very harsh conditions, including heavily salt-laden soils and extreme winds.

The species native to Australia, coastal salt bush (*A. cinerea*), grows into a dense thicket about 1.5 m (5 ft) round and has attractive, quite ornamental grey foliage. Although the leaves themselves are not fit for human consumption, in extreme conditions they're renowned as sheep

fodder and, in turn, the meat of the stock has a salty flavour that is highly valued.

It is mountain spinach (*A. hortensis*), a native plant of Asia that has naturalised in many temperate regions, which is most popular with humans. This plant can grow to 2 m (6$\frac{1}{2}$ ft). There are very ornamental golden- or red-leafed forms; one particularly beautiful variety is *A. hortensis* var. *rubra*. Cook it in the same way you would spinach.

Purslane

Purslane (*Portulaca oleracea*) is another weed that, although native to India, has

Above left: The prickly hairs on stinging nettle contain a substance that is a mixture of histamine and formic acid.

Above: Stinging nettle grows to more than 1 m (3 ft) and bears greenish flowers.

managed to spread everywhere. It is a succulent, related to the ornamental portulaca. This one, however, has very small flowers and a sprawling ground-hugging habit that quickly covers any bare earth. Although it grows best in the sun, purslane also copes well with shade, and only struggles in very wet conditions. The best way to control purslane is to manually remove it, leaving no part behind. The new shoots can be eaten in salads and have quite a nice, crisp texture. There is also a golden form.

Sorrel and dock

French sorrel (*Rumex scutatus*) is a member of the knot weed family, one with many weedy members that have spread right around the world, thanks to their floating seeds. It is a perennial to 50 cm (20 in) that grows in a clump in damp soil in full sun or shade.

Rosy dock (*R. vesicarius*) is one of the worst of these, but even the common garden sorrel (*R. acetosa*) can become weedy. Its arrow-shaped foliage can be added to salads or cooked, but it is the French sorrel that is valued as a culinary herb. The apple-green leaves have a lemony flavour that is commonly teamed with eggs and cream in France, where sorrel is commercially available.

One of the few greens available in winter, sorrel is useful as young leaves or sprouts in salads. The older leaves can be used in soups or steamed with fish. They have a sweetish overtone, a bit like rhubarb, to which it is also related.

Stinging nettles

Stinging nettles (*Urtica dioica*) don't sound at all appealing — just touching their tiny hairs will sting. After cooking, however, stinging nettles lose their bite and are very popular with wild food enthusiasts. The very young shoots are best eaten cooked as a vegetable or added to soups. They are very hardy, hence their ability to become such successful weeds, and will adapt to most soils and positions easily.

root herbs

Sometimes the most useful parts of plants can be found underground, where you least expect to find them. The roots of many plants make great flours and thickeners, even vegetables, and some have a delicious fragrance that is synonymous with Asian cuisine.

Arrowroot

The tuber of arrowroot (*Maranta arundinacea*) is used as a flour to thicken soups and sauces, and also in baked goods such as pastries and biscuits. Its other common names are West Indian arrowroot and prayer plant, so named because the leaves close up at night, as if in silent prayer. They are often grown as indoor plants for their attractively marked, blotchy sword-shaped leaves.

Native to the West Indies and Central America, arrowroot grows to about 1.6 m (5¼ ft). It has white flowers in spring, and in warm temperate climates makes a good groundcover under trees.

Cultivating arrowroot

To grow arrowroot successfully, find a frost-free position in rich, well drained sandy loam and, after all chance of cool weather has gone, plant tubers about 5 to 7.5 cm (2 to 3 in) deep and 30 cm (1 ft) apart. Ten to twelve months later, when the leaves turn yellow and fall over, they are easy to harvest. To do this, dig

Above: Grate fresh ginger root and use it in stir-fries and marinades.

Left: Lemon grass is a perennial that is native to tropical climates.

them up carefully so you don't damage the skins; they can also be eaten raw, or baked or cooked in curries.

To make arrowroot flour, add water to the tuber and pulverise into a pulp, then pass this through a sieve to remove any fibres, and dry it in the sun.

Chinese keys

Like other members of the ginger family, Zingiberaceae, this root herb has beautiful, aromatic, dark green foliage and pinkish purple, orchid-like flowers. Also known as fingerroot, Chinese keys (*Boesenbergia pandurata* syn. *Kaempferia pandurata*) grows to about 50 cm (20 in).

It is popular in Thailand for the aromatic, spicy flavour of the finger-like storage roots on its rhizomes — similar to ginger but not as strong — which are used in cooking to enhance fish dishes. It is also often used raw in salads, served as a side dish with rice or cooked in stews, soups and curries.

Cultivating Chinese keys

Chinese keys is suitable for growing in subtropical and tropical areas, and won't stand any frost. Native to Java and Sumatra, it grows best in a well drained fertile soil with lots of compost, manure and water — in fact, it requires 1.5 m (5 ft) of annual water.

To grow Chinese keys, plant rhizomes into warm soil in spring 5 cm (2 in) deep and 30 cm (1 ft) apart. The rhizomes look like bunched carrots, except that they are yellow, not orange. Harvest them when the leaves yellow and die off. Scrape away the brown skin before using the long, cylindrical roots. The shoots are also edible.

did you know? Arrowroot's common name may derive from the fact that it was once used to treat wounds caused by poisoned arrows. It's also interesting to note that arrowroot was also used to make a photo-sensitive paper.

Above left: Galangal is a key ingredient in ras el hanout, another Moroccan spice blend.

Above: Turmeric is an ingredient in chermoula, a Moroccan spice blend.

Right: Store galangal in a cool, dark ventilated cupboard or in the fridge.

Below: The flowers of evening primrose — which can also be white, pink or red — open towards the end of the day, hence its common name. This one is *Oenothera biennis*. Its stems, leaves and flower buds are edible.

Opposite: Fresh ginger (top) and galangal.

Evening primrose

Evening primrose (*Oenothera* sp.) is usually grown for its many medicinal properties as well as its ornamental qualities. It's a very pretty garden plant with lovely clear yellow flowers in spring. The roots can be boiled and eaten like parsnips, or pickled and added to salads.

Cultivating evening primrose

Evening primrose is easy to grow and can become slightly invasive in some areas, as it self-seeds readily. It prefers full sun and light, well drained soil with regular water, but will also cope happily with less suitable conditions, even drought.

Galangal

Galangal (*Alpinia galanga*) is native to the Malay Peninsula, but was probably introduced to Europe more than 1000 years ago by Arabic physicians via China. The name 'galangal' is thought to be derived from the Arabic word *Khalanjan*, which in turn is derived from the Chinese word meaning 'mild ginger'.

This perennial herb grows to 1 to 2 m (3 to 6½ ft), and has long, narrow, blade-like foliage as well as white flowers with red streaks that appear at the top of the plant in summer. The rhizomes are used fresh or dried and have a wonderful aroma, something like a cross between pepper and ginger. The texture is quite woody, so add pieces to curries and soups, then remove them before serving.

Cultivating galangal

To grow galangal, plant sections of the rhizomes 10 cm (4 in) deep and 30 cm (1 ft) apart in spring after all frost has gone. Harvest the plant ten months after the leaves die down. It likes rich soil and will cope with some shade.

Ginger

Native to tropical rainforests, ginger (*Zingiber officinale*) has spectacular yellowish green flowers with a deep purple lip, which show up brilliantly against the reed-like foliage. Of course it is the edible rhizome that is used — in baking and as a condiment and spice, particularly in Asian cuisine.

You can store ginger in the fridge for some time or, alternatively, scrape the skin off the rhizome before covering it with wine vinegar or sherry and storing it in an airtight container in the fridge.

Cultivating ginger

To grow ginger, choose either a frost-free position outside or a tub, which can be brought inside for protection over winter. Gingers like a good peaty mix and added sharp sand for drainage, as wet 'feet' can cause rot. They grow to about 3 m (10 ft) tall, but are unlikely to reach this size if they are grown in a container. Divide them in spring.

did you know? Another yellow-flowered herb is elecampane or scabwort (*Inula helenium*). In ancient Rome and Elizabethan England, its roots were candied, but they can also be cooked as a vegetable. Elecampane was named after Helen of Troy: according to the legend, it grew wherever her tears fell.

Horseradish and wasabi

Horseradish and wasabi are two root crops in the Brassicaceae family. Horseradish or red cole (*Armoracia rusticana*) has a very deep taproot. Its white flesh is commonly made into a condiment by grating it and adding cream, vinegar and mustard. The plant itself grows to 60 cm (2 ft) and has whorls of deeply divided leaves and small white flowers, which can be removed to encourage the plant to grow larger rootstock. High in vitamin C, the root is used to flavour meat, dips and sauces.

Wasabi or Japanese horseradish (*Wasabia japonica*) is another member of the Brassicaceae family that is famous for a paste made from its root, but in fact every part is edible, including the leaves. It grows naturally in moist soils along riverbeds and in mountain gullies in Japan, and, like other members of the family, is best grown quickly with a plentiful water supply so the root doesn't become woody and fibrous.

Wasabi root is usually grated finely, then combined with fish and rice in sushi so it keeps its colour and flavour, as it oxidises quickly when left exposed to

Ginseng

The carrot-shaped root of ginseng (*Panax* sp.), a member of the Ivy (Araliaceae) family, is native to both Asia and North America. Notoginseng (*P. pseudoginseng*) — a haemostatic herb, not a culinary one — is usually available in dried form, either whole or sliced, but can also be pickled.

Ginseng is used for medicinal purposes and as an aphrodisiac, and is included in some energy drinks. In Korea it's used in a soup called *samgyetang*, which is served as a cure-all against illness and also as an antidote to heat on the hottest days of the year.

Ginseng grows to about 30 x 30 cm (1 x 1 ft) and likes a shady position with regular water and fertiliser.

Kuzu

Kuzu (*Pueraria lobata*) is a prized thickening agent that's made from the root of the hardy wild kuzu plant, which is native to Asia. The dried root is crushed, then dissolved in cold water, as you would dissolve corn flour, before being used in soups, custards and broths. Japanese arrowroot, as it is also known, is an extremely vigorous climber in the Fabaceae family. It is sometimes called 'the vine that ate the south' so, before planting, carefully consider whether you really want to grow it in your garden.

the air, but it can be processed and sold in tubes; however, this commercial product is often artificially flavoured and coloured. Japanese chefs also pickle them overnight in salt and vinegar and deep-fry the leaves in tempura batter, which helps to retain some of their spiciness.

Japan now consumes so much wasabi that it imports it from other countries, such as New Zealand. The rest of the world has caught on too, adding the spicy avocado-coloured condiment to everything, from mayonnaise to ice cream.

Cultivating horseradish and wasabi

Horseradish dies back in winter but is a perennial that grows in any moist, humus-rich, well drained soil, but it does tend to romp if it finds itself at home. One of three members of this genus, it enjoys any temperate climate.

Sow wasabi seeds in spring, and plant them out when they're large enough, but take special care to keep them moist and not let them dry out. It will be 4 to 5 years before the roots are worth harvesting, by which stage they will be about 20 cm (8 in) long. Used fresh, frozen or dried, wasabi has a heat that is similar to mustard.

Lemon grass

Lemon grass (*Cymbopogon citratus*) is a graceful grass with a lemony tang to both the foliage, which is used in teas, and the base of the leaf blade, which is juicier and more suitable for cooking; it is particularly popular in Asian cuisines.

Cultivating lemon grass

Native to India and Sri Lanka, lemon grass grows to about 1 to 1.5 m (3 to 5 ft), and likes regular water and free-draining soil in a full sun, humid position. The best way to grow it is to take root divisions in late spring, and you can buy specific varieties better suited to either leaf or leaf-base production. Harvest the leaves at any time, but cut the stems in autumn.

Above left: If using whole stems of lemon grass, bruise them first to release the flavour but remove them before serving.

Left: Horseradish is a very efficient remedy for a blocked nose.

Opposite, top: The leaves of a horseradish plant.

Right: Turmeric, some-times known as Indian saffron and haldi, has a complex flavour.

Opposite, top: Tiny flowers appear among showy, leafy bracts on a turmeric plant.

Turmeric

With its clump of large apple-green leaves about 1.2 m (4 ft) tall and stunning white and greenish yellow orchid-like flowers in summer, turmeric (*Curcuma longa* syn. *C. domestica*) is a highly ornamental plant in the garden.

Once its root has been boiled and then dried, turmeric provides the yellow colour in curry powders; it is also used for dyeing cloth, especially in India where it is used to colour saris. The leaves are used for wrapping fish and the shoots are also edible.

Cultivating turmeric

Like Chinese keys (see page 401), turmeric grows naturally in high rainfall areas in the tropics and needs 1 to 2 m (3 to 6½ ft) of water annually.

To grow this member of the ginger family, you need to live in a frost-free climate. Find a sunny position with good free-draining, fertile soil and plant the small rhizomes or setts 5 to 7 cm (2 to 2¾ in) deep and 40 to 50 cm (16 to 20 in) apart in spring.

Ten months later, after the white and yellow flowers appear, the leaves yellow and the stems start falling over, your plants will be ready to harvest. Once your clump is established, you can dig up fresh turmeric from the perimeter of the clump at will, providing you cover the roots straightaway so the clump doesn't dry out.

Marsh mallow

Marsh mallow (*Althaea officinalis*), sometimes called sweet weed, belongs to the Hibiscus family, and the mucilage in its roots was once the major ingredient of the confectionery, marshmallow. From its native habitat in Europe, this hardy perennial has spread all over the world, becoming wild in many areas. Its young leaves may be eaten fresh or boiled, and the flowers, which are also edible, are very pretty and look similar to hollyhocks, to which they are related, although they don't grow on tall spires. The flowers are followed by round, flat fruit with the curious name of 'cheeses'.

It is both salt- and frost-hardy, so it's rarely bothered by climatic restraints, and suffers from few diseases. It can also be used as an edible savoury vegetable — just parboil the roots before lightly frying them in butter. The Romans regarded marsh mallow as a delicacy with the additional benefit of medicinal properties. However, don't eat this plant if you are pregnant or breastfeeding.

Dry curry paste

2 dried long red chillis, about
  13 cm (5 in) long
2 lemon grass stalks, white
  part only, finely diced
2.5-cm (1-in) piece of galangal,
  finely chopped
3–4 Asian shallots, finely chopped
5–6 coriander (cilantro) shoots,
  finely chopped
1 teaspoon shrimp paste
1 teaspoon ground cumin,
  dry-roasted
3 tablespoons unsalted peanuts,
  chopped

Remove the stems from the chillis
and slit them in half lengthways with
a sharp knife. Discard the seeds and
soak the chillis in hot water for about
1 to 2 minutes, or until soft. Drain and
roughly chop.

Using a mortar and pestle, pound
the chillis, lemon grass and galangal
into a paste. Add the remaining
ingredients one at a time and pound
until the mixture forms a very smooth
paste. Alternatively, use a food processor
to blend all the ingredients together
into as smooth a paste as possible. Add
cooking oil, as required, to assist with
the blending.

Store the curry paste in an airtight
jar and use as required.

Makes 80 g (1/3 cup).

Drying turmeric

Harvesting turmeric is a simple matter
of lifting the roots, then washing and
drying them.

1 Pull up the roots.

2 Trim them.

3 Wash them in a bucket of water.

4 Place them on a rack to dry.

Buds and flowers

Sadly, the knowledge of which flowers are edible and how to use them in cooking has been eroded over the centuries. However, it's certainly worth doing a little research to find out which flowers and buds can be eaten safely.

Edible blooms

Best known of the edible blooms are borage flowers (*Borago officinalis*), whose intense blue blooms are often crystallised and used in cake decorations, in a similar way to pinks (*Dianthus* sp.), which look and taste lovely when prepared in a similar fashion, provided you first remove the bitter heal.

But over the centuries there have been many others — flowers such as pot marigold (*Calendula officinalis*), nasturtium (*Tropaeolum majus*), *Cercis* sp., violets and pansies (*Viola* sp.), orange blossom (*Citrus* sp.), roses (*Rosa* sp.) and lavender (*Lavandula* sp.). All have been eaten as fragrant additions to various dishes or else imbibed in intoxicating distillations and beverages.

Other edible flowers include echiums (*Echium vulgare*), sweet rocket (*Hesperis matronalis*), hyssop (*Hyssopus* sp.), chicory (*Cichorium intybus*), honeysuckle (*Lonicera japonica*) and cowslips (*Primula veris* and *P. vulgaris*). Some flowers, such as those of meadowsweet (*Filipendula ulmaria*) and

Above: Hyssop bears blue flowers in summer.

Left: Popular edible flowers include borage and pot marigold.

elderflower (*Sambucus* sp.), can be dipped into batter and then fried, while lavender (*Lavandula* sp.) can be added to pastry.

Other flowers are either distilled for their oil or used to flavour beer and liqueurs (see page 429). These include roses (*Rosa* sp.), meadowsweet and the Judas tree (*Cercis siliquastrum*), whose individual flowers resemble those on the pendulous racemes of wisteria.

Globe artichokes

The globe artichoke (*Cynara scolymus*), which grows to 1.5 m (5 ft), is a herbaceous perennial grown for its thistle-like blooms. Although it demands space, it's well worth the effort to create some room for it. Not only are the lower bracts and heart, or base, a prized delicacy, but the plant itself is also wonderfully ornamental, with deeply cut silver leaves. Once topped with the mauve bloom, they form a rosette of some beauty.

Native to North Africa, this plant has spread across the Mediterranean, where it is featured in many dishes. There are a few different varieties of artichoke, but one of the most spectacular types is a cultivar called 'Violetto', which has dark purple-black flowers.

The flower contains the fleshy edible segment. To prepare it for cooking, first remove the hairy 'choke' from inside the flower head. This will reveal the edible heart. The stems, or chards as they are

Above: The delicate flowers of *Viola tricolor* can be crystallised and used as decorations on cakes and desserts.

Above left: *Rosa rugosa*.

Below: Sweet violet (*Viola odorata*).

edible flowers

1 Nasturtium   **2** *Dianthus* sp.   **3** Borage   **4** Judas tree   **5** Lavender   **6** Pot marigold   **7** *Pyrus* sp.
8 Globe artichoke   **9** Spice geranium (nutmeg)   **10** Violets   **11** Pansy   **12** Chives   **13** Artichoke

known, can also be eaten. To do this, wait until after the plant has stopped producing flowers well — after about four years — then cut the plant down to the ground in late autumn as usual.

When the new shoots appear, wait until they are about 60 cm (2 ft) tall, then tie them together and wrap them in black plastic. This blanching technique is used on chicory, asparagus, celery and cardoons, their relatives, and will make the shoots whiter and sweeter. They are then cooked and eaten in a similar way.

Cultivating globe artichokes

Globe artichokes can be planted by seed (sown in autumn/winter/spring), but as this produces variable plants, offsets are usually used. These are taken from the mother plant in spring and placed 75 to 90 cm (30 to 36 in) apart. Take care not to change the soil level from the old position to the new, and keep the soil moist while they take root.

Globe artichokes like a rich, well drained soil, so work in plenty of manure or compost to help build it up before planting, and even side-dress with blood and bone, as your plants will grow in the same site for 3 to 4 years.

They are fast-growing and you can expect six flower heads from each plant from their second year onwards. If your plant produces more flower heads than this, disbud them as they appear, otherwise the size and quality of each bloom will be compromised.

did you know? In 1947, Marilyn Monroe was crowned the first Artichoke Queen of Castroville, the self-proclaimed artichoke capital of the United States.

Feeding

Keep globe artichokes mulched each spring with well rotted manure or compost, and promote more blooms by feeding them with liquid fertiliser every two weeks as soon as the first flower is cut.

Pruning

To increase the quality of the remaining blooms, pinch out the smaller side shoots that appear on each flowering stem. After about six flowering stems appear, cut them off so that the remainder develop into the biggest flowers.

In late autumn, when the leaves have started to die and wither naturally, cut back your plants and mulch heavily with more manure or, in cold climates, use straw to protect the crowns from the cold.

Harvesting

To harvest, first remove the top bloom, which will be the largest of all the heads. Do this after the plant is fully grown, but before it changes colour. Use secateurs to remove the bloom, leaving a short stem. Then cut back each stem by about half, which will encourage another crop of flowers; at this point, use liquid fertiliser fortnightly to encourage flowering.

To prepare artichokes, bring a large saucepan of salted water to the boil, and add lemon juice. Break off the stalks, pulling out any strings at the same time, then trim the bases flat. Add the artichokes to the water, keeping them submerged with a small plate on top. Simmer until a leaf from the base comes away easily, about 20 to 25 minutes. Cool quickly under cold running water, then drain upside down.

Problems

Watch for snails and slugs (see page 59), fungus gnat (page 54) and petal blight.

Right: Rosella sepals, preserved in sugar syrup, are delicious in champagne.

Below: *Lavandula canariensis* 'Sidonie'.

Opposite, top: A young rosella seedling.

Lavender

Lavender flowers (*Lavandula* sp.) can be used for a variety of culinary purposes, from biscuit baking to herb jellies. Pick them the moment they open and hang them in small bunches to dry in an airy position. Growing lavender is popular worldwide, not just for the flowers, but also because the ornamental foliage has such a delicious fragrance. Lavender needs full sun to grow successfully, as well as free-draining, limed soil.

There are many different varieties of lavender grown, each with its own particular colour, scent, season and habit, but all must be pruned back lightly each year after they finish flowering to stop them from becoming woody.

Rosella

Rosella (*Hibiscus sabdariffa*) is an annual bush that grows to 2 m (6½ ft), producing very showy flowers with a lovely dark eye. To grow rosella, sow the seeds in spring, and water well during summer. They grow to about 1.2 m (4 ft) and need full sun in order to flower.

Use the sepals to make jams, jellies, chutneys and wine, or preserve the buds in sugar syrup. Other hibiscus, such as *H. rosa-sinensis*, or Hawaiian hibiscus, are also eaten in some areas. Marsh mallow (*Althaea officinalis*) is also in the hibiscus family. This herb is mostly known for its root (see page 406), but the flowers can be eaten fresh in salads.

Cotton lavender

Santolina or cotton lavender (*Santolina chamaecyparissus*) is not related to lavender at all. Instead it has the characteristic small button, daisy-like yellow flowers of the daisy family. The leaves can be used to flavour biscuits instead of rosemary, but otherwise it's usually grown for its ornamental and insect-repelling qualities. The green (*S. rosmarinifolia*) and grey foliage forms (*S. chamaecyparissus*) also make beautiful hedges.

Like its namesake lavender, cotton lavender likes a full sun position and fairly poor, well drained soil. Clip it regularly to encourage it to stay bushy, tight and healthy; however, if you live in a cold area, avoid doing this in late autumn.

Caper berry

Capparis spinosa, Capparaceae family

Caper berry is a scrambling vine, growing over rocky crags and cliffs around the Mediterranean. Although it does produce an edible berry, it's actually the flower buds, pickled or preserved in salt, that are sold as capers. A low-growing plant, it sprawls about 3 m (10 ft) in diameter and, if the buds are not removed, they open into very pretty stamenous white flowers.

There are also two Australian native species, called bush caper berries. *Capparis arborea* is native to the warm rainforest regions of the east coast, and bumbil or wild orange (*C. mitchellii*) is native to the desert and suitable for dry-climate gardens. Both species cope with extreme heat and bear edible fruit that is eaten by Aboriginals.

Climate: Long, hot, dry summers are required. In a cold climate, grow it in a pot and overwinter it under glass.

Culture: Caper berries are very popular in local cuisines all around the Mediterranean.

Colours: White flowers with purple stamens.

Height: 1 m tall x 3 m wide (3 x 10 ft).

Planting time: Plant out struck cuttings or hardened off seedlings in early autumn.

Soil: Prefers slightly alkaline, reasonably fertile, free-draining, open soil among rocks.

Position: Full sun.

Fertiliser: Apply lime if the soil is too acid.

Pests and diseases: Caper berries are disease-free.

Propagation: Sow fresh seeds in spring or plant semi-hardwood cuttings in summer.

Harvesting and storing: Harvest unopened buds early in the morning then pickle them either in salt or in a salt and vinegar solution. Use them as a garnish and in sauces and butters. If caper berries are unavailable you can substitute pickled nasturtium buds (see page 396). The fruit can also be eaten and pickled.

Expensive tastes

It takes up to 250,000 flowers, each one hand-picked, to make half a kilo (1 lb) of saffron (*Crocus sativus*). The world's most expensive spice is made from the dried stigmas of the flower. Native to South-East Asia, it has been used in various ways since ancient Egyptian times – in perfumes and medicines, as a fabric dye and to colour food a rich golden yellow. If you can't afford saffron, try turmeric (see page 406) instead.

Spices

Until the fifteenth century, spices were traded overland between Europe and Asia, but during the European Age of Discovery, explorers roamed the seas, opening up maritime trading routes that resulted in the introduction of new but expensive spices.

The spice trade

Spices are made from the dried leaves, roots, fruit, bark and seeds of plants, and are used to flavour, colour and preserve food, and also as ingredients in cosmetics, perfumery and medicines. Some can be used whole or ground into a powder — for example, cinnamon, one of the first spices traded in the Middle East, about 4000 years ago, is a powder that is ground from the bark of the cinnamon tree.

During the Middle Ages, Venice controlled the extremely lucrative spice trade between Europe and the Middle East, but in the fifteenth century, as explorers started to discover new sea routes, the trade spread to India and the Orient, falling under the control of the Portuguese, the English and, eventually, the Dutch.

These days you can buy spices and spice mixes from your local supermarket, but it's so much more satisfying to make your own from scratch. The aromas of fresh spices are truly a delight.

Above: Allspice is so named because it tastes like a combination of spices.

Left: You can use star anise whole, broken up or in powder form.

Allspice

Ground allspice isn't a spice blend, as the name suggests, but the dried green fruit of *Pimenta dioica*. When dry, the fruit are brown, and resemble large brown peppercorns; in fact, they were confused with pepper when they were discovered in South America and Mexico. They are used in everything from cakes to chutneys, but the leaves can also be used in a similar way to bay leaves: add them to dishes to infuse their flavour but remove them before serving.

Cloves

These are the dried form of the unopened flower bud of *Syzygium aromaticum*. A close relative of lilly pilly trees (*Syzygium* sp.), this species, like its cousin, grows into a large tree about 20 m (66 ft) tall in its native rainforest habitat, but smaller in home gardens, which makes them easier to pick and air dry. When the buds are bright red, they're ready for harvesting.

Native to Indonesia, cloves are used in many different cuisines, where their fragrance is valued in rice dishes, cakes and curries, and also in famous spice mixes such as Chinese five spice (see page 421) and *quatre épices*. In Europe, a pomander, an orange studded with cloves and cure-dried, is used to repel moths and impart a fresh smell to stored clothes and linen.

Above left: Garlic, fresh coriander and cumin seeds, some of the ingredients of the spice mix, chermoula.

Above: Ras el hanout, another spice mix, includes coriander seeds and black peppercorns.

Below: Dried cloves and clove powder.

did you know? The name 'cloves' derives from the Latin word *clavus* for 'nail', which they resemble.

Nutmeg and mace

Nutmeg is actually more like an almond kernel than a traditional 'nut', as it lies inside the fruit of the *Myristica fragrans* tree, a tropical evergreen that is native to the Banda Islands in eastern Indonesia. When nutmeg is fresh, a special covering, known as an aril or arillus, wraps around this seed. Known as mace, it has a distinct purplish red hue and is extracted separately as a milder-flavoured version of the 'nut'. The fruit that surrounds this kernel is pulpy and tough, but in Indonesia it is used to make a fragrant jam called *selei buah pala*.

Nutmeg is surrounded by an aril, which is known as mace.

did you know? An aril may also be fruit-like: the flesh surrounding a pomegranate seed is actually an aril. Longans and lychees are two other examples.

Cumin

Although they look similar, the taste of cumin (*Cuminum cyminum*) is much spicier than that of caraway, its close relative and another member of the Apiaceae family, and the seed is lighter and slightly larger. Used for thousands of years in Middle Eastern and Indian cuisines, cumin made its way across the Atlantic to Mexico with the Spaniards, becoming one of the distinctive flavours in that cuisine as well as in Cuban cooking.

Cultivating cumin

This small plant, which grows to about 20 to 30 cm (8 to 12 in) and bears fine, feathery foliage, is an annual, so each year in spring you need to replant it from seed. Cumin will go to seed in a few months of hot, dry weather, which it loves. It is these seeds that are harvested and used after being dry roasted; indeed, they were once so popular for seasoning food that the ancient Greeks kept them on their tables in much the same way as we use a pepper grinder today.

Peppers

Although black and white pepper are among the most commonly used spices in Western cooking, there are also other peppers that are key ingredients in Asian cuisines. And you may not realise that green, white, black and pink peppercorns all come from the same tree.

Green, white and black peppercorns

Native to India, pepper (*Piper nigrum*) is one of the world's great travellers, and has been traded along the spice routes for hundreds of years. It is a climbing perennial vine with fragrant leaves and green flowers that develop into dark red fruit, and it's the various stages of this fruit that are sold as commercial pepper.

Green peppercorns are picked when the fruit is unripe. White pepper, on the other hand, is made by soaking the fruit for about a week, so that the pulp is removed, leaving the seeds, which are then dried. Black pepper is processed from the dried unripe green seeds.

Pepper needs a frost-free position, but can successfully grow under cover or in indoor positions. The shiny, heart-shaped leaves are quite attractive, but the plant is very vigorous, growing some 8 m (26 ft) tall if allowed. It is related to peperomia (*Peperomia* sp.), the indoor plant, which is sometimes called flowering pepper.

Pink peppercorns

Pink peppercorns, on the other hand, are native to Central and South America, and actually produced by the pepper tree (*Schinus molle*), a large shade tree that's often planted on rural properties or in city streets, due to its drought tolerance, graceful weeping habit and substantial size — about 15 x 15 m (49 x 49 ft). Its foliage, which is said to be fly-repelling,

is used as stock fodder during drought. They are in the same family as the cashew nut (Anacardiaceae), and there is also another species known as the Brazilian pepper tree (*S. terebinthifolius*), which grows to about 6 m (20 ft) and has much broader leaves and red berries.

Sichuan pepper

Another pepper tree is the famous Chinese spice, Sichuan pepper (*Zanthoxylum* sp.), which has a flavour not dissimilar to white pepper. Used in Chinese five spice (see the box on page 421), it's in the same family as citrus, and there are about five species that bear the spicy, edible fruits. They produce aromatic foliage as well as fruit. Most grow to about 6 m (20 ft).

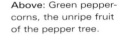

Above: Green peppercorns, the unripe fruit of the pepper tree.

Below left: Black, white and pink peppercorns.

Below right: The pepper tree (*Schinus molle*) has a graceful habit.

Opposite, top: Cumin seeds and powder.

tip

Cumin is ready for harvesting when the plant turns a yellowish brown. Pull up the whole plant, then dry it before removing the seeds.

Cubeb pepper

Cubeb pepper or tailed pepper (*Piper cubeba*) has been used in Asian and Moroccan dishes since ancient times. It has mostly kept to its homeland of Java, hence its other common name, Javanese pepper. The African version is actually another tailed species, also called false cubeb pepper (*Piper guineense* syn. *P. clusii*), which is native to Central Africa. Its fruit, sometimes known as ashanti pepper, strongly resemble cubeb berries, but are smaller, smoother and somewhat reddish-coloured. The tail is curved and the taste is fresher and less bitter.

Star anise

Star anise (*Illicium verum*), one of the famous Asian spices, bears beautiful star-shaped seeds that are an essential ingredient in garam masala and Chinese five spice (see the box, right). Japanese anise (*I. anisatum*) has very similar glossy foliage, the same whitish yellow flowers in mid-spring and glossy brown fruit in summer, which are virtually indistinguishable when dried, so buy clearly labelled plants from a reliable supplier. Both trees grow to 8 m (26 ft).

Za'atar

   2 tablespoons sesame seeds, toasted
   1 tablespoon dried thyme
   2 teaspoons sumac
   1/4 teaspoon salt

Grind the seeds and thyme in a spice grinder, or with a mortar and pestle, to a coarse texture. Stir in the sumac and salt.

   Store it in an airtight container for up to one month.

   Makes 4 tablespoons.

Herb and spice blends

Some cuisines feature classic herb mixes or blends. The best known is bouquet garni — a bundle of parsley stalks, thyme sprigs and bay leaves that is perfect for slow-cooked dishes such as casseroles. Another culinary mainstay in French cuisine is *fines herbes* — made with fresh parsley, chives, tarragon and chervil — which is added to dishes at the last minute. Marjoram, cress, sweet cicely or lemon balm may be added to *fines herbes*, and the marjoram and tarragon may be dried.

Za'atar is a mixture of herbs (dried thyme, oregano or marjoram) and spices (salt and sesame seeds) that is used as a condiment in the Middle East. Other ingredients vary, depending on the region — for example, in Lebanon it is mixed with sumac berries, which gives it a distinctive red colour. Other recipes include savory, cumin, coriander or fennel seeds. (For our recipe, see below left.) Throughout the Arab world, it's eaten for breakfast with bread alongside a cheese made of yoghurt.

Garam masala, a blend used in many Indian cuisines, is a mixture of cardamom, cloves, mace, cinnamon, cumin, coriander, fennel, black peppercorns and fenugreek seeds. It is highly aromatic but not hot, and is usually added to a dish towards the end of the cooking process.

Chinese five spice, a traditional ingredient in Chinese cooking, is made by roasting Sichuan peppercorns, then combining them with star anise, cloves, cinnamon and fennel seeds. These are all ground together to form a fine powder, which is used to flavour Cantonese roast duck and many other Chinese dishes.

Opposite: Star anise (in the bowl), Sichuan pepper and cubeb pepper, with their little tails.

Tamarind

Although tamarind (*Tamarindus indica*)
was well known to the ancient Egyptians
and the Greeks as far back as 4 BCE, it is
actually native to tropical Africa, in places
such as the Sudan and Madagascar, but
was introduced to India so long ago that its
common name is Indian date; of course,
its botanical name *indica* attributes its
origin to India. It is now naturalised in
the East Indies, some islands of the
Pacific and tropical America.

Tamarinds are related to cassias and,
like many of them, have soft ferny leaves
and pea-shaped yellow flowers, tinged with
red. It is the pod, however, that is the spice.

The edible pulp inside is popular in
both Asian and Latin American cuisines,
and is also an important ingredient in
Worcestershire and HP sauces. The hard
green pulp of the young fruit is very tart
and acidic, and is most often used as an
ingredient in savoury dishes. The ripened
fruit is sweeter, yet still distinctively sour,
and can be used in desserts and sweetened
drinks, or as a snack.

In Thailand, there is a carefully
cultivated sweet variety, with little to
no tartness, that is grown specifically
for its fresh fruit.

Cultivating tamarind

This highly ornamental evergreen,
which grows to 20 m tall x 10 m wide
(66 x 33 ft), can drop its leaves, depending
on the rainfall. It also tolerates a wide
range of soil types. In less desirable
climates, it can be grown under glass.

Tamarind copycats

Horse tamarind (*Leucaena glauca*), a low scrubby tree that grows to
about 9 m (30 ft), is from tropical and subtropical North America. It
bears long flattened pods and white flowers tinged with yellow that
resemble mimosa flowers (*Acacia* sp.). The leaves and flower buds
are edible, and the dried seeds can be used as a coffee substitute.

The small-leafed tamarind (*Diploglottis campbellii*) is a large tree
to 18 m (59 ft) from South Australia. In spring it produces creamy
flowers, followed in late summer and autumn by edible red fruit
that can be made into sweet jams and drinks.

Edible pods

The discovery of the Americas introduced Europeans to many new flavours, including cocoa, the base for chocolate and one of the world's most popular confections.

Cardamom

Cardamom (*Elettaria cardamomum*) is a member of the ginger family; however, only its seeds are used, not its roots. The green seed pods of the plant are dried and the seeds inside are used in many Indian dishes, as well as *masala chai*, a spiced herbal tea. It is also used in the Middle East as a flavour additive in tea and coffee.

Cardamom plants are wonderful additions to the shady garden, where they thrive as long as they receive regular water. They grow to anywhere between 1 and 3 m (3 and 10 ft), depending on the variety and the conditions. The pod containing these precious seeds develops after the flowers, which are white with blue streaks.

Cocoa

Cocoa is the dried and fermented bean of the cacao pod. The cacao (*Theobroma cacao*), a small tree to 4 to 8 m (13 to 26 ft), is thought to be from the Amazon, where it grows as an understorey plant in the rainforest. Long ago it travelled further afield to south-eastern Mexico; it was an important commodity in Meso-America.

Like many other rainforest species, the cacao tree is cauliferous, flowering directly from the trunk and main branches. After it flowers, it develops huge seed structures (pods) that weigh 500 g (1 lb), and it can bear twice a year. These pods contain a fluffy white material that cushions the beans or seeds themselves. It is the seeds, rich in fat and flavour, that make chocolate so irresistible. Cacao trees grow in any frost-free position.

did you know? Cacao is Aztec for 'food of the gods'. When the Spaniards conquered Mexico in 1521, Montezuma II, the king of the Aztecs, was reported to drink an amazing 50 chocolate drinks a day.

Edible bark

Cinnamon is a spice ground from the inner layer of bark that has been stripped off a cinnamon tree (*Cinnamomum vernum*). This is hand-peeled and dried into quills, which is then ground or left whole, depending on the recipe. Like bay laurel, the cinnamon tree is a member of the Lauraceae family. It's very hardy and copes with many different soils and a wide range of climates. You can grow cinnamon from seed or cuttings, and even aerial layers, but keep them moist until they root well. A close relative is the camphor laurel (*Cinnamomum camphora*), whose timber is used in cabinetry, in particular hope chests, as the moth-deterring, scented timber is ideal for storing fabrics.

Cassia (*Cinnamomum zeylanicum*), sometimes known as Ceylon cinnamon, originates from Sri Lanka and can be used in a similar way to cinnamon, while the leaves can be used like bay leaves. Unless you live on a large property, all species of cinnamon are too large for the home garden: these spectacular trees grow to about 10 m wide x 20 m tall (33 x 66 ft). Camphor laurel can become invasive in certain climates, so plant with caution.

The bark of the cinnamon tree, which is used to make the spice.

Carob

Until the discovery of chocolate, carob (*Ceratonia siliqua*) was a popular Middle Eastern and Mediterranean treat. Rich in sugar and protein, it is still sold in health food stores, as it contains less fat and more tannins than chocolate. Carob trees grow to 8 m (26 ft), and the leathery brown pods can reach about 30 cm (1 ft) in length. These pods are only produced on female or hermaphrodite trees, so make sure you know the sex of your plants before planting them out, or you could be disappointed. Once established, the trees are extremely drought-tolerant, although more regular waterings will produce better crops.

Icecream bean tree

One of the most surprising plants is icecream bean tree (*Inga edulis*), from tropical areas such as the West Indies, Mexico and the north of South America. A small tree, growing very quickly to only about 4 m (13 ft), it starts producing edible pods after four years. These pods contain shiny black seeds, which are discarded, leaving the pulpy edible white flesh that tastes just like fibrousy vanilla ice cream.

Tonka beans

Tonka beans (*Dipteryx odorata*), the dried seeds of a tree from the northern part of South America, have a strong, fragrant, almost bitter almond aroma, and are used in a similar way to vanilla beans. Their fragrance is a tantalising mix of cinnamon, almond, cloves and vanilla.

For those who grew up in the Caribbean, both chewing and playing with tonka beans was part of childhood; however, they can be toxic in large doses, so they're banned in both the United States and the United Kingdom, although they are still used to make perfume.

Vanilla

Vanilla from the vanilla orchid (*Vanilla planifolia*) is the second most expensive spice after saffron, due to the extensive labour required to grow the seed pods used in its manufacture. Outside its native habitat, where a fly does the work, this climber must be hand-pollinated.

The vanilla orchid needs a frost-free position and is best grown on a sheltered trellis or up a tree that has low branches; a she-oak (*Casuarina* sp.) is ideal.

To give cakes and desserts such as ice cream a vanilla flavour, you can use either vanilla essence, which is readily available in supermarkets, or the more intense flavour of dried vanilla pods — just scrape the tiny seeds out of the pod.

did you know? Siliqua is the modern name given to small, thin, silver Roman coins that were produced from the fourth century. The term comes from *siliqua graeca*, the seed of the carob tree, which was a weight system in Roman times.

Above left: New foliage on an icecream bean tree, with its characteristic leaf-covered petiole.

Above: Vanilla orchid is native to Central America and the West Indies.

Below: Dried vanilla pods with vanilla essence.

Teas, tonics and tinctures

There are many effective ways of extracting the volatile, essential oils from plants so that you can use them as a beverage or tonic, or enjoy them in classic tinctures.

Teas

Perhaps the easiest method of doing so is to make a tea, which can be drunk either hot or cold. Teas are made by infusing plant leaves, stems or flowers in hot water. Typically, boiling water is poured over the plant matter, then steeped for a while, decanted and drunk, either cool or hot, and sometimes sweetened with sugar or honey.

Apart from water, the world's most popular drink is tea, which is made from the dried leaves of *Camellia sinensis*, or the tea camellia. Green tea is made from the same plant, although it is processed differently, so the leaves retain more of their antioxidant properties. Flavoured preparations are made by adding other plants — for example, Earl Grey tea contains bergamot (*Monarda didyma*).

Herbal tea, made from plants other than *Camellia sinensis*, has long been a popular beverage in many cultures around the world. For example, the Oswego Indians of North America used bergamot to make a medicinal tea.

Above: Rue, which is used to make grappa, is a very bitter-tasting herb.

Left: *Camellia sinensis* leaves, from which China tea, the world's most popular beverage, is made.

Herbal teas include lemon verbena (*Aloysia triphylla*), which is also made into jellies and ice cream; calamint (*Calamintha* sp.); chamomile (*Chamaemelum nobile*); peppermint (*Mentha x piperita*); sage tea (*Salvia* sp.); ground ivy (*Glechoma hederacea*); nettle (*Urtica* sp.); and catmint (*Nepeta* sp.), which was enjoyed as a tea before China tea was introduced to the West.

Coffee

Of course, you can't go very far without mentioning coffee (*Coffea* sp.), the beverage of choice for many Westerners today. Originally from Ethiopia, coffee copes well in full sun or part shade.

The best quality beans for roasting are produced by *Coffea arabica*, and the beans, once ripe, are simply removed from the berry and dry roasted in a pan to bring out the flavour. In Ethiopia this is conducted as a special ceremony in much the same way as tea ceremonies play an important role in Japanese culture. Ethiopians make a tincture out of the leaves, which also contain caffeine.

The plants themselves are highly ornamental and worth growing. They are in the same family as gardenias and citrus (Rutaceae), and have the same

Above left and right: Roman chamomile (left) and lemon verbena (right). Both plants are popular in herbal teas.

Below left: The glossy foliage of the coffee tree.

did you know? Between them, China and India produce the world's largest amount of tea.

Above: Traditionally used as a herbal treatment for intestinal worms, wormwood should not be consumed, unless it is used as an ingredient in a spirit such as absinthe.

Above right: The pretty blue-green leaves of rue complement its small yellow flowers.

glossy foliage — but on coffee trees it is larger and deeply veined — and sweetly scented flowers in spring. These are white, of a similar shape to jasmine, borne down the branches' leaf axils in late spring. They last only a few weeks, and the cherry-red berries that develop afterwards are also very pretty. It is inside these berries that the two precious coffee beans lie.

Cultivating coffee

Coffee plants only take three years to bear, need protection from frost, and can even be grown indoors in a bright position. They can also be hedged and pleached easily. The dwarf cultivar 'Catui' is ideal for growing in a pot but, even when ground-grown, this variety is a prolific and easy to pick cropper. You'll need to roast the ripe berries before using them.

Coffee substitutes

If you want a hot drink that's not coffee, you could consider a beverage of old. For centuries chicory has been made into a slightly nutty hot drink, as have dandelion root and iris seeds. Chicory or witlof (*Cichorium intybus*) is a hardy biennial with a white taproot. While its green leaves are used in salads and cooking, the roots are roasted and used as a coffee substitute. They are dug throughout summer and autumn, washed thoroughly, sliced and then dried off in a slow oven before being ground into a powder. (See also page 240.)

The roasted seeds of iris yellow flag (*Iris pseudacorus*) also make a reasonable coffee substitute. These are gathered in early summer and autumn, then air-dried.

Mesquite (*Prosopis pubescens*), also called screwbean because of the shape

Guarana

Guarana (*Paulinia cupana*), an ingredient in energy drinks, is a climber that grows to about 3 x 3 m (10 x 10 ft). Inside the fruit are three black seeds, which contain five times more caffeine than coffee beans.

of its twisted legumes, was used by Native Americans to make a sweet, rich drink, but dandelion roots, dug in autumn before being dried and powdered, possibly come closest to an authentic coffee flavour.

Tinctures

These are a solution of a plant extract or chemical in alcohol. Some well known tinctures include gin (made with *Juniperus* sp. and other herbs); Benedictine (flavoured with angelica, *Angelica archangelica*); vermouth and aperitifs such as absinthe, which are flavoured with wormwood (*Artemisia absinthium*); grappa, whose classic ingredient is rue (*Ruta* sp.); Lion's milk (*raki*), where the licorice flavour comes from the dried seeds of anise (*Pimpinella anisum*); crème de menthe (mint, *Mentha* sp.); and the German liqueur Kummel, made with caraway (*Carum carvi*) and cumin (*Cuminum cyminum*). Wall germander (*Teucrium* x *lucidrys*) is also used for flavouring liqueurs.

Other herbs are made into wine or added to beer. For example, hops (*Humulus lupulus*) help keep beer longer; licorice (*Glycyrrhiza glabra*) is used to flavour some beers, in particular Guinness; and betony (*Stachys officinalis*), wild bog myrtle (*Myrica gale*) and clove pinks (*Dianthus* sp.) were once all used to flavour home-brewed ale in much the same way as hops are.

Above: Yellow or water flag iris is perfect for growing in a boggy area or on the edge of a pond.

Left: The tender new growth of hops.

did you know? Tonics are drinks designed to lift your spirits or make you feel generally better. For example, tonic water originally contained quinine, and was used as a preventative against malaria. These days the amount of quinine is insignificant, but it still lends this popular carbonated drink its bitter taste.

Index

Acknowledgments

I would like to thank my publisher, Kay Scarlett; Greenpatch Organic Seeds, Glenthorne NSW; Gilberts Nursery, Moorland NSW; Lorne Valley Macadamia Farm and Café, Lorne via Kendall NSW; Dave Gray, Historic Houses Trust (Vaucluse House, Vaucluse NSW); Michael Bradford; Mark Engall, Engall's Nursery, Dural NSW; David Fonteyn, Glover's Garden, Leichhardt NSW; Mickey Robertson (Glenmore House, Camden NSW); Gunther and Gitta Rembel (Reverie, Dural NSW); Cedric Lethbridge (Bilpin Spring Orchard, Bilpin NSW); Royal Botanic Gardens, Sydney NSW; Tim Robson; Ali Mentesh and Wayne Morissey (Red Cow Farm, Sutton Forest NSW); and Caroline Flood (Woodcote, Wedderburn NSW).

My special thanks go to Tim Robson and Kenneth Bottomley (Westward House, Suffolk, UK) for their contagious enthusiasm and inspirational advice.

Picture credits

All photographs by **Sue Stubbs**, except for the following.
Alan Benson 113 btm; 117 btm r; 123 c; 126 top; 129 btm; 199 top; 309 btm r; 353 top r; 363 btm; 369 top l; 401 l; 422 r.
Joe Filshie 46; 64; 93 top; 142 top r; 235 top r; 241 btm l; 329 btm r; 341; 362 btm r; 369 top r; 371 top r; 378 c; 379 l; 382 top; 387 r; 389 btm l; 400 btm; 414 btm.
Denise Greig 59 r; 153; 157 r.
Ian Hofstetter 415 btm l & top r; 421 c.
istockphoto.com/OlegPrikhodo 35 top l.
Chris L Jones 87 l; 140 r; 142 top l; 196; 324 btm.
Natasha Milne 78 top l & btm l; 92 btm r; 104; 106 btm; 107 top r; 112 top; 136; 142 btm r; 151 r; 161 btm c; 163 top l & btm l; 166 top l; 174 btm l; 183 l; 193 btm l; 195; 200 l; 206; 207; 208 l; 210 top; 212 l; 220; 233 top l; 249 r; 250 top; 259 top l & r; 262 btm l & c; 267 top l; 270 top; 276 c; 284 top; 307; 309 btm l; 310 btm; 316; 329 top r; 344 l; 404 btm; 416 btm; 418 l.
Murdoch Books Photo Library 42; 43; 44 top c; 51 (all but top l); 52 btm c; 55 btm l; 63; 68 l; 69 c; 80 r; 90 top c; 91 top r; 92 top; 96; 99 r; 101 btm r; 106 top; 109 btm; 112 btm; 115 btm l & top r; 117 top l; 119 top l; 121 btm r; 134 r; 137 top c & btm; 138 top; 143 top; 148; 161 top r; 168 r; 170; 173 btm; 175; 182 r; 186 top; 187 top; 200 r; 205 btm l; 209; 212 r; 213 r; 218 top; 232 r; 233 btm; 234 btm; 237 btm; 238 top; 240 btm; 241 top; 242; 245 btm; 253 btm; 258 top; 259 btm; 262 top; 266 r; 267 btm r; 268 top; 275 btm; 277; 278 top l & btm; 280 r; 285 top l; 286 r; 291 btm; 296 top; 297 btm l; 300 top; 301 btm l; 302 top; 309 top; 310 top; 312 top; 315 top; 319 top; 320; 325 top l; 326 r; 327 btm r; 328; 332 btm l; 336 r; 338 btm; 339 top; 343 top; 344 r; 348 top; 350 top l & btm; 351 btm l & r; 352 btm; 353 btm; 355 top; 356 top l & r; 357 l; 358 r; 368 top; 368 r; 369 btm; 374 btm; 377 btm; 380; 385 top; 386; 388; 392 top; 394 r; 395 top l & btm; 396; 398 btm; 400 top; 401 r; 402 r; 405 btm; 406 top; 408 top; 409 btm; 412; 414 top; 416 top; 417 btm; 418 r; 419 r & btm l; 421 top & btm; 422 l; 425 btm; 426 top.
Lorna Rose 21 l; 55 (all but btm l); 58; 59 l; 61 top; 68 c & r; 69 top & btm; 93 c; 108 btm l; 118 btm l; 120; 121 top l & top r; 123 l; 126 btm; 131 l; 133; 137 top r; 140 l; 146 l; 160 top; 191 btm; 223 r; 311 r; 361; 389 top r; 402 l; 429 top.
Shutterstock 88 top l; 90 btm l.

The publisher would like to acknowledge photography in the following gardens and nurseries: Alstonville Tropical Fruit Research Station, Alstonville NSW; Austral Watergardens, Cowan NSW; Burnbank, Wagga Wagga NSW; F. Cavenett; Ray, Myrtle and Ron Charter, members of Brisbane Organic Growers, Inc.; Chicago Botanic Garden; The Garden in a Forest, Stanley Vic; Ian Jewell, Glenreagh NSW; Kennerton Green, Mittagong NSW; Kiwi Down Under Organic Fruit Farm, Bonville NSW; Noel Outerbridge, Alstonville NSW; Moidart, Bowral NSW; Rainbow Ridge Nursery, Dural NSW; Renaissance Herbs, Warnervale NSW; Linda Ross, Kurrajong NSW; Royal Botanic Gardens, Sydney NSW; Shoalmarra Quandong Farm, Tumby Bay SA; Sally and Mel Siddall, Morayfield Qld; Anne Thomson, Pymble NSW; and Tropical Fruit World, Duranbah NSW.